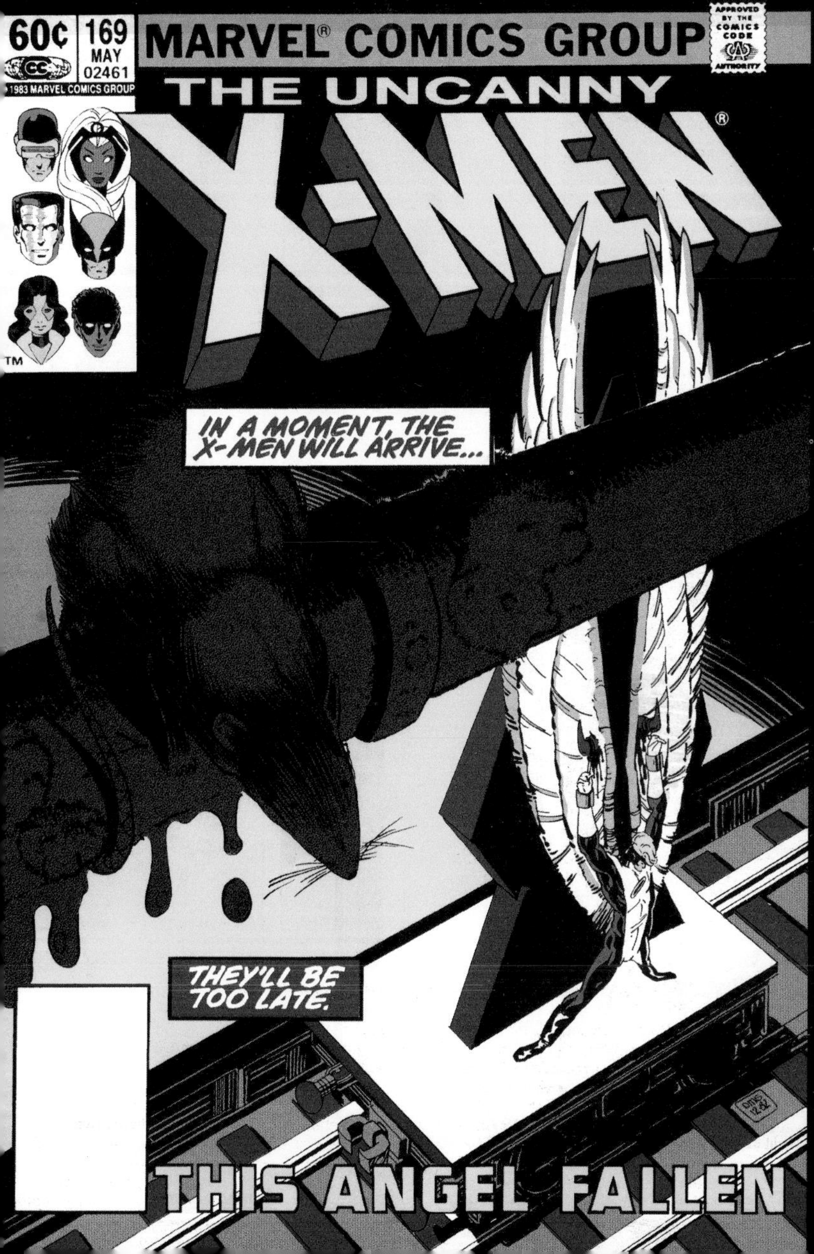
60¢
169
MAY
02461
©1983 MARVEL COMICS GROUP
MARVEL® COMICS GROUP
APPROVED BY THE COMICS CODE AUTHORITY
THE UNCANNY
X-MEN®
IN A MOMENT, THE X-MEN WILL ARRIVE...
THEY'LL BE TOO LATE.
THIS ANGEL FALLEN

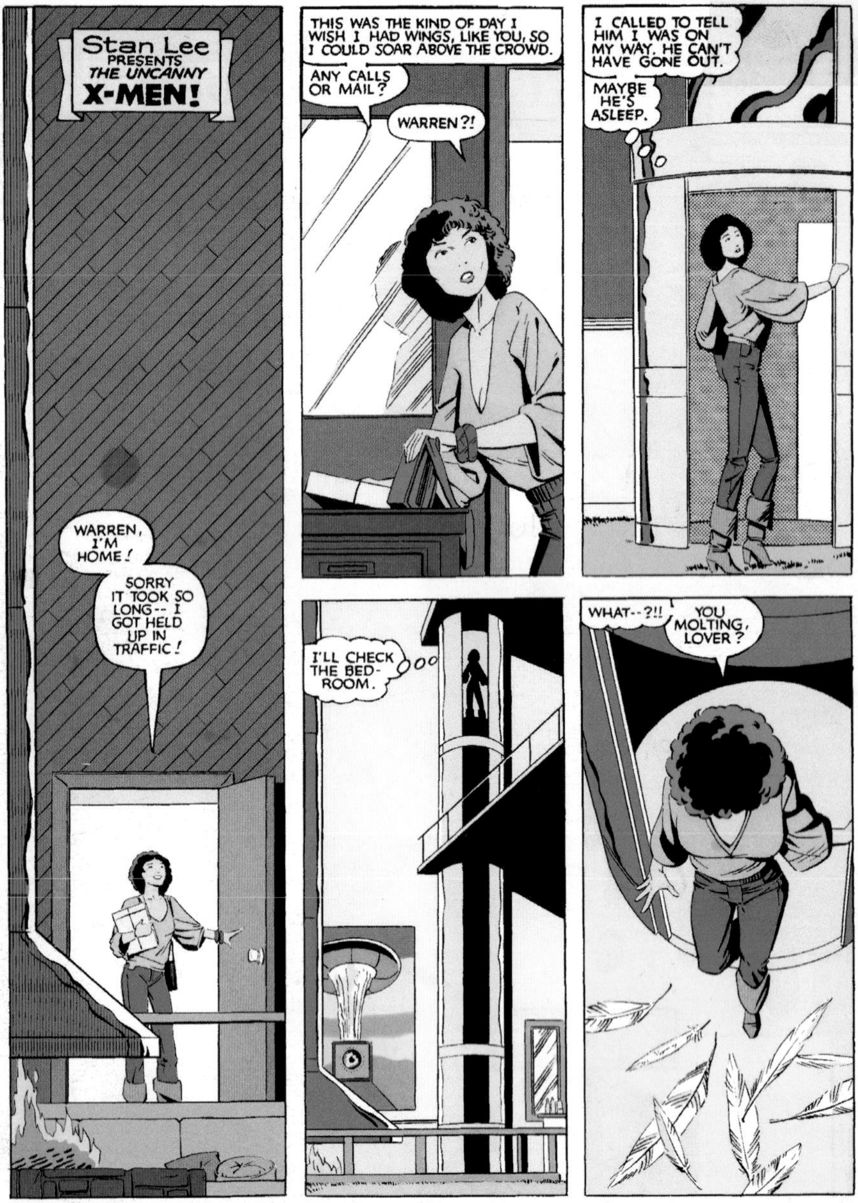
Stan Lee PRESENTS THE UNCANNY X-MEN!
WARREN, I'M HOME!
SORRY IT TOOK SO LONG-- I GOT HELD UP IN TRAFFIC!
THIS WAS THE KIND OF DAY I WISH I HAD WINGS, LIKE YOU, SO I COULD SOAR ABOVE THE CROWD.
ANY CALLS OR MAIL?
WARREN?!
I CALLED TO TELL HIM I WAS ON MY WAY. HE CAN'T HAVE GONE OUT.
MAYBE HE'S ASLEEP.
I'LL CHECK THE BED-ROOM.
WHAT--?!!
YOU MOLTING, LOVER?

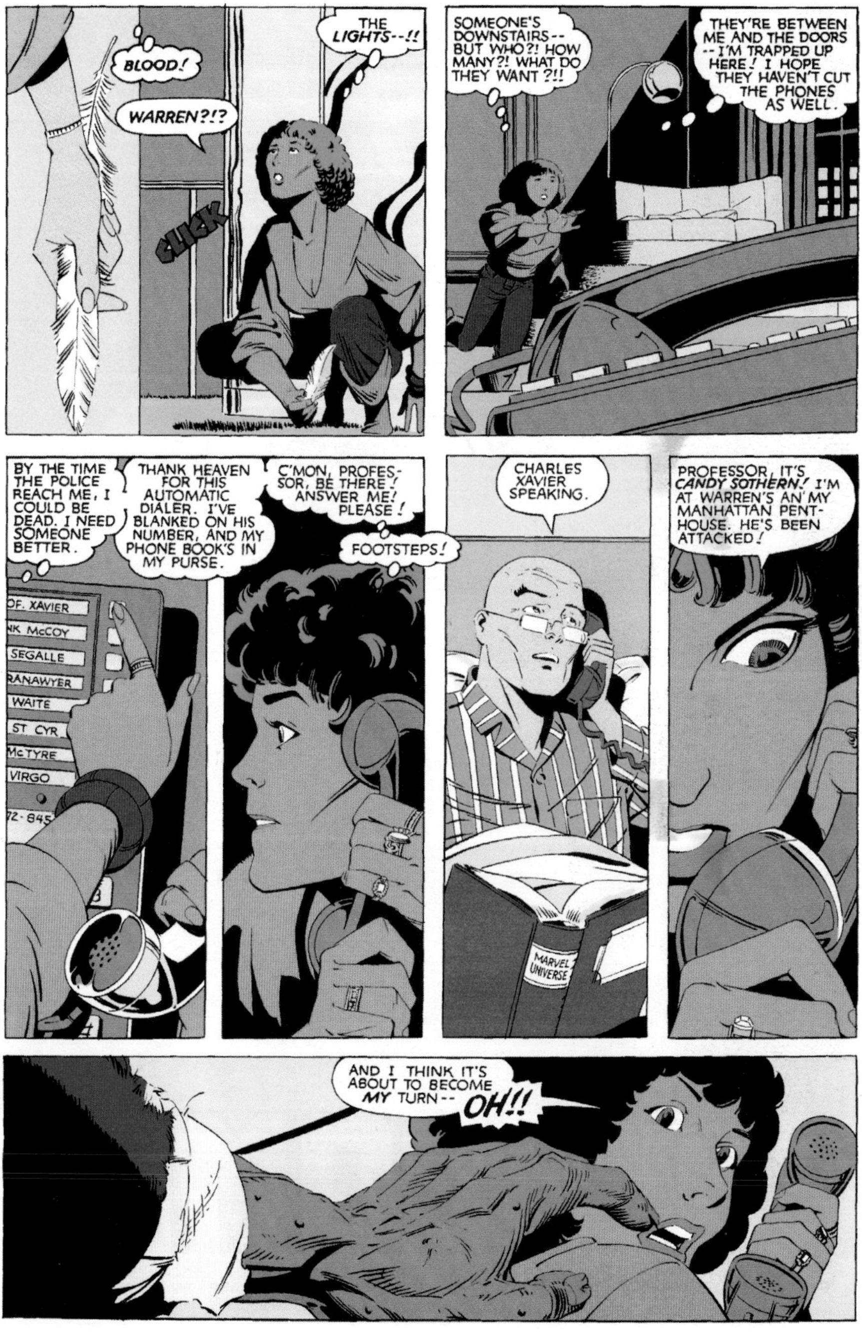
BLOOD!
WARREN?!?
CLICK
THE LIGHTS--!!
SOMEONE'S DOWNSTAIRS-- BUT WHO?! HOW MANY?! WHAT DO THEY WANT?!!
THEY'RE BETWEEN ME AND THE DOORS -- I'M TRAPPED UP HERE! I HOPE THEY HAVEN'T CUT THE PHONES AS WELL.
BY THE TIME THE POLICE REACH ME, I COULD BE DEAD. I NEED SOMEONE BETTER.
THANK HEAVEN FOR THIS AUTOMATIC DIALER. I'VE BLANKED ON HIS NUMBER, AND MY PHONE BOOK'S IN MY PURSE.
OF. XAVIER
NK McCOY
SEGALLE
RANAWYER
WAITE
ST. CYR
McTYRE
VIRGO
72-845
C'MON, PROFESSOR, BE THERE! ANSWER ME! PLEASE!
FOOTSTEPS!
CHARLES XAVIER SPEAKING.
MARVEL UNIVERSE
PROFESSOR, IT'S CANDY SOTHERN! I'M AT WARREN'S AN' MY MANHATTAN PENTHOUSE. HE'S BEEN ATTACKED!
AND I THINK IT'S ABOUT TO BECOME MY TURN-- OH!!

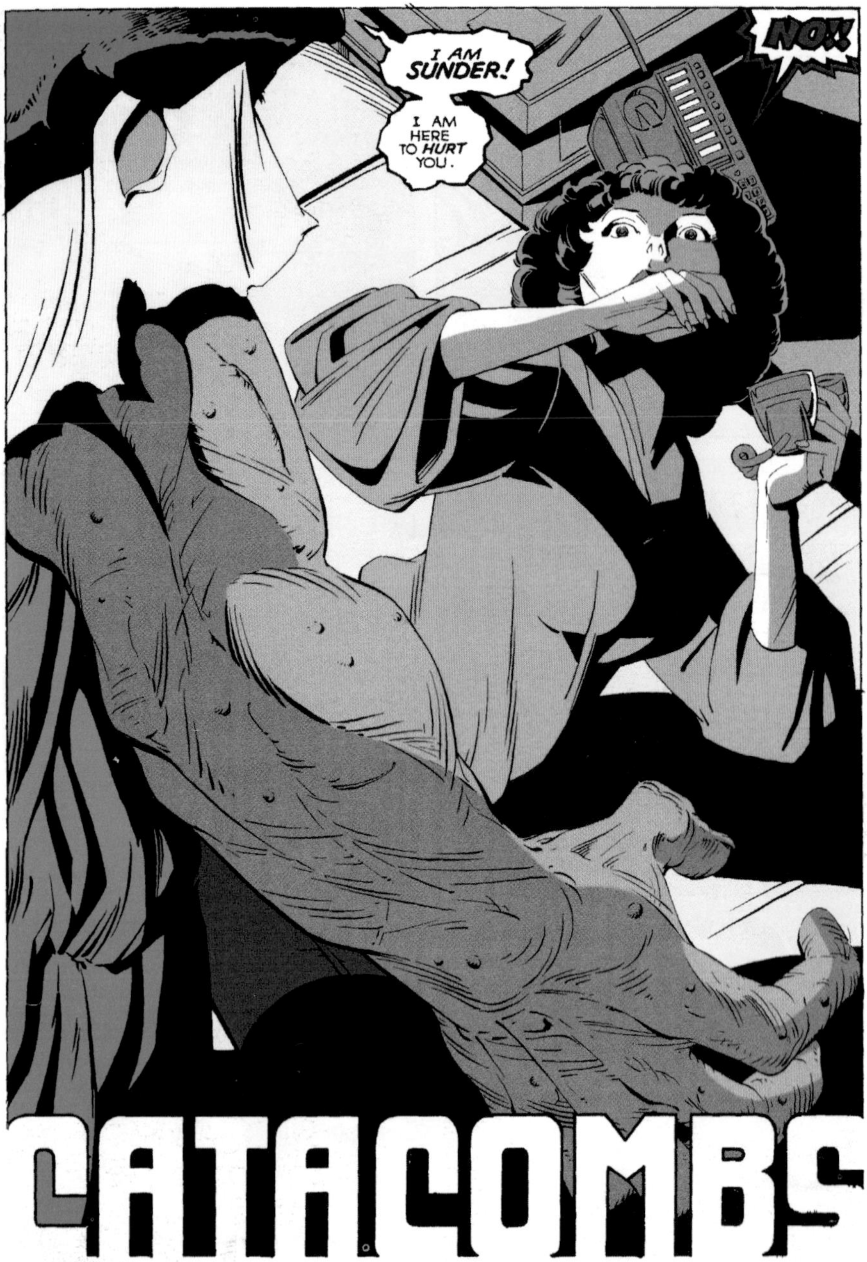
I AM SUNDER!
I AM HERE TO HURT YOU.
NO!!

CATACOMBS

CHRIS CLAREMONT *WRITER* · PAUL SMITH *PENCILLER* · BOB WIACEK *INKER* · BOB SHAREN *COLORIST* · TOM ORZECHOWSKI *LETTERER* · LOUISE JONES *EDITOR* · JIM SHOOTER *EDITOR-IN-CHIEF*

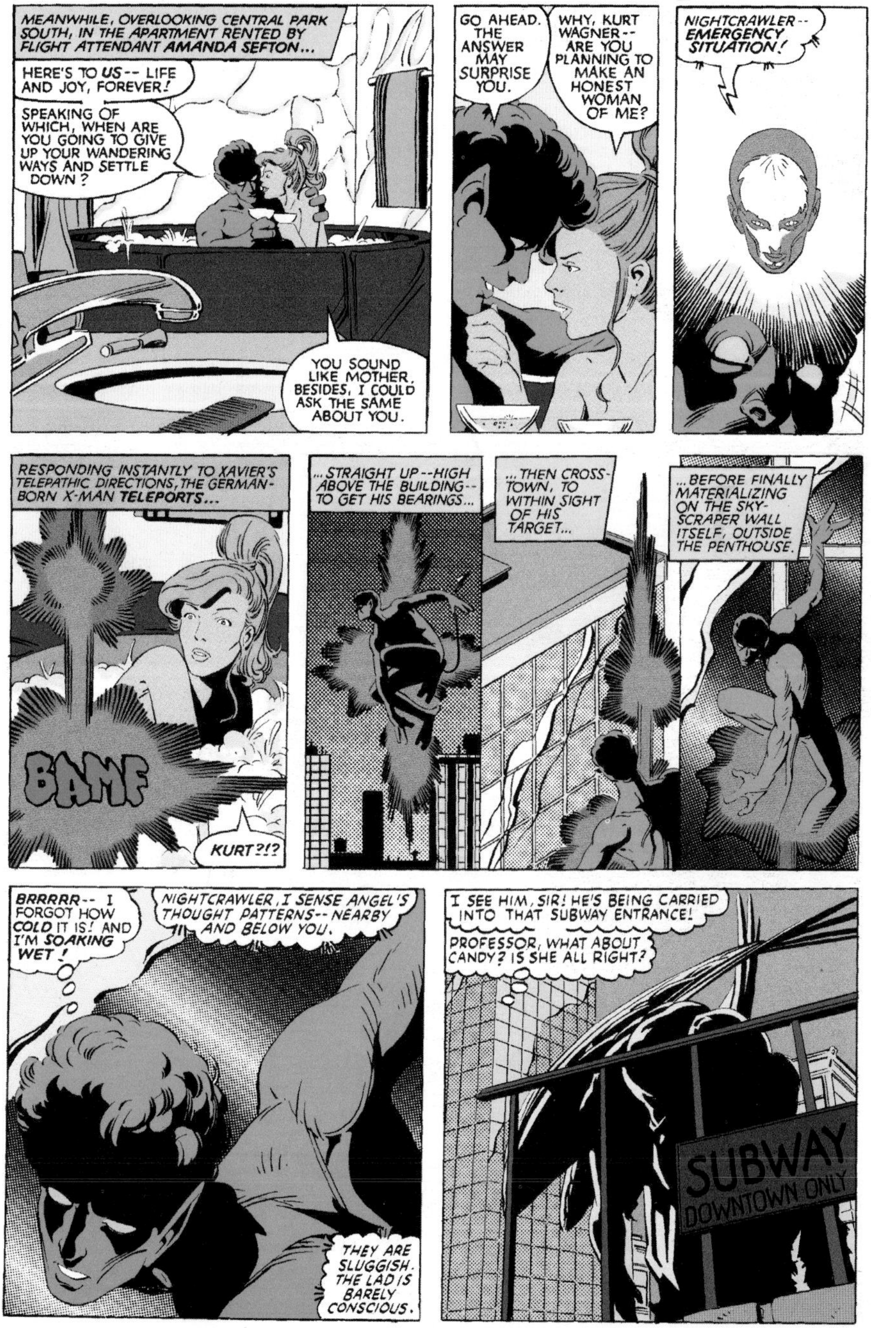
MEANWHILE, OVERLOOKING CENTRAL PARK SOUTH, IN THE APARTMENT RENTED BY FLIGHT ATTENDANT AMANDA SEFTON...
HERE'S TO US -- LIFE AND JOY, FOREVER!
SPEAKING OF WHICH, WHEN ARE YOU GOING TO GIVE UP YOUR WANDERING WAYS AND SETTLE DOWN?
YOU SOUND LIKE MOTHER. BESIDES, I COULD ASK THE SAME ABOUT YOU.
WHY, KURT WAGNER -- ARE YOU PLANNING TO MAKE AN HONEST WOMAN OF ME?
GO AHEAD. THE ANSWER MAY SURPRISE YOU.
NIGHTCRAWLER -- EMERGENCY SITUATION!
RESPONDING INSTANTLY TO XAVIER'S TELEPATHIC DIRECTIONS, THE GERMAN-BORN X-MAN TELEPORTS...
BAMF
KURT?!?
...STRAIGHT UP -- HIGH ABOVE THE BUILDING -- TO GET HIS BEARINGS...
...THEN CROSS-TOWN, TO WITHIN SIGHT OF HIS TARGET...
...BEFORE FINALLY MATERIALIZING ON THE SKY-SCRAPER WALL ITSELF, OUTSIDE THE PENTHOUSE.
BRRRRR -- I FORGOT HOW COLD IT IS! AND I'M SOAKING WET!
NIGHTCRAWLER, I SENSE ANGEL'S THOUGHT PATTERNS -- NEARBY AND BELOW YOU.
THEY ARE SLUGGISH. THE LAD IS BARELY CONSCIOUS.
I SEE HIM, SIR! HE'S BEING CARRIED INTO THAT SUBWAY ENTRANCE!
PROFESSOR, WHAT ABOUT CANDY? IS SHE ALL RIGHT?
SUBWAY
DOWNTOWN ONLY

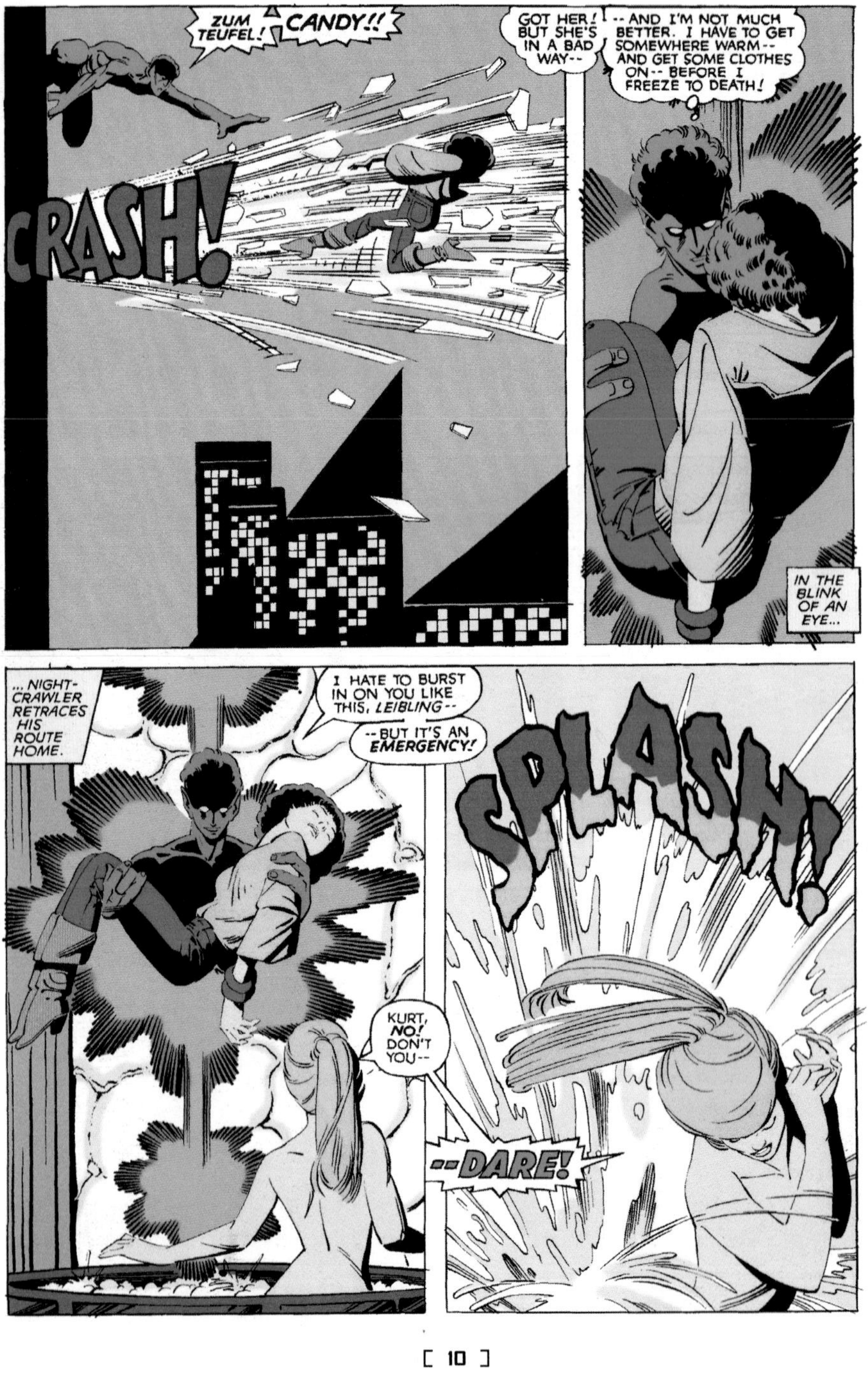
ZUM TEUFEL!
CANDY!!
CRASH!
GOT HER! BUT SHE'S IN A BAD WAY--
-- AND I'M NOT MUCH BETTER. I HAVE TO GET SOMEWHERE WARM-- AND GET SOME CLOTHES ON-- BEFORE I FREEZE TO DEATH!
IN THE BLINK OF AN EYE...
...NIGHT-CRAWLER RETRACES HIS ROUTE HOME.
I HATE TO BURST IN ON YOU LIKE THIS, LEIBLING--
--BUT IT'S AN EMERGENCY!
KURT, NO! DON'T YOU--
SPLASH!
--DARE!

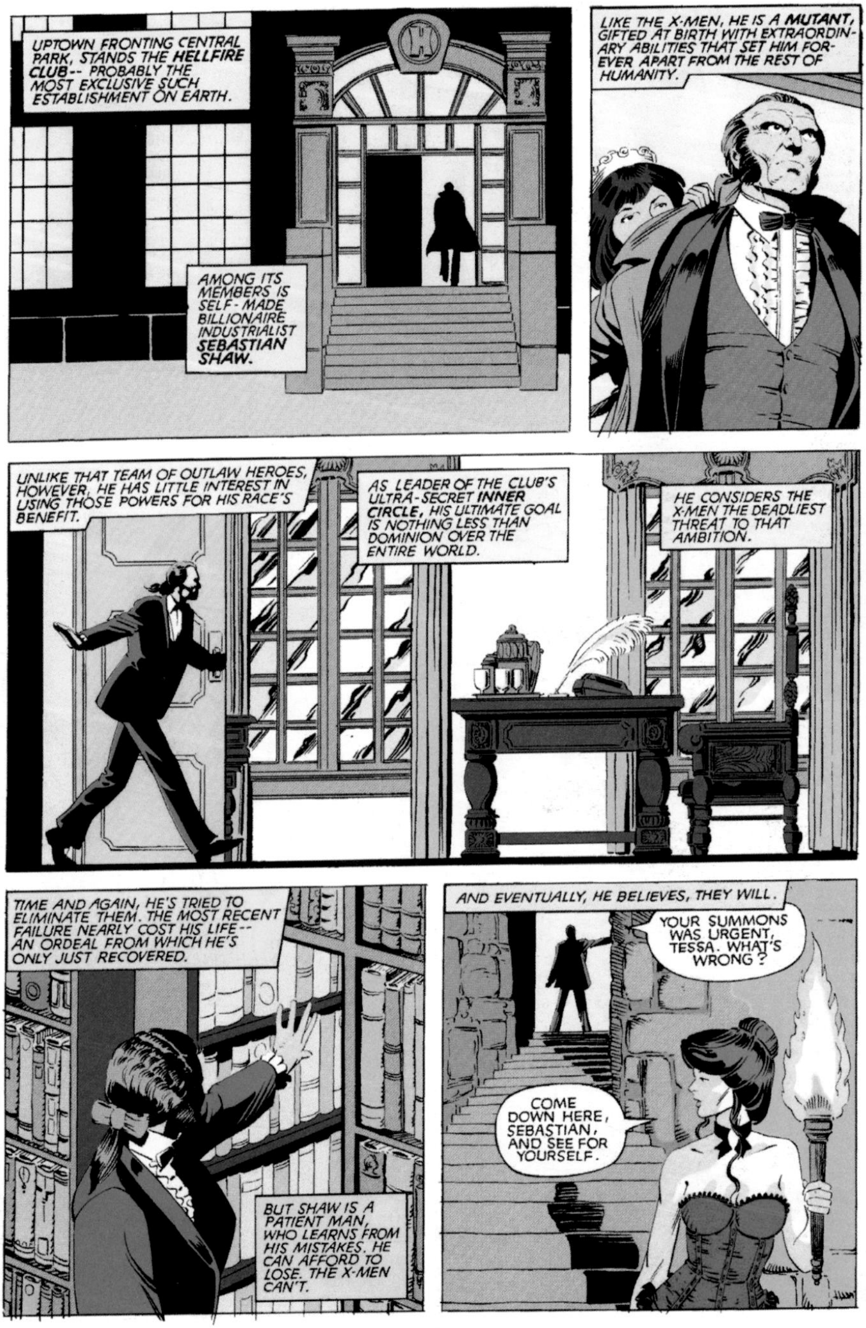
UPTOWN FRONTING CENTRAL PARK, STANDS THE **HELLFIRE CLUB**-- PROBABLY THE MOST EXCLUSIVE SUCH ESTABLISHMENT ON EARTH.
AMONG ITS MEMBERS IS SELF-MADE BILLIONAIRE INDUSTRIALIST **SEBASTIAN SHAW.**
LIKE THE X-MEN, HE IS A **MUTANT,** GIFTED AT BIRTH WITH EXTRAORDINARY ABILITIES THAT SET HIM FOREVER APART FROM THE REST OF HUMANITY.
UNLIKE THAT TEAM OF OUTLAW HEROES, HOWEVER, HE HAS LITTLE INTEREST IN USING THOSE POWERS FOR HIS RACE'S BENEFIT.
AS LEADER OF THE CLUB'S ULTRA-SECRET **INNER CIRCLE,** HIS ULTIMATE GOAL IS NOTHING LESS THAN DOMINION OVER THE ENTIRE WORLD.
HE CONSIDERS THE X-MEN THE DEADLIEST THREAT TO THAT AMBITION.
TIME AND AGAIN, HE'S TRIED TO ELIMINATE THEM. THE MOST RECENT FAILURE NEARLY COST HIS LIFE-- AN ORDEAL FROM WHICH HE'S ONLY JUST RECOVERED.
BUT SHAW IS A PATIENT MAN, WHO LEARNS FROM HIS MISTAKES. HE CAN AFFORD TO LOSE. THE X-MEN CAN'T.
AND EVENTUALLY, HE BELIEVES, THEY WILL.
YOUR SUMMONS WAS URGENT, TESSA. WHAT'S WRONG?
COME DOWN HERE, SEBASTIAN, AND SEE FOR YOURSELF.

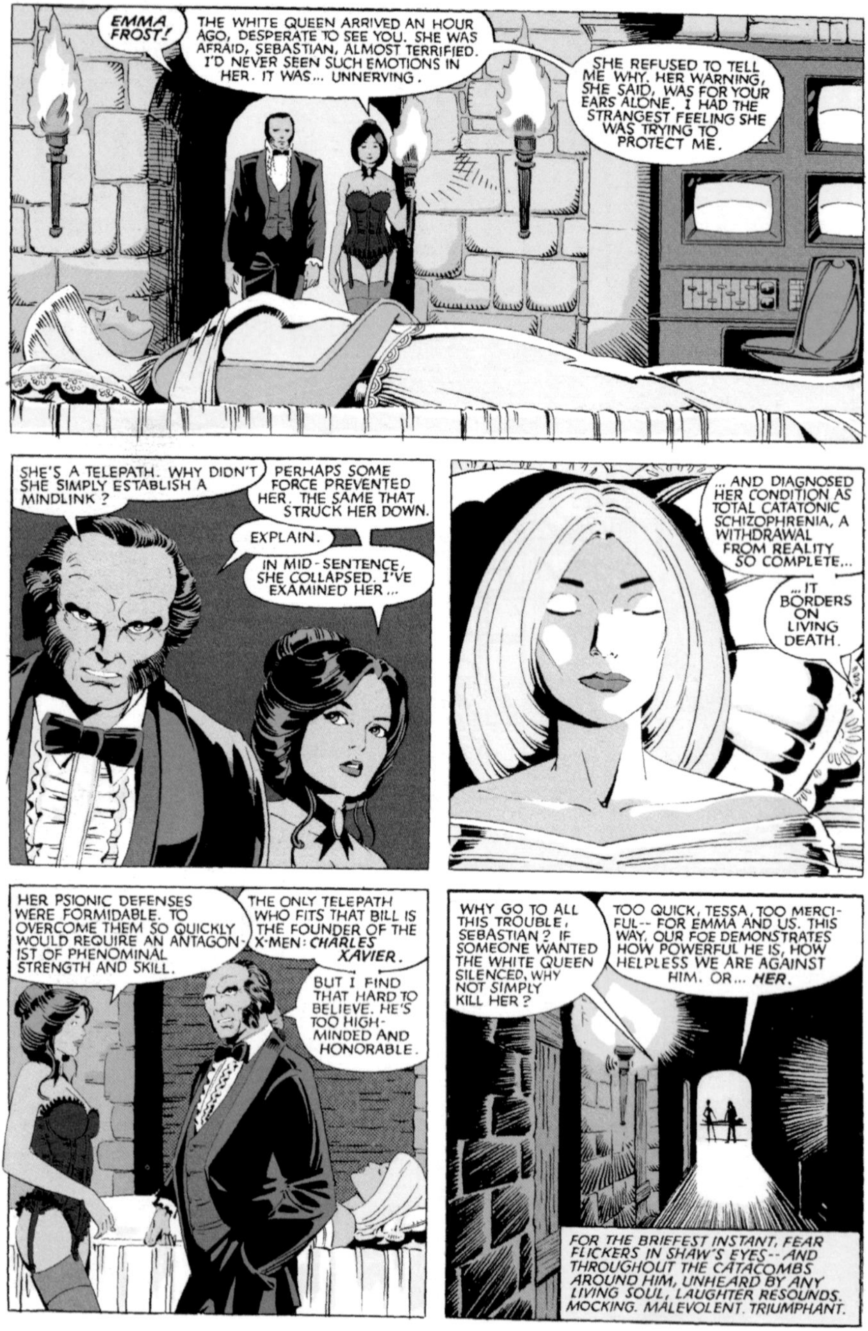
EMMA FROST!
THE WHITE QUEEN ARRIVED AN HOUR AGO, DESPERATE TO SEE YOU. SHE WAS AFRAID, SEBASTIAN, ALMOST TERRIFIED. I'D NEVER SEEN SUCH EMOTIONS IN HER. IT WAS... UNNERVING.
SHE REFUSED TO TELL ME WHY. HER WARNING, SHE SAID, WAS FOR YOUR EARS ALONE. I HAD THE STRANGEST FEELING SHE WAS TRYING TO PROTECT ME.
SHE'S A TELEPATH. WHY DIDN'T SHE SIMPLY ESTABLISH A MINDLINK?
PERHAPS SOME FORCE PREVENTED HER. THE SAME THAT STRUCK HER DOWN.
EXPLAIN.
IN MID-SENTENCE, SHE COLLAPSED. I'VE EXAMINED HER...
... AND DIAGNOSED HER CONDITION AS TOTAL CATATONIC SCHIZOPHRENIA, A WITHDRAWAL FROM REALITY SO COMPLETE...
... IT BORDERS ON LIVING DEATH.
HER PSIONIC DEFENSES WERE FORMIDABLE. TO OVERCOME THEM SO QUICKLY WOULD REQUIRE AN ANTAGON-IST OF PHENOMINAL STRENGTH AND SKILL.
THE ONLY TELEPATH WHO FITS THAT BILL IS THE FOUNDER OF THE X-MEN: CHARLES XAVIER.
BUT I FIND THAT HARD TO BELIEVE. HE'S TOO HIGH-MINDED AND HONORABLE.
WHY GO TO ALL THIS TROUBLE, SEBASTIAN? IF SOMEONE WANTED THE WHITE QUEEN SILENCED, WHY NOT SIMPLY KILL HER?
TOO QUICK, TESSA, TOO MERCIFUL-- FOR EMMA AND US. THIS WAY, OUR FOE DEMONSTRATES HOW POWERFUL HE IS, HOW HELPLESS WE ARE AGAINST HIM. OR... HER.
FOR THE BRIEFEST INSTANT, FEAR FLICKERS IN SHAW'S EYES--AND THROUGHOUT THE CATACOMBS AROUND HIM, UNHEARD BY ANY LIVING SOUL, LAUGHTER RESOUNDS. MOCKING. MALEVOLENT. TRIUMPHANT.

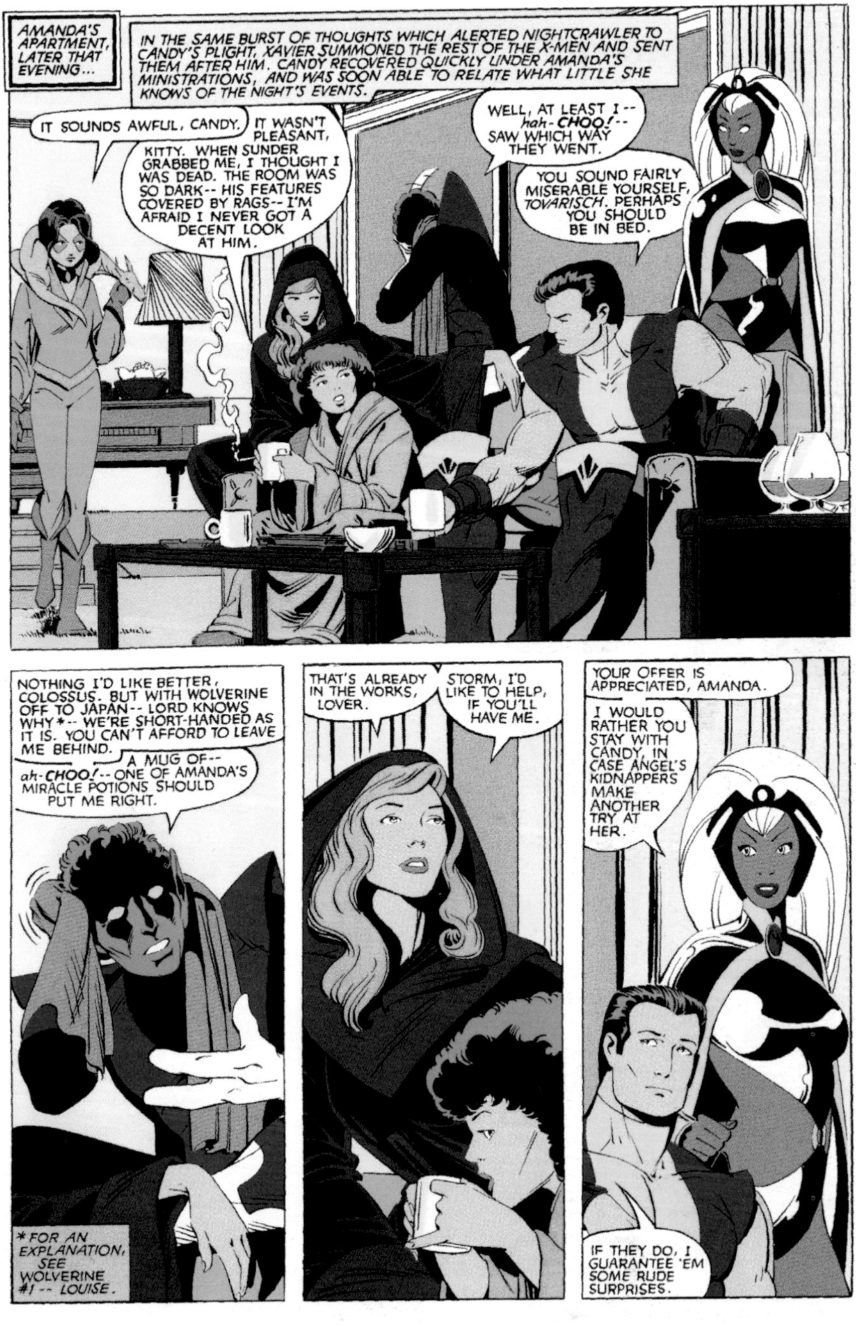
AMANDA'S APARTMENT, LATER THAT EVENING...
IN THE SAME BURST OF THOUGHTS WHICH ALERTED NIGHTCRAWLER TO CANDY'S PLIGHT, XAVIER SUMMONED THE REST OF THE X-MEN AND SENT THEM AFTER HIM. CANDY RECOVERED QUICKLY UNDER AMANDA'S MINISTRATIONS, AND WAS SOON ABLE TO RELATE WHAT LITTLE SHE KNOWS OF THE NIGHT'S EVENTS.
IT SOUNDS AWFUL, CANDY.
IT WASN'T PLEASANT, KITTY. WHEN SUNDER GRABBED ME, I THOUGHT I WAS DEAD. THE ROOM WAS SO DARK-- HIS FEATURES COVERED BY RAGS-- I'M AFRAID I NEVER GOT A DECENT LOOK AT HIM.
WELL, AT LEAST I -- hah-CHOO!-- SAW WHICH WAY THEY WENT.
YOU SOUND FAIRLY MISERABLE YOURSELF, TOVARISCH. PERHAPS YOU SHOULD BE IN BED.
NOTHING I'D LIKE BETTER, COLOSSUS. BUT WITH WOLVERINE OFF TO JAPAN-- LORD KNOWS WHY*-- WE'RE SHORT-HANDED AS IT IS. YOU CAN'T AFFORD TO LEAVE ME BEHIND.
A MUG OF-- ah-CHOO!-- ONE OF AMANDA'S MIRACLE POTIONS SHOULD PUT ME RIGHT.
*FOR AN EXPLANATION, SEE WOLVERINE #1 -- LOUISE.
THAT'S ALREADY IN THE WORKS, LOVER.
STORM, I'D LIKE TO HELP, IF YOU'LL HAVE ME.
YOUR OFFER IS APPRECIATED, AMANDA.
I WOULD RATHER YOU STAY WITH CANDY, IN CASE ANGEL'S KIDNAPPERS MAKE ANOTHER TRY AT HER.
IF THEY DO, I GUARANTEE 'EM SOME RUDE SURPRISES.

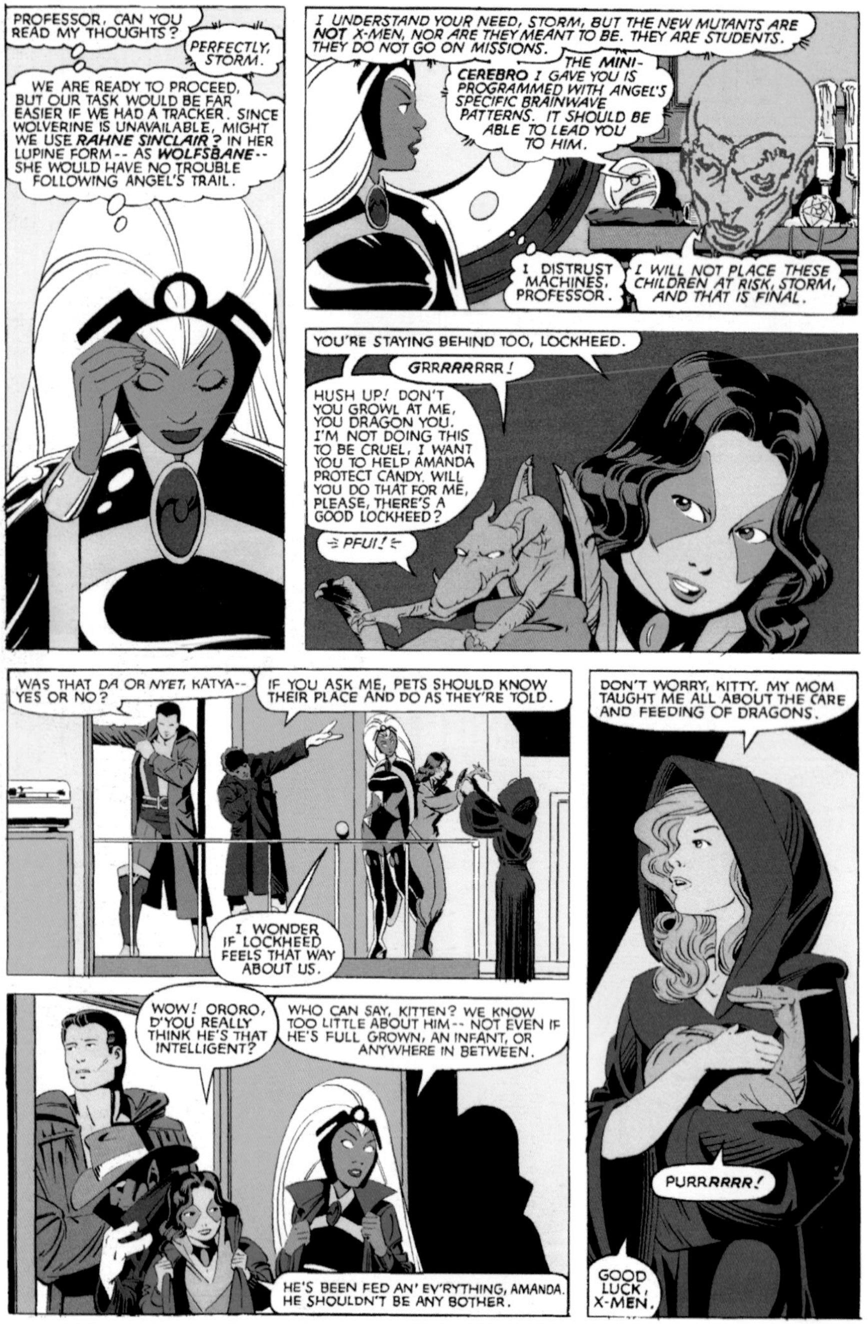
PROFESSOR, CAN YOU READ MY THOUGHTS?
PERFECTLY, STORM.
WE ARE READY TO PROCEED, BUT OUR TASK WOULD BE FAR EASIER IF WE HAD A TRACKER. SINCE WOLVERINE IS UNAVAILABLE, MIGHT WE USE RAHNE SINCLAIR? IN HER LUPINE FORM -- AS WOLFSBANE -- SHE WOULD HAVE NO TROUBLE FOLLOWING ANGEL'S TRAIL.
I UNDERSTAND YOUR NEED, STORM, BUT THE NEW MUTANTS ARE NOT X-MEN, NOR ARE THEY MEANT TO BE. THEY ARE STUDENTS. THEY DO NOT GO ON MISSIONS.
THE MINI-CEREBRO I GAVE YOU IS PROGRAMMED WITH ANGEL'S SPECIFIC BRAINWAVE PATTERNS. IT SHOULD BE ABLE TO LEAD YOU TO HIM.
I DISTRUST MACHINES, PROFESSOR.
I WILL NOT PLACE THESE CHILDREN AT RISK, STORM, AND THAT IS FINAL.
YOU'RE STAYING BEHIND TOO, LOCKHEED.
GRRRRRRRR!
HUSH UP! DON'T YOU GROWL AT ME, YOU DRAGON YOU. I'M NOT DOING THIS TO BE CRUEL. I WANT YOU TO HELP AMANDA PROTECT CANDY. WILL YOU DO THAT FOR ME, PLEASE, THERE'S A GOOD LOCKHEED?
PFUI!
WAS THAT DA OR NYET, KATYA -- YES OR NO?
IF YOU ASK ME, PETS SHOULD KNOW THEIR PLACE AND DO AS THEY'RE TOLD.
I WONDER IF LOCKHEED FEELS THAT WAY ABOUT US.
WOW! ORORO, D'YOU REALLY THINK HE'S THAT INTELLIGENT?
WHO CAN SAY, KITTEN? WE KNOW TOO LITTLE ABOUT HIM -- NOT EVEN IF HE'S FULL GROWN, AN INFANT, OR ANYWHERE IN BETWEEN.
HE'S BEEN FED AN' EV'RYTHING, AMANDA. HE SHOULDN'T BE ANY BOTHER.
DON'T WORRY, KITTY. MY MOM TAUGHT ME ALL ABOUT THE CARE AND FEEDING OF DRAGONS.
PURRRRRR!
GOOD LUCK, X-MEN.

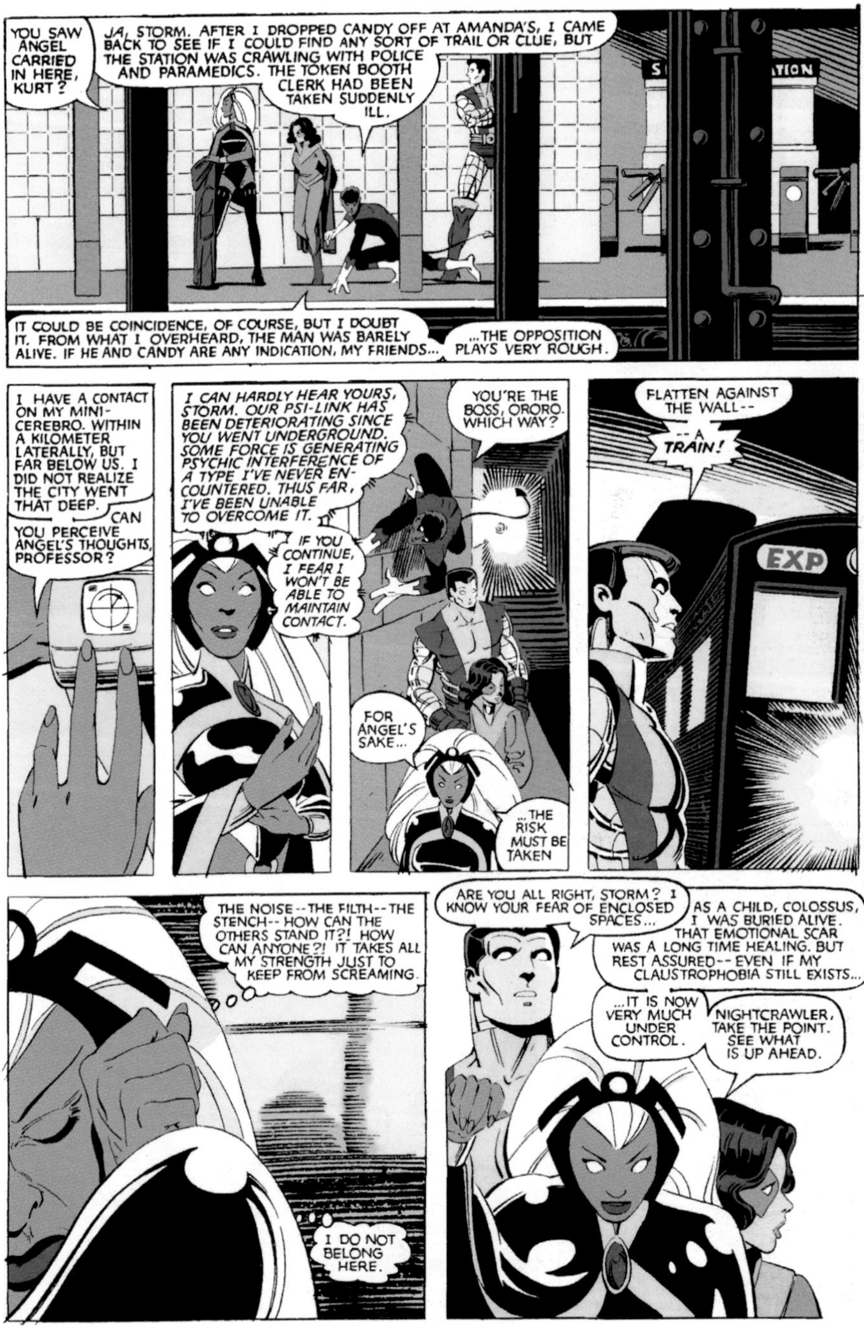
YOU SAW ANGEL CARRIED IN HERE, KURT?
JA, STORM. AFTER I DROPPED CANDY OFF AT AMANDA'S, I CAME BACK TO SEE IF I COULD FIND ANY SORT OF TRAIL OR CLUE, BUT THE STATION WAS CRAWLING WITH POLICE AND PARAMEDICS. THE TOKEN BOOTH CLERK HAD BEEN TAKEN SUDDENLY ILL.
IT COULD BE COINCIDENCE, OF COURSE, BUT I DOUBT IT. FROM WHAT I OVERHEARD, THE MAN WAS BARELY ALIVE. IF HE AND CANDY ARE ANY INDICATION, MY FRIENDS...
...THE OPPOSITION PLAYS VERY ROUGH.
I HAVE A CONTACT ON MY MINI-CEREBRO. WITHIN A KILOMETER LATERALLY, BUT FAR BELOW US. I DID NOT REALIZE THE CITY WENT THAT DEEP.
CAN YOU PERCEIVE ANGEL'S THOUGHTS, PROFESSOR?
I CAN HARDLY HEAR YOURS, STORM. OUR PSI-LINK HAS BEEN DETERIORATING SINCE YOU WENT UNDERGROUND. SOME FORCE IS GENERATING PSYCHIC INTERFERENCE OF A TYPE I'VE NEVER ENCOUNTERED. THUS FAR, I'VE BEEN UNABLE TO OVERCOME IT.
IF YOU CONTINUE, I FEAR I WON'T BE ABLE TO MAINTAIN CONTACT.
YOU'RE THE BOSS, ORORO. WHICH WAY?
FOR ANGEL'S SAKE...
...THE RISK MUST BE TAKEN
FLATTEN AGAINST THE WALL--
--A TRAIN!
EXP
THE NOISE--THE FILTH--THE STENCH--HOW CAN THE OTHERS STAND IT?! HOW CAN ANYONE?! IT TAKES ALL MY STRENGTH JUST TO KEEP FROM SCREAMING.
I DO NOT BELONG HERE.
ARE YOU ALL RIGHT, STORM? I KNOW YOUR FEAR OF ENCLOSED SPACES...
AS A CHILD, COLOSSUS, I WAS BURIED ALIVE. THAT EMOTIONAL SCAR WAS A LONG TIME HEALING. BUT REST ASSURED--EVEN IF MY CLAUSTROPHOBIA STILL EXISTS...
...IT IS NOW VERY MUCH UNDER CONTROL.
NIGHTCRAWLER, TAKE THE POINT. SEE WHAT IS UP AHEAD.

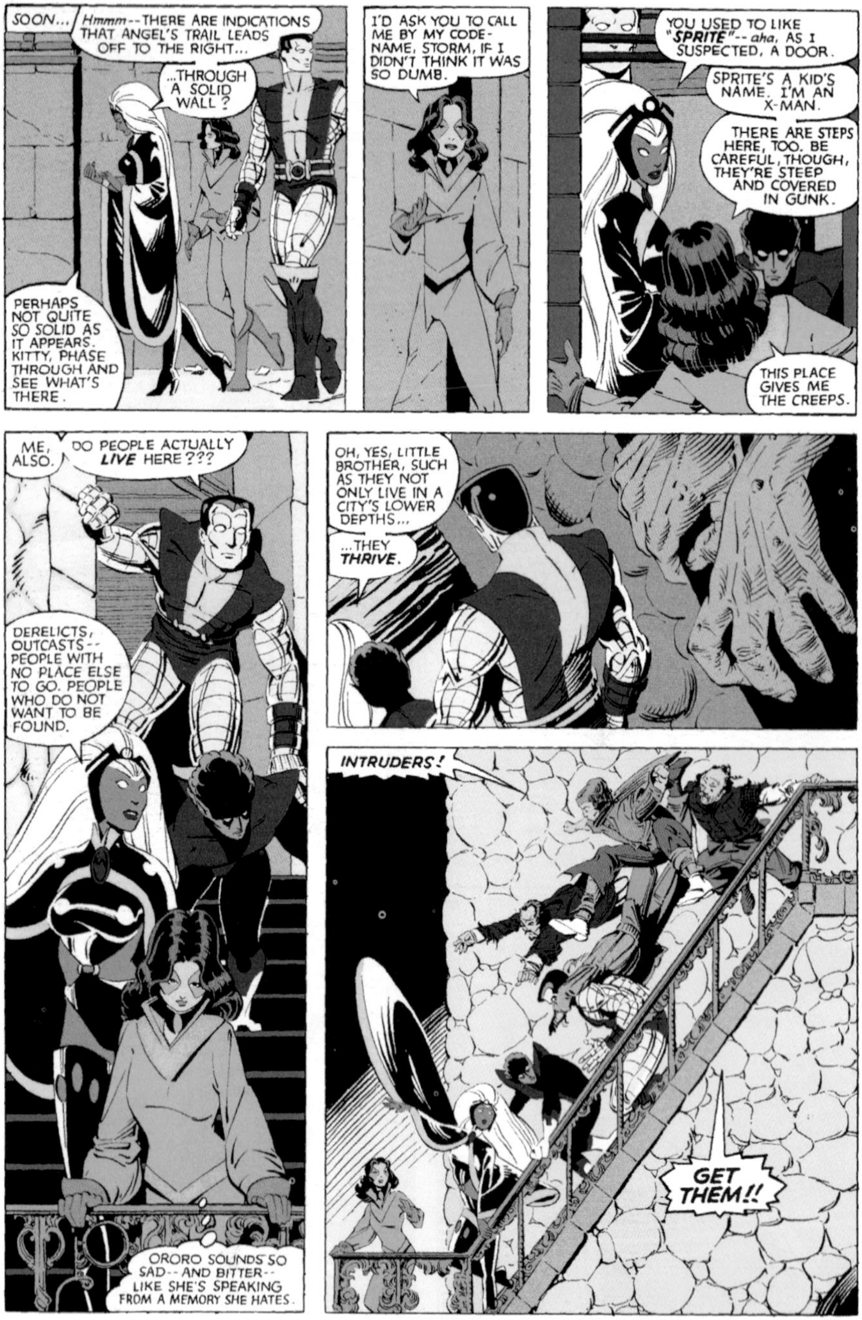

SOON...
Hmmm--THERE ARE INDICATIONS THAT ANGEL'S TRAIL LEADS OFF TO THE RIGHT...
...THROUGH A SOLID WALL ?
PERHAPS NOT QUITE SO SOLID AS IT APPEARS. KITTY, PHASE THROUGH AND SEE WHAT'S THERE.
I'D ASK YOU TO CALL ME BY MY CODE-NAME, STORM, IF I DIDN'T THINK IT WAS SO DUMB.
YOU USED TO LIKE "SPRITE"-- aha, AS I SUSPECTED, A DOOR.
SPRITE'S A KID'S NAME. I'M AN X-MAN.
THERE ARE STEPS HERE, TOO. BE CAREFUL, THOUGH, THEY'RE STEEP AND COVERED IN GUNK.
THIS PLACE GIVES ME THE CREEPS.
ME, ALSO.
DO PEOPLE ACTUALLY LIVE HERE???
DERELICTS, OUTCASTS-- PEOPLE WITH NO PLACE ELSE TO GO. PEOPLE WHO DO NOT WANT TO BE FOUND.
ORORO SOUNDS SO SAD-- AND BITTER-- LIKE SHE'S SPEAKING FROM A MEMORY SHE HATES.
OH, YES, LITTLE BROTHER, SUCH AS THEY NOT ONLY LIVE IN A CITY'S LOWER DEPTHS...
...THEY THRIVE.
INTRUDERS!
GET THEM!!

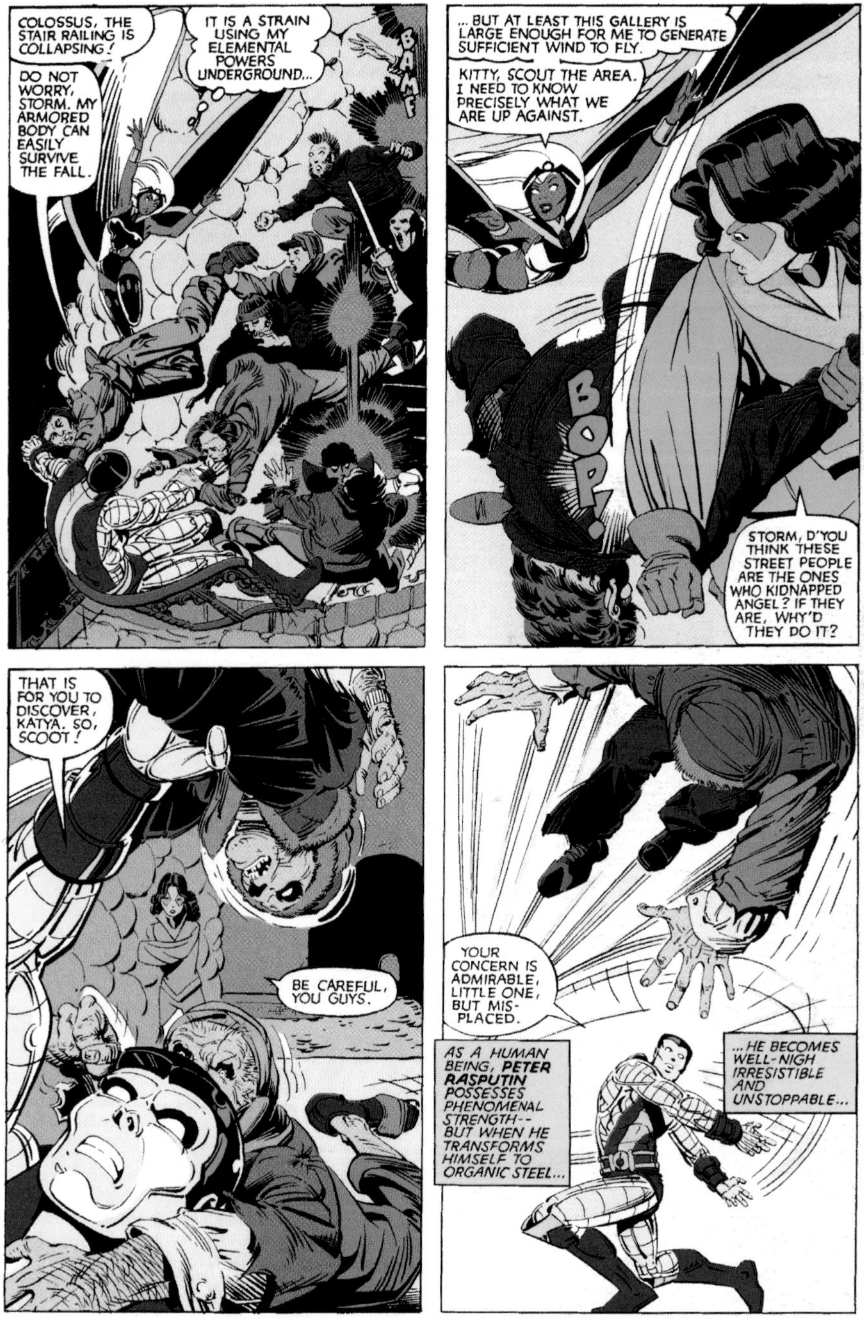
COLOSSUS, THE STAIR RAILING IS COLLAPSING!
IT IS A STRAIN USING MY ELEMENTAL POWERS UNDERGROUND...
DO NOT WORRY, STORM. MY ARMORED BODY CAN EASILY SURVIVE THE FALL.
BAMF
... BUT AT LEAST THIS GALLERY IS LARGE ENOUGH FOR ME TO GENERATE SUFFICIENT WIND TO FLY.
KITTY, SCOUT THE AREA. I NEED TO KNOW PRECISELY WHAT WE ARE UP AGAINST.
BOP!
STORM, D'YOU THINK THESE STREET PEOPLE ARE THE ONES WHO KIDNAPPED ANGEL? IF THEY ARE, WHY'D THEY DO IT?
THAT IS FOR YOU TO DISCOVER, KATYA. SO, SCOOT!
BE CAREFUL, YOU GUYS.
YOUR CONCERN IS ADMIRABLE, LITTLE ONE, BUT MISPLACED.
AS A HUMAN BEING, PETER RASPUTIN POSSESSES PHENOMENAL STRENGTH-- BUT WHEN HE TRANSFORMS HIMSELF TO ORGANIC STEEL...
...HE BECOMES WELL-NIGH IRRESISTIBLE AND UNSTOPPABLE...

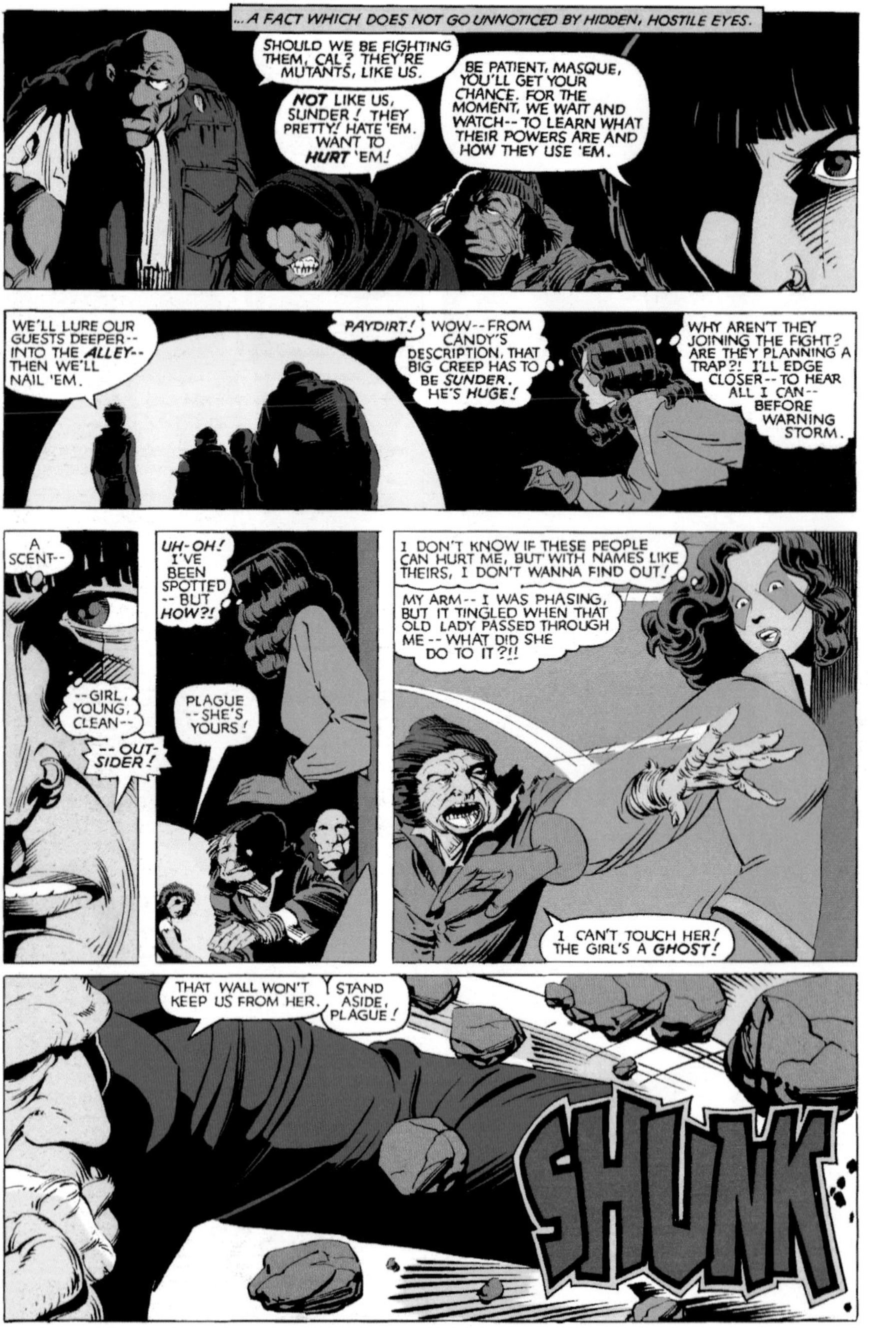
...A FACT WHICH DOES NOT GO UNNOTICED BY HIDDEN, HOSTILE EYES.
SHOULD WE BE FIGHTING THEM, CAL? THEY'RE MUTANTS, LIKE US.
NOT LIKE US, SUNDER! THEY PRETTY! HATE 'EM. WANT TO HURT 'EM!
BE PATIENT, MASQUE, YOU'LL GET YOUR CHANCE. FOR THE MOMENT, WE WAIT AND WATCH-- TO LEARN WHAT THEIR POWERS ARE AND HOW THEY USE 'EM.
WE'LL LURE OUR GUESTS DEEPER-- INTO THE ALLEY-- THEN WE'LL NAIL 'EM.
PAYDIRT!
WOW--FROM CANDY'S DESCRIPTION, THAT BIG CREEP HAS TO BE SUNDER. HE'S HUGE!
WHY AREN'T THEY JOINING THE FIGHT? ARE THEY PLANNING A TRAP?! I'LL EDGE CLOSER--TO HEAR ALL I CAN-- BEFORE WARNING STORM.
A SCENT--
--GIRL, YOUNG, CLEAN--
--OUT-SIDER!
UH-OH! I'VE BEEN SPOTTED --BUT HOW?!
PLAGUE --SHE'S YOURS!
I DON'T KNOW IF THESE PEOPLE CAN HURT ME, BUT WITH NAMES LIKE THEIRS, I DON'T WANNA FIND OUT!
MY ARM-- I WAS PHASING, BUT IT TINGLED WHEN THAT OLD LADY PASSED THROUGH ME-- WHAT DID SHE DO TO IT?!!
I CAN'T TOUCH HER! THE GIRL'S A GHOST!
THAT WALL WON'T KEEP US FROM HER.
STAND ASIDE, PLAGUE!
SHUNK

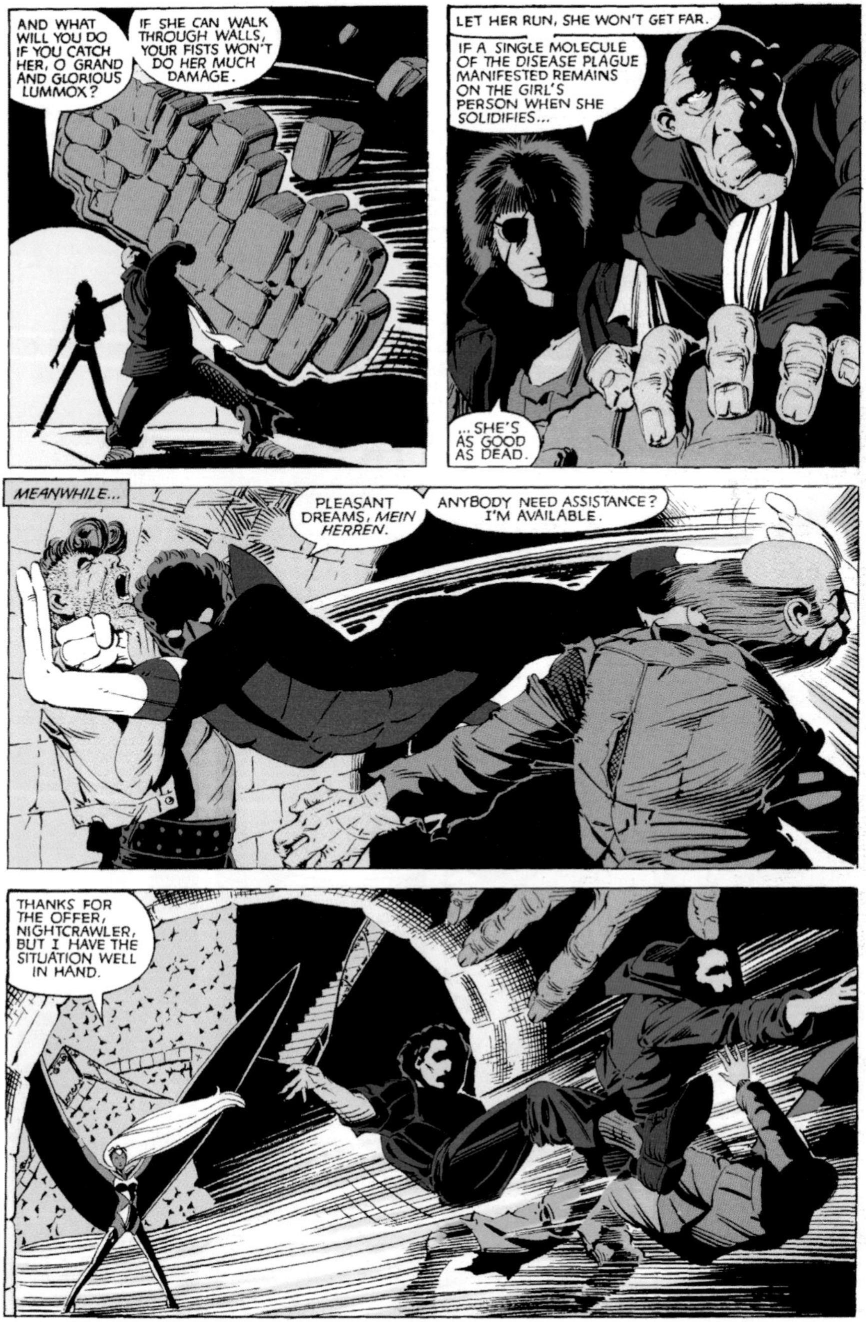
AND WHAT WILL YOU DO IF YOU CATCH HER, O GRAND AND GLORIOUS LUMMOX?
IF SHE CAN WALK THROUGH WALLS, YOUR FISTS WON'T DO HER MUCH DAMAGE.
LET HER RUN, SHE WON'T GET FAR.
IF A SINGLE MOLECULE OF THE DISEASE PLAGUE MANIFESTED REMAINS ON THE GIRL'S PERSON WHEN SHE SOLIDIFIES...
...SHE'S AS GOOD AS DEAD.
MEANWHILE...
PLEASANT DREAMS, MEIN HERREN.
ANYBODY NEED ASSISTANCE? I'M AVAILABLE.
THANKS FOR THE OFFER, NIGHTCRAWLER, BUT I HAVE THE SITUATION WELL IN HAND.

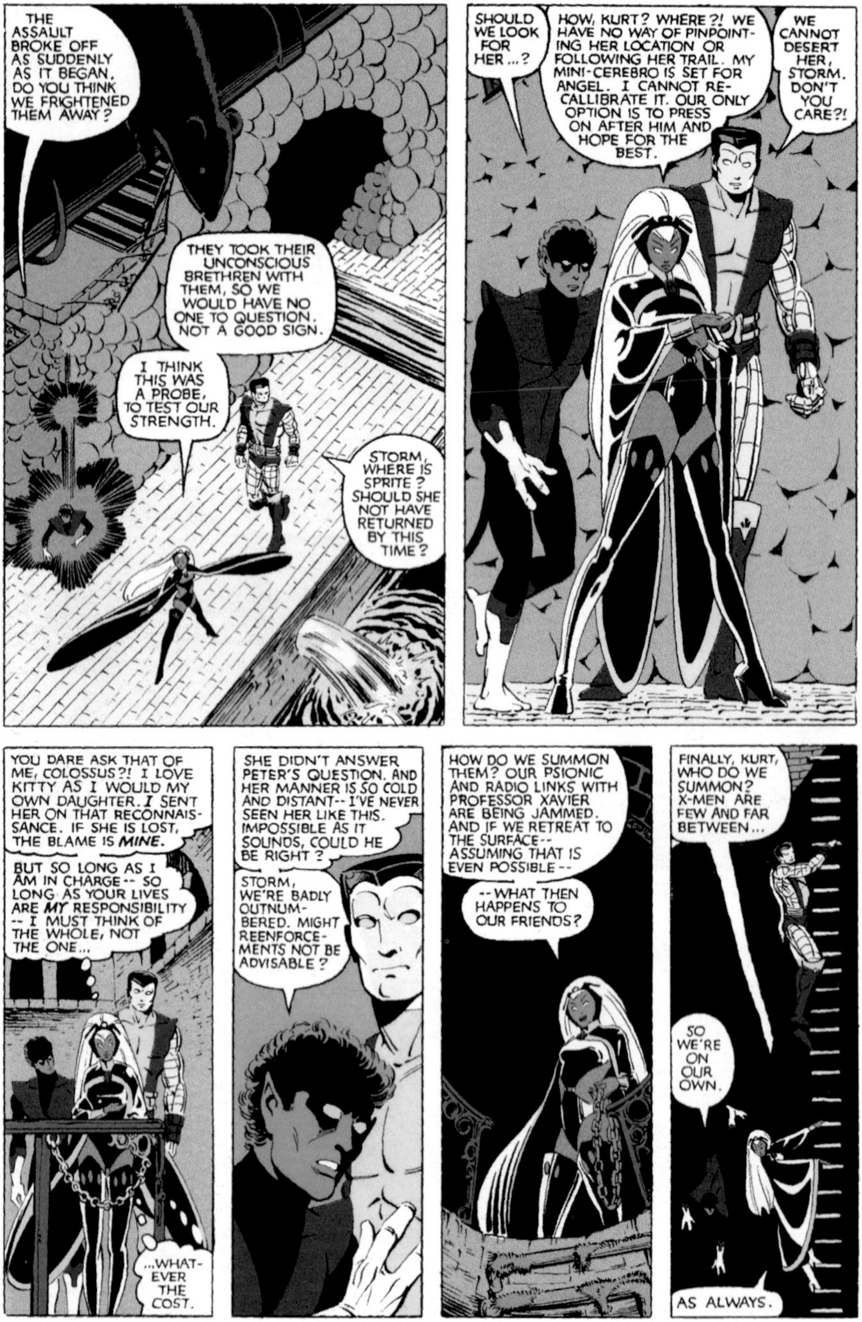
THE ASSAULT BROKE OFF AS SUDDENLY AS IT BEGAN. DO YOU THINK WE FRIGHTENED THEM AWAY?
THEY TOOK THEIR UNCONSCIOUS BRETHREN WITH THEM, SO WE WOULD HAVE NO ONE TO QUESTION. NOT A GOOD SIGN.
I THINK THIS WAS A PROBE, TO TEST OUR STRENGTH.
STORM, WHERE IS SPRITE? SHOULD SHE NOT HAVE RETURNED BY THIS TIME?
SHOULD WE LOOK FOR HER...?
HOW, KURT? WHERE?! WE HAVE NO WAY OF PINPOINTING HER LOCATION OR FOLLOWING HER TRAIL. MY MINI-CEREBRO IS SET FOR ANGEL. I CANNOT RE-CALLIBRATE IT. OUR ONLY OPTION IS TO PRESS ON AFTER HIM AND HOPE FOR THE BEST.
WE CANNOT DESERT HER, STORM. DON'T YOU CARE?!
YOU DARE ASK THAT OF ME, COLOSSUS?! I LOVE KITTY AS I WOULD MY OWN DAUGHTER. I SENT HER ON THAT RECONNAISSANCE. IF SHE IS LOST, THE BLAME IS *MINE*.
BUT SO LONG AS I AM IN CHARGE -- SO LONG AS YOUR LIVES ARE *MY* RESPONSIBILITY -- I MUST THINK OF THE WHOLE, NOT THE ONE...
...WHATEVER THE COST.
SHE DIDN'T ANSWER PETER'S QUESTION. AND HER MANNER IS SO COLD AND DISTANT -- I'VE NEVER SEEN HER LIKE THIS. IMPOSSIBLE AS IT SOUNDS, COULD HE BE RIGHT?
STORM, WE'RE BADLY OUTNUMBERED. MIGHT REENFORCEMENTS NOT BE ADVISABLE?
HOW DO WE SUMMON THEM? OUR PSIONIC AND RADIO LINKS WITH PROFESSOR XAVIER ARE BEING JAMMED. AND IF WE RETREAT TO THE SURFACE -- ASSUMING THAT IS EVEN POSSIBLE --
-- WHAT THEN HAPPENS TO OUR FRIENDS?
FINALLY, KURT, WHO DO WE SUMMON? X-MEN ARE FEW AND FAR BETWEEN...
SO WE'RE ON OUR OWN.
AS ALWAYS.

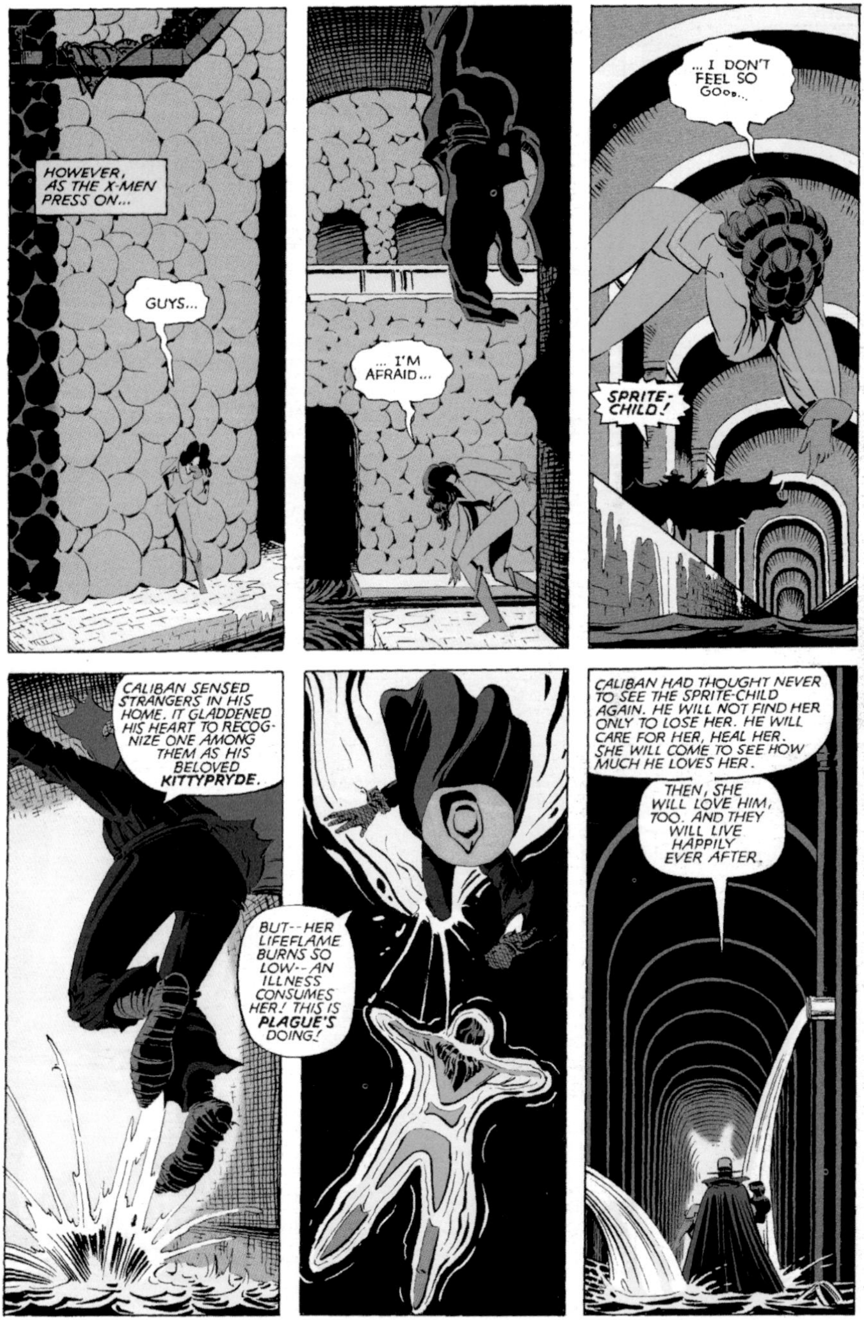
HOWEVER, AS THE X-MEN PRESS ON...
GUYS...
... I'M AFRAID...
... I DON'T FEEL SO GOOD...
SPRITE-CHILD!
CALIBAN SENSED STRANGERS IN HIS HOME. IT GLADDENED HIS HEART TO RECOGNIZE ONE AMONG THEM AS HIS BELOVED KITTYPRYDE.
BUT--HER LIFEFLAME BURNS SO LOW--AN ILLNESS CONSUMES HER! THIS IS PLAGUE'S DOING!
CALIBAN HAD THOUGHT NEVER TO SEE THE SPRITE-CHILD AGAIN. HE WILL NOT FIND HER ONLY TO LOSE HER. HE WILL CARE FOR HER, HEAL HER. SHE WILL COME TO SEE HOW MUCH HE LOVES HER.
THEN, SHE WILL LOVE HIM, TOO. AND THEY WILL LIVE HAPPILY EVER AFTER.

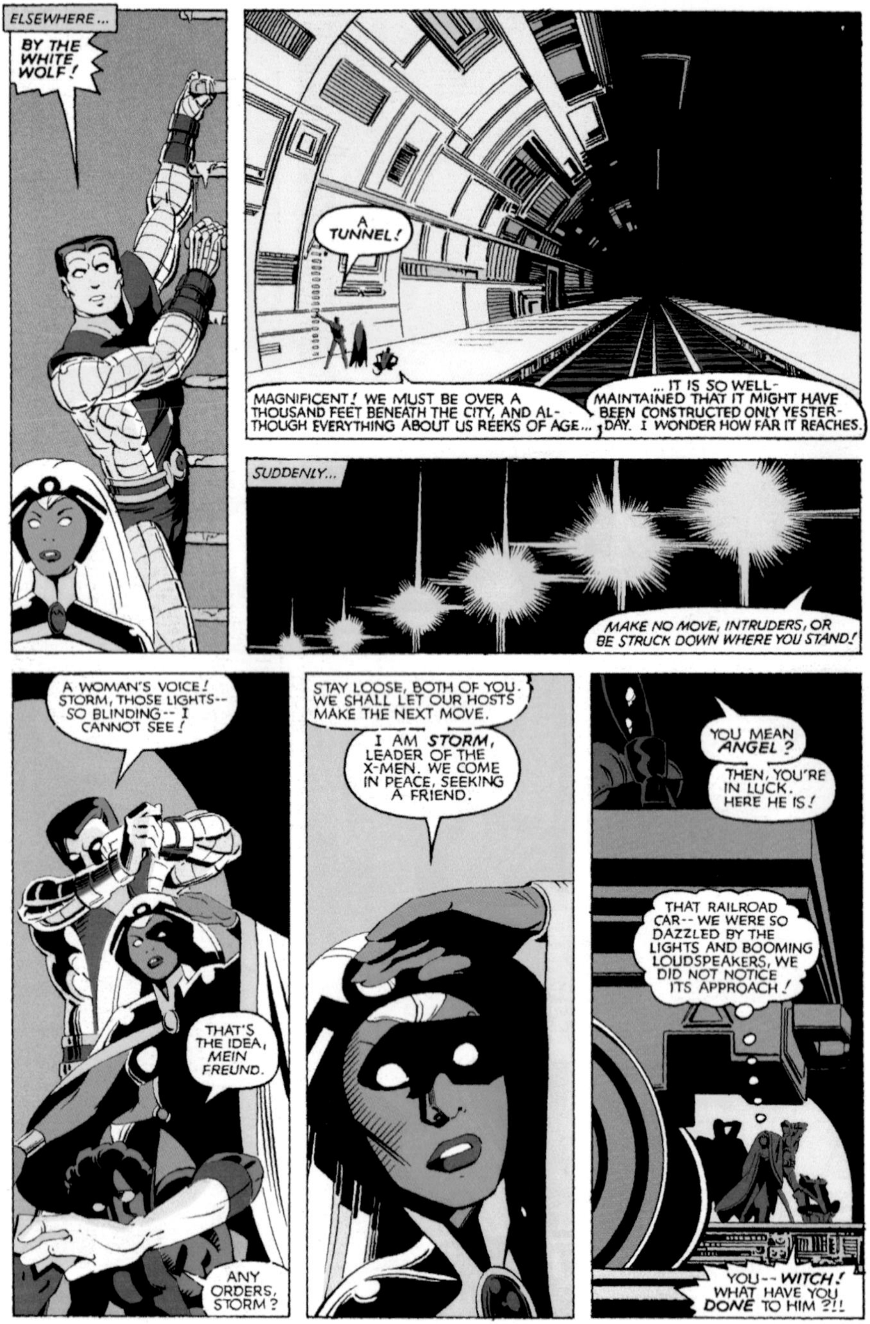
ELSEWHERE...
BY THE WHITE WOLF!
A TUNNEL!
MAGNIFICENT! WE MUST BE OVER A THOUSAND FEET BENEATH THE CITY, AND ALTHOUGH EVERYTHING ABOUT US REEKS OF AGE...
... IT IS SO WELL-MAINTAINED THAT IT MIGHT HAVE BEEN CONSTRUCTED ONLY YESTERDAY. I WONDER HOW FAR IT REACHES.
SUDDENLY...
MAKE NO MOVE, INTRUDERS, OR BE STRUCK DOWN WHERE YOU STAND!
A WOMAN'S VOICE! STORM, THOSE LIGHTS-- SO BLINDING-- I CANNOT SEE!
THAT'S THE IDEA, MEIN FREUND.
ANY ORDERS, STORM?
STAY LOOSE, BOTH OF YOU. WE SHALL LET OUR HOSTS MAKE THE NEXT MOVE.
I AM STORM, LEADER OF THE X-MEN. WE COME IN PEACE, SEEKING A FRIEND.
YOU MEAN ANGEL?
THEN, YOU'RE IN LUCK. HERE HE IS!
THAT RAILROAD CAR-- WE WERE SO DAZZLED BY THE LIGHTS AND BOOMING LOUDSPEAKERS, WE DID NOT NOTICE ITS APPROACH!
YOU-- WITCH! WHAT HAVE YOU DONE TO HIM?!!

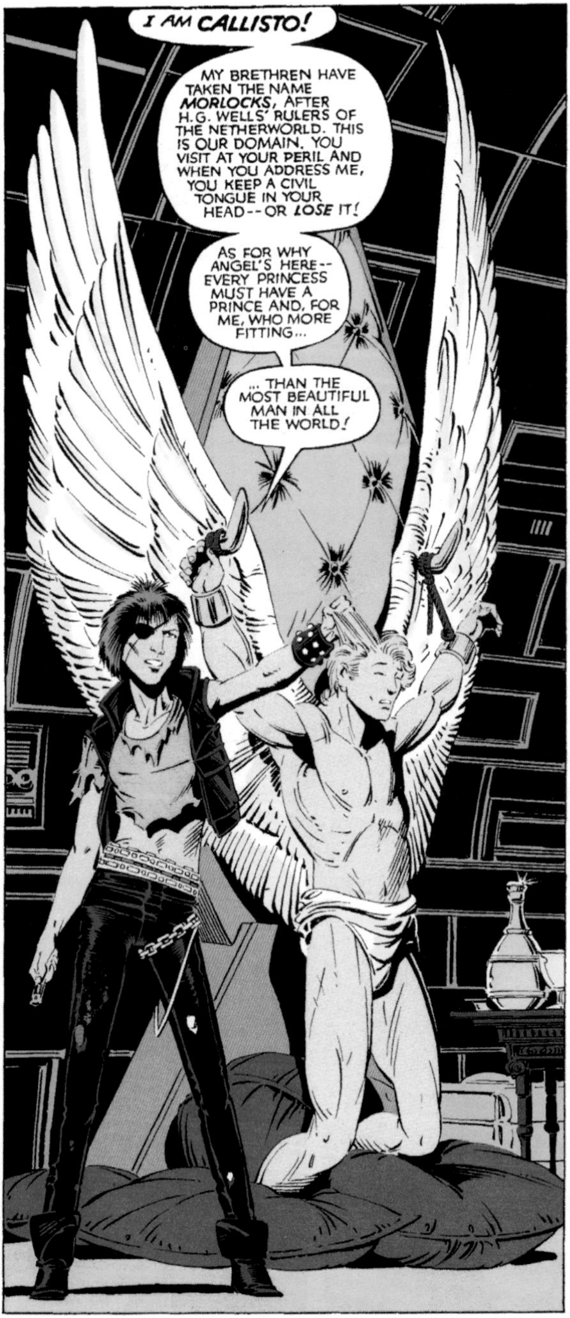
I AM CALLISTO!
MY BRETHREN HAVE TAKEN THE NAME MORLOCKS, AFTER H.G. WELLS' RULERS OF THE NETHERWORLD. THIS IS OUR DOMAIN. YOU VISIT AT YOUR PERIL AND WHEN YOU ADDRESS ME, YOU KEEP A CIVIL TONGUE IN YOUR HEAD--OR LOSE IT!
AS FOR WHY ANGEL'S HERE--EVERY PRINCESS MUST HAVE A PRINCE AND, FOR ME, WHO MORE FITTING...
... THAN THE MOST BEAUTIFUL MAN IN ALL THE WORLD!

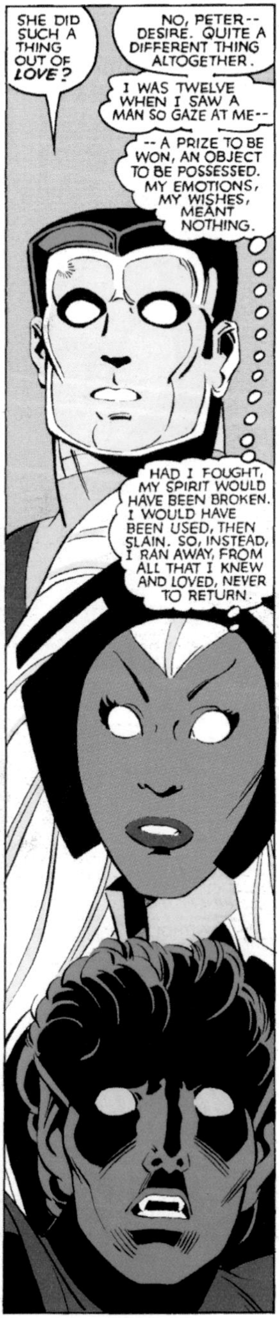
SHE DID SUCH A THING OUT OF LOVE?
NO, PETER--DESIRE. QUITE A DIFFERENT THING ALTOGETHER.
I WAS TWELVE WHEN I SAW A MAN SO GAZE AT ME--
--A PRIZE TO BE WON, AN OBJECT TO BE POSSESSED. MY EMOTIONS, MY WISHES, MEANT NOTHING.
HAD I FOUGHT, MY SPIRIT WOULD HAVE BEEN BROKEN. I WOULD HAVE BEEN USED, THEN SLAIN. SO, INSTEAD, I RAN AWAY, FROM ALL THAT I KNEW AND LOVED, NEVER TO RETURN.

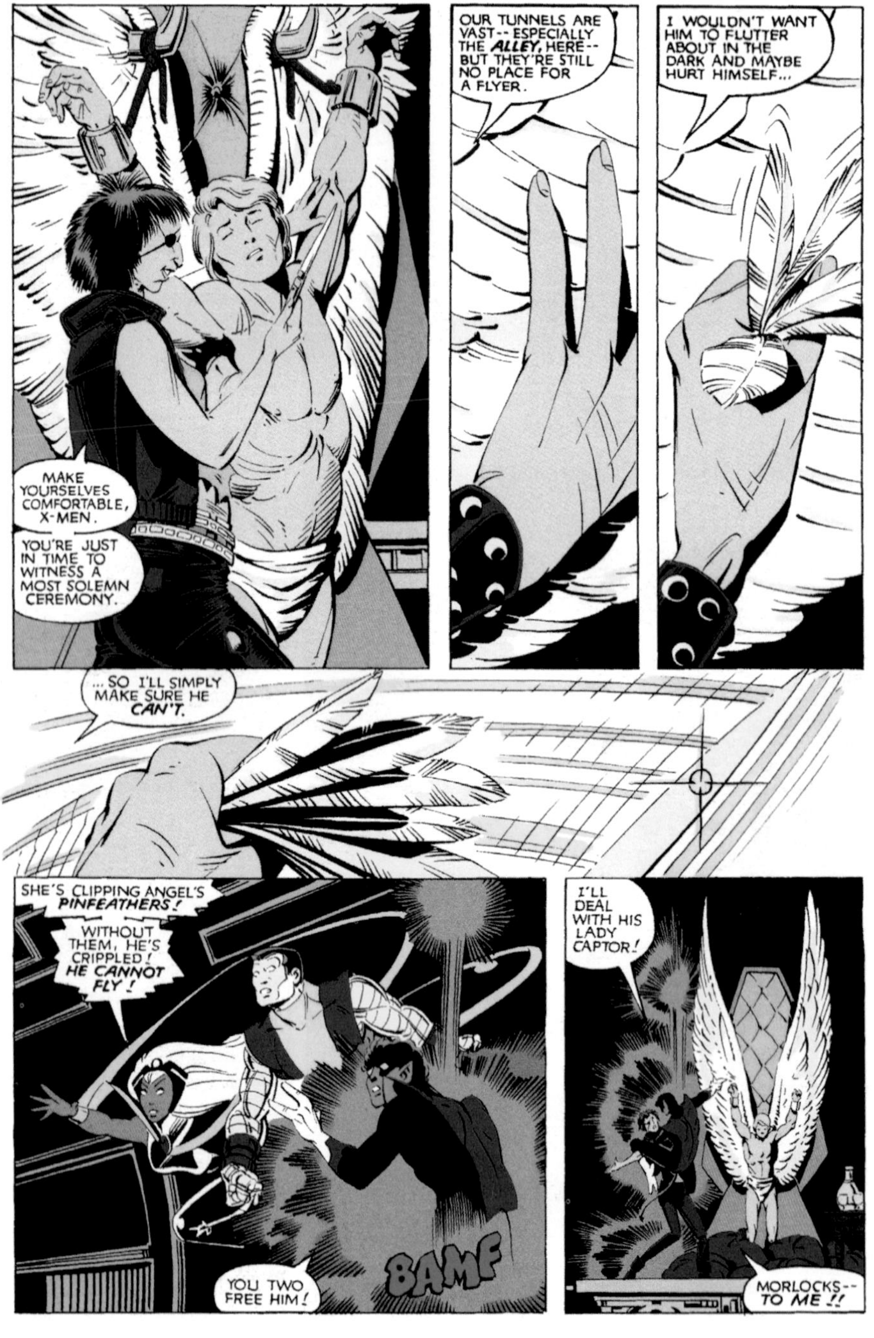
MAKE YOURSELVES COMFORTABLE, X-MEN.
YOU'RE JUST IN TIME TO WITNESS A MOST SOLEMN CEREMONY.
OUR TUNNELS ARE VAST-- ESPECIALLY THE ALLEY, HERE-- BUT THEY'RE STILL NO PLACE FOR A FLYER.
I WOULDN'T WANT HIM TO FLUTTER ABOUT IN THE DARK AND MAYBE HURT HIMSELF...
...SO I'LL SIMPLY MAKE SURE HE CAN'T.
SHE'S CLIPPING ANGEL'S PINFEATHERS!
WITHOUT THEM, HE'S CRIPPLED! HE CANNOT FLY!
YOU TWO FREE HIM!
BAMF
I'LL DEAL WITH HIS LADY CAPTOR!
MORLOCKS-- TO ME!!

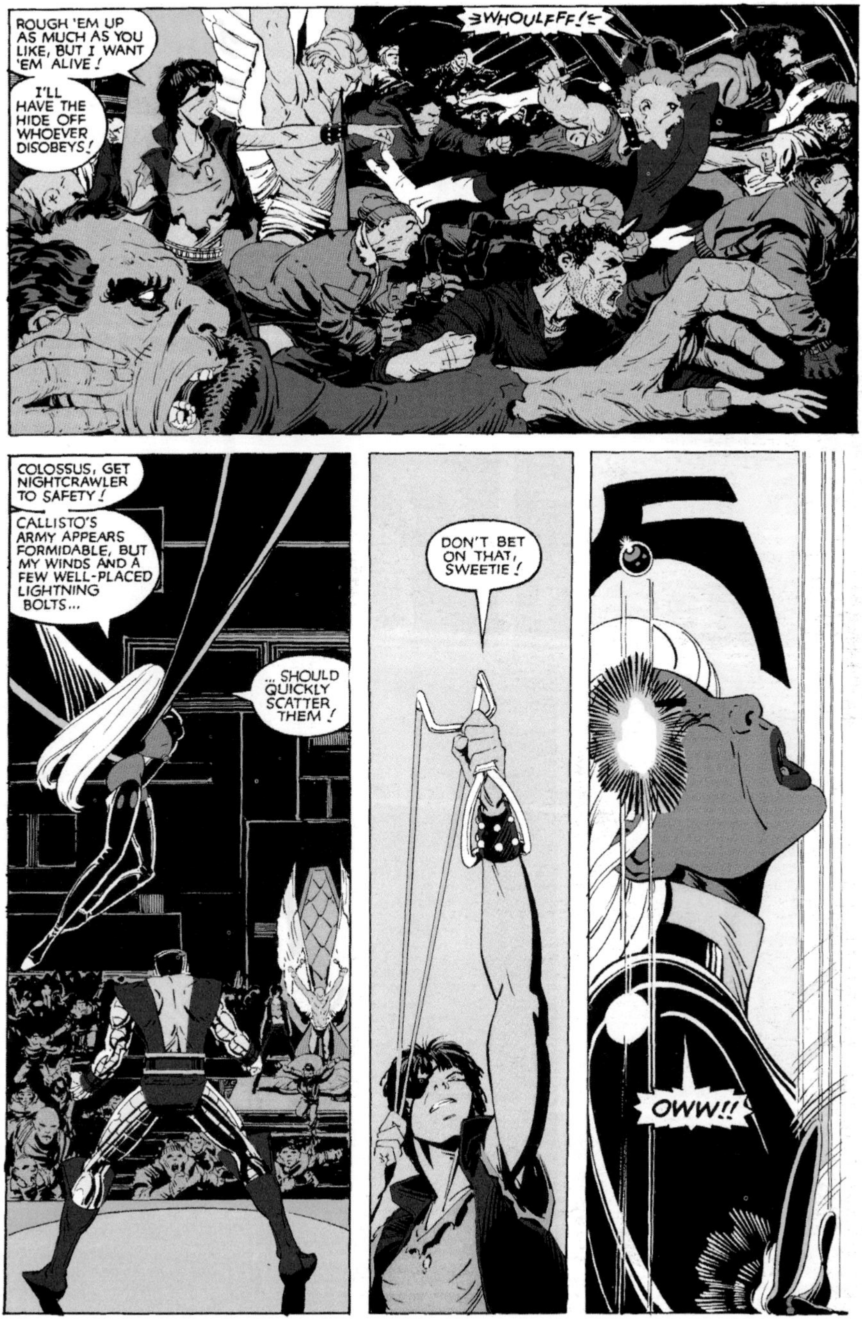
ROUGH 'EM UP AS MUCH AS YOU LIKE, BUT I WANT 'EM ALIVE!
I'LL HAVE THE HIDE OFF WHOEVER DISOBEYS!
WHOULFFF!
COLOSSUS, GET NIGHTCRAWLER TO SAFETY!
CALLISTO'S ARMY APPEARS FORMIDABLE, BUT MY WINDS AND A FEW WELL-PLACED LIGHTNING BOLTS...
...SHOULD QUICKLY SCATTER THEM!
DON'T BET ON THAT, SWEETIE!
OWW!!

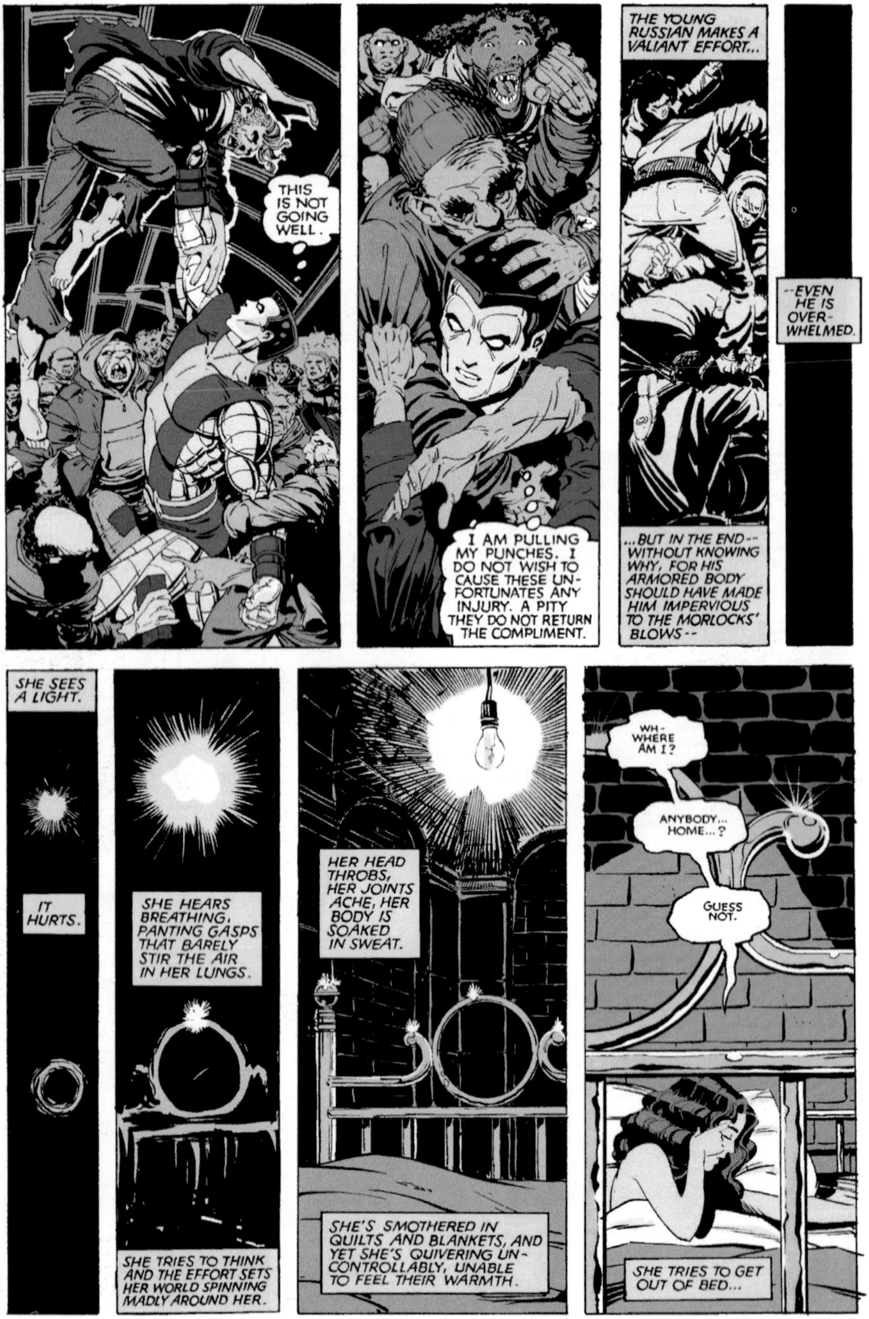
THIS IS NOT GOING WELL.
I AM PULLING MY PUNCHES. I DO NOT WISH TO CAUSE THESE UNFORTUNATES ANY INJURY. A PITY THEY DO NOT RETURN THE COMPLIMENT.
THE YOUNG RUSSIAN MAKES A VALIANT EFFORT...
...BUT IN THE END-- WITHOUT KNOWING WHY, FOR HIS ARMORED BODY SHOULD HAVE MADE HIM IMPERVIOUS TO THE MORLOCKS' BLOWS--
--EVEN HE IS OVERWHELMED.
SHE SEES A LIGHT.
IT HURTS.
SHE HEARS BREATHING, PANTING GASPS THAT BARELY STIR THE AIR IN HER LUNGS.
SHE TRIES TO THINK AND THE EFFORT SETS HER WORLD SPINNING MADLY AROUND HER.
HER HEAD THROBS, HER JOINTS ACHE, HER BODY IS SOAKED IN SWEAT.
SHE'S SMOTHERED IN QUILTS AND BLANKETS, AND YET SHE'S QUIVERING UNCONTROLLABLY, UNABLE TO FEEL THEIR WARMTH.
WH- WHERE AM I?
ANYBODY... HOME...?
GUESS NOT.
SHE TRIES TO GET OUT OF BED...

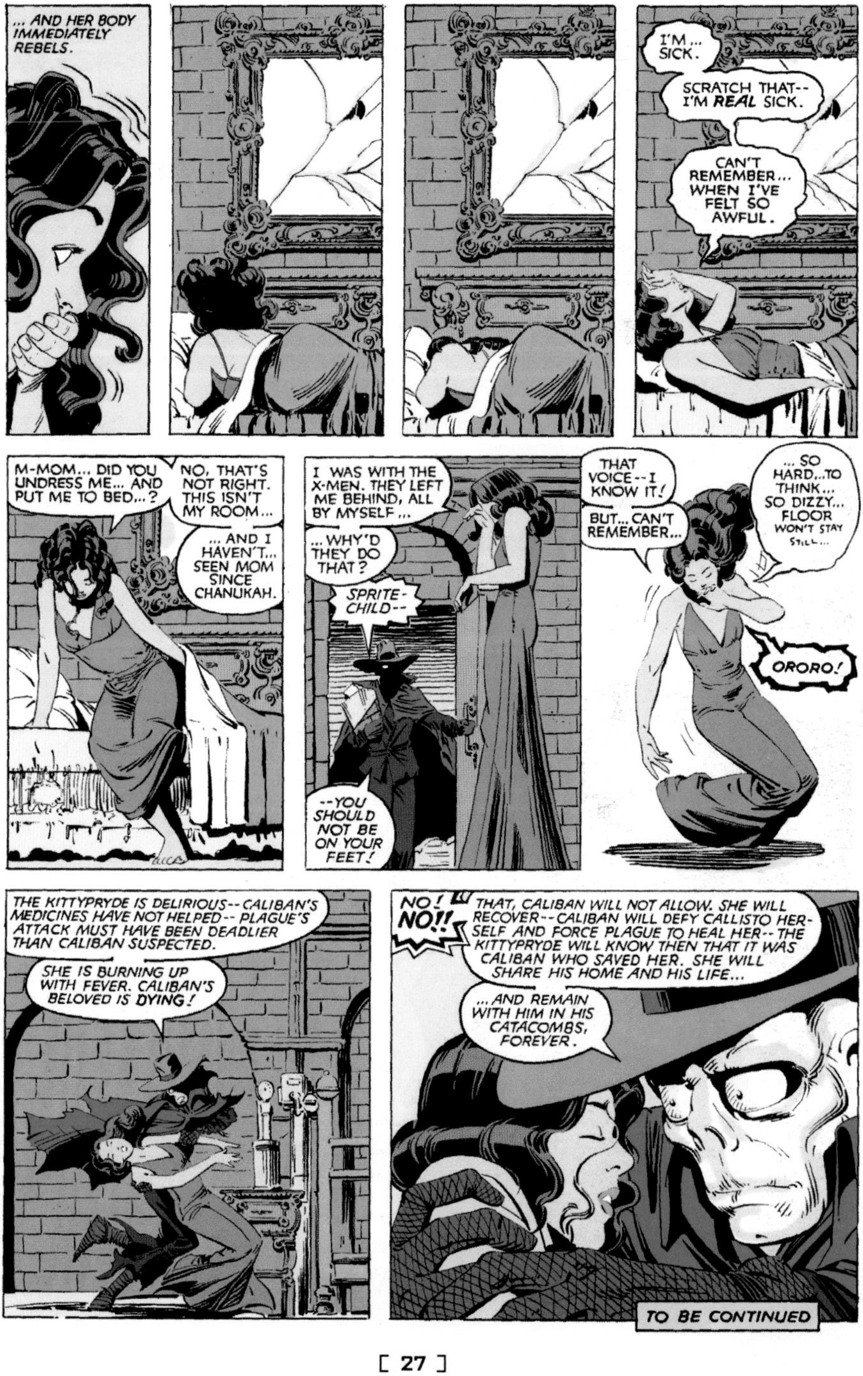

... AND HER BODY IMMEDIATELY REBELS.
I'M... SICK.
SCRATCH THAT-- I'M REAL SICK.
CAN'T REMEMBER... WHEN I'VE FELT SO AWFUL.
M-MOM... DID YOU UNDRESS ME... AND PUT ME TO BED...?
NO, THAT'S NOT RIGHT. THIS ISN'T MY ROOM...
... AND I HAVEN'T... SEEN MOM SINCE CHANUKAH.
I WAS WITH THE X-MEN. THEY LEFT ME BEHIND, ALL BY MYSELF...
... WHY'D THEY DO THAT?
SPRITE-CHILD--
--YOU SHOULD NOT BE ON YOUR FEET!
THAT VOICE--I KNOW IT!
BUT... CAN'T REMEMBER...
... SO HARD... TO THINK... SO DIZZY... FLOOR WON'T STAY STILL...
ORORO!
THE KITTYPRYDE IS DELIRIOUS--CALIBAN'S MEDICINES HAVE NOT HELPED--PLAGUE'S ATTACK MUST HAVE BEEN DEADLIER THAN CALIBAN SUSPECTED.
SHE IS BURNING UP WITH FEVER. CALIBAN'S BELOVED IS DYING!
NO! NO!!
THAT, CALIBAN WILL NOT ALLOW. SHE WILL RECOVER--CALIBAN WILL DEFY CALLISTO HERSELF AND FORCE PLAGUE TO HEAL HER--THE KITTYPRYDE WILL KNOW THEN THAT IT WAS CALIBAN WHO SAVED HER. SHE WILL SHARE HIS HOME AND HIS LIFE...
... AND REMAIN WITH HIM IN HIS CATACOMBS, FOREVER.
TO BE CONTINUED

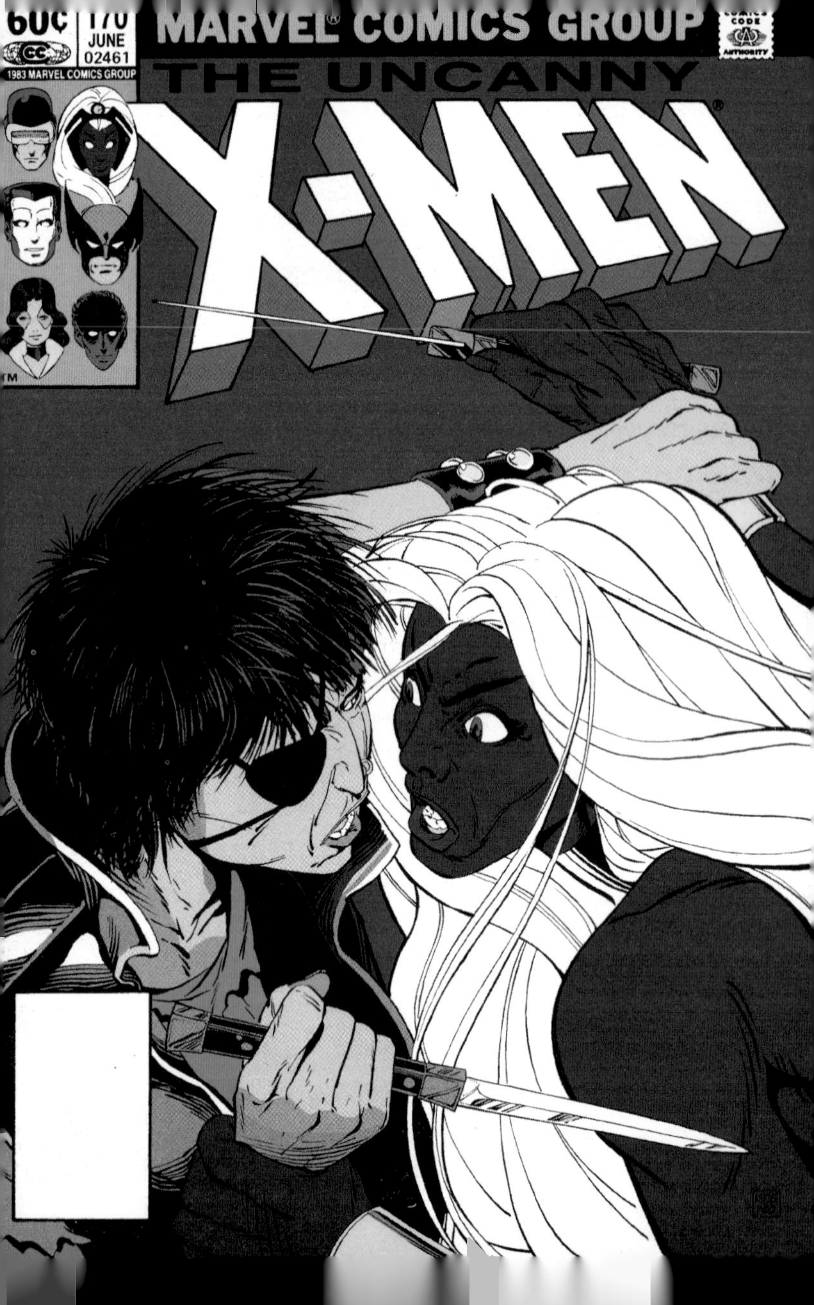

60¢
170
JUNE
02461
CC
1983 MARVEL COMICS GROUP
MARVEL COMICS GROUP
COMICS CODE AUTHORITY
THE UNCANNY
X-MEN
TM

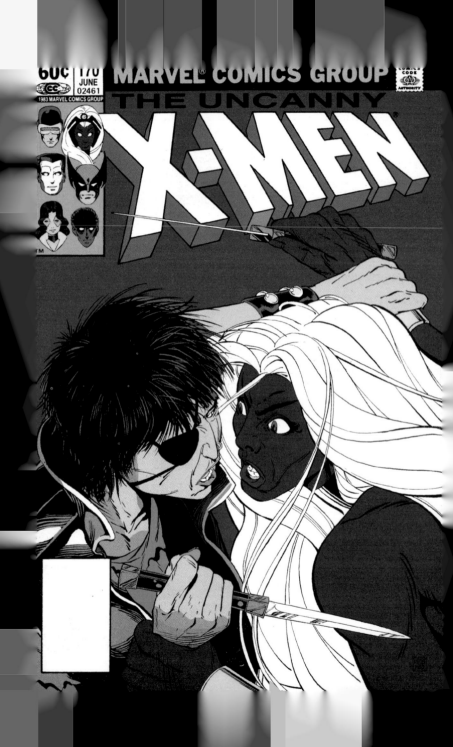

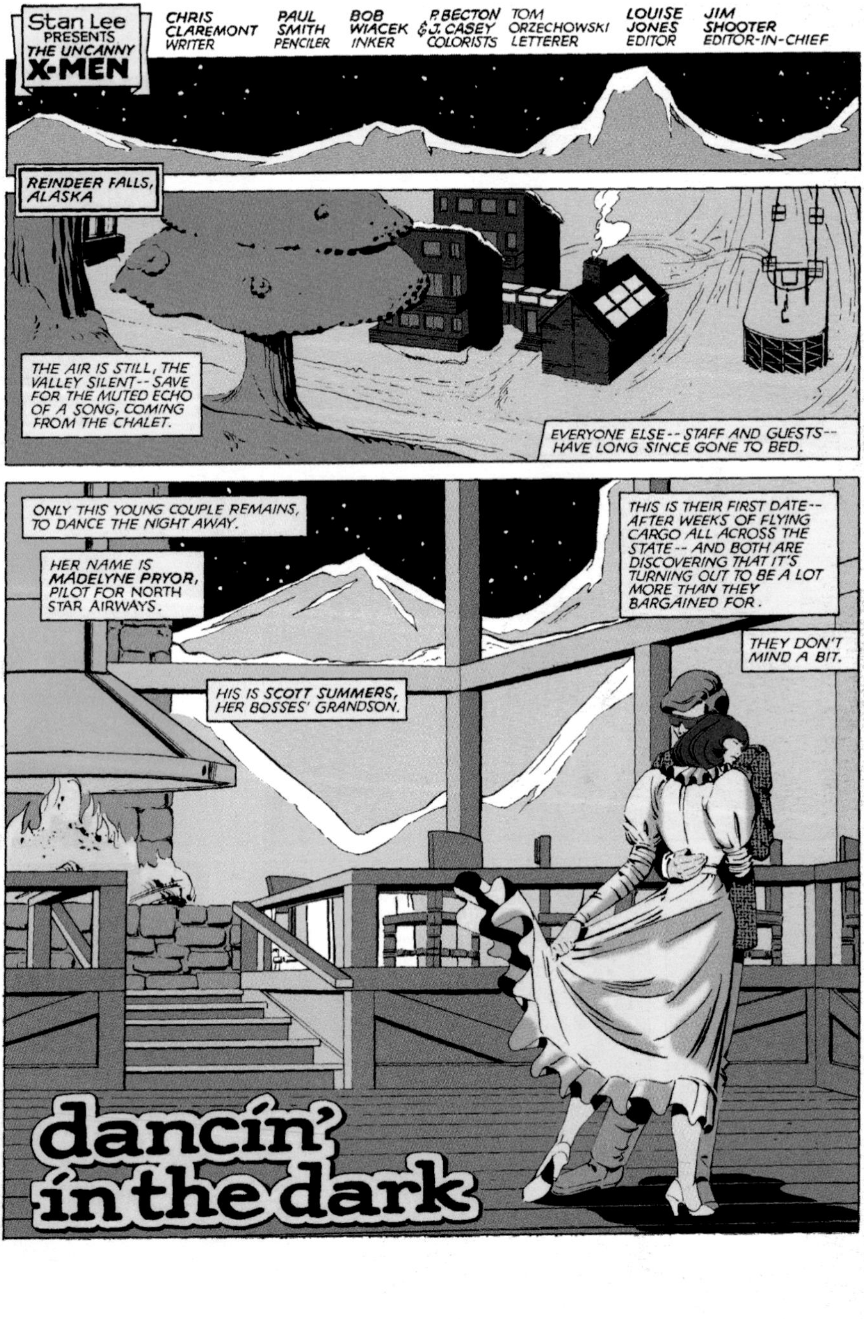

Stan Lee PRESENTS THE UNCANNY X-MEN
CHRIS CLAREMONT WRITER
PAUL SMITH PENCILER
BOB WIACEK INKER
P. BECTON & J. CASEY COLORISTS
TOM ORZECHOWSKI LETTERER
LOUISE JONES EDITOR
JIM SHOOTER EDITOR-IN-CHIEF
REINDEER FALLS, ALASKA
THE AIR IS STILL, THE VALLEY SILENT-- SAVE FOR THE MUTED ECHO OF A SONG, COMING FROM THE CHALET.
EVERYONE ELSE-- STAFF AND GUESTS-- HAVE LONG SINCE GONE TO BED.
ONLY THIS YOUNG COUPLE REMAINS, TO DANCE THE NIGHT AWAY.
HER NAME IS MADELYNE PRYOR, PILOT FOR NORTH STAR AIRWAYS.
HIS IS SCOTT SUMMERS, HER BOSSES' GRANDSON.
THIS IS THEIR FIRST DATE-- AFTER WEEKS OF FLYING CARGO ALL ACROSS THE STATE-- AND BOTH ARE DISCOVERING THAT IT'S TURNING OUT TO BE A LOT MORE THAN THEY BARGAINED FOR.
THEY DON'T MIND A BIT.
dancin' in the dark

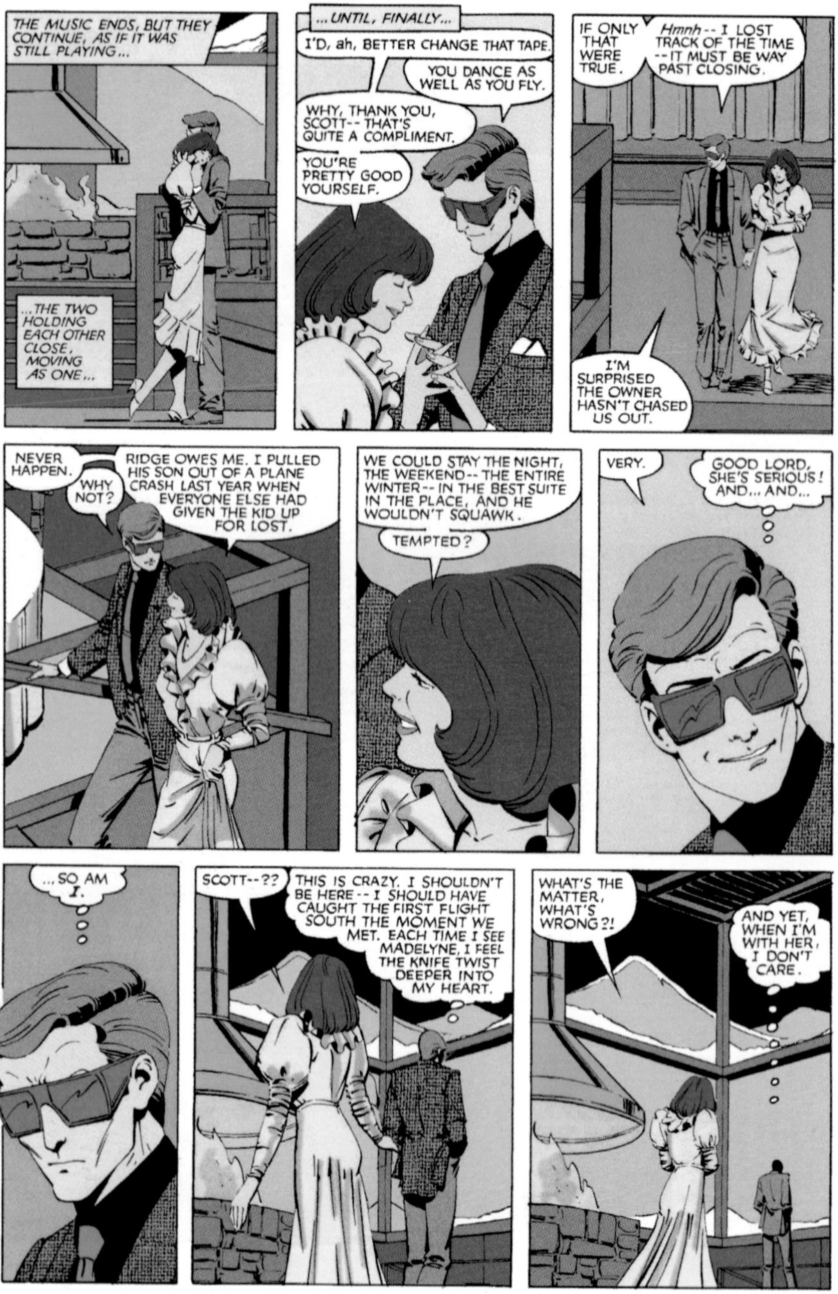
THE MUSIC ENDS, BUT THEY CONTINUE, AS IF IT WAS STILL PLAYING...
...THE TWO HOLDING EACH OTHER CLOSE, MOVING AS ONE...
...UNTIL, FINALLY...
I'D, ah, BETTER CHANGE THAT TAPE.
YOU DANCE AS WELL AS YOU FLY.
WHY, THANK YOU, SCOTT-- THAT'S QUITE A COMPLIMENT.
YOU'RE PRETTY GOOD YOURSELF.
IF ONLY THAT WERE TRUE.
Hmnh-- I LOST TRACK OF THE TIME --IT MUST BE WAY PAST CLOSING.
I'M SURPRISED THE OWNER HASN'T CHASED US OUT.
NEVER HAPPEN.
WHY NOT?
RIDGE OWES ME. I PULLED HIS SON OUT OF A PLANE CRASH LAST YEAR WHEN EVERYONE ELSE HAD GIVEN THE KID UP FOR LOST.
WE COULD STAY THE NIGHT, THE WEEKEND-- THE ENTIRE WINTER-- IN THE BEST SUITE IN THE PLACE, AND HE WOULDN'T SQUAWK.
TEMPTED?
VERY.
GOOD LORD, SHE'S SERIOUS! AND... AND...
...SO AM I.
SCOTT--??
THIS IS CRAZY. I SHOULDN'T BE HERE-- I SHOULD HAVE CAUGHT THE FIRST FLIGHT SOUTH THE MOMENT WE MET. EACH TIME I SEE MADELYNE, I FEEL THE KNIFE TWIST DEEPER INTO MY HEART.
WHAT'S THE MATTER, WHAT'S WRONG?!
AND YET, WHEN I'M WITH HER, I DON'T CARE.

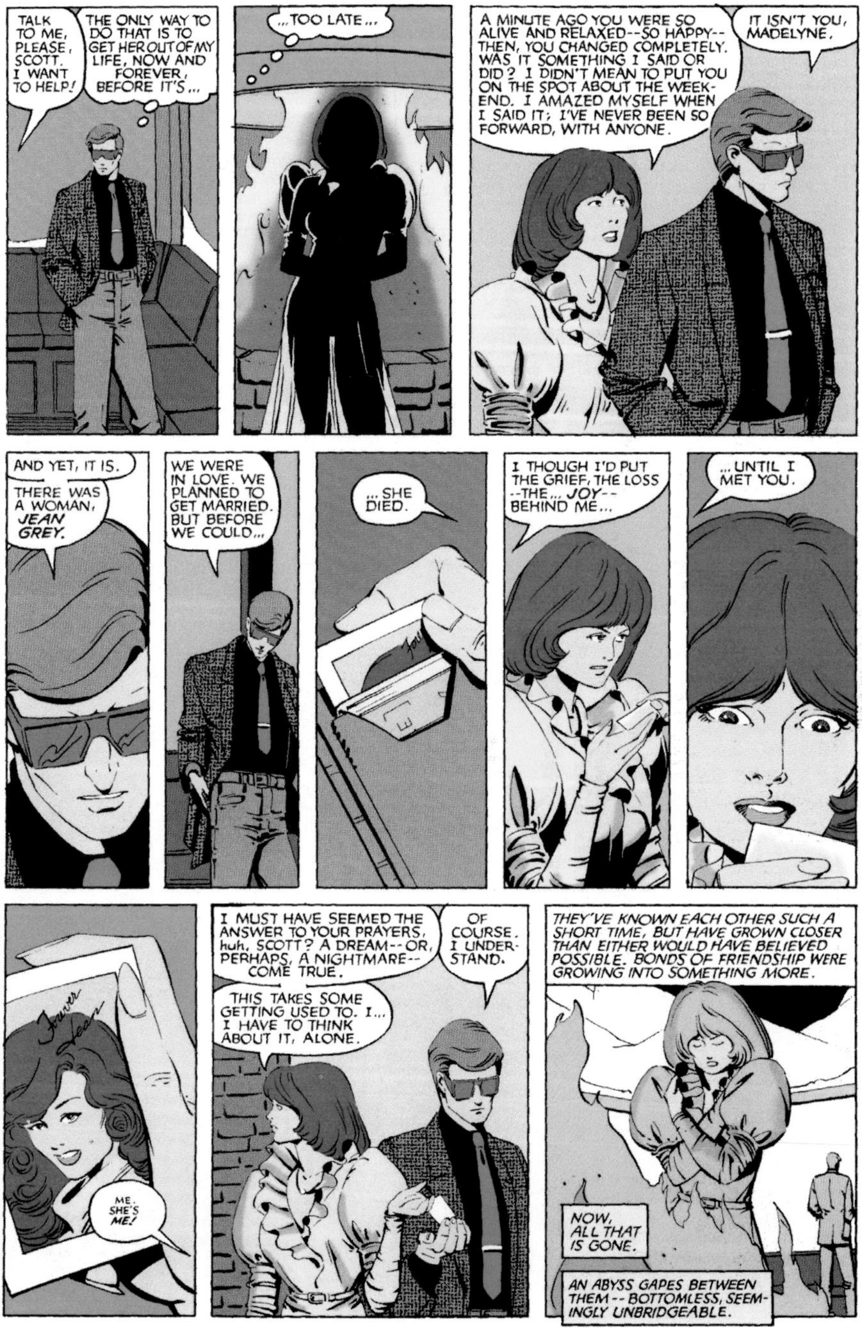
TALK TO ME, PLEASE, SCOTT. I WANT TO HELP!
THE ONLY WAY TO DO THAT IS TO GET HER OUT OF MY LIFE, NOW AND FOREVER, BEFORE IT'S...
...TOO LATE...
A MINUTE AGO YOU WERE SO ALIVE AND RELAXED--SO HAPPY--THEN, YOU CHANGED COMPLETELY. WAS IT SOMETHING I SAID OR DID? I DIDN'T MEAN TO PUT YOU ON THE SPOT ABOUT THE WEEK-END. I AMAZED MYSELF WHEN I SAID IT; I'VE NEVER BEEN SO FORWARD, WITH ANYONE.
IT ISN'T YOU, MADELYNE.
AND YET, IT IS.
THERE WAS A WOMAN, JEAN GREY.
WE WERE IN LOVE. WE PLANNED TO GET MARRIED. BUT BEFORE WE COULD...
...SHE DIED.
I THOUGH I'D PUT THE GRIEF, THE LOSS --THE... JOY-- BEHIND ME...
...UNTIL I MET YOU.
Forever Jean
ME. SHE'S ME!
I MUST HAVE SEEMED THE ANSWER TO YOUR PRAYERS, huh, SCOTT? A DREAM--OR, PERHAPS, A NIGHTMARE--COME TRUE.
OF COURSE. I UNDERSTAND.
THIS TAKES SOME GETTING USED TO. I... I HAVE TO THINK ABOUT IT, ALONE.
THEY'VE KNOWN EACH OTHER SUCH A SHORT TIME, BUT HAVE GROWN CLOSER THAN EITHER WOULD HAVE BELIEVED POSSIBLE. BONDS OF FRIENDSHIP WERE GROWING INTO SOMETHING MORE.
NOW, ALL THAT IS GONE.
AN ABYSS GAPES BETWEEN THEM--BOTTOMLESS, SEEMINGLY UNBRIDGEABLE.

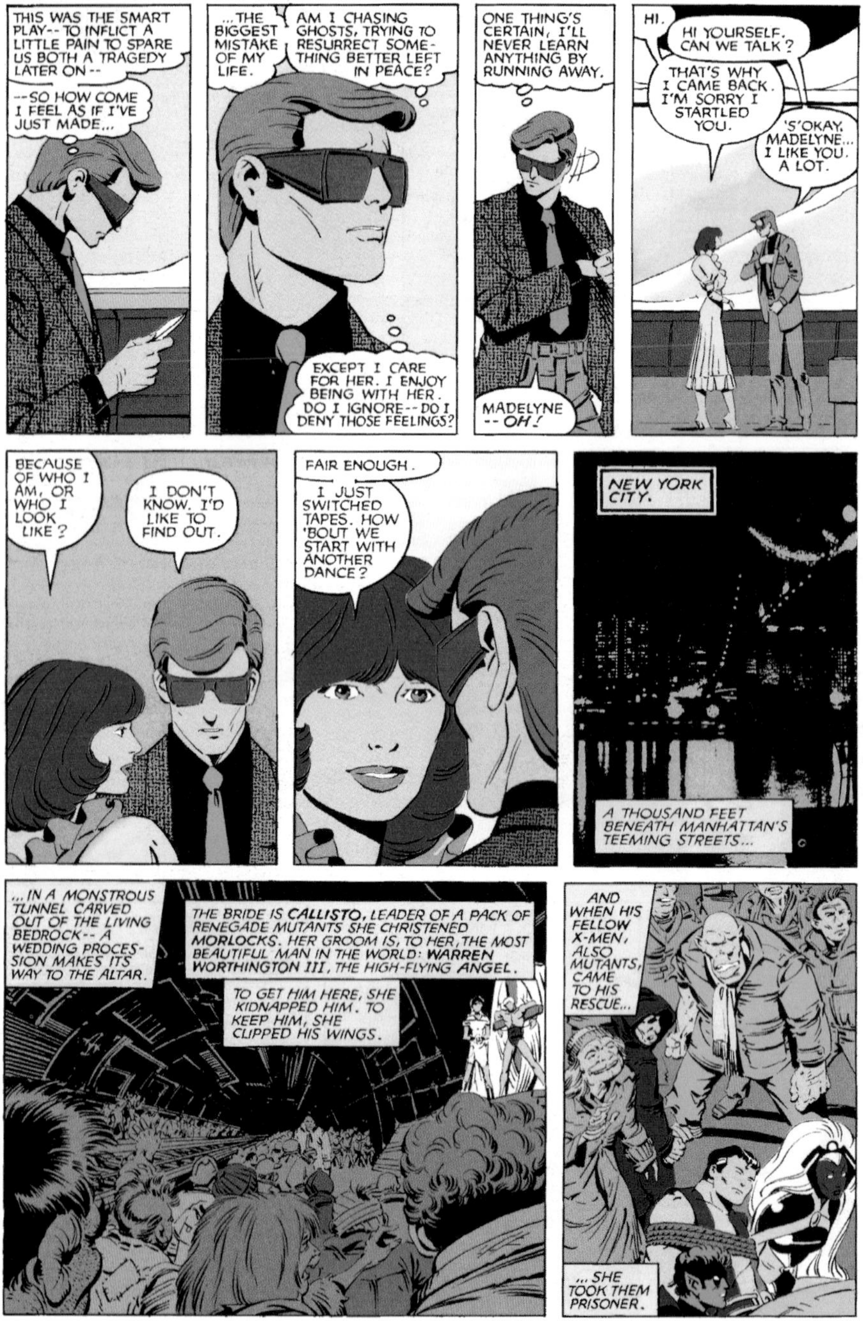
THIS WAS THE SMART PLAY-- TO INFLICT A LITTLE PAIN TO SPARE US BOTH A TRAGEDY LATER ON --
--SO HOW COME I FEEL AS IF I'VE JUST MADE...
...THE BIGGEST MISTAKE OF MY LIFE.
AM I CHASING GHOSTS, TRYING TO RESURRECT SOMETHING BETTER LEFT IN PEACE?
EXCEPT I CARE FOR HER. I ENJOY BEING WITH HER. DO I IGNORE--DO I DENY THOSE FEELINGS?
ONE THING'S CERTAIN, I'LL NEVER LEARN ANYTHING BY RUNNING AWAY.
MADELYNE --OH!
HI.
HI YOURSELF. CAN WE TALK?
THAT'S WHY I CAME BACK. I'M SORRY I STARTLED YOU.
'S'OKAY, MADELYNE... I LIKE YOU. A LOT.
BECAUSE OF WHO I AM, OR WHO I LOOK LIKE?
I DON'T KNOW. I'D LIKE TO FIND OUT.
FAIR ENOUGH.
I JUST SWITCHED TAPES. HOW 'BOUT WE START WITH ANOTHER DANCE?
NEW YORK CITY.
A THOUSAND FEET BENEATH MANHATTAN'S TEEMING STREETS...
...IN A MONSTROUS TUNNEL CARVED OUT OF THE LIVING BEDROCK-- A WEDDING PROCESSION MAKES ITS WAY TO THE ALTAR.
THE BRIDE IS CALLISTO, LEADER OF A PACK OF RENEGADE MUTANTS SHE CHRISTENED MORLOCKS. HER GROOM IS, TO HER, THE MOST BEAUTIFUL MAN IN THE WORLD: WARREN WORTHINGTON III, THE HIGH-FLYING ANGEL.
TO GET HIM HERE, SHE KIDNAPPED HIM. TO KEEP HIM, SHE CLIPPED HIS WINGS.
AND WHEN HIS FELLOW X-MEN, ALSO MUTANTS, CAME TO HIS RESCUE...
...SHE TOOK THEM PRISONER.

COMFY, MY PRETTY-PRETTY? LOOKING FORWARD TO OUR WEDDING NIGHT?

I CERTAINLY AM.

CALLISTO-- *STOP!*

ANGEL IS A HUMAN BEING, NOT SOME PET OR TOY! YOU HAVE NO RIGHT TO TREAT HIM LIKE THIS!

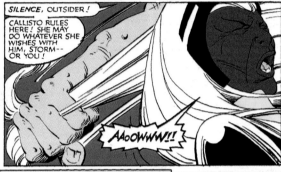

SILENCE, OUTSIDER!

CALLISTO RULES HERE! SHE MAY DO WHATEVER SHE WISHES WITH HIM, STORM-- OR YOU!

AAoOWWW!!

IN THAT CASE, *HERR* SUNDER, PERHAPS IT'S TIME CALLISTO'S RULE WAS BROUGHT TO AN END.

IT WILL BE MY PLEASURE, NIGHT-CRAWLER.

SHE'S MINE, COLOSSUS! CAN YOU HANDLE THE REST?!

AN EXPLOSIVE BURST OF BRIMSTONE AND FIRE HERALDS NIGHTCRAWLER'S DEPARTURE, AS HE TELEPORTS OUT OF HIS BONDS...

...WHILE HIS RUSSIAN TEAM-MATE TRANSFORMS FROM FLESH-AND-BLOOD TO SUPER-STRONG ORGANIC STEEL.

BAMF

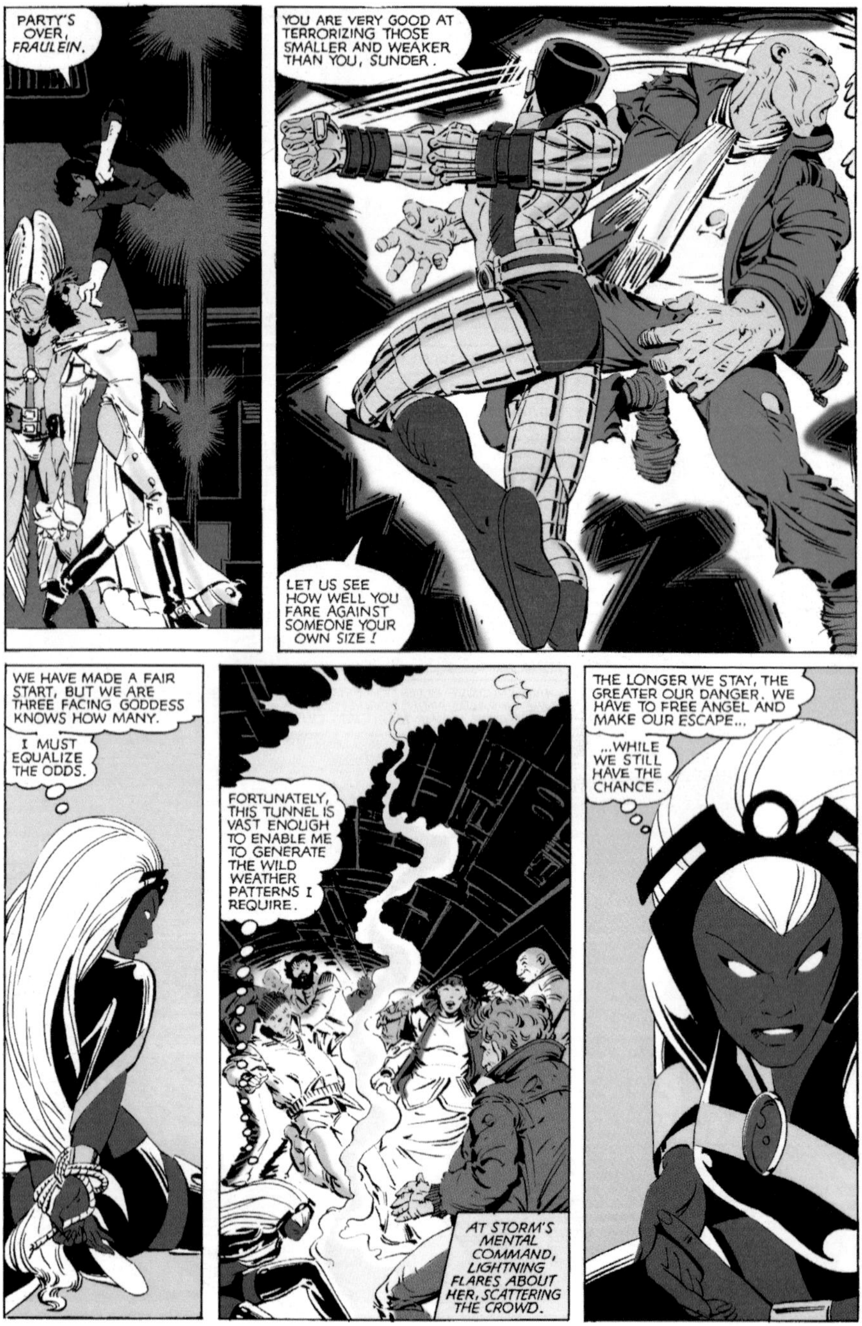
PARTY'S OVER, FRAULEIN.
YOU ARE VERY GOOD AT TERRORIZING THOSE SMALLER AND WEAKER THAN YOU, SUNDER.
LET US SEE HOW WELL YOU FARE AGAINST SOMEONE YOUR OWN SIZE!
WE HAVE MADE A FAIR START, BUT WE ARE THREE FACING GODDESS KNOWS HOW MANY.
I MUST EQUALIZE THE ODDS.
FORTUNATELY, THIS TUNNEL IS VAST ENOUGH TO ENABLE ME TO GENERATE THE WILD WEATHER PATTERNS I REQUIRE.
AT STORM'S MENTAL COMMAND, LIGHTNING FLARES ABOUT HER, SCATTERING THE CROWD.
THE LONGER WE STAY, THE GREATER OUR DANGER. WE HAVE TO FREE ANGEL AND MAKE OUR ESCAPE...
...WHILE WE STILL HAVE THE CHANCE.

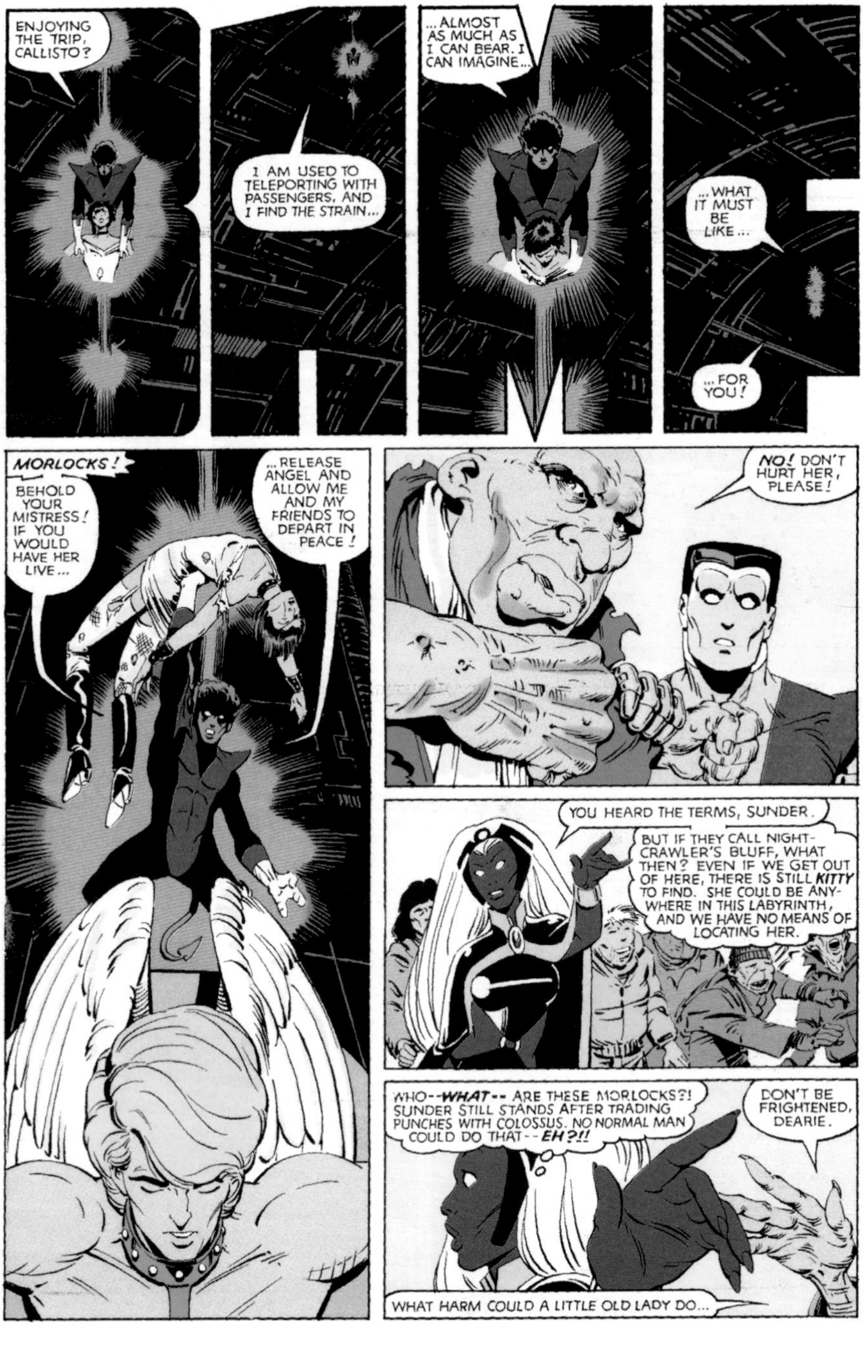
ENJOYING THE TRIP, CALLISTO?
I AM USED TO TELEPORTING WITH PASSENGERS, AND I FIND THE STRAIN...
...ALMOST AS MUCH AS I CAN BEAR. I CAN IMAGINE...
...WHAT IT MUST BE LIKE...
...FOR YOU!
MORLOCKS!
BEHOLD YOUR MISTRESS! IF YOU WOULD HAVE HER LIVE...
...RELEASE ANGEL AND ALLOW ME AND MY FRIENDS TO DEPART IN PEACE!
NO! DON'T HURT HER, PLEASE!
YOU HEARD THE TERMS, SUNDER.
BUT IF THEY CALL NIGHT-CRAWLER'S BLUFF, WHAT THEN? EVEN IF WE GET OUT OF HERE, THERE IS STILL KITTY TO FIND. SHE COULD BE ANY-WHERE IN THIS LABYRINTH, AND WE HAVE NO MEANS OF LOCATING HER.
WHO--WHAT-- ARE THESE MORLOCKS?! SUNDER STILL STANDS AFTER TRADING PUNCHES WITH COLOSSUS. NO NORMAL MAN COULD DO THAT--EH?!!
DON'T BE FRIGHTENED, DEARIE.
WHAT HARM COULD A LITTLE OLD LADY DO...

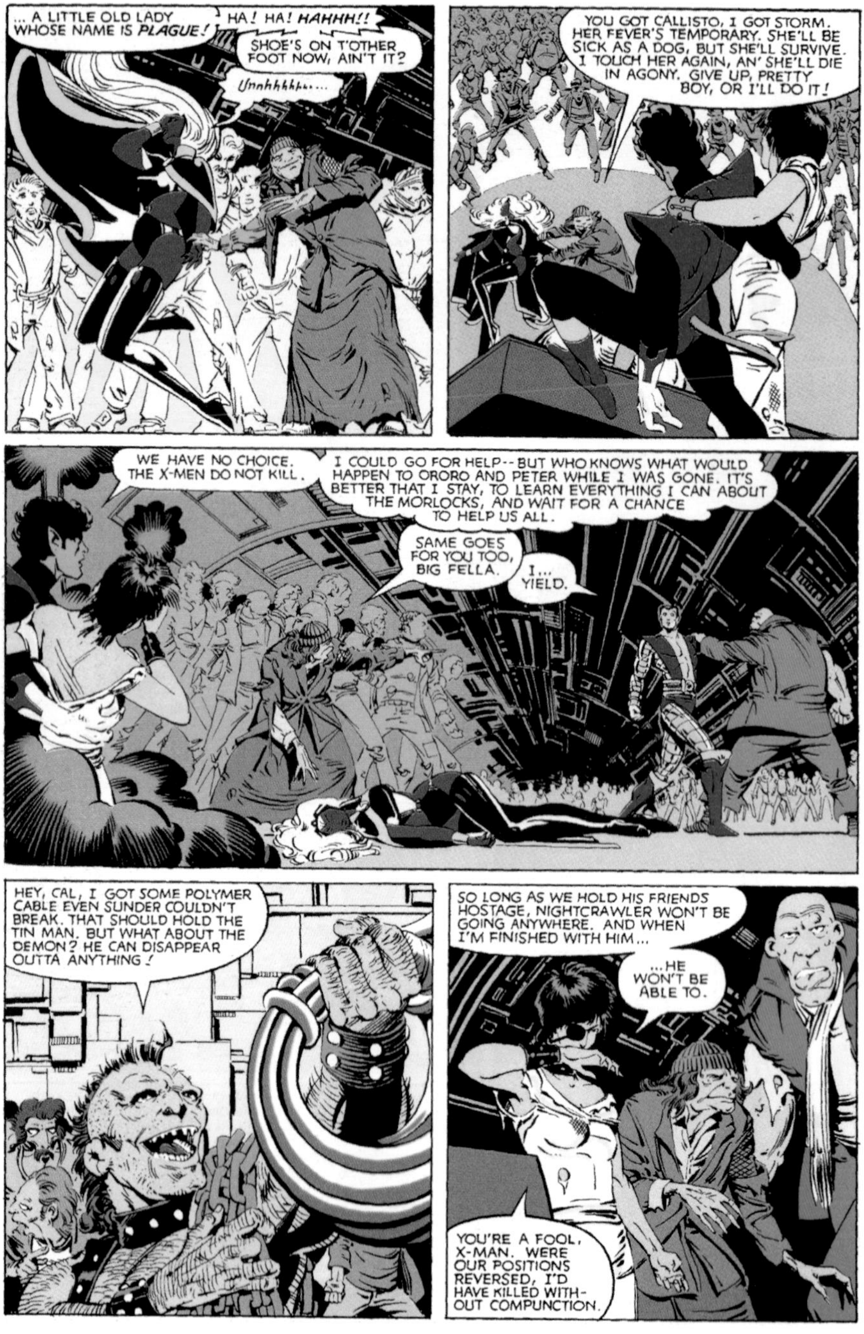
... A LITTLE OLD LADY WHOSE NAME IS PLAGUE!
HA! HA! HAHHH!!
SHOE'S ON T'OTHER FOOT NOW, AIN'T IT?
Unnhhhhhh....
YOU GOT CALLISTO, I GOT STORM. HER FEVER'S TEMPORARY. SHE'LL BE SICK AS A DOG, BUT SHE'LL SURVIVE. I TOUCH HER AGAIN, AN' SHE'LL DIE IN AGONY. GIVE UP, PRETTY BOY, OR I'LL DO IT!
WE HAVE NO CHOICE. THE X-MEN DO NOT KILL.
I COULD GO FOR HELP-- BUT WHO KNOWS WHAT WOULD HAPPEN TO ORORO AND PETER WHILE I WAS GONE. IT'S BETTER THAT I STAY, TO LEARN EVERYTHING I CAN ABOUT THE MORLOCKS, AND WAIT FOR A CHANCE TO HELP US ALL.
SAME GOES FOR YOU TOO, BIG FELLA.
I... YIELD.
HEY, CAL, I GOT SOME POLYMER CABLE EVEN SUNDER COULDN'T BREAK. THAT SHOULD HOLD THE TIN MAN. BUT WHAT ABOUT THE DEMON? HE CAN DISAPPEAR OUTTA ANYTHING!
SO LONG AS WE HOLD HIS FRIENDS HOSTAGE, NIGHTCRAWLER WON'T BE GOING ANYWHERE. AND WHEN I'M FINISHED WITH HIM...
...HE WON'T BE ABLE TO.
YOU'RE A FOOL, X-MAN. WERE OUR POSITIONS REVERSED, I'D HAVE KILLED WITHOUT COMPUNCTION.

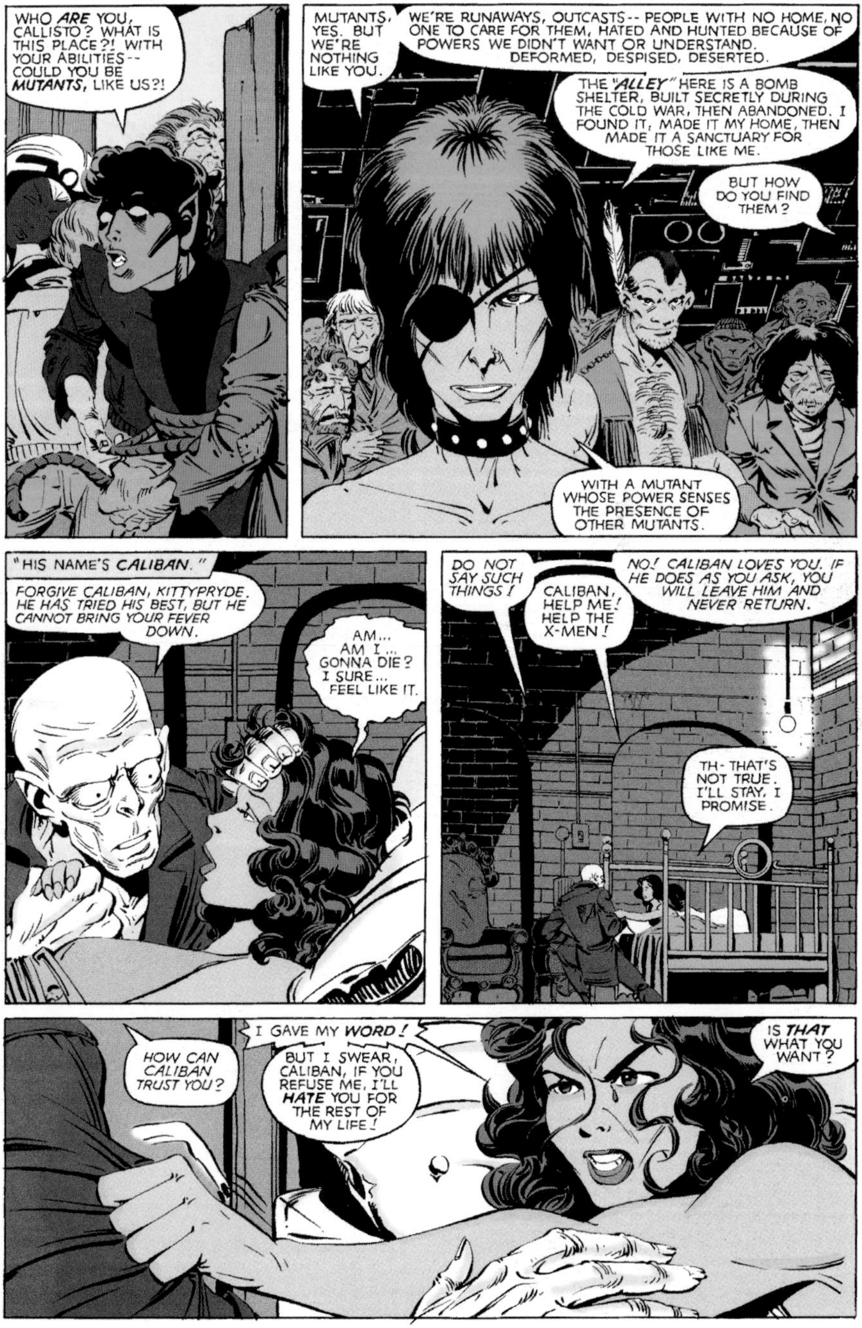
WHO ARE YOU, CALLISTO? WHAT IS THIS PLACE?! WITH YOUR ABILITIES-- COULD YOU BE MUTANTS, LIKE US?!
MUTANTS, YES. BUT WE'RE NOTHING LIKE YOU.
WE'RE RUNAWAYS, OUTCASTS-- PEOPLE WITH NO HOME, NO ONE TO CARE FOR THEM, HATED AND HUNTED BECAUSE OF POWERS WE DIDN'T WANT OR UNDERSTAND. DEFORMED, DESPISED, DESERTED.
THE "ALLEY" HERE IS A BOMB SHELTER, BUILT SECRETLY DURING THE COLD WAR, THEN ABANDONED. I FOUND IT, MADE IT MY HOME, THEN MADE IT A SANCTUARY FOR THOSE LIKE ME.
BUT HOW DO YOU FIND THEM?
WITH A MUTANT WHOSE POWER SENSES THE PRESENCE OF OTHER MUTANTS.
"HIS NAME'S CALIBAN."
FORGIVE CALIBAN, KITTYPRYDE. HE HAS TRIED HIS BEST, BUT HE CANNOT BRING YOUR FEVER DOWN.
AM... AM I... GONNA DIE? I SURE... FEEL LIKE IT.
DO NOT SAY SUCH THINGS!
CALIBAN, HELP ME! HELP THE X-MEN!
NO! CALIBAN LOVES YOU. IF HE DOES AS YOU ASK, YOU WILL LEAVE HIM AND NEVER RETURN.
TH- THAT'S NOT TRUE. I'LL STAY. I PROMISE.
HOW CAN CALIBAN TRUST YOU?
I GAVE MY WORD!
BUT I SWEAR, CALIBAN, IF YOU REFUSE ME, I'LL HATE YOU FOR THE REST OF MY LIFE!
IS THAT WHAT YOU WANT?

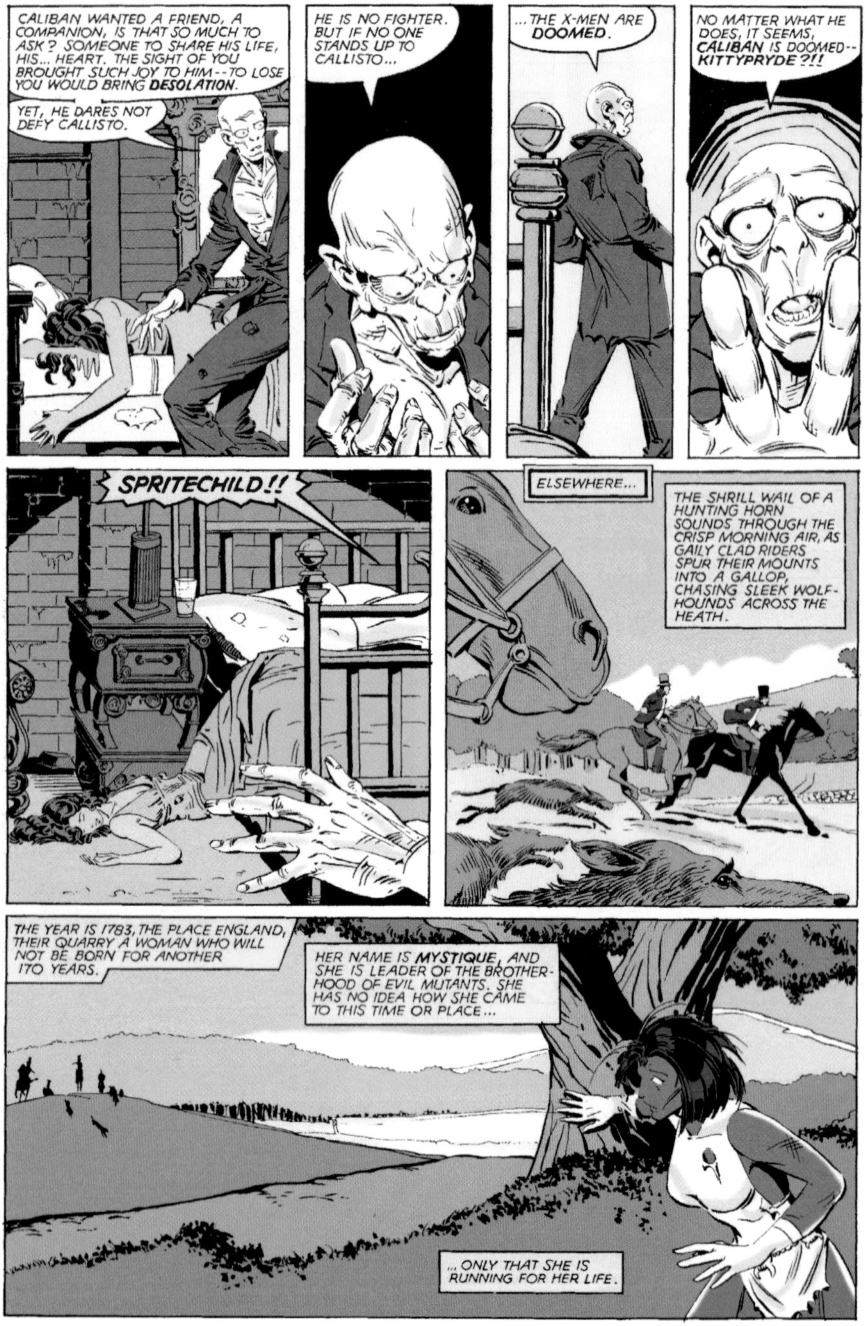
CALIBAN WANTED A FRIEND, A COMPANION, IS THAT SO MUCH TO ASK? SOMEONE TO SHARE HIS LIFE, HIS... HEART. THE SIGHT OF YOU BROUGHT SUCH JOY TO HIM--TO LOSE YOU WOULD BRING DESOLATION.
YET, HE DARES NOT DEFY CALLISTO.
HE IS NO FIGHTER. BUT IF NO ONE STANDS UP TO CALLISTO...
...THE X-MEN ARE DOOMED.
NO MATTER WHAT HE DOES, IT SEEMS, CALIBAN IS DOOMED--KITTYPRYDE?!!
SPRITECHILD!!
ELSEWHERE...
THE SHRILL WAIL OF A HUNTING HORN SOUNDS THROUGH THE CRISP MORNING AIR, AS GAILY CLAD RIDERS SPUR THEIR MOUNTS INTO A GALLOP, CHASING SLEEK WOLF-HOUNDS ACROSS THE HEATH.
THE YEAR IS 1783, THE PLACE ENGLAND, THEIR QUARRY A WOMAN WHO WILL NOT BE BORN FOR ANOTHER 170 YEARS.
HER NAME IS MYSTIQUE, AND SHE IS LEADER OF THE BROTHER-HOOD OF EVIL MUTANTS. SHE HAS NO IDEA HOW SHE CAME TO THIS TIME OR PLACE...
...ONLY THAT SHE IS RUNNING FOR HER LIFE.

THIS IS **MADNESS!**

I WAS IN BED, IN MY HOUSE-- BUT NO DREAM EVER FELT SO **REAL--**

-- MY **FOOT!**

THE ANKLE IS BROKEN. SHE'LL RUN NO MORE. AS SHE SPRAWLS INTO THE BROOK...

... SHE HEARS THE HOUNDS...

... AND MOMENTS LATER, FEELS THEIR TEETH TEARING AT CLOTHES AND FLESH.

WHOA, SATAN-- **WHOA!**

SIR JASON-- THE DOGS!

I'LL DEAL WITH 'EM, MILADY.

BACK, YOU CURS! BACK, I SAY!

Y-IPE!

WE'RE FORTUNATE INDEED, MILADY. THE BEAST STILL LIVES.

AS THE FIRST TO RUN IT TO THE GROUND, TO YOU GOES THE HONOR OF ADMINI-STERING THE COUP DE GRACE.

THANK YOU, SIR JASON.

I CAN'T REMEMBER WHEN I'VE HAD FINER SPORT, MILADY.

WITH A SMILE OF PURE JOY, LADY JEAN GREY...

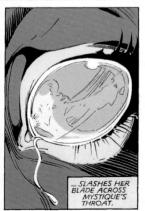

... SLASHES HER BLADE ACROSS MYSTIQUE'S THROAT.

AND THE MADNESS ENDS. FOR A TIME.

NO!

NO.

I ... LIVE!

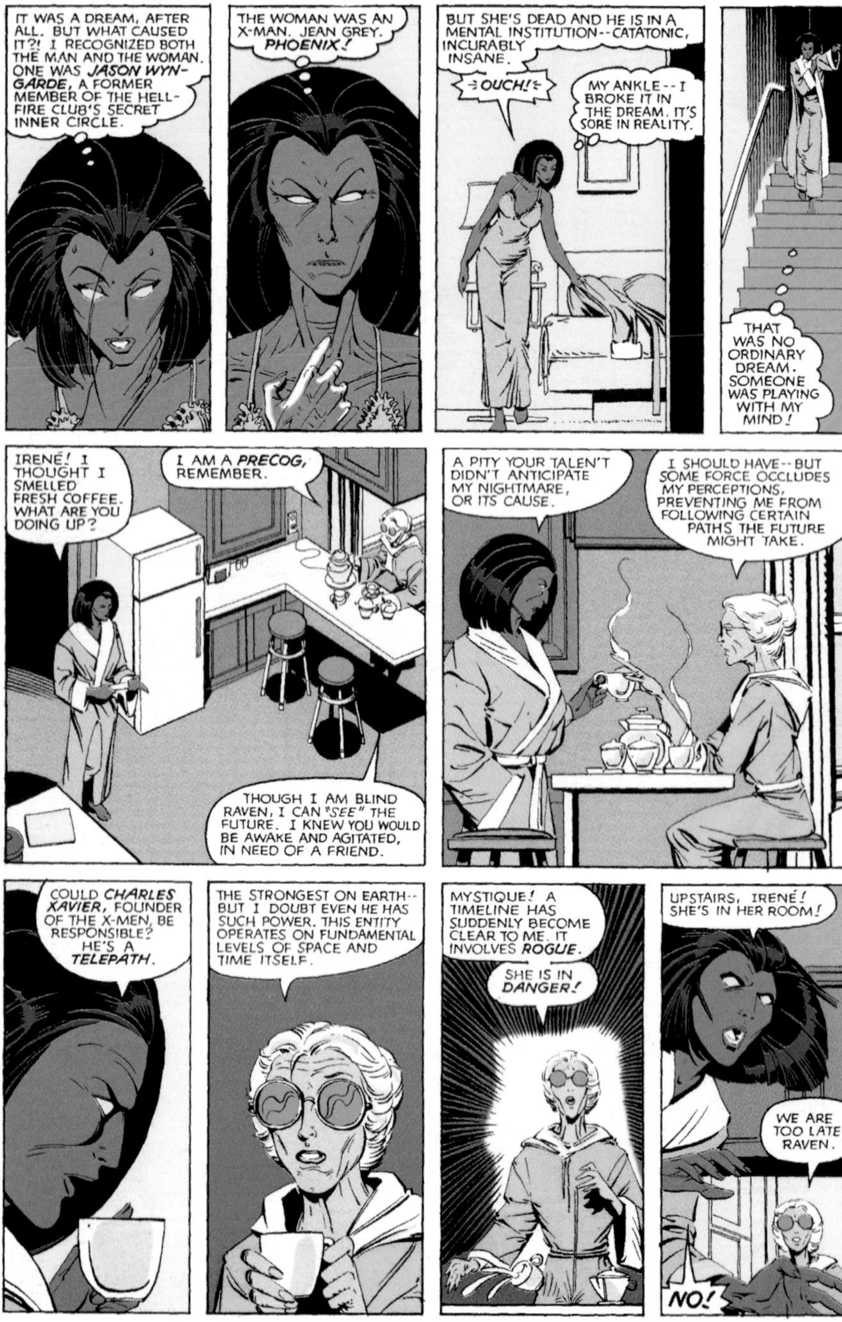
IT WAS A DREAM, AFTER ALL. BUT WHAT CAUSED IT?! I RECOGNIZED BOTH THE MAN AND THE WOMAN. ONE WAS JASON WYN-GARDE, A FORMER MEMBER OF THE HELL-FIRE CLUB'S SECRET INNER CIRCLE.
THE WOMAN WAS AN X-MAN. JEAN GREY. PHOENIX!
BUT SHE'S DEAD AND HE IS IN A MENTAL INSTITUTION--CATATONIC, INCURABLY INSANE.
OUCH!
MY ANKLE--I BROKE IT IN THE DREAM. IT'S SORE IN REALITY.
THAT WAS NO ORDINARY DREAM. SOMEONE WAS PLAYING WITH MY MIND!
IRENÉ! I THOUGHT I SMELLED FRESH COFFEE. WHAT ARE YOU DOING UP?
I AM A PRECOG, REMEMBER.
THOUGH I AM BLIND RAVEN, I CAN "SEE" THE FUTURE. I KNEW YOU WOULD BE AWAKE AND AGITATED, IN NEED OF A FRIEND.
A PITY YOUR TALEN'T DIDN'T ANTICIPATE MY NIGHTMARE, OR ITS CAUSE.
I SHOULD HAVE--BUT SOME FORCE OCCLUDES MY PERCEPTIONS, PREVENTING ME FROM FOLLOWING CERTAIN PATHS THE FUTURE MIGHT TAKE.
COULD CHARLES XAVIER, FOUNDER OF THE X-MEN, BE RESPONSIBLE? HE'S A TELEPATH.
THE STRONGEST ON EARTH--BUT I DOUBT EVEN HE HAS SUCH POWER. THIS ENTITY OPERATES ON FUNDAMENTAL LEVELS OF SPACE AND TIME ITSELF.
MYSTIQUE! A TIMELINE HAS SUDDENLY BECOME CLEAR TO ME. IT INVOLVES ROGUE.
SHE IS IN DANGER!
UPSTAIRS, IRENÉ! SHE'S IN HER ROOM!
WE ARE TOO LATE, RAVEN.
NO!

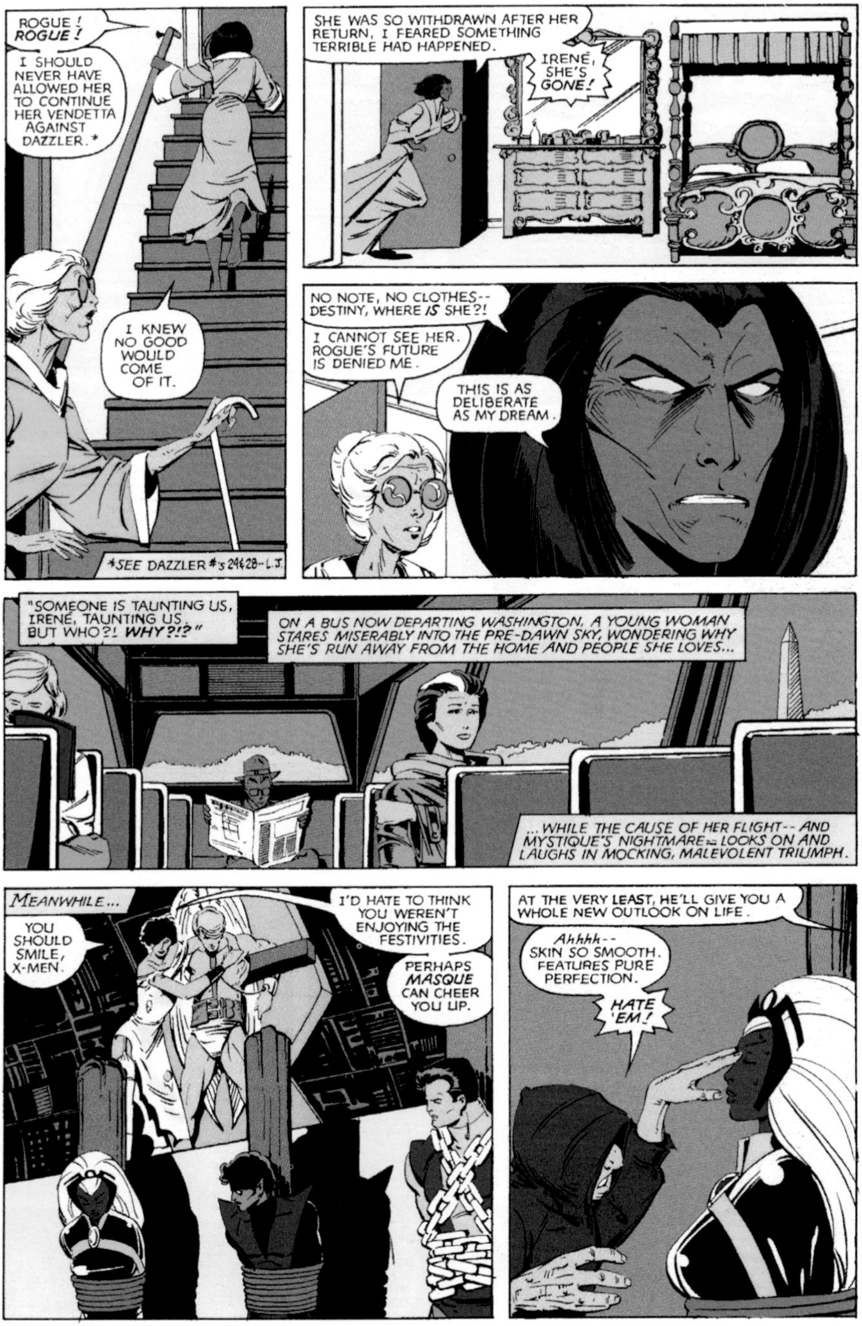

ROGUE! ROGUE!
I SHOULD NEVER HAVE ALLOWED HER TO CONTINUE HER VENDETTA AGAINST DAZZLER.*
I KNEW NO GOOD WOULD COME OF IT.
*SEE DAZZLER #'s 24&28--L.J.
SHE WAS SO WITHDRAWN AFTER HER RETURN, I FEARED SOMETHING TERRIBLE HAD HAPPENED.
IRENE, SHE'S GONE!
NO NOTE, NO CLOTHES-- DESTINY, WHERE IS SHE?!
I CANNOT SEE HER. ROGUE'S FUTURE IS DENIED ME.
THIS IS AS DELIBERATE AS MY DREAM.
"SOMEONE IS TAUNTING US, IRENE, TAUNTING US. BUT WHO?! WHY?!?"
ON A BUS NOW DEPARTING WASHINGTON, A YOUNG WOMAN STARES MISERABLY INTO THE PRE-DAWN SKY, WONDERING WHY SHE'S RUN AWAY FROM THE HOME AND PEOPLE SHE LOVES...
...WHILE THE CAUSE OF HER FLIGHT-- AND MYSTIQUE'S NIGHTMARE-- LOOKS ON AND LAUGHS IN MOCKING, MALEVOLENT TRIUMPH.
MEANWHILE...
YOU SHOULD SMILE, X-MEN.
I'D HATE TO THINK YOU WEREN'T ENJOYING THE FESTIVITIES.
PERHAPS MASQUE CAN CHEER YOU UP.
AT THE VERY LEAST, HE'LL GIVE YOU A WHOLE NEW OUTLOOK ON LIFE.
Ahhhh-- SKIN SO SMOOTH. FEATURES PURE PERFECTION.
HATE 'EM!

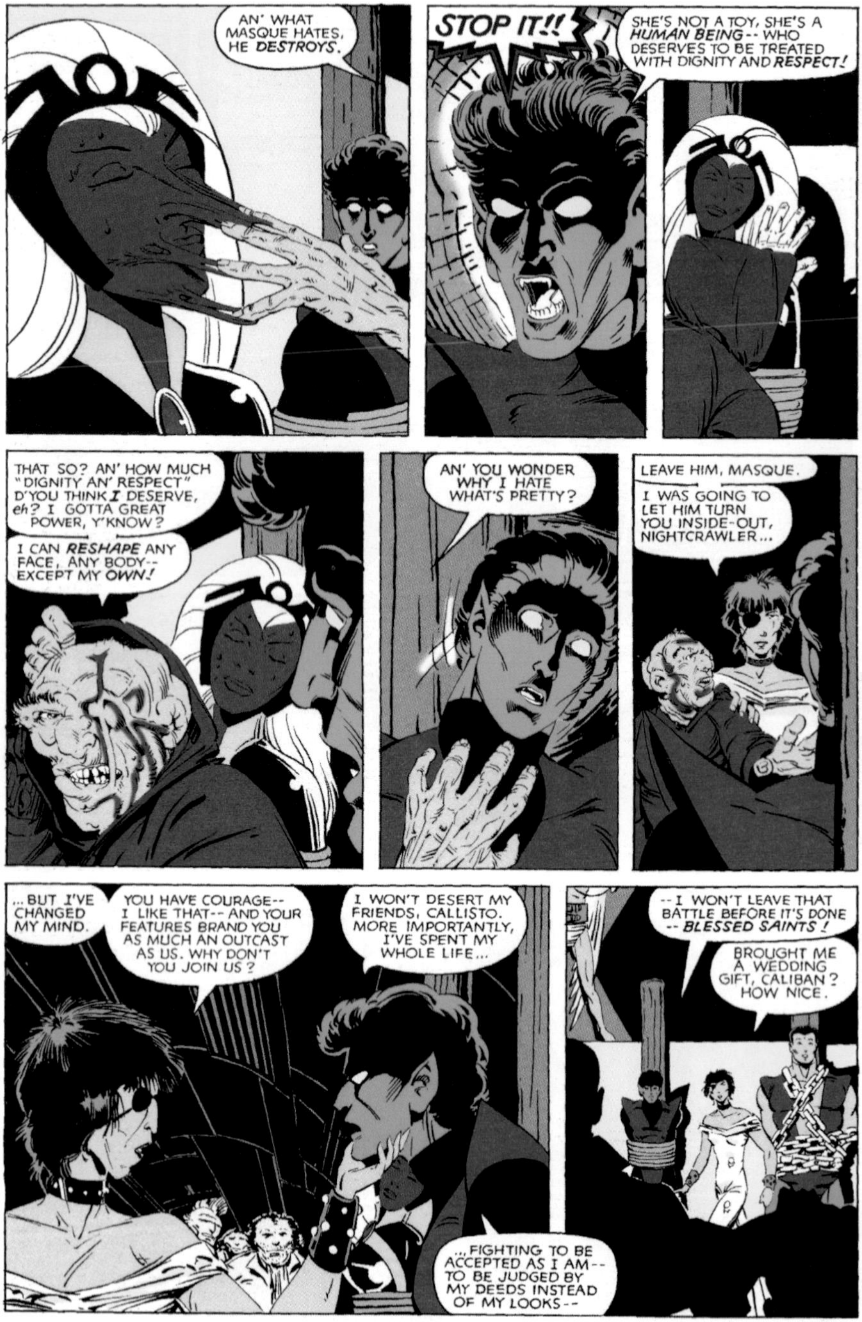

AN' WHAT MASQUE HATES, HE DESTROYS.
STOP IT!!
SHE'S NOT A TOY, SHE'S A HUMAN BEING-- WHO DESERVES TO BE TREATED WITH DIGNITY AND RESPECT!
THAT SO? AN' HOW MUCH "DIGNITY AN' RESPECT" D'YOU THINK I DESERVE, eh? I GOTTA GREAT POWER, Y'KNOW?
I CAN RESHAPE ANY FACE, ANY BODY-- EXCEPT MY OWN!
AN' YOU WONDER WHY I HATE WHAT'S PRETTY?
LEAVE HIM, MASQUE.
I WAS GOING TO LET HIM TURN YOU INSIDE-OUT, NIGHTCRAWLER...
...BUT I'VE CHANGED MY MIND.
YOU HAVE COURAGE-- I LIKE THAT-- AND YOUR FEATURES BRAND YOU AS MUCH AN OUTCAST AS US. WHY DON'T YOU JOIN US?
I WON'T DESERT MY FRIENDS, CALLISTO. MORE IMPORTANTLY, I'VE SPENT MY WHOLE LIFE...
...FIGHTING TO BE ACCEPTED AS I AM-- TO BE JUDGED BY MY DEEDS INSTEAD OF MY LOOKS--
--I WON'T LEAVE THAT BATTLE BEFORE IT'S DONE -- BLESSED SAINTS!
BROUGHT ME A WEDDING GIFT, CALIBAN? HOW NICE.

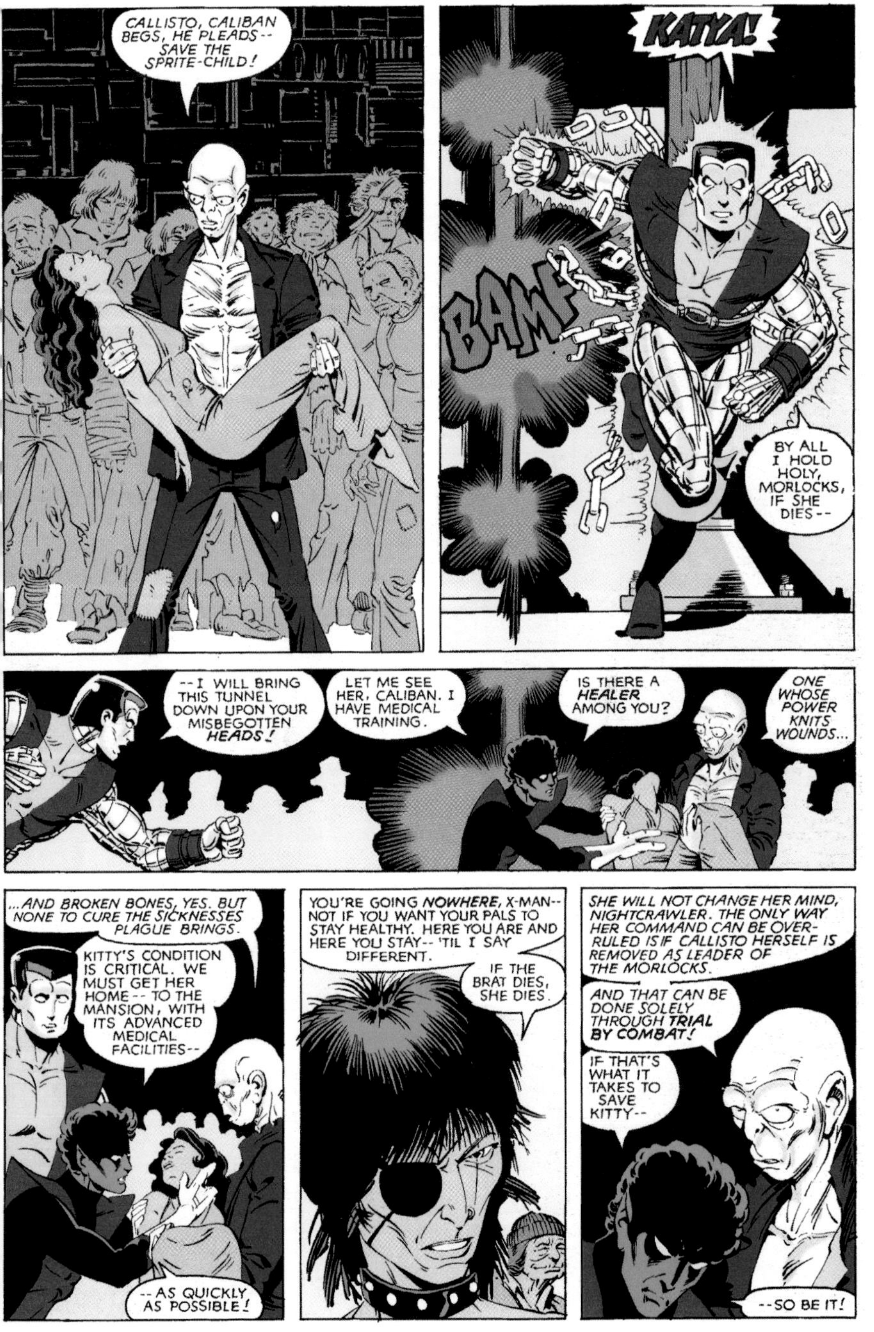

CALLISTO, CALIBAN BEGS, HE PLEADS-- SAVE THE SPRITE-CHILD!
KATYA!
BAMF
BY ALL I HOLD HOLY, MORLOCKS, IF SHE DIES--
--I WILL BRING THIS TUNNEL DOWN UPON YOUR MISBEGOTTEN HEADS!
LET ME SEE HER, CALIBAN. I HAVE MEDICAL TRAINING.
IS THERE A HEALER AMONG YOU?
ONE WHOSE POWER KNITS WOUNDS...
...AND BROKEN BONES, YES. BUT NONE TO CURE THE SICKNESSES PLAGUE BRINGS.
KITTY'S CONDITION IS CRITICAL. WE MUST GET HER HOME-- TO THE MANSION, WITH ITS ADVANCED MEDICAL FACILITIES--
--AS QUICKLY AS POSSIBLE!
YOU'RE GOING NOWHERE, X-MAN-- NOT IF YOU WANT YOUR PALS TO STAY HEALTHY. HERE YOU ARE AND HERE YOU STAY-- 'TIL I SAY DIFFERENT.
IF THE BRAT DIES, SHE DIES.
SHE WILL NOT CHANGE HER MIND, NIGHTCRAWLER. THE ONLY WAY HER COMMAND CAN BE OVER-RULED IS IF CALLISTO HERSELF IS REMOVED AS LEADER OF THE MORLOCKS.
AND THAT CAN BE DONE SOLELY THROUGH TRIAL BY COMBAT!
IF THAT'S WHAT IT TAKES TO SAVE KITTY--
--SO BE IT!

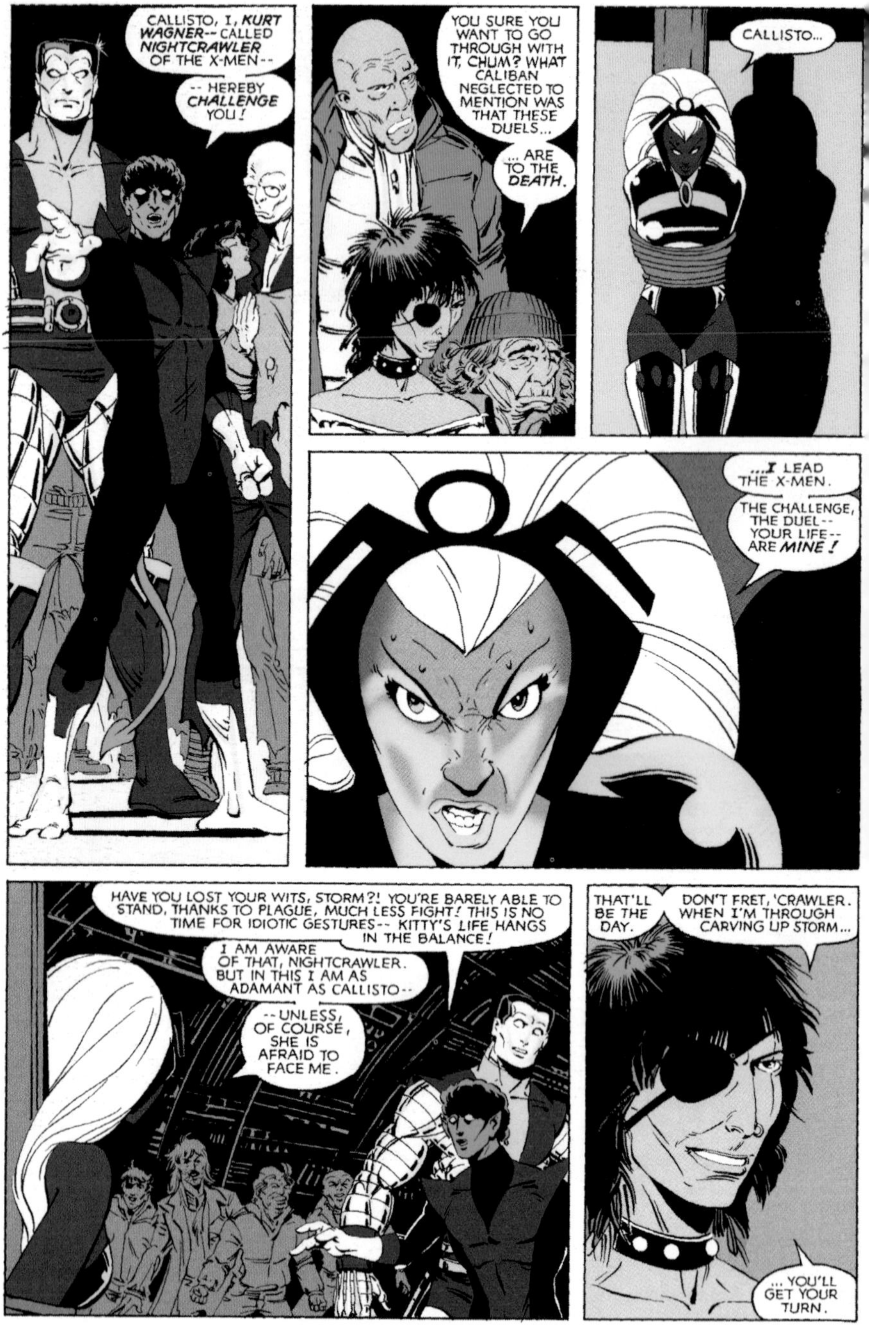

CALLISTO, I, KURT WAGNER-- CALLED NIGHTCRAWLER OF THE X-MEN--
-- HEREBY CHALLENGE YOU!
YOU SURE YOU WANT TO GO THROUGH WITH IT, CHUM? WHAT CALIBAN NEGLECTED TO MENTION WAS THAT THESE DUELS...
... ARE TO THE DEATH.
CALLISTO...
...I LEAD THE X-MEN.
THE CHALLENGE, THE DUEL-- YOUR LIFE-- ARE MINE!
HAVE YOU LOST YOUR WITS, STORM?! YOU'RE BARELY ABLE TO STAND, THANKS TO PLAGUE, MUCH LESS FIGHT! THIS IS NO TIME FOR IDIOTIC GESTURES-- KITTY'S LIFE HANGS IN THE BALANCE!
I AM AWARE OF THAT, NIGHTCRAWLER. BUT IN THIS I AM AS ADAMANT AS CALLISTO--
--UNLESS, OF COURSE, SHE IS AFRAID TO FACE ME.
THAT'LL BE THE DAY.
DON'T FRET, 'CRAWLER. WHEN I'M THROUGH CARVING UP STORM...
... YOU'LL GET YOUR TURN.

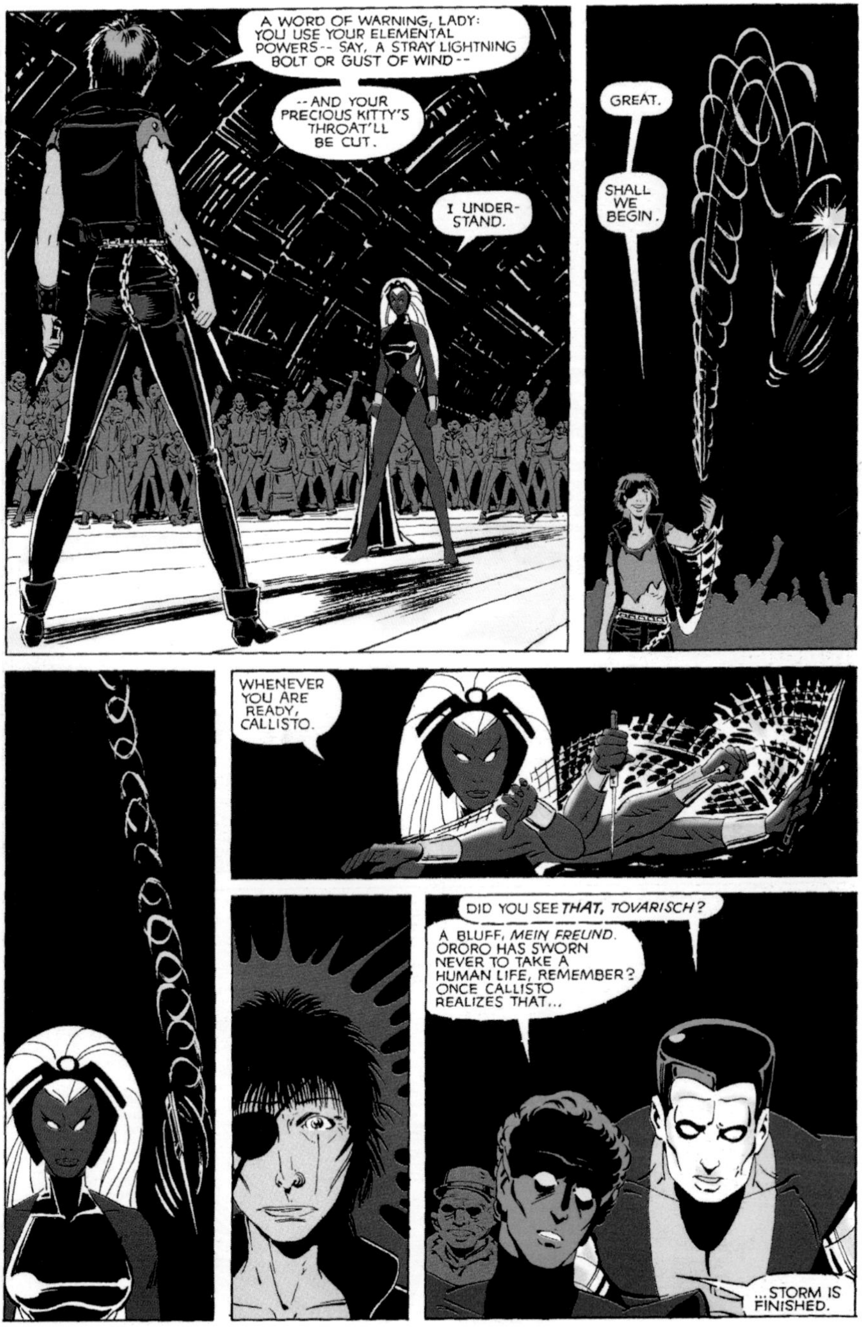

A WORD OF WARNING, LADY: YOU USE YOUR ELEMENTAL POWERS-- SAY, A STRAY LIGHTNING BOLT OR GUST OF WIND--
--AND YOUR PRECIOUS KITTY'S THROAT'LL BE CUT.
I UNDERSTAND.
GREAT.
SHALL WE BEGIN.
WHENEVER YOU ARE READY, CALLISTO.
DID YOU SEE *THAT, TOVARISCH?*
A BLUFF, *MEIN FREUND.* ORORO HAS SWORN NEVER TO TAKE A HUMAN LIFE, REMEMBER? ONCE CALLISTO REALIZES THAT...
...STORM IS FINISHED.

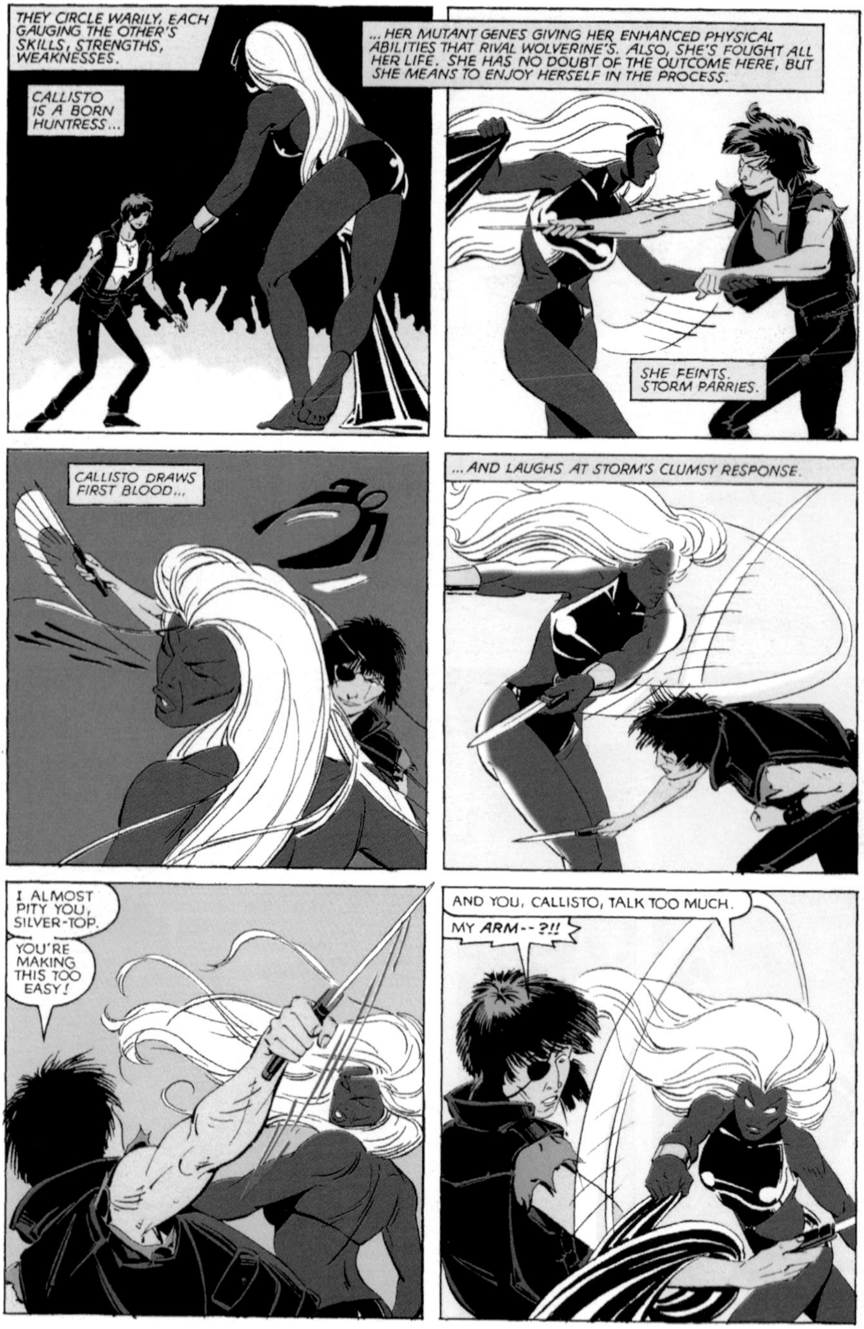
THEY CIRCLE WARILY, EACH GAUGING THE OTHER'S SKILLS, STRENGTHS, WEAKNESSES.
CALLISTO IS A BORN HUNTRESS...
...HER MUTANT GENES GIVING HER ENHANCED PHYSICAL ABILITIES THAT RIVAL WOLVERINE'S. ALSO, SHE'S FOUGHT ALL HER LIFE. SHE HAS NO DOUBT OF THE OUTCOME HERE, BUT SHE MEANS TO ENJOY HERSELF IN THE PROCESS.
SHE FEINTS. STORM PARRIES.
CALLISTO DRAWS FIRST BLOOD...
...AND LAUGHS AT STORM'S CLUMSY RESPONSE.
I ALMOST PITY YOU, SILVER-TOP.
YOU'RE MAKING THIS TOO EASY!
AND YOU, CALLISTO, TALK TOO MUCH.
MY ARM--?!!

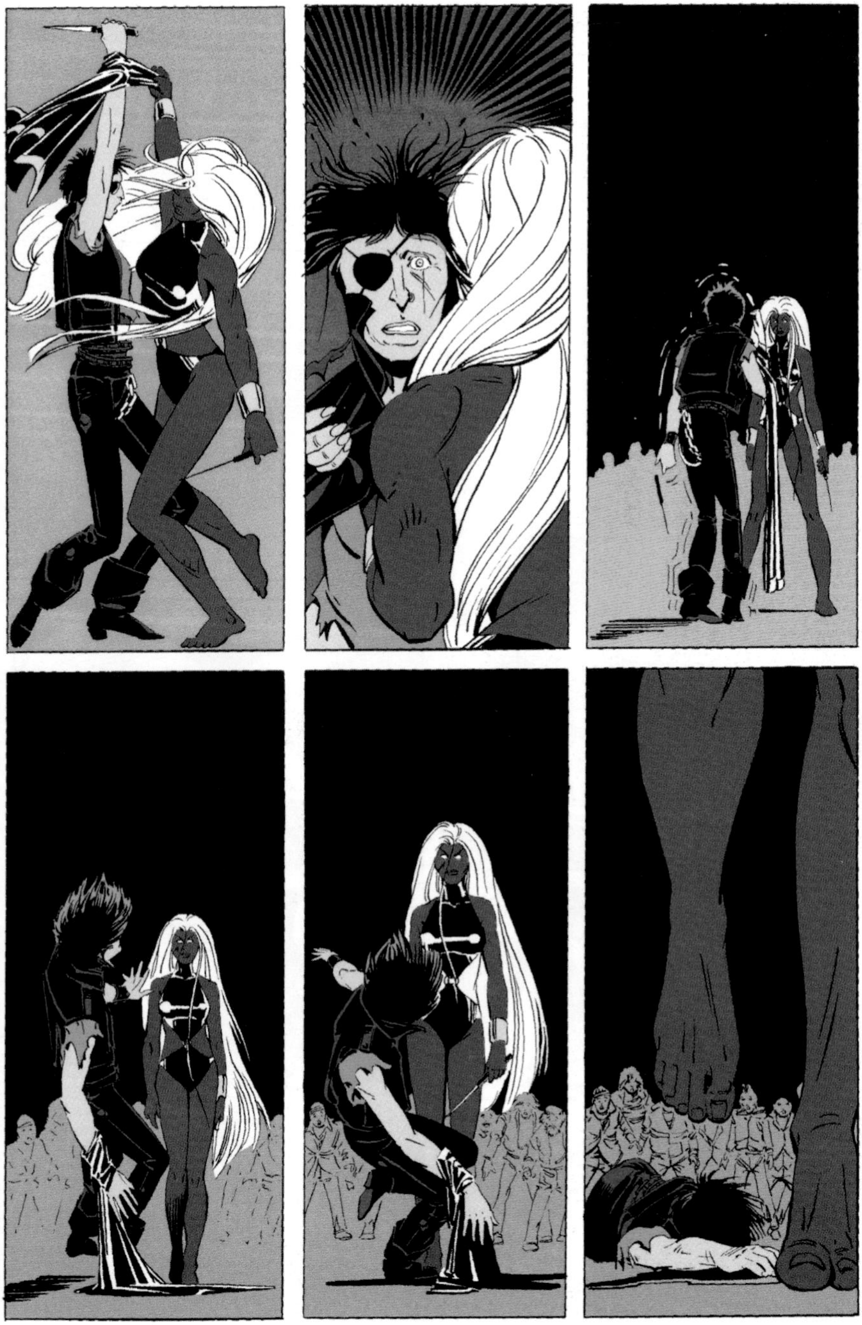

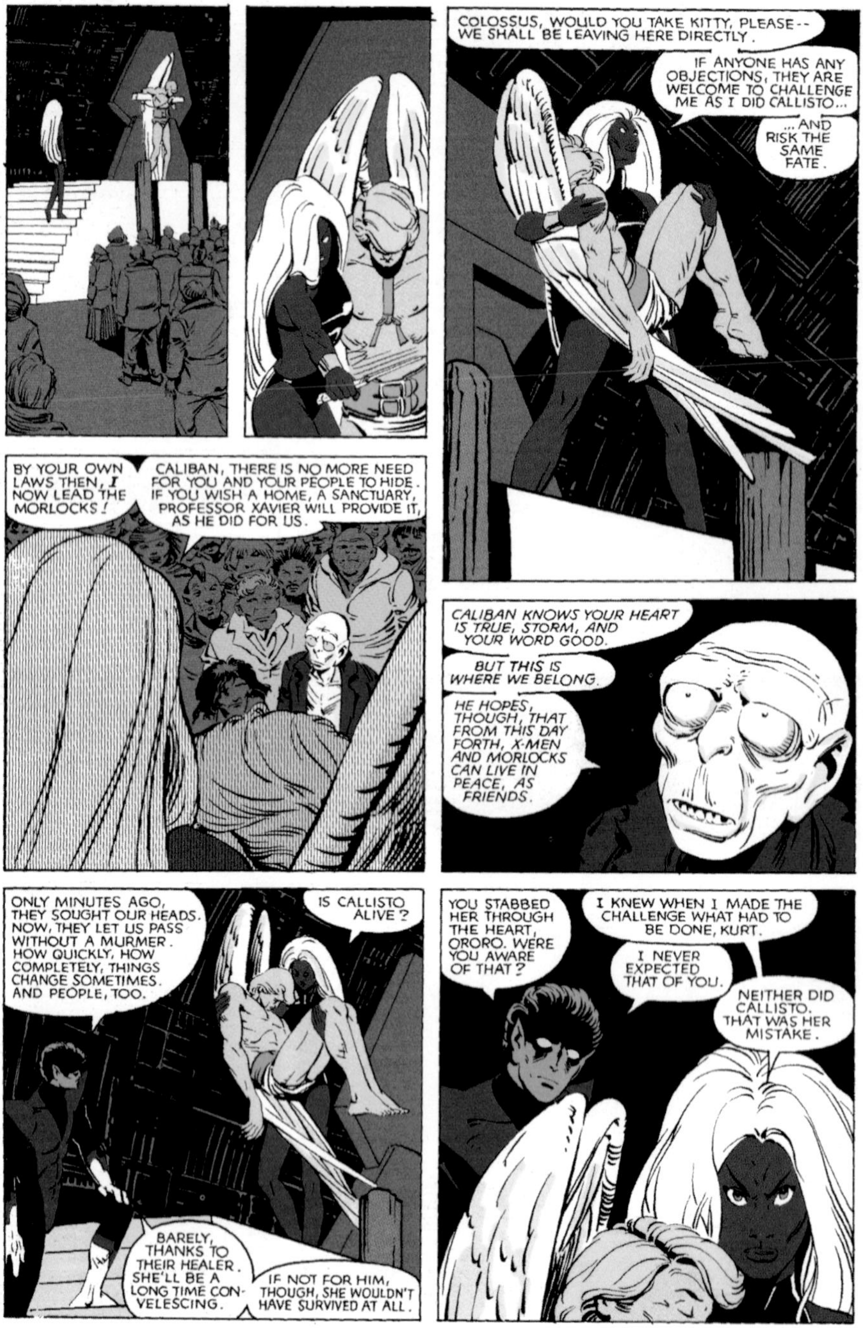
COLOSSUS, WOULD YOU TAKE KITTY, PLEASE-- WE SHALL BE LEAVING HERE DIRECTLY.
IF ANYONE HAS ANY OBJECTIONS, THEY ARE WELCOME TO CHALLENGE ME AS I DID CALLISTO...
...AND RISK THE SAME FATE.
BY YOUR OWN LAWS THEN, I NOW LEAD THE MORLOCKS!
CALIBAN, THERE IS NO MORE NEED FOR YOU AND YOUR PEOPLE TO HIDE. IF YOU WISH A HOME, A SANCTUARY, PROFESSOR XAVIER WILL PROVIDE IT, AS HE DID FOR US.
CALIBAN KNOWS YOUR HEART IS TRUE, STORM, AND YOUR WORD GOOD.
BUT THIS IS WHERE WE BELONG.
HE HOPES, THOUGH, THAT FROM THIS DAY FORTH, X-MEN AND MORLOCKS CAN LIVE IN PEACE, AS FRIENDS.
ONLY MINUTES AGO, THEY SOUGHT OUR HEADS. NOW, THEY LET US PASS WITHOUT A MURMER. HOW QUICKLY, HOW COMPLETELY, THINGS CHANGE SOMETIMES. AND PEOPLE, TOO.
IS CALLISTO ALIVE?
BARELY, THANKS TO THEIR HEALER. SHE'LL BE A LONG TIME CON-VELESCING.
IF NOT FOR HIM, THOUGH, SHE WOULDN'T HAVE SURVIVED AT ALL.
YOU STABBED HER THROUGH THE HEART, ORORO. WERE YOU AWARE OF THAT?
I KNEW WHEN I MADE THE CHALLENGE WHAT HAD TO BE DONE, KURT.
I NEVER EXPECTED THAT OF YOU.
NEITHER DID CALLISTO. THAT WAS HER MISTAKE.

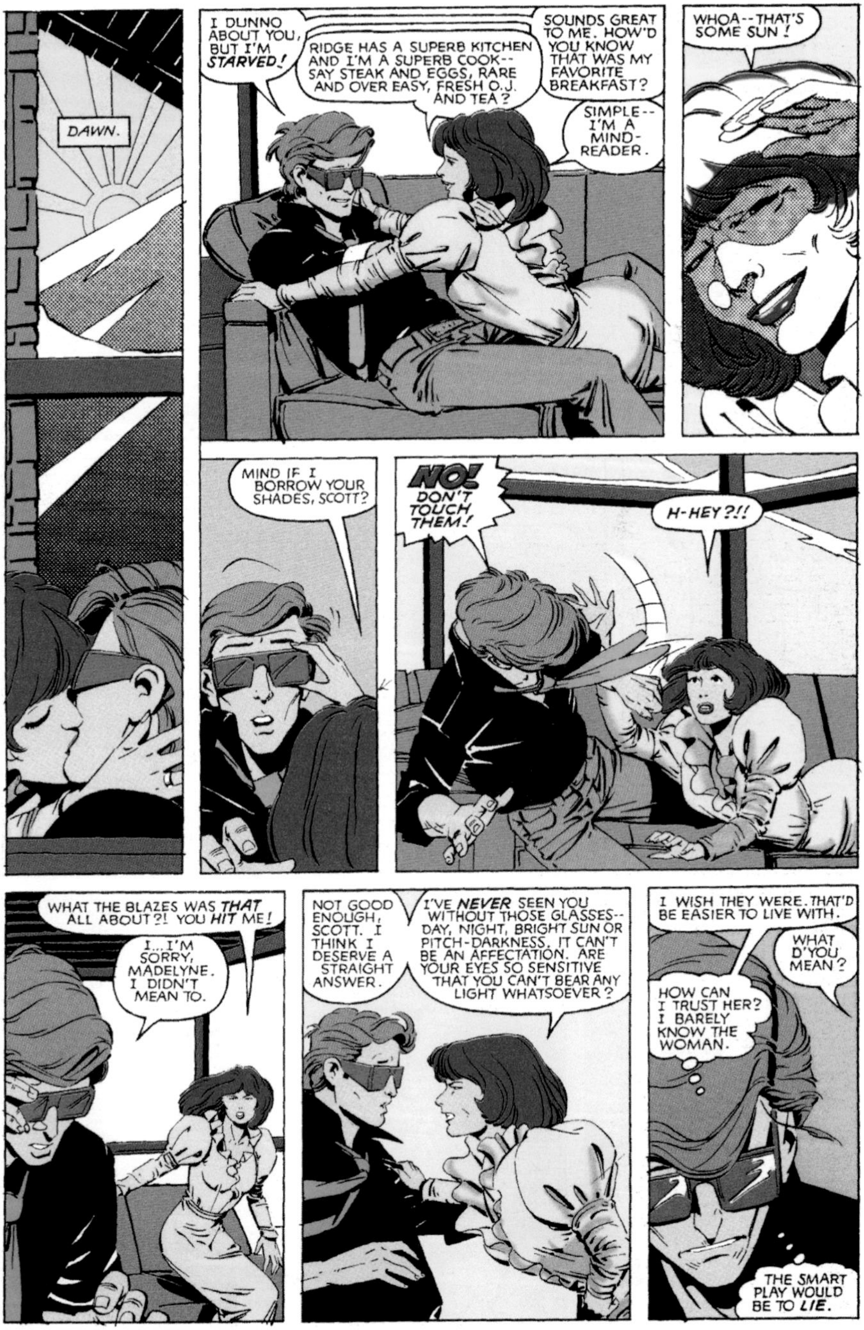

DAWN.
I DUNNO ABOUT YOU, BUT I'M STARVED!
RIDGE HAS A SUPERB KITCHEN AND I'M A SUPERB COOK-- SAY STEAK AND EGGS, RARE AND OVER EASY, FRESH O.J. AND TEA?
SOUNDS GREAT TO ME. HOW'D YOU KNOW THAT WAS MY FAVORITE BREAKFAST?
SIMPLE-- I'M A MIND-READER.
WHOA--THAT'S SOME SUN!
MIND IF I BORROW YOUR SHADES, SCOTT?
NO! DON'T TOUCH THEM!
H-HEY?!!
WHAT THE BLAZES WAS THAT ALL ABOUT?! YOU HIT ME!
I...I'M SORRY, MADELYNE. I DIDN'T MEAN TO.
NOT GOOD ENOUGH, SCOTT. I THINK I DESERVE A STRAIGHT ANSWER.
I'VE NEVER SEEN YOU WITHOUT THOSE GLASSES-- DAY, NIGHT, BRIGHT SUN OR PITCH-DARKNESS. IT CAN'T BE AN AFFECTATION. ARE YOUR EYES SO SENSITIVE THAT YOU CAN'T BEAR ANY LIGHT WHATSOEVER?
I WISH THEY WERE. THAT'D BE EASIER TO LIVE WITH.
WHAT D'YOU MEAN?
HOW CAN I TRUST HER? I BARELY KNOW THE WOMAN.
THE SMART PLAY WOULD BE TO LIE.

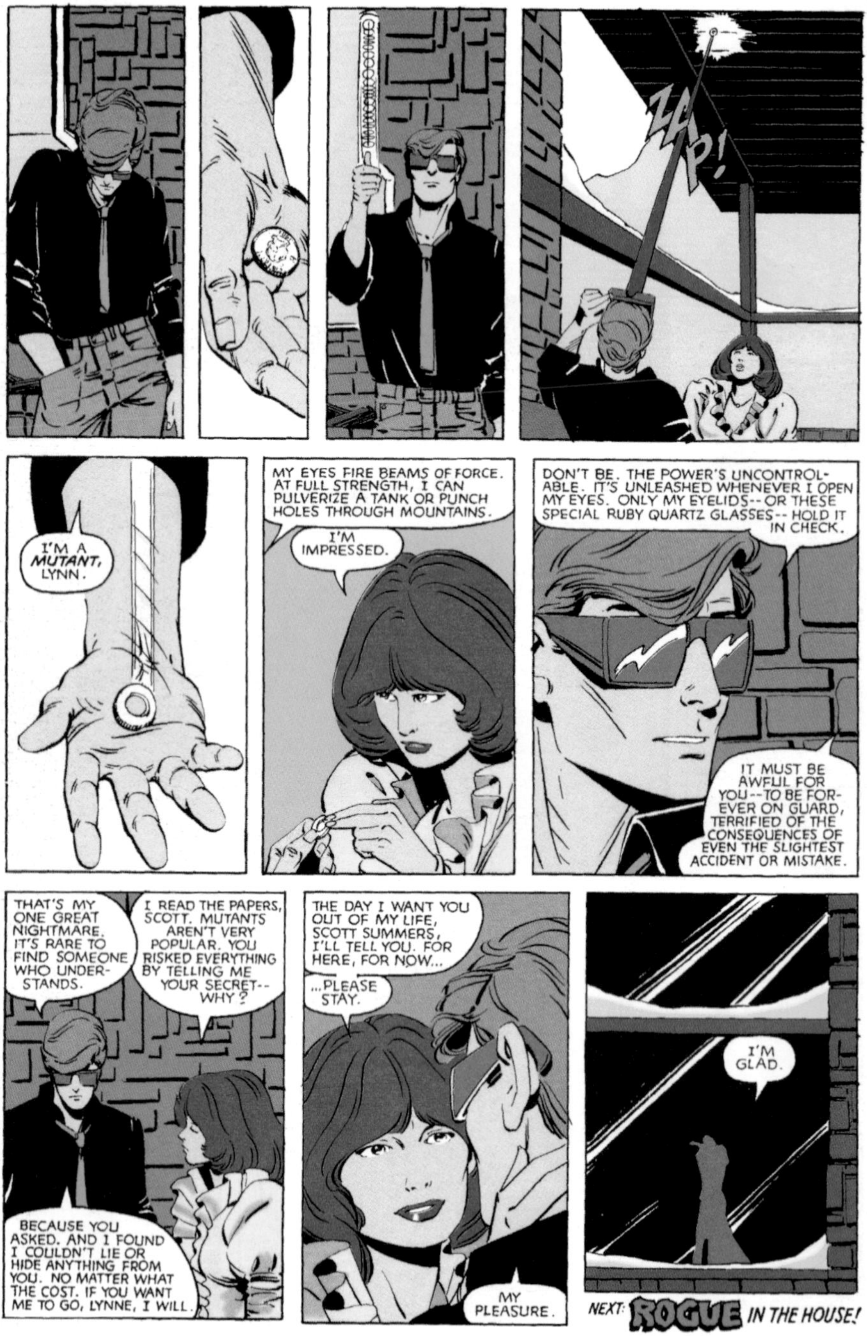
ZAP!
I'M A MUTANT, LYNN.
MY EYES FIRE BEAMS OF FORCE. AT FULL STRENGTH, I CAN PULVERIZE A TANK OR PUNCH HOLES THROUGH MOUNTAINS.
I'M IMPRESSED.
DON'T BE. THE POWER'S UNCONTROLABLE. IT'S UNLEASHED WHENEVER I OPEN MY EYES. ONLY MY EYELIDS--OR THESE SPECIAL RUBY QUARTZ GLASSES--HOLD IT IN CHECK.
IT MUST BE AWFUL FOR YOU--TO BE FOREVER ON GUARD, TERRIFIED OF THE CONSEQUENCES OF EVEN THE SLIGHTEST ACCIDENT OR MISTAKE.
THAT'S MY ONE GREAT NIGHTMARE. IT'S RARE TO FIND SOMEONE WHO UNDERSTANDS.
I READ THE PAPERS, SCOTT. MUTANTS AREN'T VERY POPULAR. YOU RISKED EVERYTHING BY TELLING ME YOUR SECRET--WHY?
BECAUSE YOU ASKED. AND I FOUND I COULDN'T LIE OR HIDE ANYTHING FROM YOU. NO MATTER WHAT THE COST. IF YOU WANT ME TO GO, LYNNE, I WILL.
THE DAY I WANT YOU OUT OF MY LIFE, SCOTT SUMMERS, I'LL TELL YOU. FOR HERE, FOR NOW...
...PLEASE STAY.
MY PLEASURE.
I'M GLAD.
NEXT: ROGUE IN THE HOUSE!

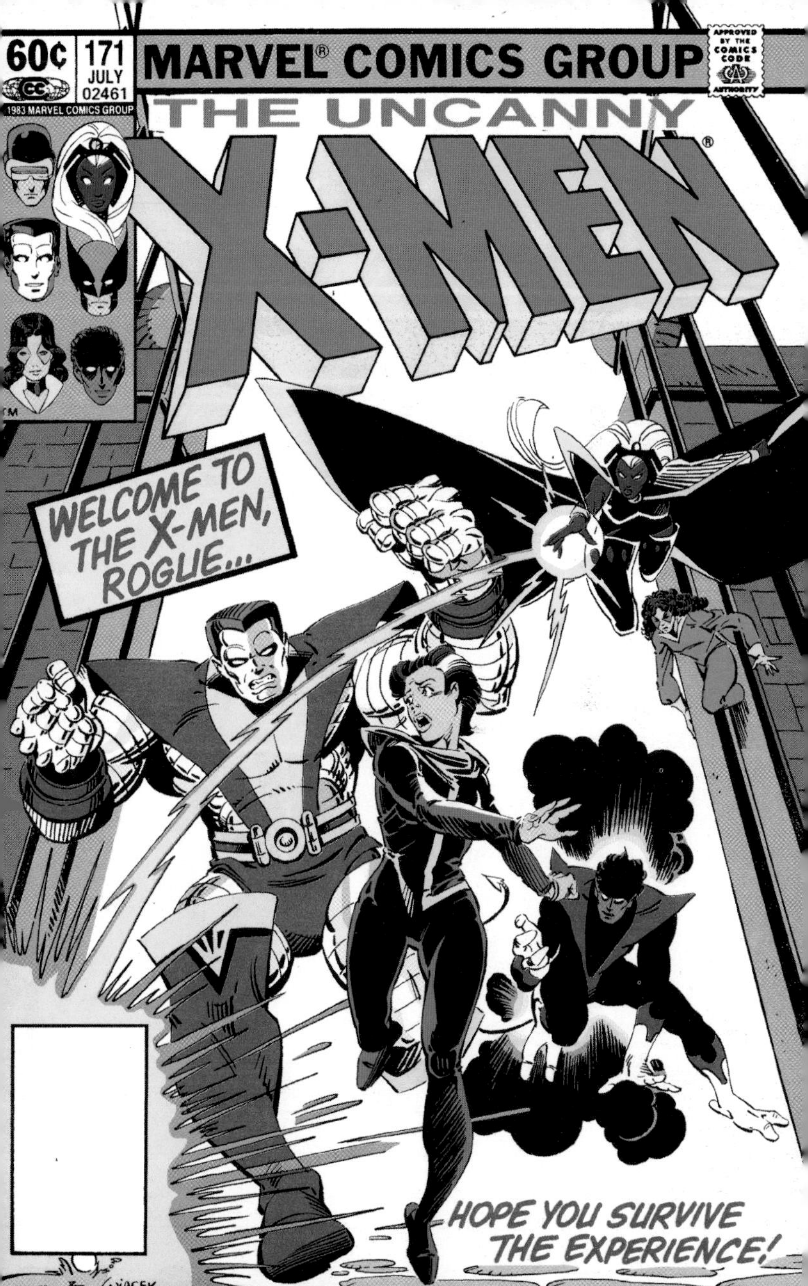

60¢
171
JULY
02461
1983 MARVEL COMICS GROUP
MARVEL® COMICS GROUP
APPROVED BY THE COMICS CODE AUTHORITY
THE UNCANNY
X-MEN®
TM
WELCOME TO THE X-MEN, ROGUE...
HOPE YOU SURVIVE THE EXPERIENCE!

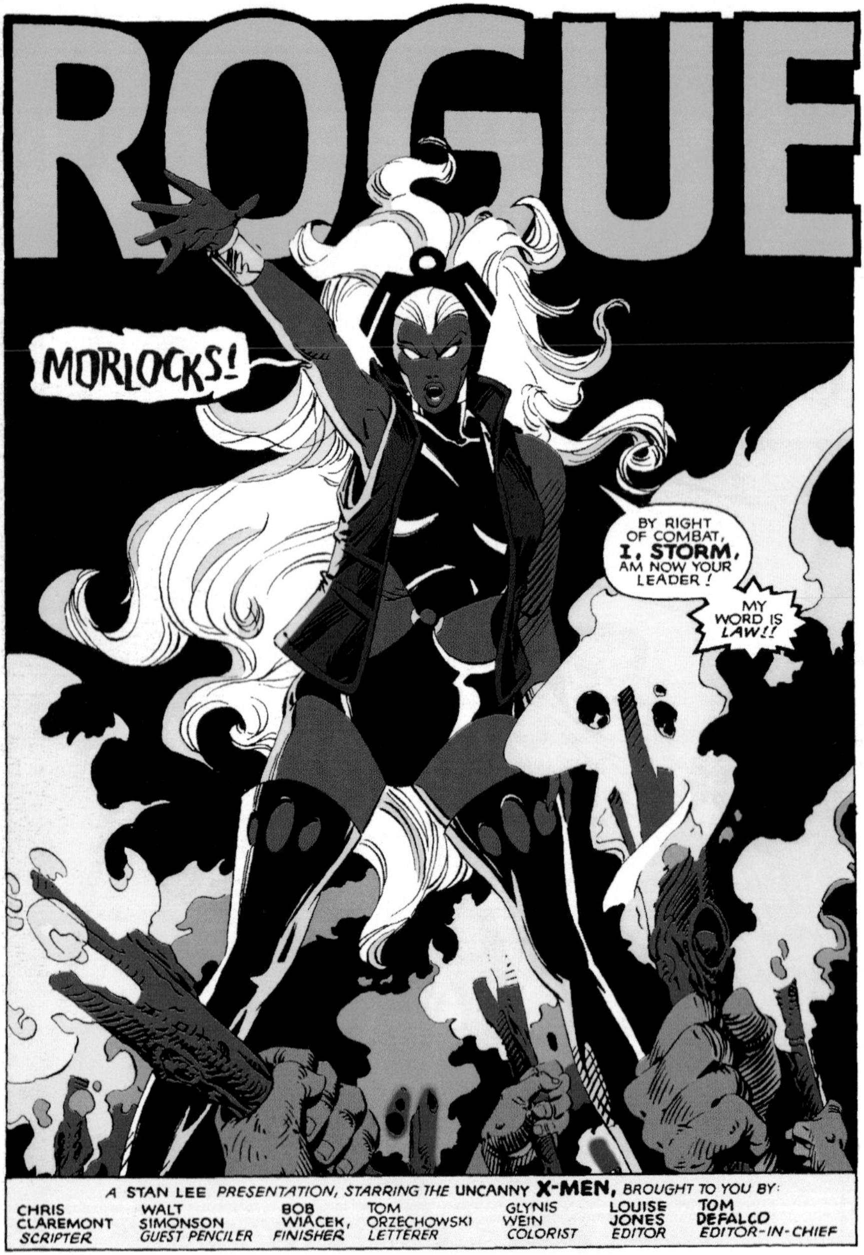
ROGUE
MORLOCKS!
BY RIGHT OF COMBAT, I, STORM, AM NOW YOUR LEADER!
MY WORD IS LAW!!
A STAN LEE PRESENTATION, STARRING THE UNCANNY X-MEN, BROUGHT TO YOU BY:
CHRIS CLAREMONT SCRIPTER
WALT SIMONSON GUEST PENCILER
BOB WIACEK, FINISHER
TOM ORZECHOWSKI LETTERER
GLYNIS WEIN COLORIST
LOUISE JONES EDITOR
TOM DEFALCO EDITOR-IN-CHIEF

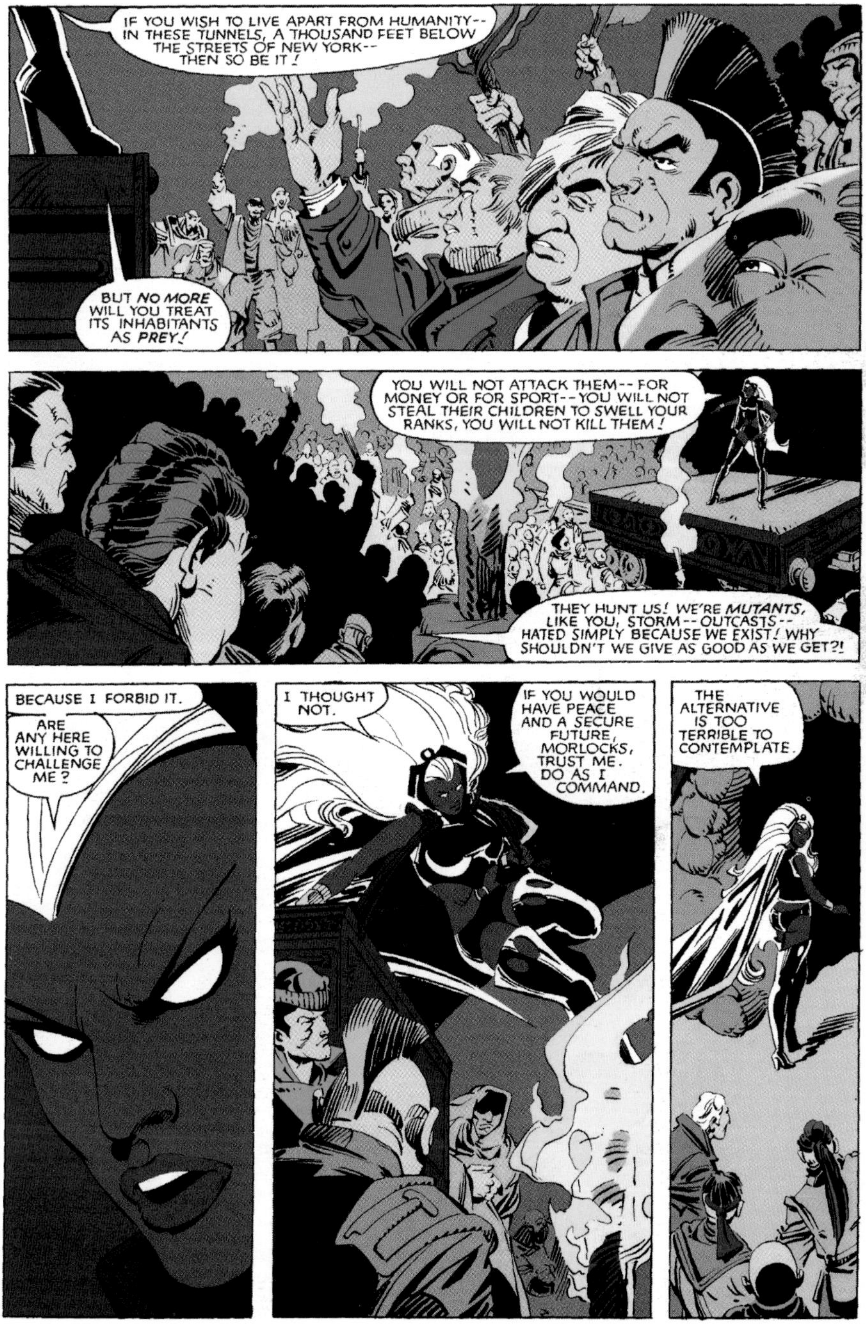
IF YOU WISH TO LIVE APART FROM HUMANITY-- IN THESE TUNNELS, A THOUSAND FEET BELOW THE STREETS OF NEW YORK-- THEN SO BE IT!
BUT NO MORE WILL YOU TREAT ITS INHABITANTS AS PREY!
YOU WILL NOT ATTACK THEM-- FOR MONEY OR FOR SPORT-- YOU WILL NOT STEAL THEIR CHILDREN TO SWELL YOUR RANKS, YOU WILL NOT KILL THEM!
THEY HUNT US! WE'RE MUTANTS, LIKE YOU, STORM-- OUTCASTS-- HATED SIMPLY BECAUSE WE EXIST! WHY SHOULDN'T WE GIVE AS GOOD AS WE GET?!
BECAUSE I FORBID IT.
ARE ANY HERE WILLING TO CHALLENGE ME?
I THOUGHT NOT.
IF YOU WOULD HAVE PEACE AND A SECURE FUTURE, MORLOCKS, TRUST ME. DO AS I COMMAND.
THE ALTERNATIVE IS TOO TERRIBLE TO CONTEMPLATE.

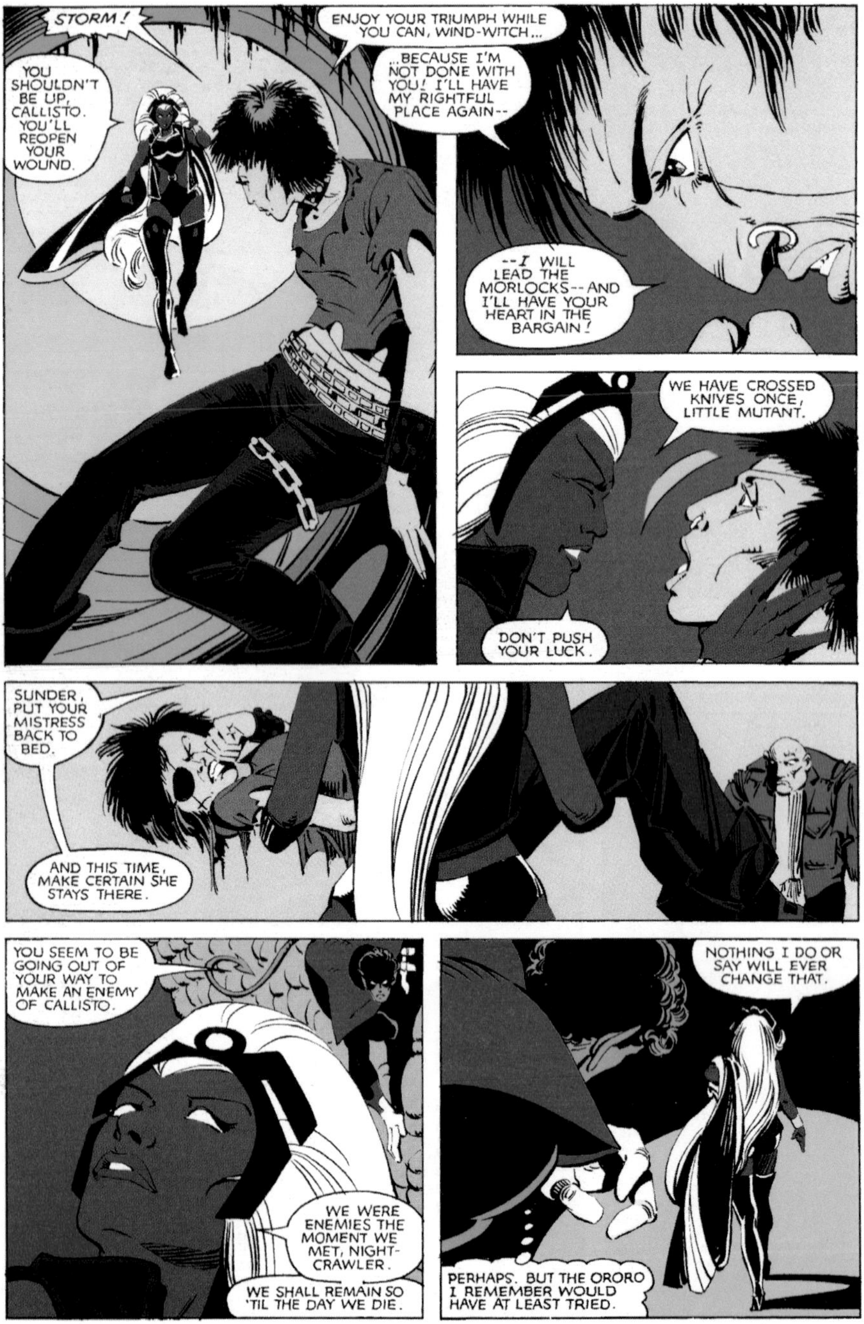
STORM!
YOU SHOULDN'T BE UP, CALLISTO. YOU'LL REOPEN YOUR WOUND.
ENJOY YOUR TRIUMPH WHILE YOU CAN, WIND-WITCH...
...BECAUSE I'M NOT DONE WITH YOU! I'LL HAVE MY RIGHTFUL PLACE AGAIN--
--I WILL LEAD THE MORLOCKS--AND I'LL HAVE YOUR HEART IN THE BARGAIN!
WE HAVE CROSSED KNIVES ONCE, LITTLE MUTANT.
DON'T PUSH YOUR LUCK.
SUNDER, PUT YOUR MISTRESS BACK TO BED.
AND THIS TIME, MAKE CERTAIN SHE STAYS THERE.
YOU SEEM TO BE GOING OUT OF YOUR WAY TO MAKE AN ENEMY OF CALLISTO.
WE WERE ENEMIES THE MOMENT WE MET, NIGHT-CRAWLER.
WE SHALL REMAIN SO 'TIL THE DAY WE DIE.
NOTHING I DO OR SAY WILL EVER CHANGE THAT.
PERHAPS. BUT THE ORORO I REMEMBER WOULD HAVE AT LEAST TRIED.

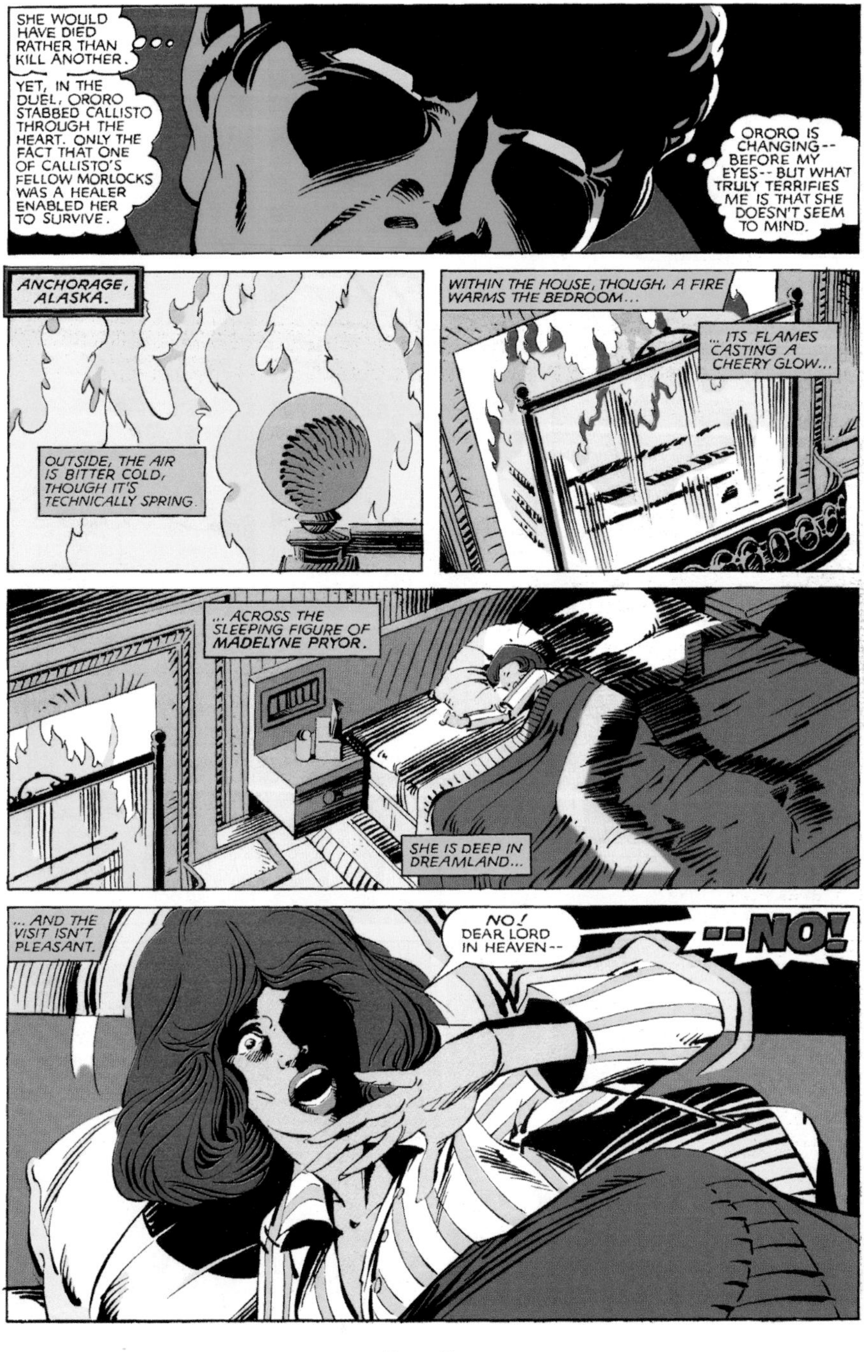
SHE WOULD HAVE DIED RATHER THAN KILL ANOTHER.
YET, IN THE DUEL, ORORO STABBED CALLISTO THROUGH THE HEART. ONLY THE FACT THAT ONE OF CALLISTO'S FELLOW MORLOCKS WAS A HEALER ENABLED HER TO SURVIVE.
ORORO IS CHANGING-- BEFORE MY EYES-- BUT WHAT TRULY TERRIFIES ME IS THAT SHE DOESN'T SEEM TO MIND.
ANCHORAGE, ALASKA.
OUTSIDE, THE AIR IS BITTER COLD, THOUGH IT'S TECHNICALLY SPRING.
WITHIN THE HOUSE, THOUGH, A FIRE WARMS THE BEDROOM...
...ITS FLAMES CASTING A CHEERY GLOW...
...ACROSS THE SLEEPING FIGURE OF MADELYNE PRYOR.
SHE IS DEEP IN DREAMLAND...
...AND THE VISIT ISN'T PLEASANT.
NO! DEAR LORD IN HEAVEN--
--NO!

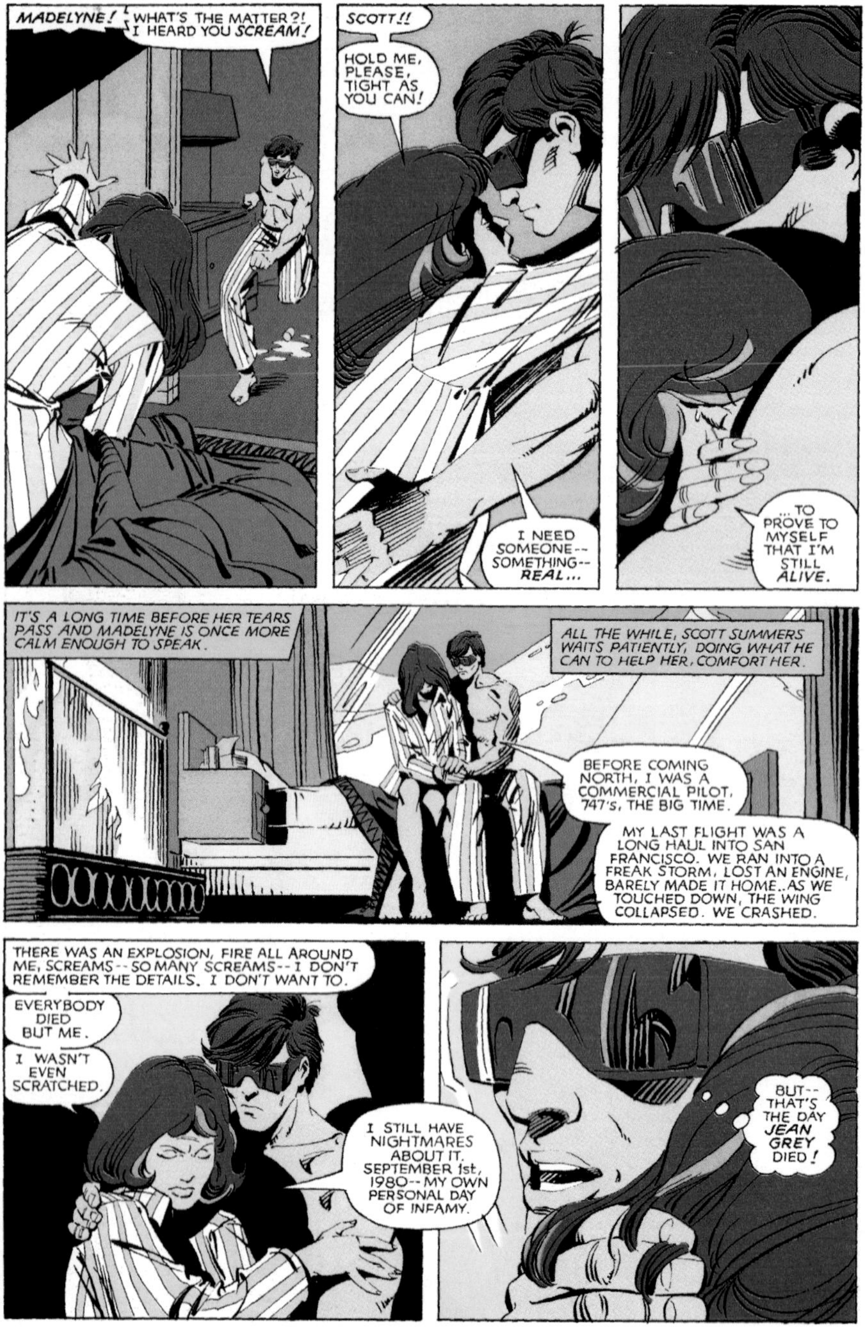
MADELYNE!
WHAT'S THE MATTER?! I HEARD YOU SCREAM!
SCOTT!!
HOLD ME, PLEASE, TIGHT AS YOU CAN!
I NEED SOMEONE-- SOMETHING-- REAL...
...TO PROVE TO MYSELF THAT I'M STILL ALIVE.
IT'S A LONG TIME BEFORE HER TEARS PASS AND MADELYNE IS ONCE MORE CALM ENOUGH TO SPEAK.
ALL THE WHILE, SCOTT SUMMERS WAITS PATIENTLY, DOING WHAT HE CAN TO HELP HER, COMFORT HER.
BEFORE COMING NORTH, I WAS A COMMERCIAL PILOT, 747's, THE BIG TIME.
MY LAST FLIGHT WAS A LONG HAUL INTO SAN FRANCISCO. WE RAN INTO A FREAK STORM, LOST AN ENGINE, BARELY MADE IT HOME..AS WE TOUCHED DOWN, THE WING COLLAPSED. WE CRASHED.
THERE WAS AN EXPLOSION, FIRE ALL AROUND ME, SCREAMS--SO MANY SCREAMS--I DON'T REMEMBER THE DETAILS. I DON'T WANT TO.
EVERYBODY DIED BUT ME.
I WASN'T EVEN SCRATCHED.
I STILL HAVE NIGHTMARES ABOUT IT. SEPTEMBER 1st, 1980--MY OWN PERSONAL DAY OF INFAMY.
BUT--THAT'S THE DAY JEAN GREY DIED!

BEVERLY, MASSACHUSETTS-- A SUBURB OF BOSTON--THE HOME OF *JOSEPH* AND *MARIE DANVERS*...

WHEN'LL WE SEE YOU NEXT, CAROL?

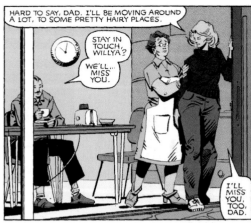

HARD TO SAY, DAD. I'LL BE MOVING AROUND A LOT, TO SOME PRETTY HAIRY PLACES.

STAY IN TOUCH, WILLYA?

WE'LL... MISS YOU.

I'LL MISS YOU, TOO, DAD.

TAKE CARE, CAROL. EVEN SUPER HEROES AREN'T IMMORTAL.

DON'T I KNOW IT.

IS EVERYTHING ALL RIGHT, DEAR? YOU'VE SEEMED... DIFFERENT LATELY.

I'M FINE, MOM, REALLY.

I NEVER COULD FOOL HER. WHEN I WAS *MS. MARVEL*, SHE RECOGNIZED ME RIGHT OFF THE BAT. AND NOW, SHE KNOWS I'VE CHANGED.

IF ONLY SHE KNEW HOW MUCH-- FOR GOOD AND ILL. CHARLES XAVIER DID HIS BEST TO RESTORE MY MEMORIES-- AFTER *ROGUE* HAD STRIPPED THEM AND MY POWERS FROM ME-- THANKS TO HIM, I REMEMBER PRETTY MUCH ALL OF WHO AND WHAT I WAS.

BUT THERE ARE NO EMOTIONS TO GO ALONG WITH THEM.

WHERE ONCE I LOVED THEM, WITH ALL MY HEART, I FEEL A VAGUE AFFECTION. THAT'S WHAT MOM NOTICED -- WHAT DISTURBED MOM AND OUTRAGES ME --

-- A LOSS THAT CAN NEVER BE REPLACED.

BUT WHAT'S DONE IS DONE-- FEELING SORRY FOR MYSELF WON'T MAKE IT ANY BETTER.

MY LIFE AS *CAROL DANVERS* MAY BE OVER.

BUT *BINARY'S* HAS JUST *BEGUN!*

[57]

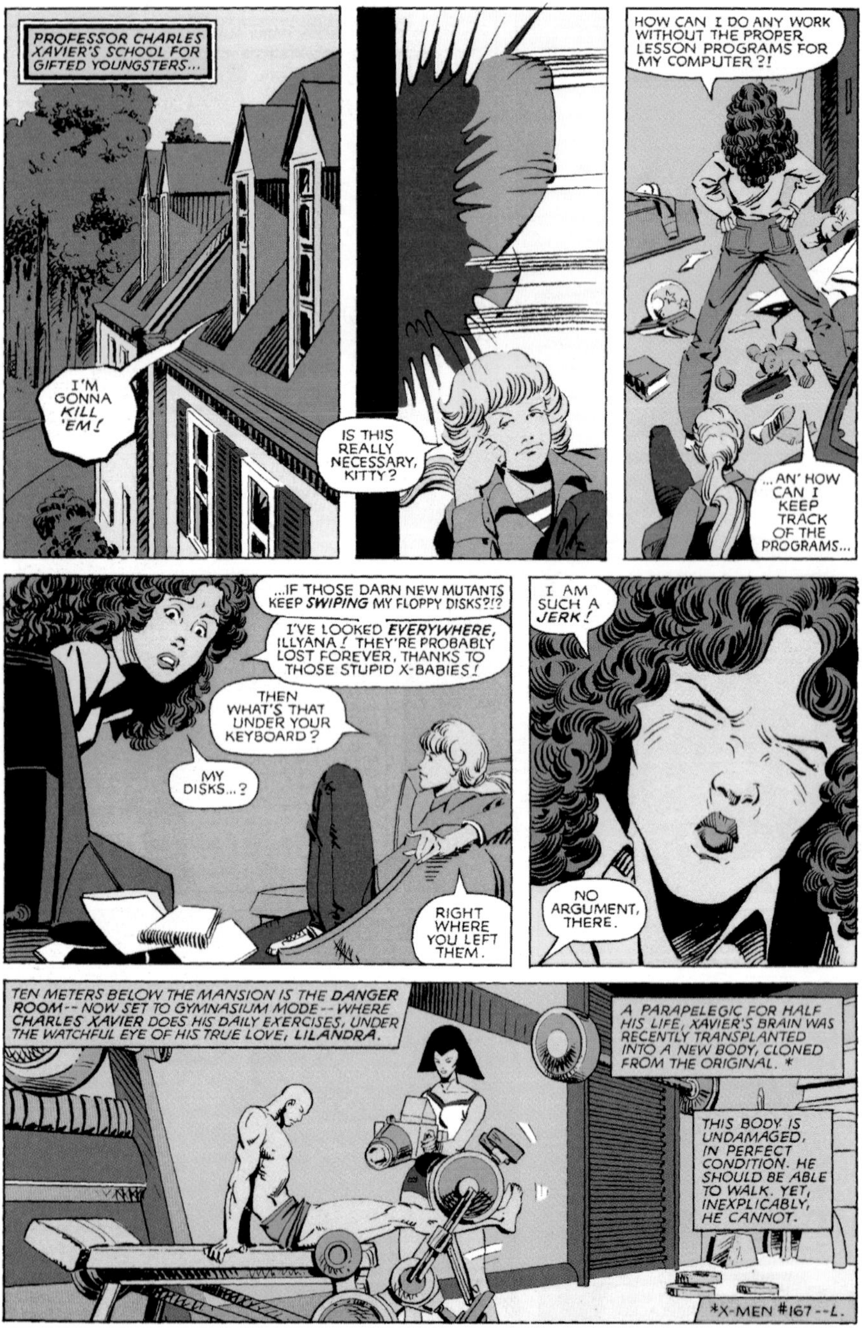
PROFESSOR CHARLES XAVIER'S SCHOOL FOR GIFTED YOUNGSTERS...
I'M GONNA KILL 'EM!
IS THIS REALLY NECESSARY, KITTY?
HOW CAN I DO ANY WORK WITHOUT THE PROPER LESSON PROGRAMS FOR MY COMPUTER?!
...AN' HOW CAN I KEEP TRACK OF THE PROGRAMS...
...IF THOSE DARN NEW MUTANTS KEEP SWIPING MY FLOPPY DISKS?!?
I'VE LOOKED EVERYWHERE, ILLYANA! THEY'RE PROBABLY LOST FOREVER, THANKS TO THOSE STUPID X-BABIES!
THEN WHAT'S THAT UNDER YOUR KEYBOARD?
MY DISKS...?
RIGHT WHERE YOU LEFT THEM.
I AM SUCH A JERK!
NO ARGUMENT, THERE.
TEN METERS BELOW THE MANSION IS THE DANGER ROOM-- NOW SET TO GYMNASIUM MODE-- WHERE CHARLES XAVIER DOES HIS DAILY EXERCISES, UNDER THE WATCHFUL EYE OF HIS TRUE LOVE, LILANDRA.
A PARAPELEGIC FOR HALF HIS LIFE, XAVIER'S BRAIN WAS RECENTLY TRANSPLANTED INTO A NEW BODY, CLONED FROM THE ORIGINAL. *
THIS BODY IS UNDAMAGED, IN PERFECT CONDITION. HE SHOULD BE ABLE TO WALK. YET, INEXPLICABLY, HE CANNOT.
*X-MEN #167--L.

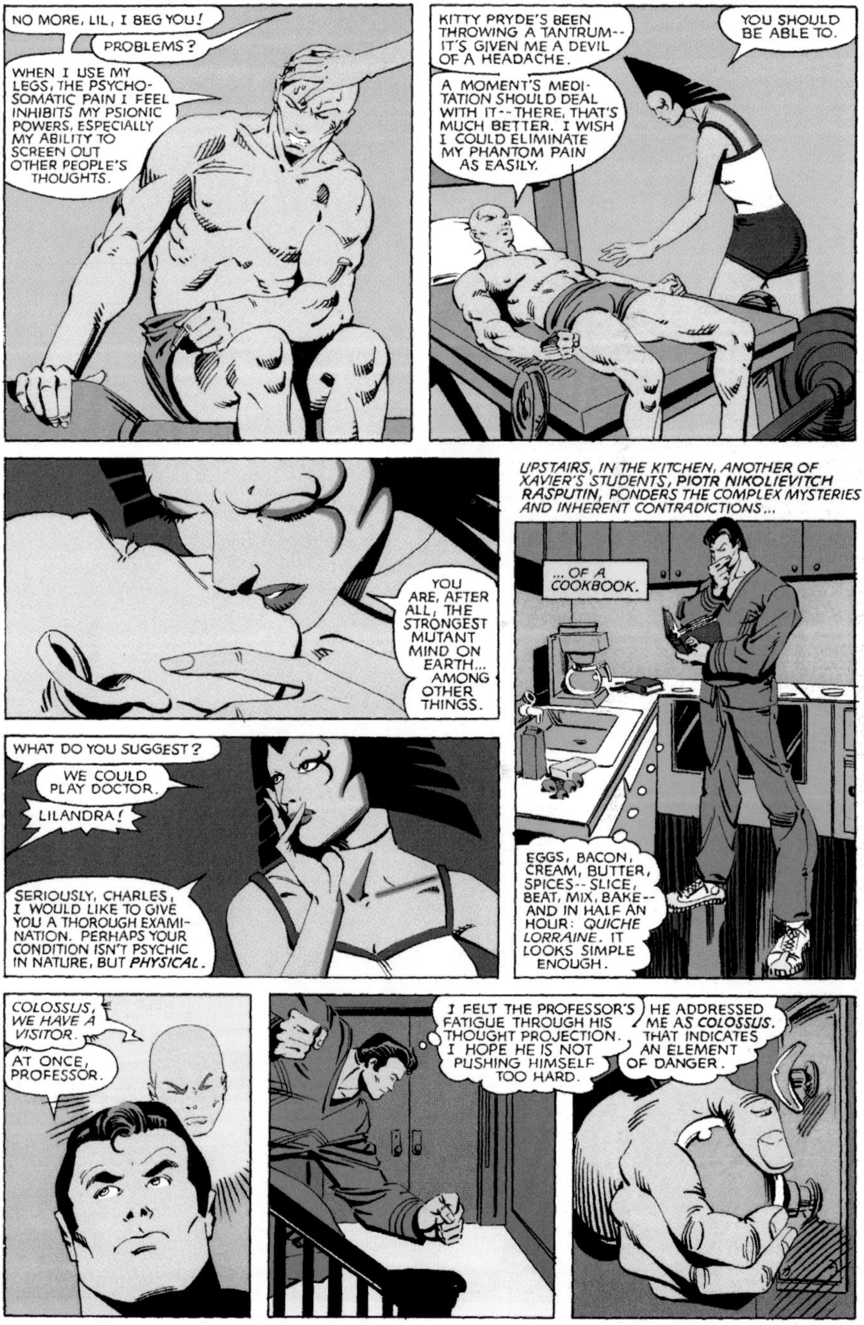
NO MORE, LIL, I BEG YOU!
PROBLEMS?
WHEN I USE MY LEGS, THE PSYCHO-SOMATIC PAIN I FEEL INHIBITS MY PSIONIC POWERS, ESPECIALLY MY ABILITY TO SCREEN OUT OTHER PEOPLE'S THOUGHTS.
KITTY PRYDE'S BEEN THROWING A TANTRUM-- IT'S GIVEN ME A DEVIL OF A HEADACHE.
YOU SHOULD BE ABLE TO.
A MOMENT'S MEDI-TATION SHOULD DEAL WITH IT--THERE, THAT'S MUCH BETTER. I WISH I COULD ELIMINATE MY PHANTOM PAIN AS EASILY.
YOU ARE, AFTER ALL, THE STRONGEST MUTANT MIND ON EARTH... AMONG OTHER THINGS.
WHAT DO YOU SUGGEST?
WE COULD PLAY DOCTOR.
LILANDRA!
SERIOUSLY, CHARLES, I WOULD LIKE TO GIVE YOU A THOROUGH EXAMI-NATION. PERHAPS YOUR CONDITION ISN'T PSYCHIC IN NATURE, BUT PHYSICAL.
UPSTAIRS, IN THE KITCHEN, ANOTHER OF XAVIER'S STUDENTS, PIOTR NIKOLIEVITCH RASPUTIN, PONDERS THE COMPLEX MYSTERIES AND INHERENT CONTRADICTIONS...
...OF A COOKBOOK.
EGGS, BACON, CREAM, BUTTER, SPICES--SLICE, BEAT, MIX, BAKE-- AND IN HALF AN HOUR: QUICHE LORRAINE. IT LOOKS SIMPLE ENOUGH.
COLOSSUS, WE HAVE A VISITOR.
AT ONCE, PROFESSOR.
I FELT THE PROFESSOR'S FATIGUE THROUGH HIS THOUGHT PROJECTION. I HOPE HE IS NOT PUSHING HIMSELF TOO HARD.
HE ADDRESSED ME AS COLOSSUS. THAT INDICATES AN ELEMENT OF DANGER.

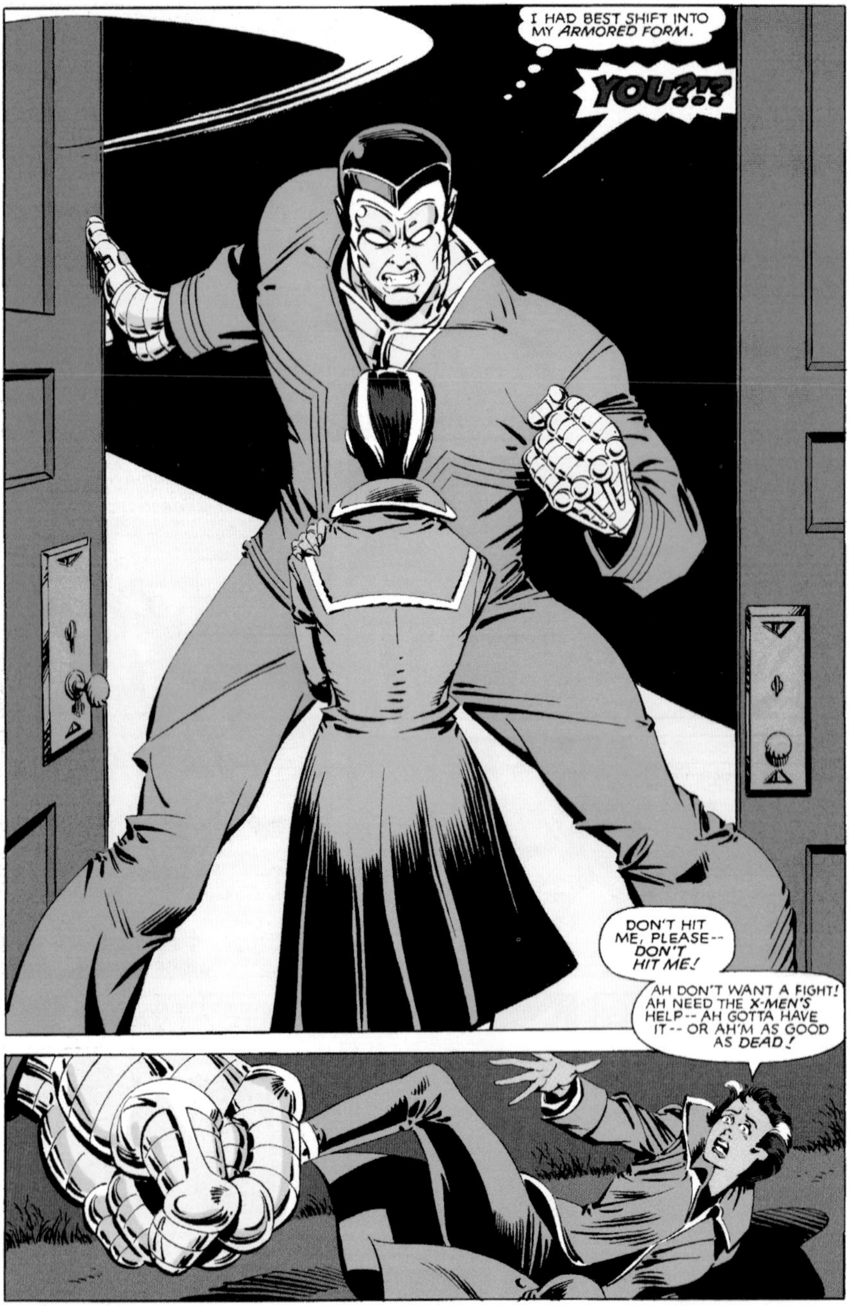
I HAD BEST SHIFT INTO MY ARMORED FORM.
YOU?!?
DON'T HIT ME, PLEASE-- DON'T HIT ME!
AH DON'T WANT A FIGHT! AH NEED THE X-MEN'S HELP-- AH GOTTA HAVE IT-- OR AH'M AS GOOD AS DEAD!

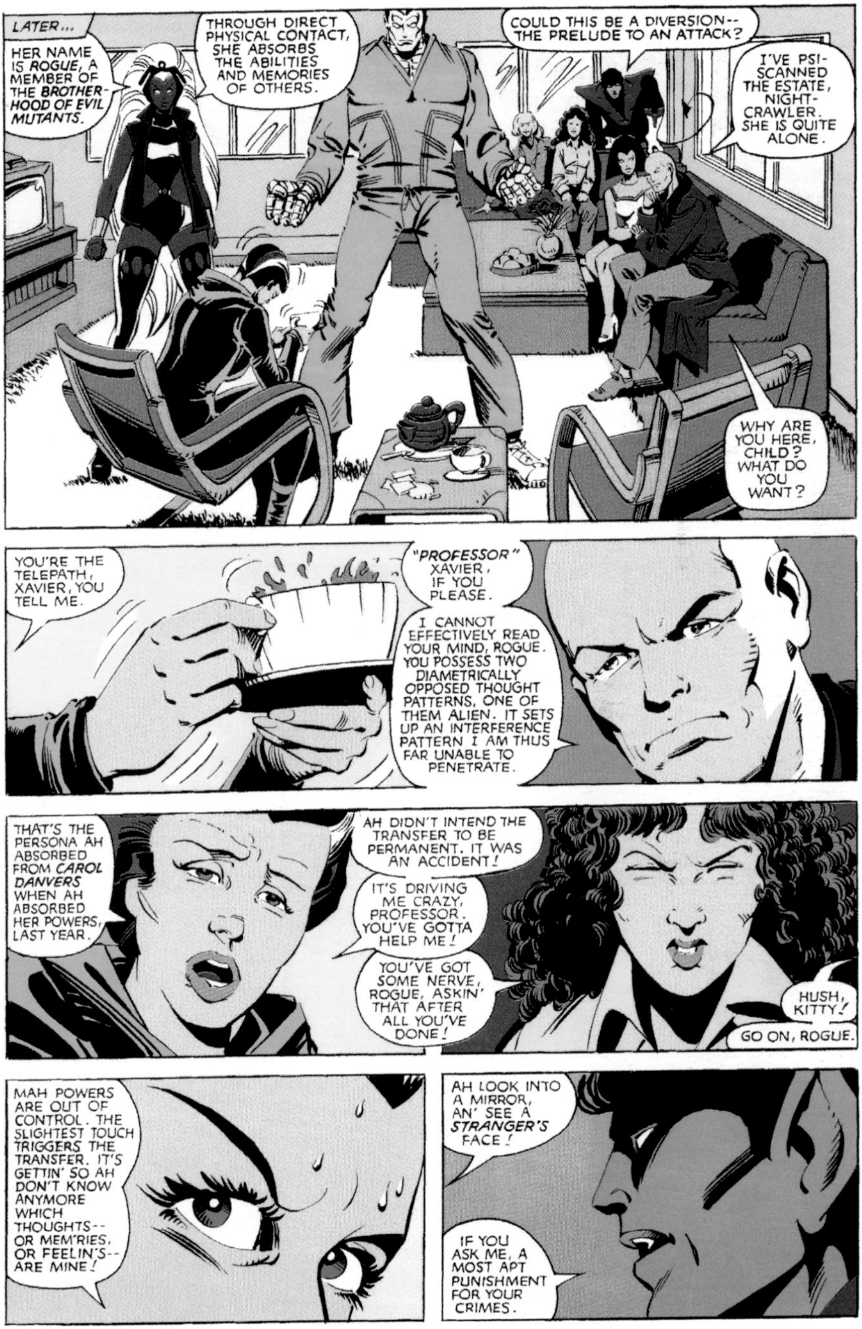
LATER...
HER NAME IS ROGUE, A MEMBER OF THE BROTHERHOOD OF EVIL MUTANTS.
THROUGH DIRECT PHYSICAL CONTACT, SHE ABSORBS THE ABILITIES AND MEMORIES OF OTHERS.
COULD THIS BE A DIVERSION-- THE PRELUDE TO AN ATTACK?
I'VE PSI-SCANNED THE ESTATE, NIGHTCRAWLER. SHE IS QUITE ALONE.
WHY ARE YOU HERE, CHILD? WHAT DO YOU WANT?
YOU'RE THE TELEPATH, XAVIER, YOU TELL ME.
"PROFESSOR" XAVIER, IF YOU PLEASE.
I CANNOT EFFECTIVELY READ YOUR MIND, ROGUE. YOU POSSESS TWO DIAMETRICALLY OPPOSED THOUGHT PATTERNS, ONE OF THEM ALIEN. IT SETS UP AN INTERFERENCE PATTERN I AM THUS FAR UNABLE TO PENETRATE.
THAT'S THE PERSONA AH ABSORBED FROM CAROL DANVERS WHEN AH ABSORBED HER POWERS, LAST YEAR.
AH DIDN'T INTEND THE TRANSFER TO BE PERMANENT. IT WAS AN ACCIDENT!
IT'S DRIVING ME CRAZY, PROFESSOR. YOU'VE GOTTA HELP ME!
YOU'VE GOT SOME NERVE, ROGUE, ASKIN' THAT AFTER ALL YOU'VE DONE!
HUSH, KITTY!
GO ON, ROGUE.
MAH POWERS ARE OUT OF CONTROL. THE SLIGHTEST TOUCH TRIGGERS THE TRANSFER. IT'S GETTIN' SO AH DON'T KNOW ANYMORE WHICH THOUGHTS-- OR MEM'RIES, OR FEELIN'S-- ARE MINE!
AH LOOK INTO A MIRROR, AN' SEE A STRANGER'S FACE!
IF YOU ASK ME, A MOST APT PUNISHMENT FOR YOUR CRIMES.

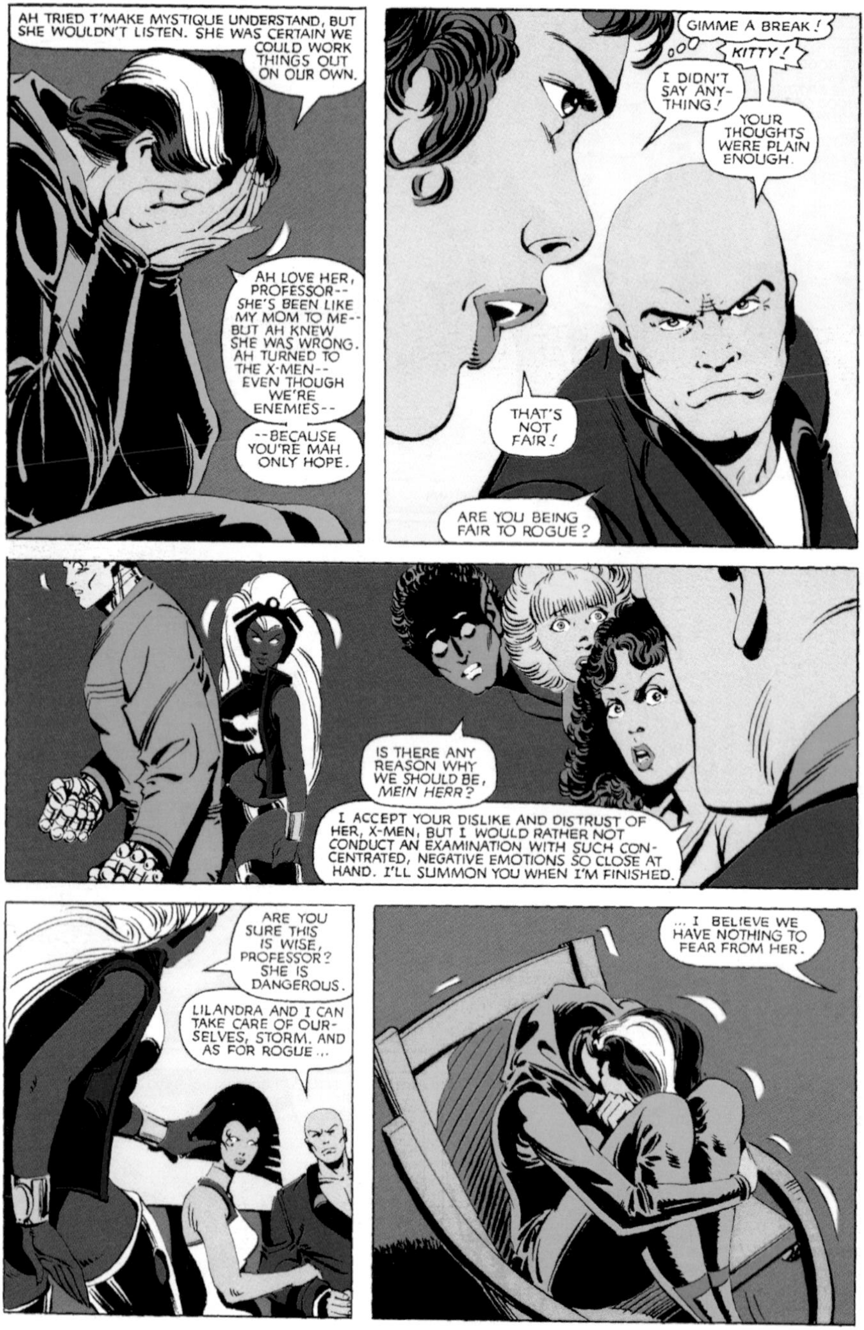
AH TRIED T'MAKE MYSTIQUE UNDERSTAND, BUT SHE WOULDN'T LISTEN. SHE WAS CERTAIN WE COULD WORK THINGS OUT ON OUR OWN.
AH LOVE HER, PROFESSOR-- SHE'S BEEN LIKE MY MOM TO ME-- BUT AH KNEW SHE WAS WRONG. AH TURNED TO THE X-MEN-- EVEN THOUGH WE'RE ENEMIES--
--BECAUSE YOU'RE MAH ONLY HOPE.
GIMME A BREAK!
KITTY!
I DIDN'T SAY ANY-THING!
YOUR THOUGHTS WERE PLAIN ENOUGH.
THAT'S NOT FAIR!
ARE YOU BEING FAIR TO ROGUE?
IS THERE ANY REASON WHY WE SHOULD BE, MEIN HERR?
I ACCEPT YOUR DISLIKE AND DISTRUST OF HER, X-MEN, BUT I WOULD RATHER NOT CONDUCT AN EXAMINATION WITH SUCH CON-CENTRATED, NEGATIVE EMOTIONS SO CLOSE AT HAND. I'LL SUMMON YOU WHEN I'M FINISHED.
ARE YOU SURE THIS IS WISE, PROFESSOR? SHE IS DANGEROUS.
LILANDRA AND I CAN TAKE CARE OF OUR-SELVES, STORM. AND AS FOR ROGUE ...
... I BELIEVE WE HAVE NOTHING TO FEAR FROM HER.

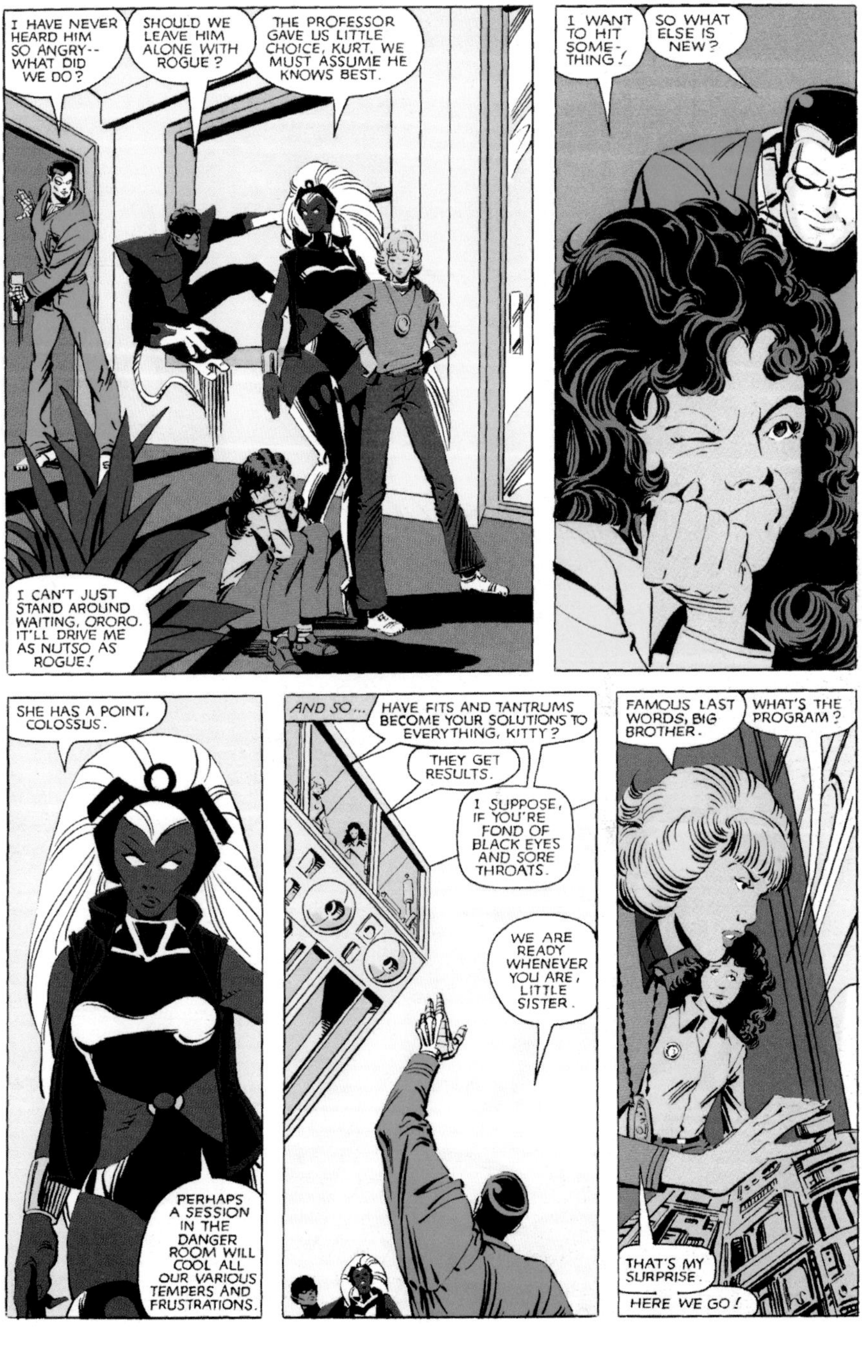

I HAVE NEVER HEARD HIM SO ANGRY-- WHAT DID WE DO?
SHOULD WE LEAVE HIM ALONE WITH ROGUE?
THE PROFESSOR GAVE US LITTLE CHOICE, KURT. WE MUST ASSUME HE KNOWS BEST.
I CAN'T JUST STAND AROUND WAITING, ORORO. IT'LL DRIVE ME AS NUTSO AS ROGUE!
I WANT TO HIT SOME-THING!
SO WHAT ELSE IS NEW?
SHE HAS A POINT, COLOSSUS.
PERHAPS A SESSION IN THE DANGER ROOM WILL COOL ALL OUR VARIOUS TEMPERS AND FRUSTRATIONS.
AND SO...
HAVE FITS AND TANTRUMS BECOME YOUR SOLUTIONS TO EVERYTHING, KITTY?
THEY GET RESULTS.
I SUPPOSE, IF YOU'RE FOND OF BLACK EYES AND SORE THROATS.
WE ARE READY WHENEVER YOU ARE, LITTLE SISTER.
FAMOUS LAST WORDS, BIG BROTHER.
WHAT'S THE PROGRAM?
THAT'S MY SURPRISE.
HERE WE GO!

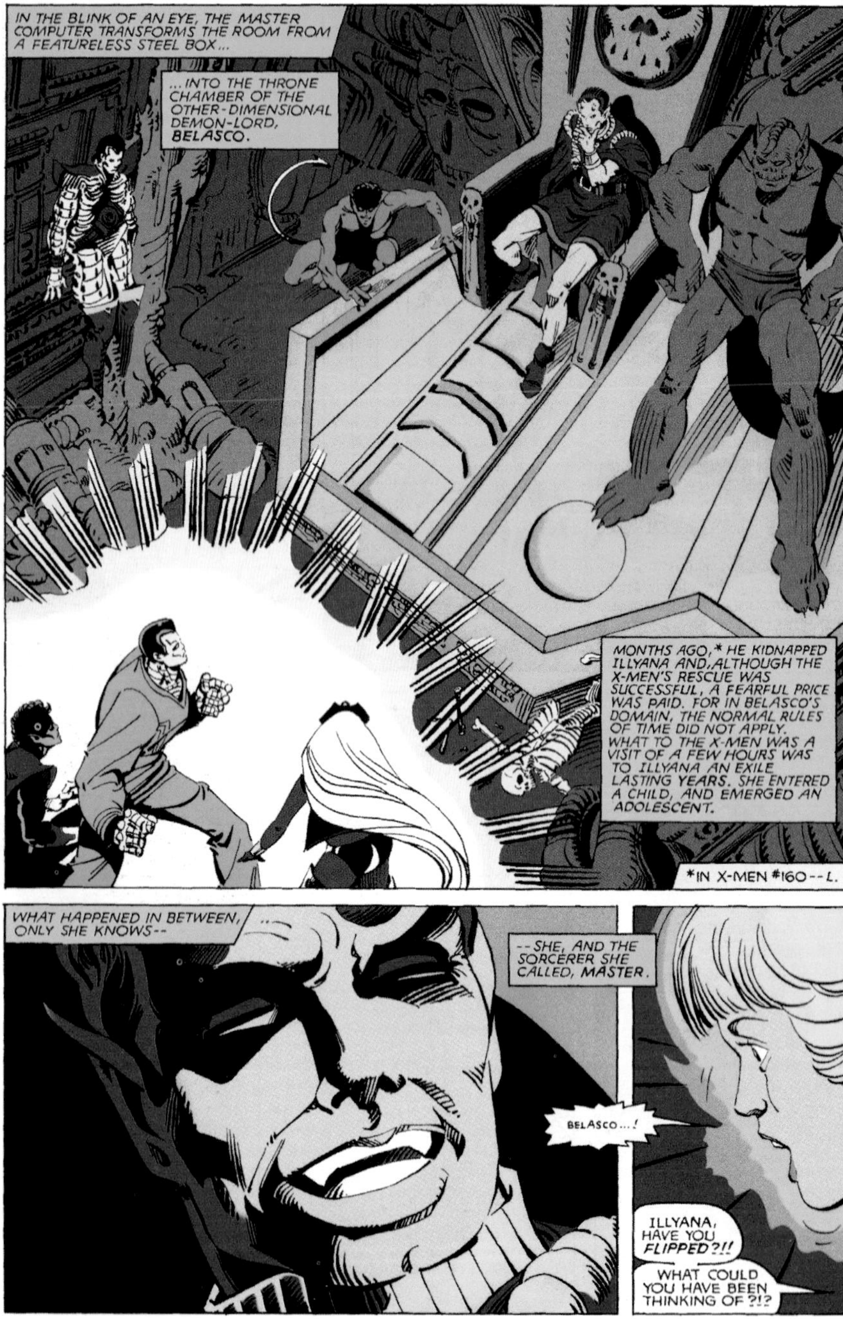

IN THE BLINK OF AN EYE, THE MASTER COMPUTER TRANSFORMS THE ROOM FROM A FEATURELESS STEEL BOX...
...INTO THE THRONE CHAMBER OF THE OTHER-DIMENSIONAL DEMON-LORD, BELASCO.
MONTHS AGO,* HE KIDNAPPED ILLYANA AND, ALTHOUGH THE X-MEN'S RESCUE WAS SUCCESSFUL, A FEARFUL PRICE WAS PAID. FOR IN BELASCO'S DOMAIN, THE NORMAL RULES OF TIME DID NOT APPLY. WHAT TO THE X-MEN WAS A VISIT OF A FEW HOURS WAS TO ILLYANA AN EXILE LASTING YEARS. SHE ENTERED A CHILD, AND EMERGED AN ADOLESCENT.
*IN X-MEN #160--L.
WHAT HAPPENED IN BETWEEN, ONLY SHE KNOWS--
--SHE, AND THE SORCERER SHE CALLED, MASTER.
BELASCO...!
ILLYANA, HAVE YOU FLIPPED?!!
WHAT COULD YOU HAVE BEEN THINKING OF?!?

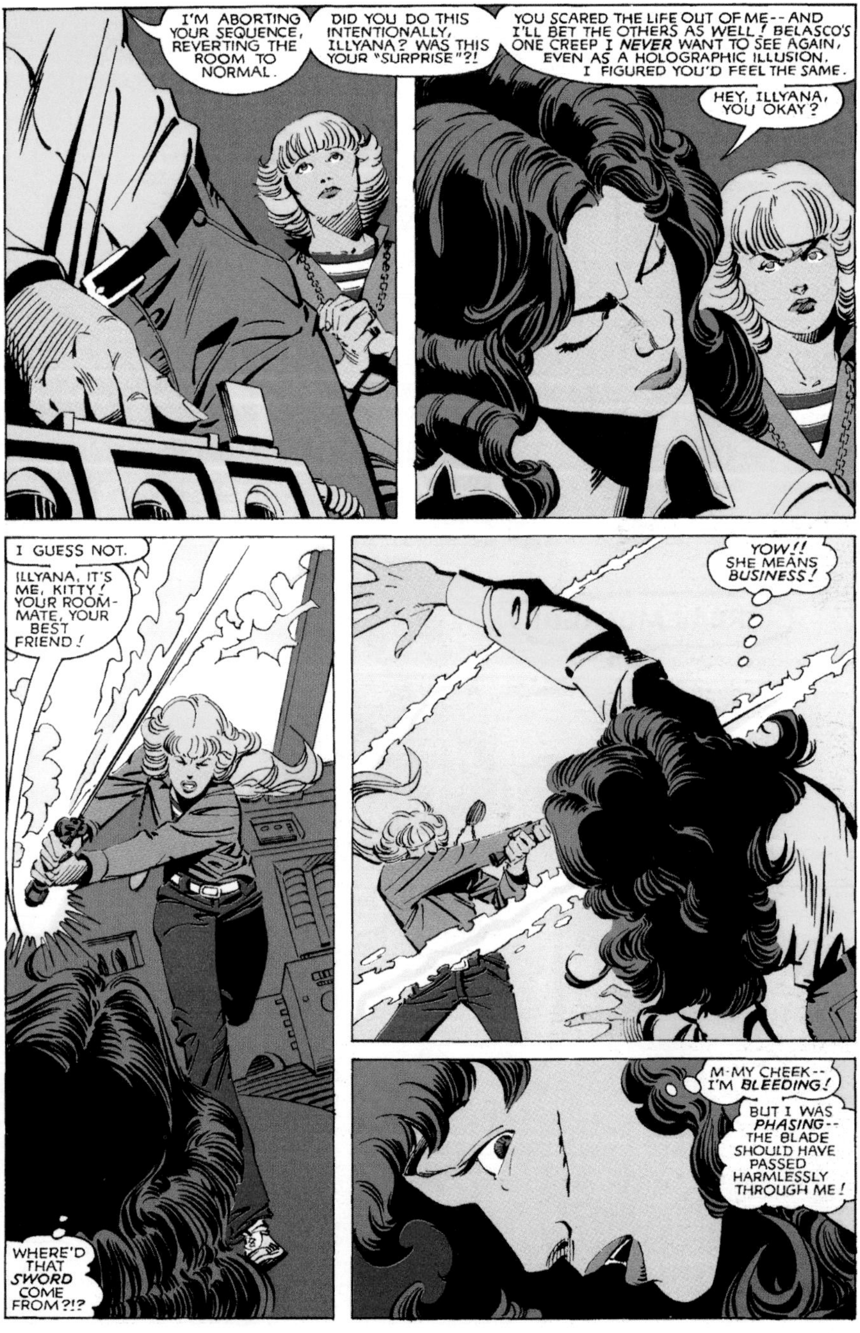
I'M ABORTING YOUR SEQUENCE, REVERTING THE ROOM TO NORMAL.
DID YOU DO THIS INTENTIONALLY, ILLYANA? WAS THIS YOUR "SURPRISE"?!
YOU SCARED THE LIFE OUT OF ME-- AND I'LL BET THE OTHERS AS WELL! BELASCO'S ONE CREEP I NEVER WANT TO SEE AGAIN, EVEN AS A HOLOGRAPHIC ILLUSION. I FIGURED YOU'D FEEL THE SAME.
HEY, ILLYANA, YOU OKAY?
I GUESS NOT.
ILLYANA, IT'S ME, KITTY! YOUR ROOM-MATE, YOUR BEST FRIEND!
WHERE'D THAT SWORD COME FROM?!?
YOW!! SHE MEANS BUSINESS!
M-MY CHEEK-- I'M BLEEDING!
BUT I WAS PHASING-- THE BLADE SHOULD HAVE PASSED HARMLESSLY THROUGH ME!

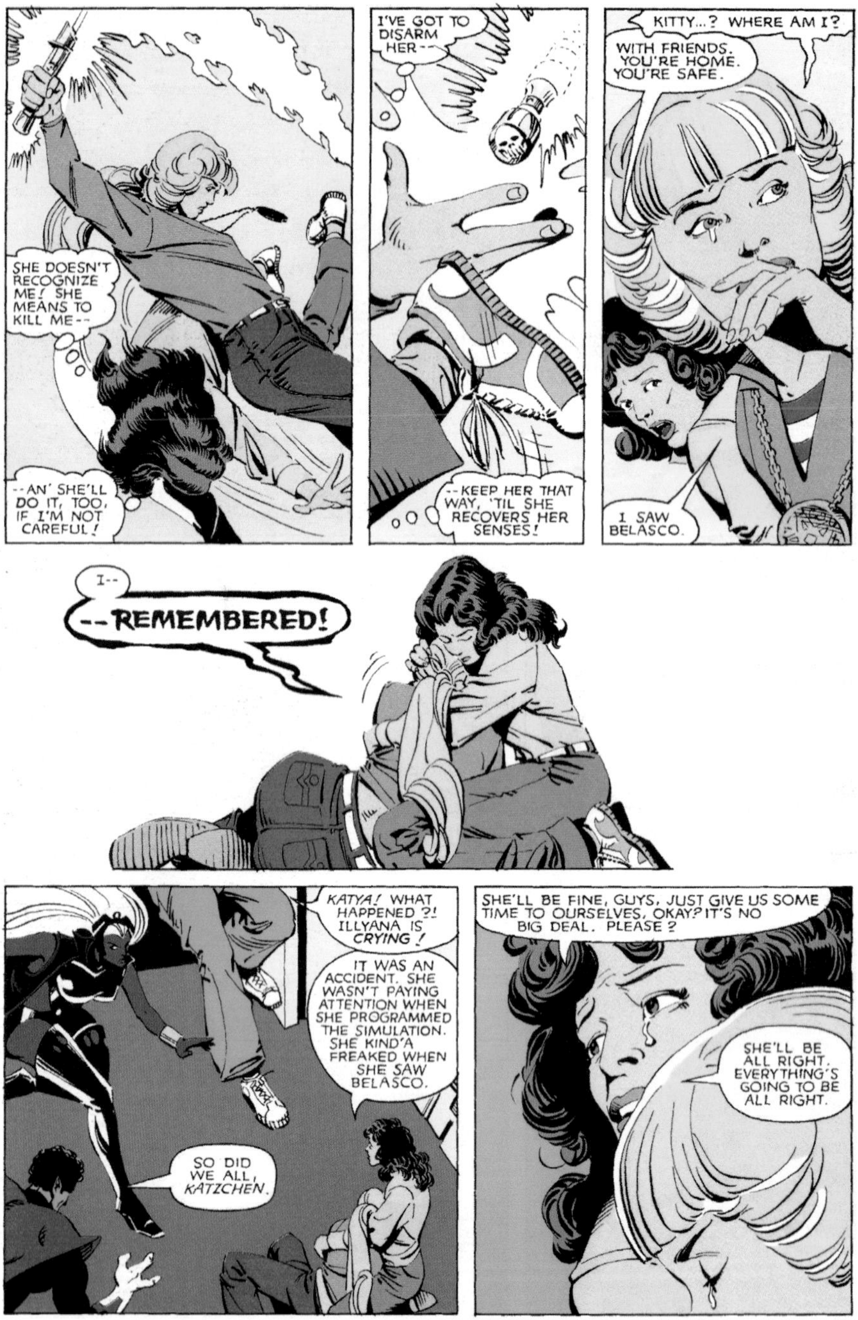
SHE DOESN'T RECOGNIZE ME! SHE MEANS TO KILL ME--
--AN' SHE'LL DO IT, TOO, IF I'M NOT CAREFUL!
I'VE GOT TO DISARM HER--
--KEEP HER THAT WAY, 'TIL SHE RECOVERS HER SENSES!
KITTY...? WHERE AM I?
WITH FRIENDS. YOU'RE HOME. YOU'RE SAFE.
I SAW BELASCO.
I--
--REMEMBERED!
KATYA! WHAT HAPPENED ?! ILLYANA IS CRYING!
IT WAS AN ACCIDENT. SHE WASN'T PAYING ATTENTION WHEN SHE PROGRAMMED THE SIMULATION. SHE KIND'A FREAKED WHEN SHE SAW BELASCO.
SO DID WE ALL, KATZCHEN.
SHE'LL BE FINE, GUYS, JUST GIVE US SOME TIME TO OURSELVES, OKAY? IT'S NO BIG DEAL. PLEASE?
SHE'LL BE ALL RIGHT. EVERYTHING'S GOING TO BE ALL RIGHT.

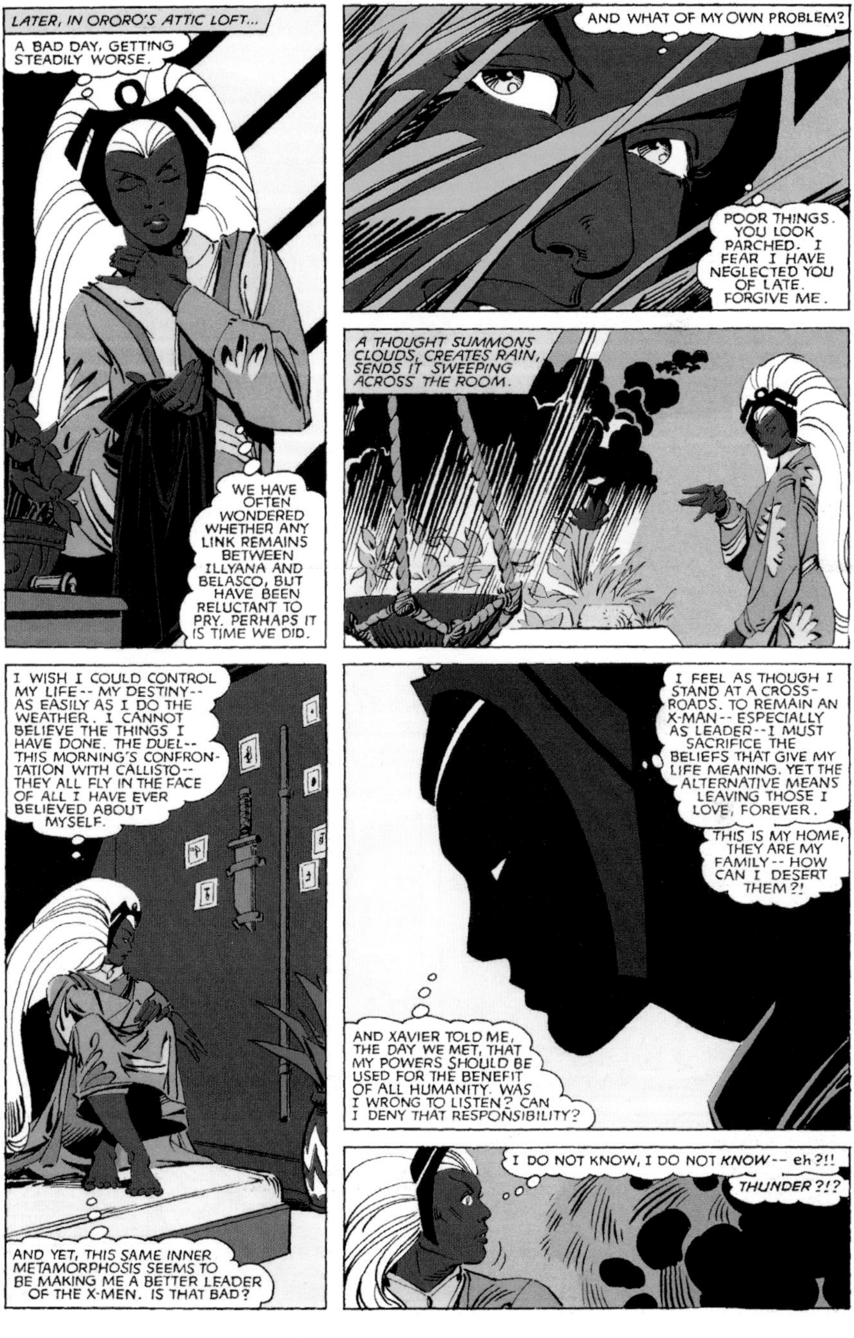
LATER, IN ORORO'S ATTIC LOFT...
A BAD DAY, GETTING STEADILY WORSE.
WE HAVE OFTEN WONDERED WHETHER ANY LINK REMAINS BETWEEN ILLYANA AND BELASCO, BUT HAVE BEEN RELUCTANT TO PRY. PERHAPS IT IS TIME WE DID.
AND WHAT OF MY OWN PROBLEM?
POOR THINGS. YOU LOOK PARCHED. I FEAR I HAVE NEGLECTED YOU OF LATE. FORGIVE ME.
A THOUGHT SUMMONS CLOUDS, CREATES RAIN, SENDS IT SWEEPING ACROSS THE ROOM.
I WISH I COULD CONTROL MY LIFE -- MY DESTINY -- AS EASILY AS I DO THE WEATHER. I CANNOT BELIEVE THE THINGS I HAVE DONE. THE DUEL -- THIS MORNING'S CONFRONTATION WITH CALLISTO -- THEY ALL FLY IN THE FACE OF ALL I HAVE EVER BELIEVED ABOUT MYSELF.
AND YET, THIS SAME INNER METAMORPHOSIS SEEMS TO BE MAKING ME A BETTER LEADER OF THE X-MEN. IS THAT BAD?
I FEEL AS THOUGH I STAND AT A CROSSROADS. TO REMAIN AN X-MAN -- ESPECIALLY AS LEADER -- I MUST SACRIFICE THE BELIEFS THAT GIVE MY LIFE MEANING. YET THE ALTERNATIVE MEANS LEAVING THOSE I LOVE, FOREVER.
THIS IS MY HOME, THEY ARE MY FAMILY -- HOW CAN I DESERT THEM?!
AND XAVIER TOLD ME, THE DAY WE MET, THAT MY POWERS SHOULD BE USED FOR THE BENEFIT OF ALL HUMANITY. WAS I WRONG TO LISTEN? CAN I DENY THAT RESPONSIBILITY?
I DO NOT KNOW, I DO NOT KNOW -- eh?!!
THUNDER?!?

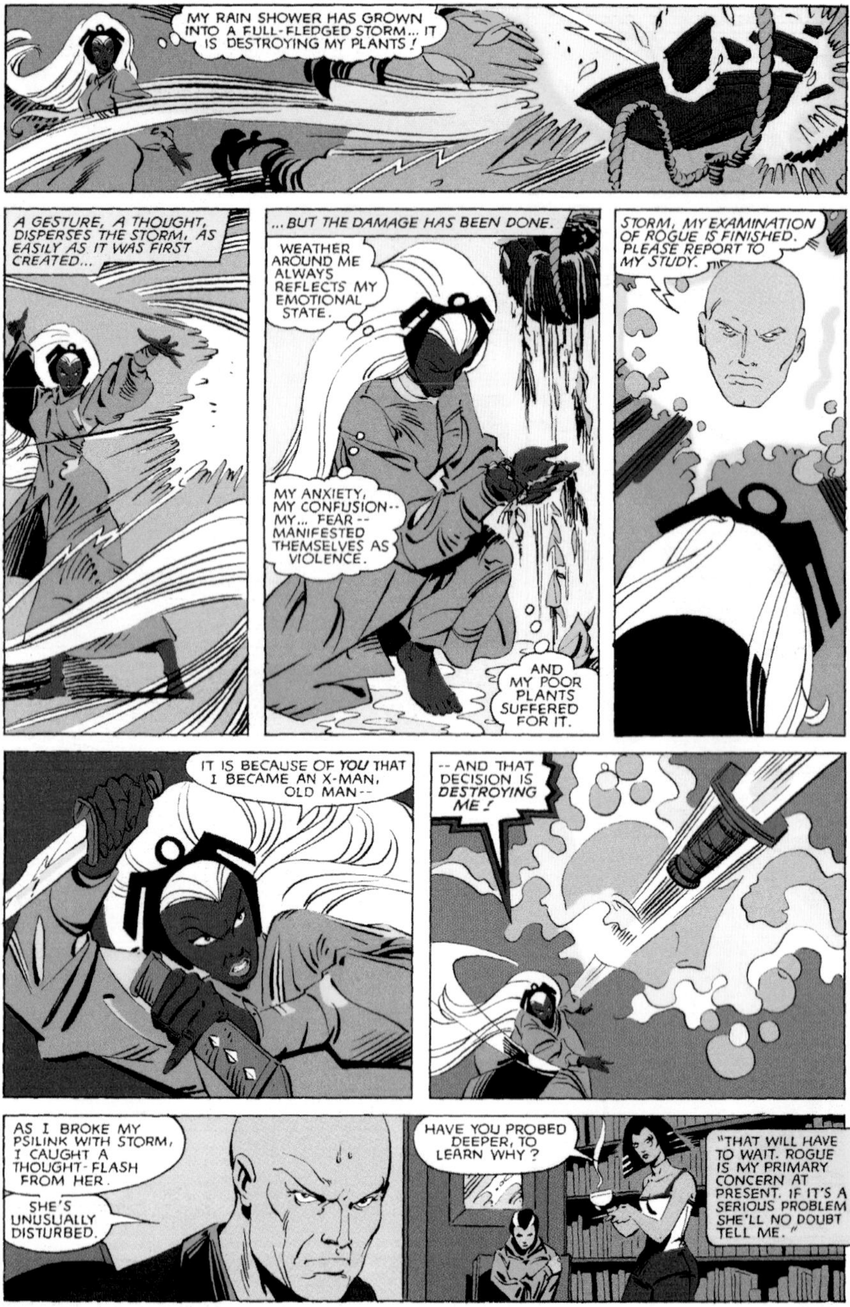
MY RAIN SHOWER HAS GROWN INTO A FULL-FLEDGED STORM... IT IS DESTROYING MY PLANTS!
A GESTURE, A THOUGHT, DISPERSES THE STORM, AS EASILY AS IT WAS FIRST CREATED...
...BUT THE DAMAGE HAS BEEN DONE.
WEATHER AROUND ME ALWAYS REFLECTS MY EMOTIONAL STATE.
MY ANXIETY, MY CONFUSION-- MY... FEAR-- MANIFESTED THEMSELVES AS VIOLENCE.
AND MY POOR PLANTS SUFFERED FOR IT.
STORM, MY EXAMINATION OF ROGUE IS FINISHED. PLEASE REPORT TO MY STUDY.
IT IS BECAUSE OF YOU THAT I BECAME AN X-MAN, OLD MAN--
--AND THAT DECISION IS DESTROYING ME!
AS I BROKE MY PSILINK WITH STORM, I CAUGHT A THOUGHT-FLASH FROM HER.
SHE'S UNUSUALLY DISTURBED.
HAVE YOU PROBED DEEPER, TO LEARN WHY?
"THAT WILL HAVE TO WAIT. ROGUE IS MY PRIMARY CONCERN AT PRESENT. IF IT'S A SERIOUS PROBLEM, SHE'LL NO DOUBT TELL ME."

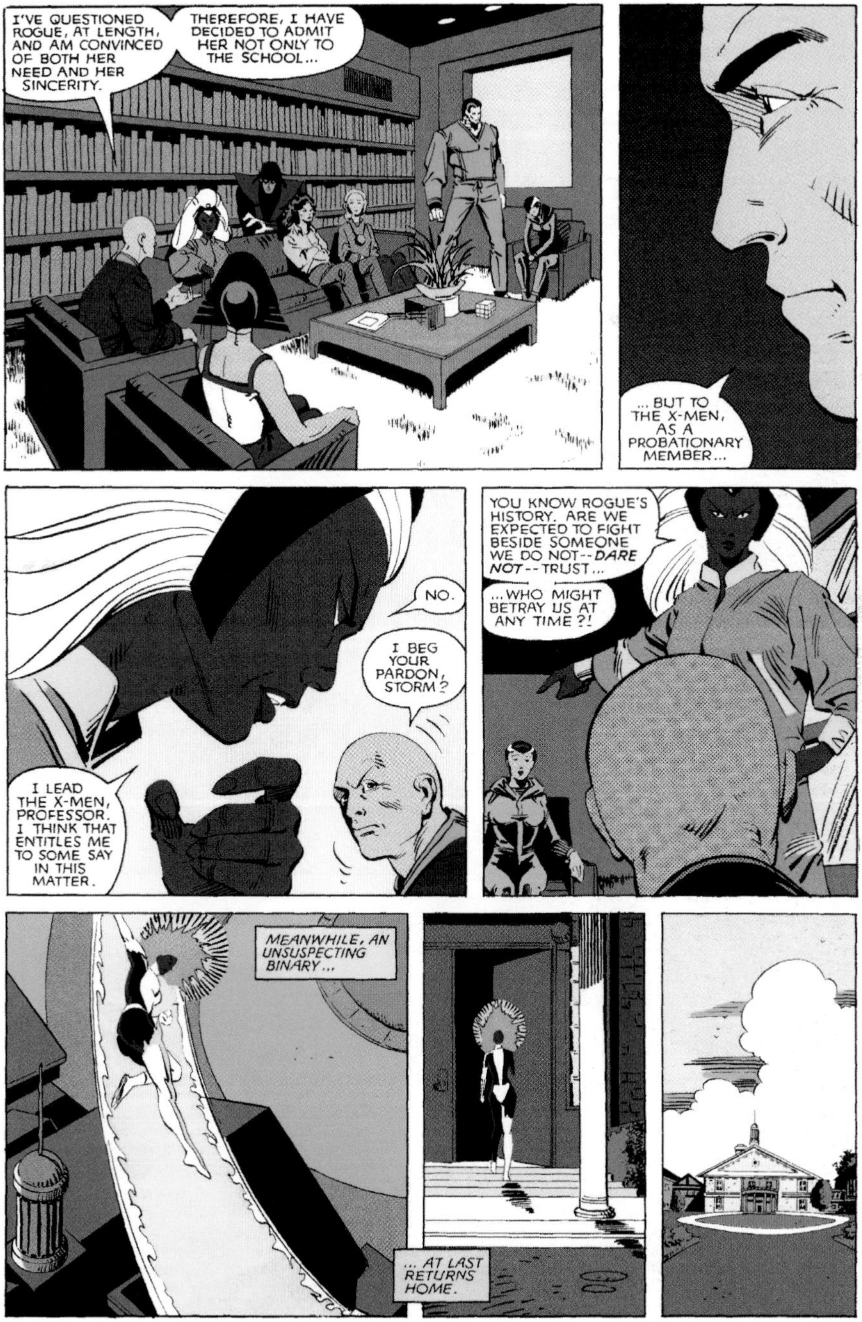
I'VE QUESTIONED ROGUE, AT LENGTH, AND AM CONVINCED OF BOTH HER NEED AND HER SINCERITY.
THEREFORE, I HAVE DECIDED TO ADMIT HER NOT ONLY TO THE SCHOOL...
...BUT TO THE X-MEN, AS A PROBATIONARY MEMBER...
NO.
I BEG YOUR PARDON, STORM?
I LEAD THE X-MEN, PROFESSOR. I THINK THAT ENTITLES ME TO SOME SAY IN THIS MATTER.
YOU KNOW ROGUE'S HISTORY. ARE WE EXPECTED TO FIGHT BESIDE SOMEONE WE DO NOT--DARE NOT--TRUST...
...WHO MIGHT BETRAY US AT ANY TIME?!
MEANWHILE, AN UNSUSPECTING BINARY...
...AT LAST RETURNS HOME.

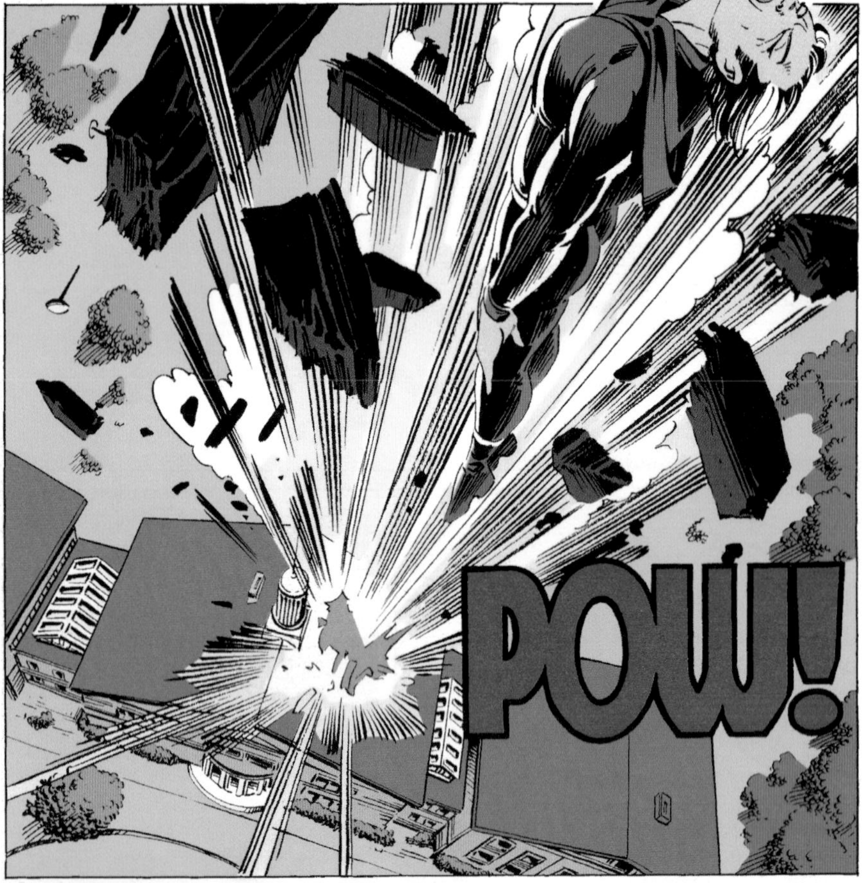
POW!

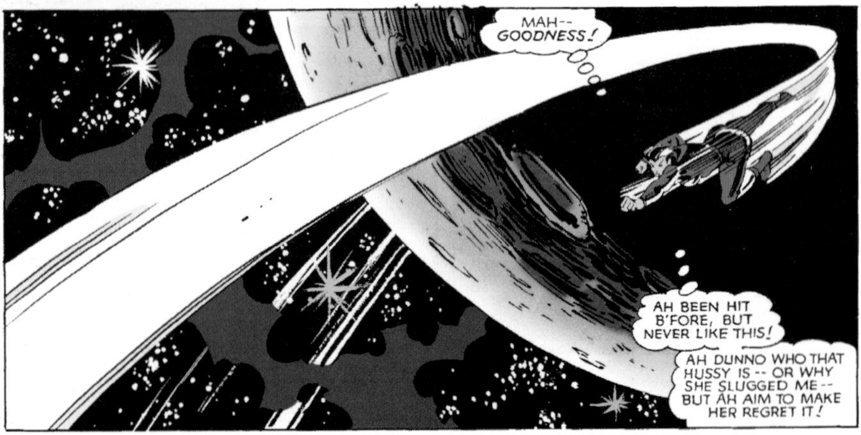
MAH--
GOODNESS!
AH BEEN HIT B'FORE, BUT NEVER LIKE THIS!
AH DUNNO WHO THAT HUSSY IS -- OR WHY SHE SLUGGED ME -- BUT AH AIM TO MAKE HER REGRET IT!

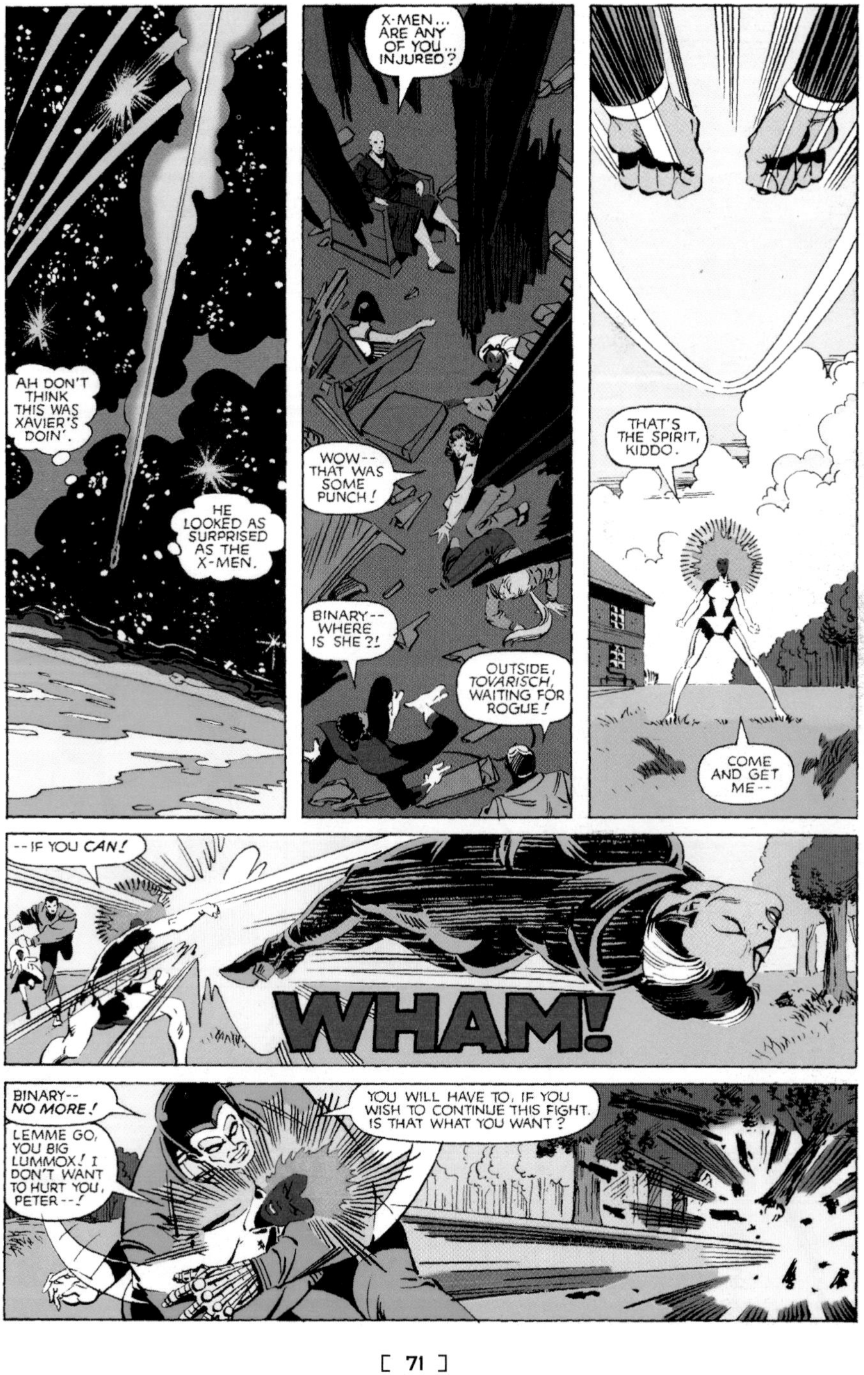
AH DON'T THINK THIS WAS XAVIER'S DOIN'.
HE LOOKED AS SURPRISED AS THE X-MEN.
X-MEN... ARE ANY OF YOU... INJURED?
WOW--THAT WAS SOME PUNCH!
BINARY--WHERE IS SHE?!
OUTSIDE, *TOVARISCH,* WAITING FOR ROGUE!
THAT'S THE SPIRIT, KIDDO.
COME AND GET ME--
--IF YOU *CAN!*
WHAM!
BINARY--*NO MORE!*
LEMME GO, YOU BIG LUMMOX! I DON'T WANT TO HURT YOU, PETER--!
YOU WILL HAVE TO, IF YOU WISH TO CONTINUE THIS FIGHT. IS THAT WHAT YOU WANT?

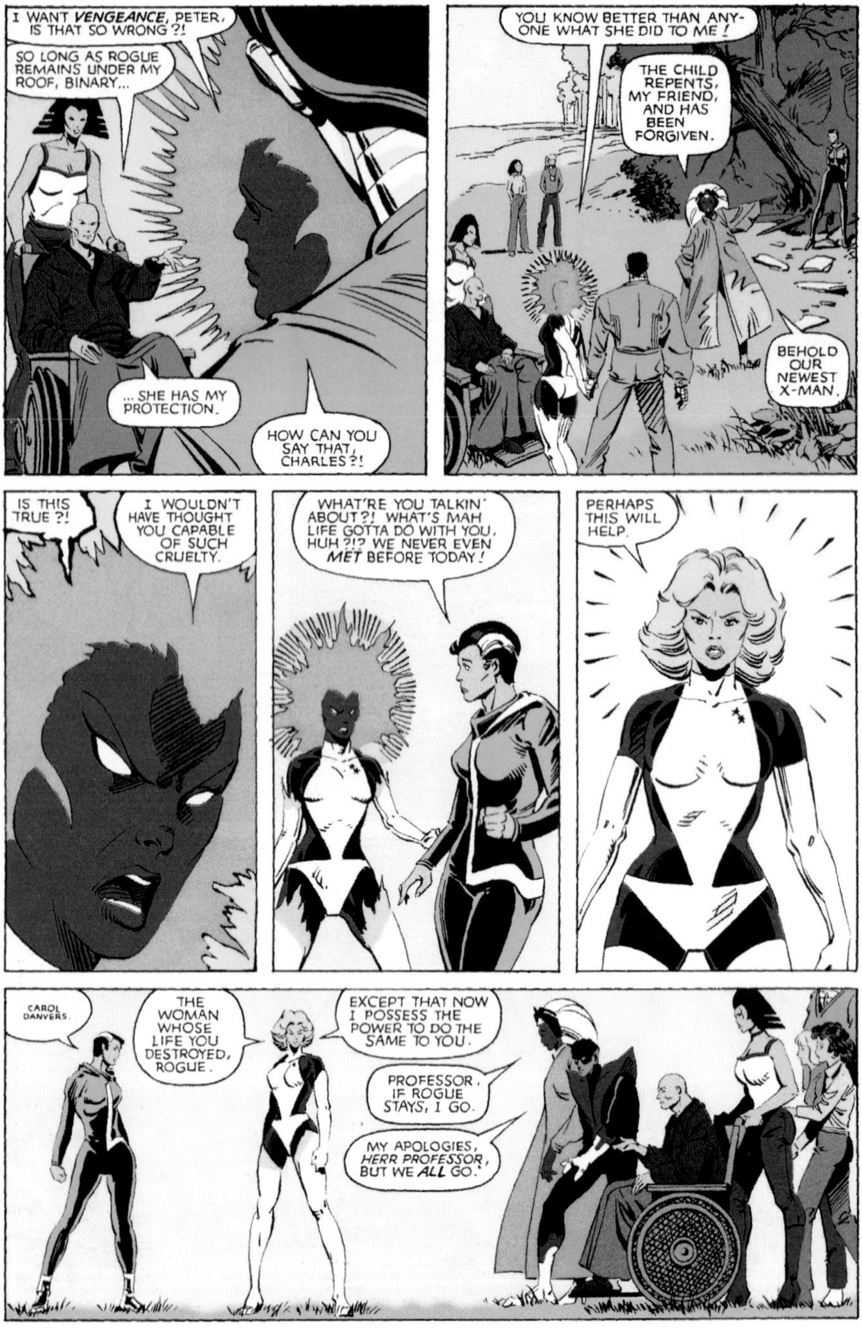

I WANT VENGEANCE, PETER, IS THAT SO WRONG?!
SO LONG AS ROGUE REMAINS UNDER MY ROOF, BINARY...
...SHE HAS MY PROTECTION.
HOW CAN YOU SAY THAT, CHARLES?!
YOU KNOW BETTER THAN ANYONE WHAT SHE DID TO ME!
THE CHILD REPENTS, MY FRIEND, AND HAS BEEN FORGIVEN.
BEHOLD OUR NEWEST X-MAN.
IS THIS TRUE?!
I WOULDN'T HAVE THOUGHT YOU CAPABLE OF SUCH CRUELTY.
WHAT'RE YOU TALKIN' ABOUT?! WHAT'S MAH LIFE GOTTA DO WITH YOU, HUH?!? WE NEVER EVEN MET BEFORE TODAY!
PERHAPS THIS WILL HELP.
CAROL DANVERS.
THE WOMAN WHOSE LIFE YOU DESTROYED, ROGUE.
EXCEPT THAT NOW I POSSESS THE POWER TO DO THE SAME TO YOU.
PROFESSOR, IF ROGUE STAYS, I GO.
MY APOLOGIES, HERR PROFESSOR, BUT WE ALL GO.

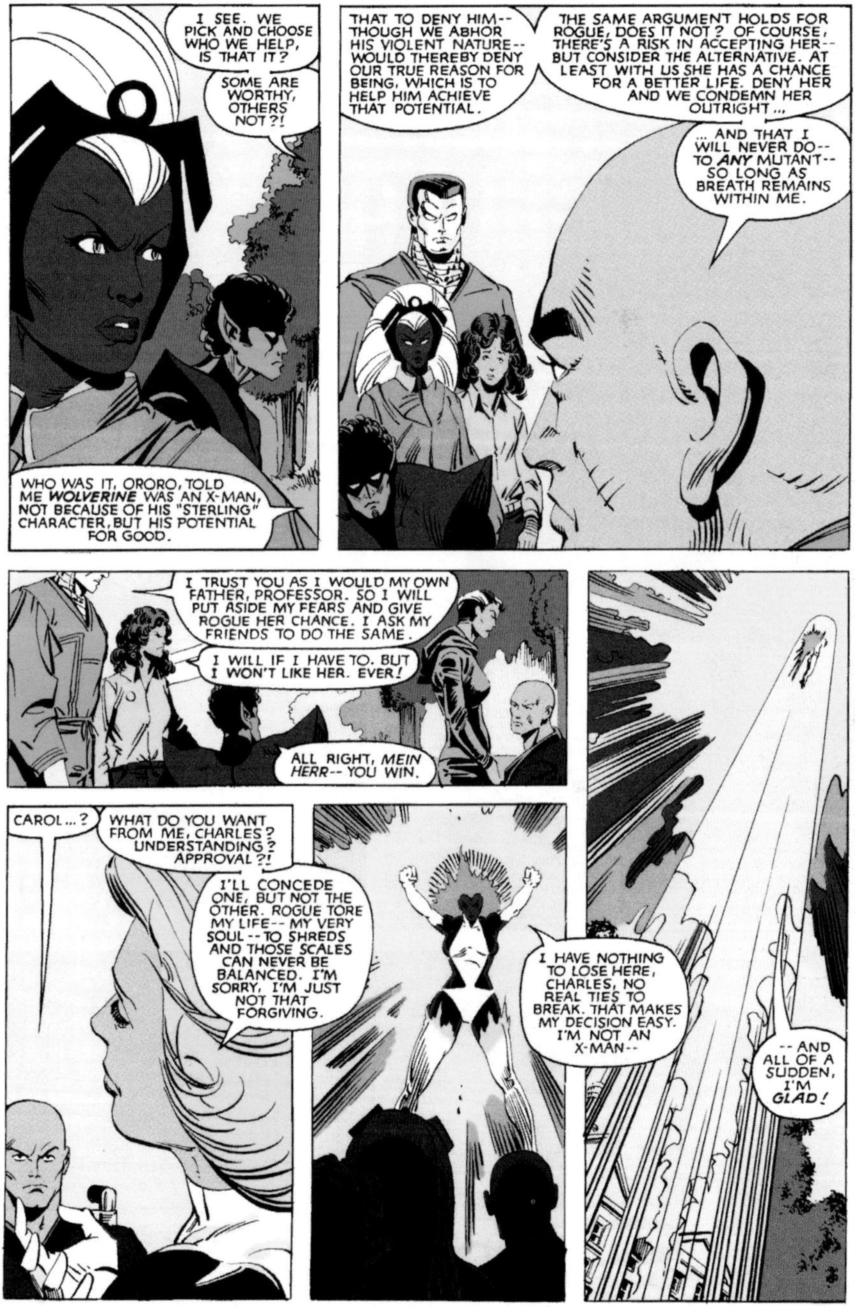

I SEE. WE PICK AND CHOOSE WHO WE HELP, IS THAT IT?
SOME ARE WORTHY, OTHERS NOT?!
WHO WAS IT, ORORO, TOLD ME WOLVERINE WAS AN X-MAN, NOT BECAUSE OF HIS "STERLING" CHARACTER, BUT HIS POTENTIAL FOR GOOD.
THAT TO DENY HIM-- THOUGH WE ABHOR HIS VIOLENT NATURE-- WOULD THEREBY DENY OUR TRUE REASON FOR BEING, WHICH IS TO HELP HIM ACHIEVE THAT POTENTIAL.
THE SAME ARGUMENT HOLDS FOR ROGUE, DOES IT NOT? OF COURSE, THERE'S A RISK IN ACCEPTING HER-- BUT CONSIDER THE ALTERNATIVE. AT LEAST WITH US SHE HAS A CHANCE FOR A BETTER LIFE. DENY HER AND WE CONDEMN HER OUTRIGHT...
... AND THAT I WILL NEVER DO-- TO ANY MUTANT-- SO LONG AS BREATH REMAINS WITHIN ME.
I TRUST YOU AS I WOULD MY OWN FATHER, PROFESSOR. SO I WILL PUT ASIDE MY FEARS AND GIVE ROGUE HER CHANCE. I ASK MY FRIENDS TO DO THE SAME.
I WILL IF I HAVE TO. BUT I WON'T LIKE HER. EVER!
ALL RIGHT, MEIN HERR-- YOU WIN.
CAROL...?
WHAT DO YOU WANT FROM ME, CHARLES? UNDERSTANDING? APPROVAL?!
I'LL CONCEDE ONE, BUT NOT THE OTHER. ROGUE TORE MY LIFE-- MY VERY SOUL-- TO SHREDS AND THOSE SCALES CAN NEVER BE BALANCED. I'M SORRY, I'M JUST NOT THAT FORGIVING.
I HAVE NOTHING TO LOSE HERE, CHARLES, NO REAL TIES TO BREAK. THAT MAKES MY DECISION EASY. I'M NOT AN X-MAN--
-- AND ALL OF A SUDDEN, I'M GLAD!

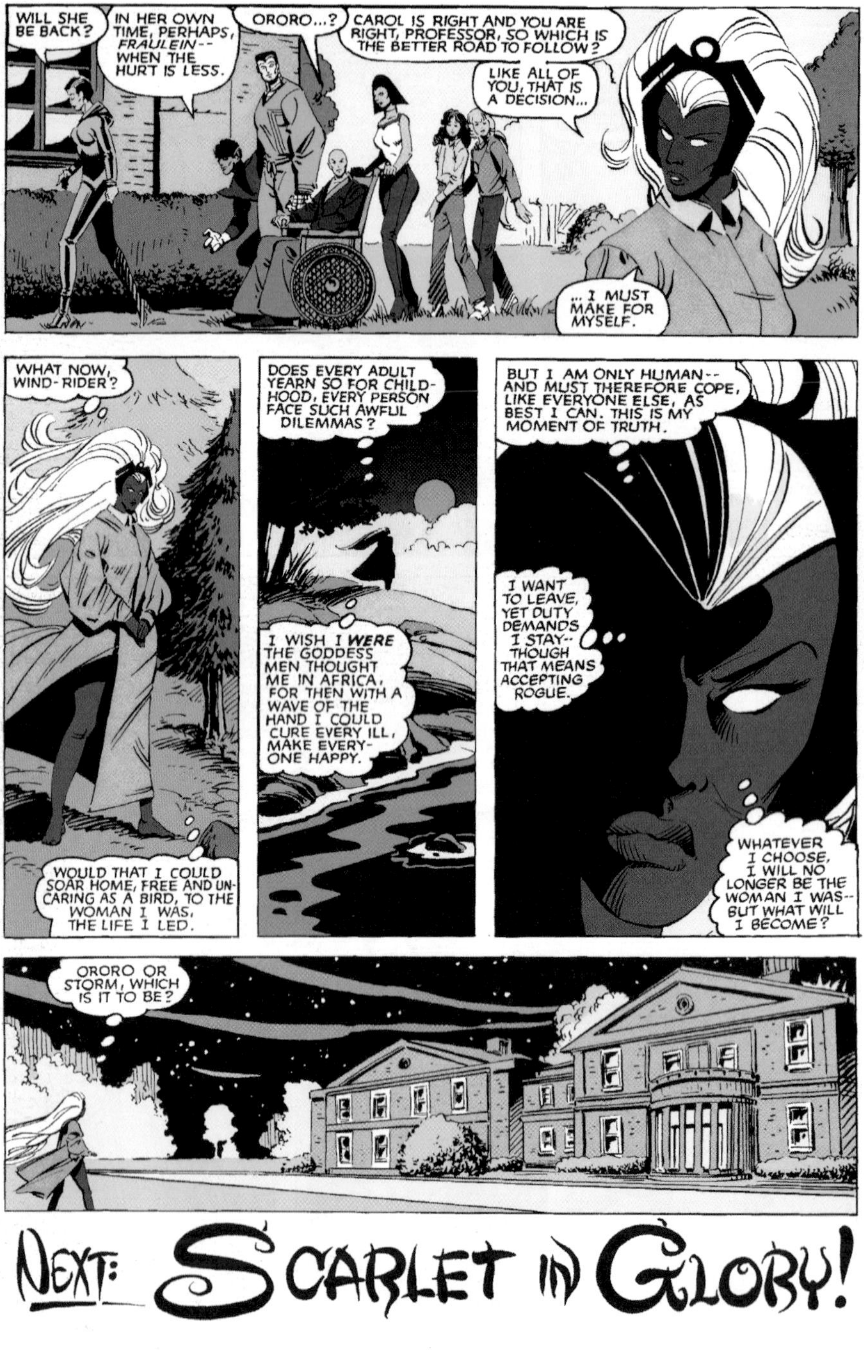
WILL SHE BE BACK?
IN HER OWN TIME, PERHAPS, *FRAULEIN*-- WHEN THE HURT IS LESS.
ORORO...?
CAROL IS RIGHT AND YOU ARE RIGHT, PROFESSOR, SO WHICH IS THE BETTER ROAD TO FOLLOW?
LIKE ALL OF YOU, THAT IS A DECISION...
... I MUST MAKE FOR MYSELF.
WHAT NOW, WIND-RIDER?
WOULD THAT I COULD SOAR HOME, FREE AND UNCARING AS A BIRD, TO THE WOMAN I WAS, THE LIFE I LED.
DOES EVERY ADULT YEARN SO FOR CHILDHOOD, EVERY PERSON FACE SUCH AWFUL DILEMMAS?
I WISH I **WERE** THE GODDESS MEN THOUGHT ME IN AFRICA, FOR THEN WITH A WAVE OF THE HAND I COULD CURE EVERY ILL, MAKE EVERYONE HAPPY.
BUT I AM ONLY HUMAN-- AND MUST THEREFORE COPE, LIKE EVERYONE ELSE, AS BEST I CAN. THIS IS MY MOMENT OF TRUTH.
I WANT TO LEAVE, YET DUTY DEMANDS I STAY-- THOUGH THAT MEANS ACCEPTING ROGUE.
WHATEVER I CHOOSE, I WILL NO LONGER BE THE WOMAN I WAS-- BUT WHAT WILL I BECOME?
ORORO OR STORM, WHICH IS IT TO BE?
NEXT: SCARLET IN GLORY!

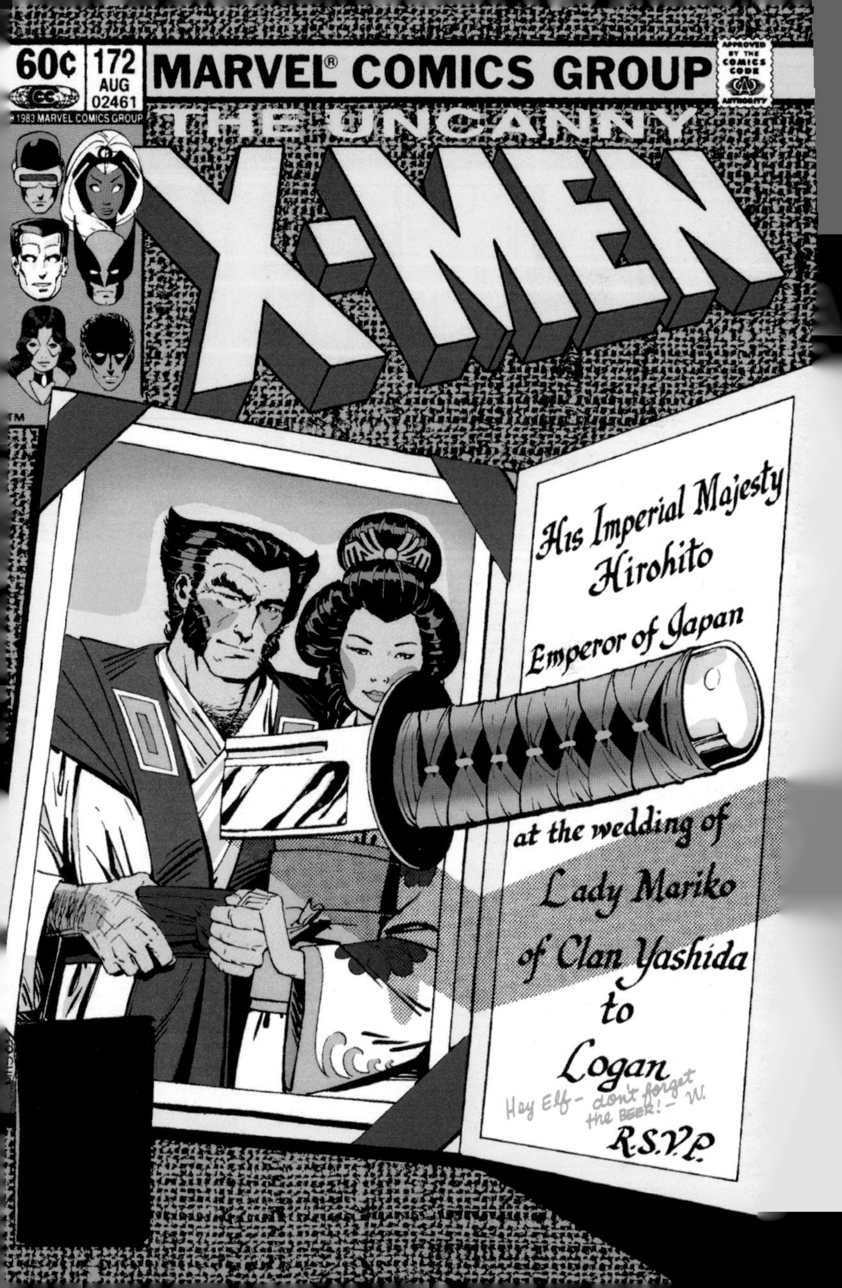

60¢
172
AUG
02461
© 1983 MARVEL COMICS GROUP
MARVEL® COMICS GROUP
APPROVED BY THE COMICS CODE AUTHORITY
THE UNCANNY
X-MEN
TM
His Imperial Majesty
Hirohito
Emperor of Japan
at the wedding of
Lady Mariko
of Clan Yashida
to
Logan
Hey Elf – don't forget the BEER! – W.
R.S.V.P.

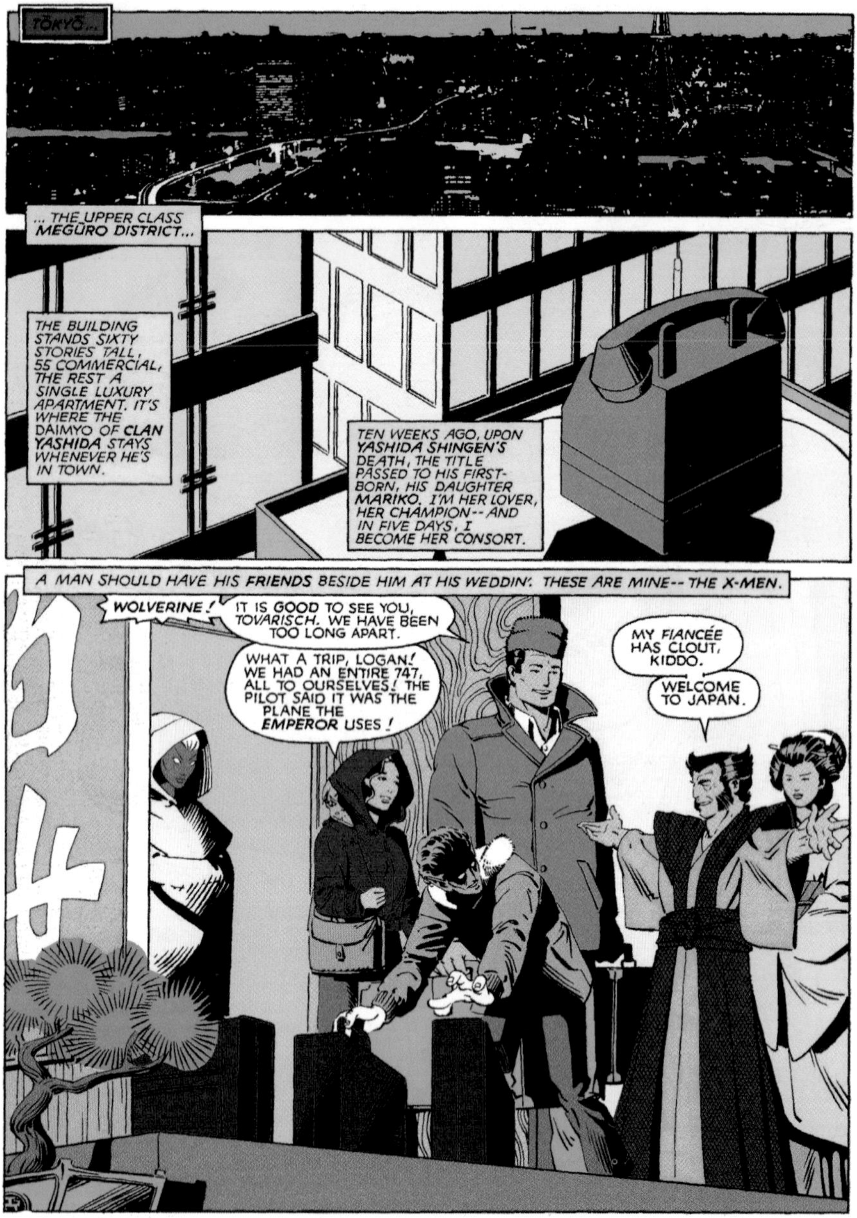
TOKYO...
... THE UPPER CLASS MEGŪRO DISTRICT...
THE BUILDING STANDS SIXTY STORIES TALL, 55 COMMERCIAL, THE REST A SINGLE LUXURY APARTMENT. IT'S WHERE THE DAIMYO OF CLAN YASHIDA STAYS WHENEVER HE'S IN TOWN.
TEN WEEKS AGO, UPON YASHIDA SHINGEN'S DEATH, THE TITLE PASSED TO HIS FIRST-BORN, HIS DAUGHTER MARIKO. I'M HER LOVER, HER CHAMPION-- AND IN FIVE DAYS, I BECOME HER CONSORT.
A MAN SHOULD HAVE HIS FRIENDS BESIDE HIM AT HIS WEDDIN'. THESE ARE MINE-- THE X-MEN.
WOLVERINE!
IT IS GOOD TO SEE YOU, TOVARISCH. WE HAVE BEEN TOO LONG APART.
WHAT A TRIP, LOGAN! WE HAD AN ENTIRE 747, ALL TO OURSELVES! THE PILOT SAID IT WAS THE PLANE THE EMPEROR USES!
MY FIANCÉE HAS CLOUT, KIDDO.
WELCOME TO JAPAN.

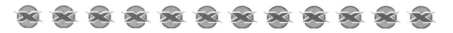

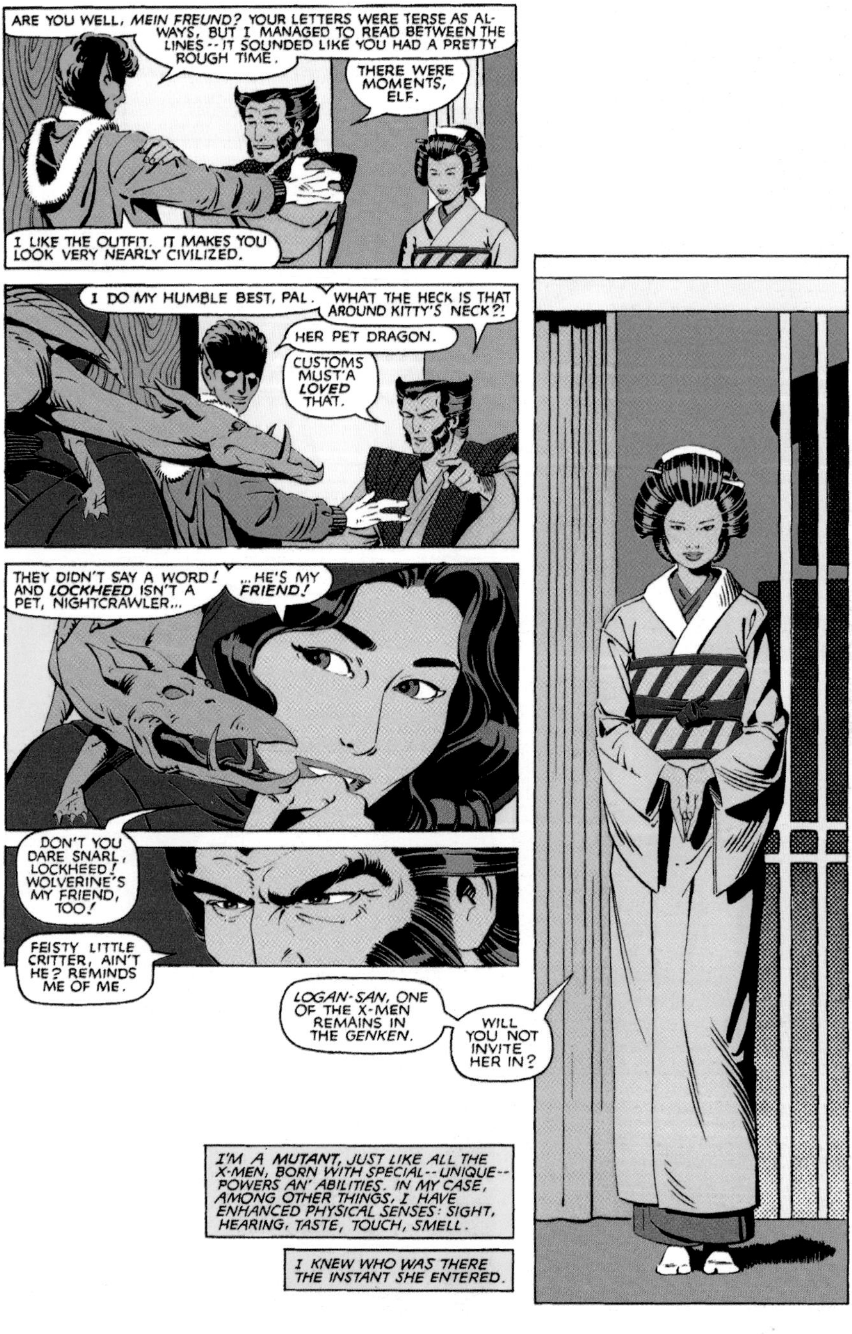
ARE YOU WELL, MEIN FREUND? YOUR LETTERS WERE TERSE AS ALWAYS, BUT I MANAGED TO READ BETWEEN THE LINES -- IT SOUNDED LIKE YOU HAD A PRETTY ROUGH TIME.
THERE WERE MOMENTS, ELF.
I LIKE THE OUTFIT. IT MAKES YOU LOOK VERY NEARLY CIVILIZED.
I DO MY HUMBLE BEST, PAL.
WHAT THE HECK IS THAT AROUND KITTY'S NECK?!
HER PET DRAGON.
CUSTOMS MUST'A LOVED THAT.
THEY DIDN'T SAY A WORD! AND LOCKHEED ISN'T A PET, NIGHTCRAWLER...
...HE'S MY FRIEND!
DON'T YOU DARE SNARL, LOCKHEED! WOLVERINE'S MY FRIEND, TOO!
FEISTY LITTLE CRITTER, AIN'T HE? REMINDS ME OF ME.
LOGAN-SAN, ONE OF THE X-MEN REMAINS IN THE GENKEN.
WILL YOU NOT INVITE HER IN?
I'M A MUTANT, JUST LIKE ALL THE X-MEN, BORN WITH SPECIAL--UNIQUE--POWERS AN' ABILITIES. IN MY CASE, AMONG OTHER THINGS, I HAVE ENHANCED PHYSICAL SENSES: SIGHT, HEARING, TASTE, TOUCH, SMELL.
I KNEW WHO WAS THERE THE INSTANT SHE ENTERED.

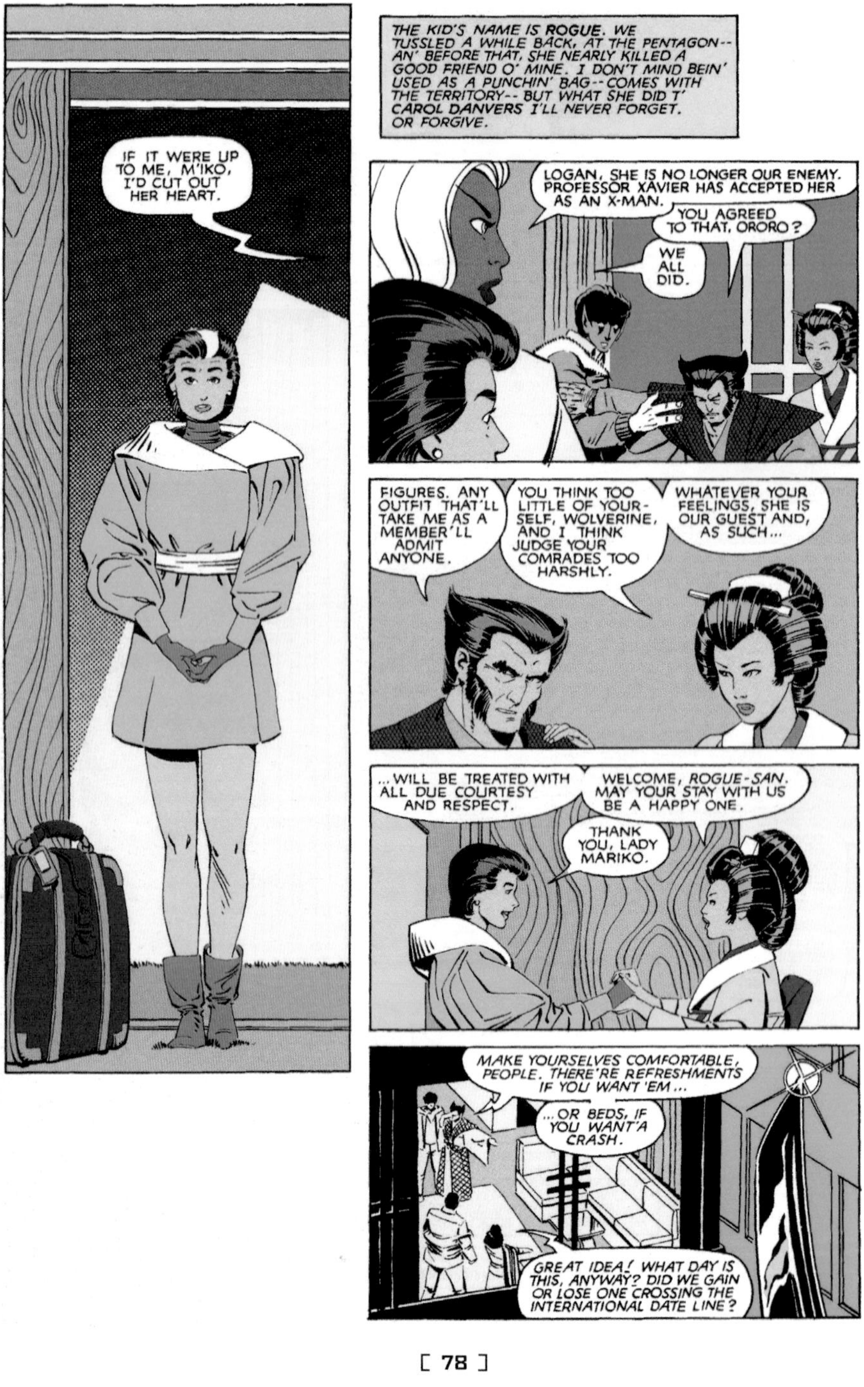
THE KID'S NAME IS ROGUE. WE TUSSLED A WHILE BACK, AT THE PENTAGON-- AN' BEFORE THAT, SHE NEARLY KILLED A GOOD FRIEND O' MINE. I DON'T MIND BEIN' USED AS A PUNCHIN' BAG--COMES WITH THE TERRITORY-- BUT WHAT SHE DID T' CAROL DANVERS I'LL NEVER FORGET. OR FORGIVE.
IF IT WERE UP TO ME, M'IKO, I'D CUT OUT HER HEART.
LOGAN, SHE IS NO LONGER OUR ENEMY. PROFESSOR XAVIER HAS ACCEPTED HER AS AN X-MAN.
YOU AGREED TO THAT, ORORO?
WE ALL DID.
FIGURES. ANY OUTFIT THAT'LL TAKE ME AS A MEMBER'LL ADMIT ANYONE.
YOU THINK TOO LITTLE OF YOURSELF, WOLVERINE, AND I THINK JUDGE YOUR COMRADES TOO HARSHLY.
WHATEVER YOUR FEELINGS, SHE IS OUR GUEST AND, AS SUCH...
...WILL BE TREATED WITH ALL DUE COURTESY AND RESPECT.
WELCOME, ROGUE-SAN. MAY YOUR STAY WITH US BE A HAPPY ONE.
THANK YOU, LADY MARIKO.
MAKE YOURSELVES COMFORTABLE, PEOPLE. THERE'RE REFRESHMENTS IF YOU WANT 'EM...
...OR BEDS, IF YOU WANT'A CRASH.
GREAT IDEA! WHAT DAY IS THIS, ANYWAY? DID WE GAIN OR LOSE ONE CROSSING THE INTERNATIONAL DATE LINE?

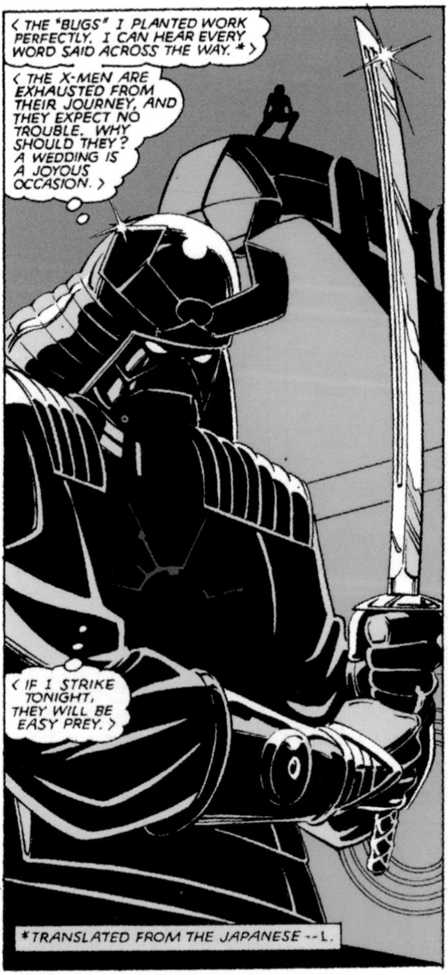
< THE "BUGS" I PLANTED WORK PERFECTLY. I CAN HEAR EVERY WORD SAID ACROSS THE WAY. * >
< THE X-MEN ARE EXHAUSTED FROM THEIR JOURNEY, AND THEY EXPECT NO TROUBLE. WHY SHOULD THEY? A WEDDING IS A JOYOUS OCCASION. >
< IF I STRIKE TONIGHT, THEY WILL BE EASY PREY. >
*TRANSLATED FROM THE JAPANESE --L.

Stan Lee PRESENTS...

Scarlet IN GLORY

CHRIS CLAREMONT *WRITER* · PAUL SMITH *PENCILER* · BOB WIACEK *INKER*

GLYNIS WEIN, *colorist* • TOM ORZECHOWSKI, *letterer*

LOUISE JONES *EDITOR* · JIM SHOOTER *EDITOR-IN-CHIEF*

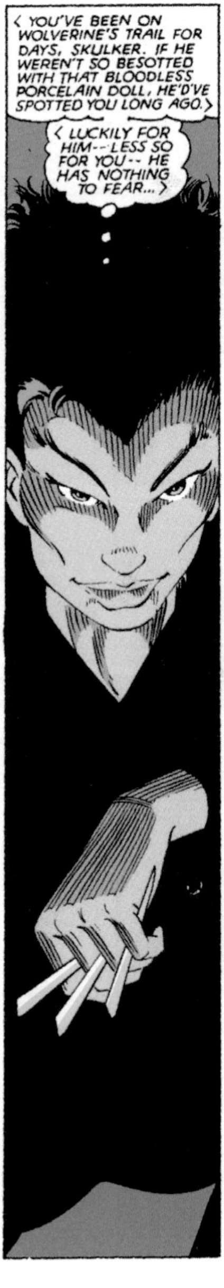
< YOU'VE BEEN ON WOLVERINE'S TRAIL FOR DAYS, SKULKER. IF HE WEREN'T SO BESOTTED WITH THAT BLOODLESS PORCELAIN DOLL, HE'D'VE SPOTTED YOU LONG AGO. >
< LUCKILY FOR HIM--LESS SO FOR YOU-- HE HAS NOTHING TO FEAR... >

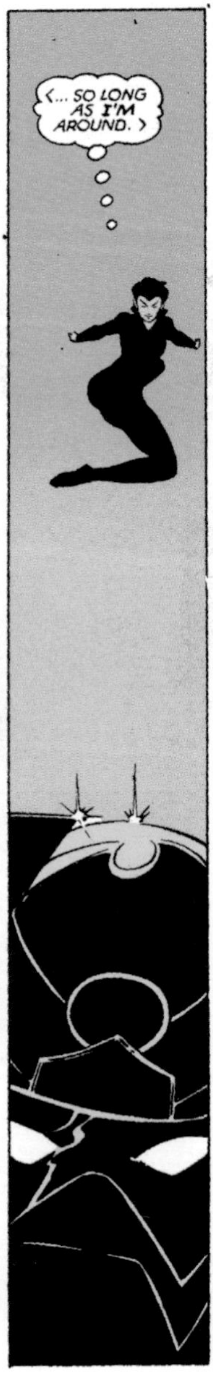
<... SO LONG AS I'M AROUND. >

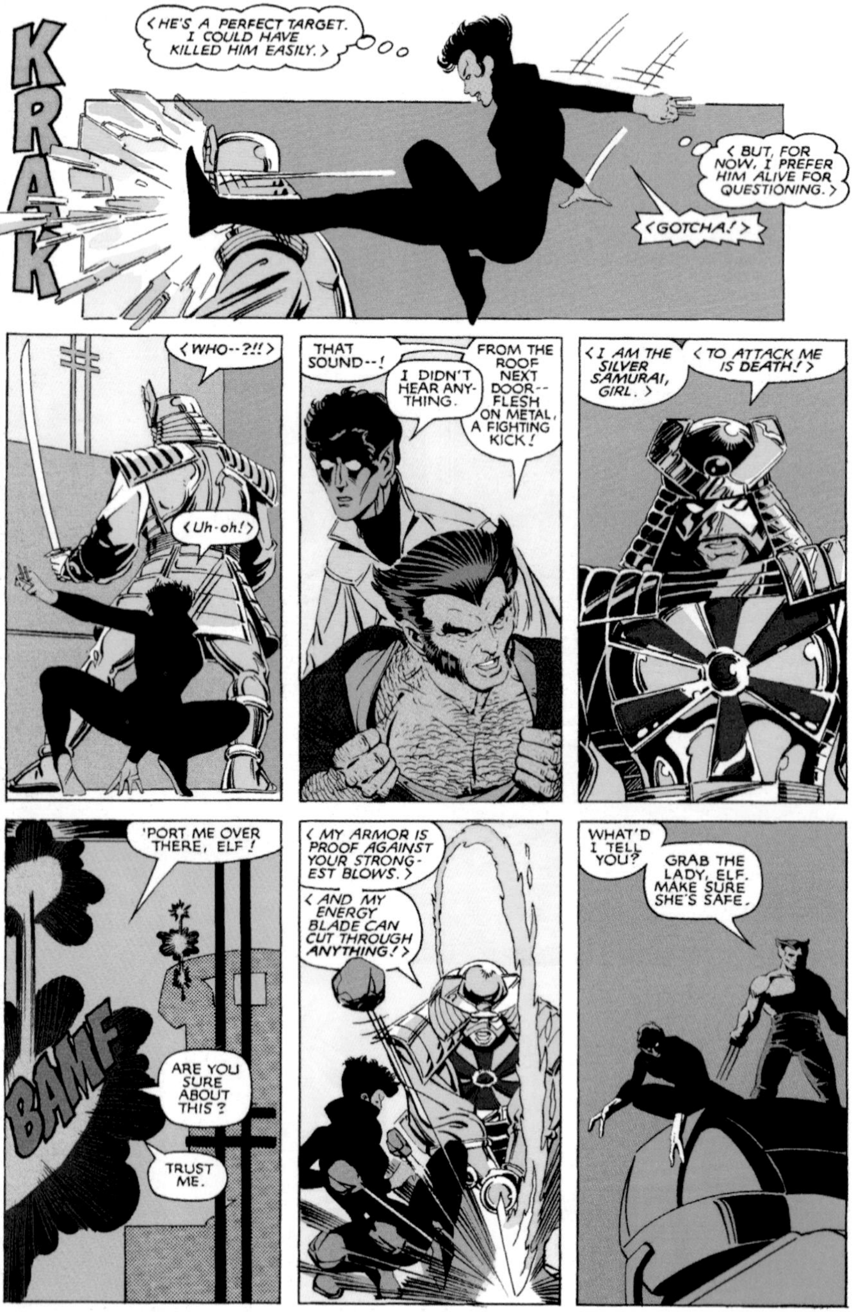
KRAK
< HE'S A PERFECT TARGET. I COULD HAVE KILLED HIM EASILY. >
< BUT, FOR NOW, I PREFER HIM ALIVE FOR QUESTIONING. >
< GOTCHA! >
< WHO--?!! >
< Uh-oh! >
THAT SOUND--!
I DIDN'T HEAR ANYTHING.
FROM THE ROOF NEXT DOOR--FLESH ON METAL, A FIGHTING KICK!
< I AM THE SILVER SAMURAI, GIRL. >
< TO ATTACK ME IS DEATH! >
'PORT ME OVER THERE, ELF!
BAMF
ARE YOU SURE ABOUT THIS?
TRUST ME.
< MY ARMOR IS PROOF AGAINST YOUR STRONGEST BLOWS. >
< AND MY ENERGY BLADE CAN CUT THROUGH ANYTHING! >
WHAT'D I TELL YOU?
GRAB THE LADY, ELF. MAKE SURE SHE'S SAFE.

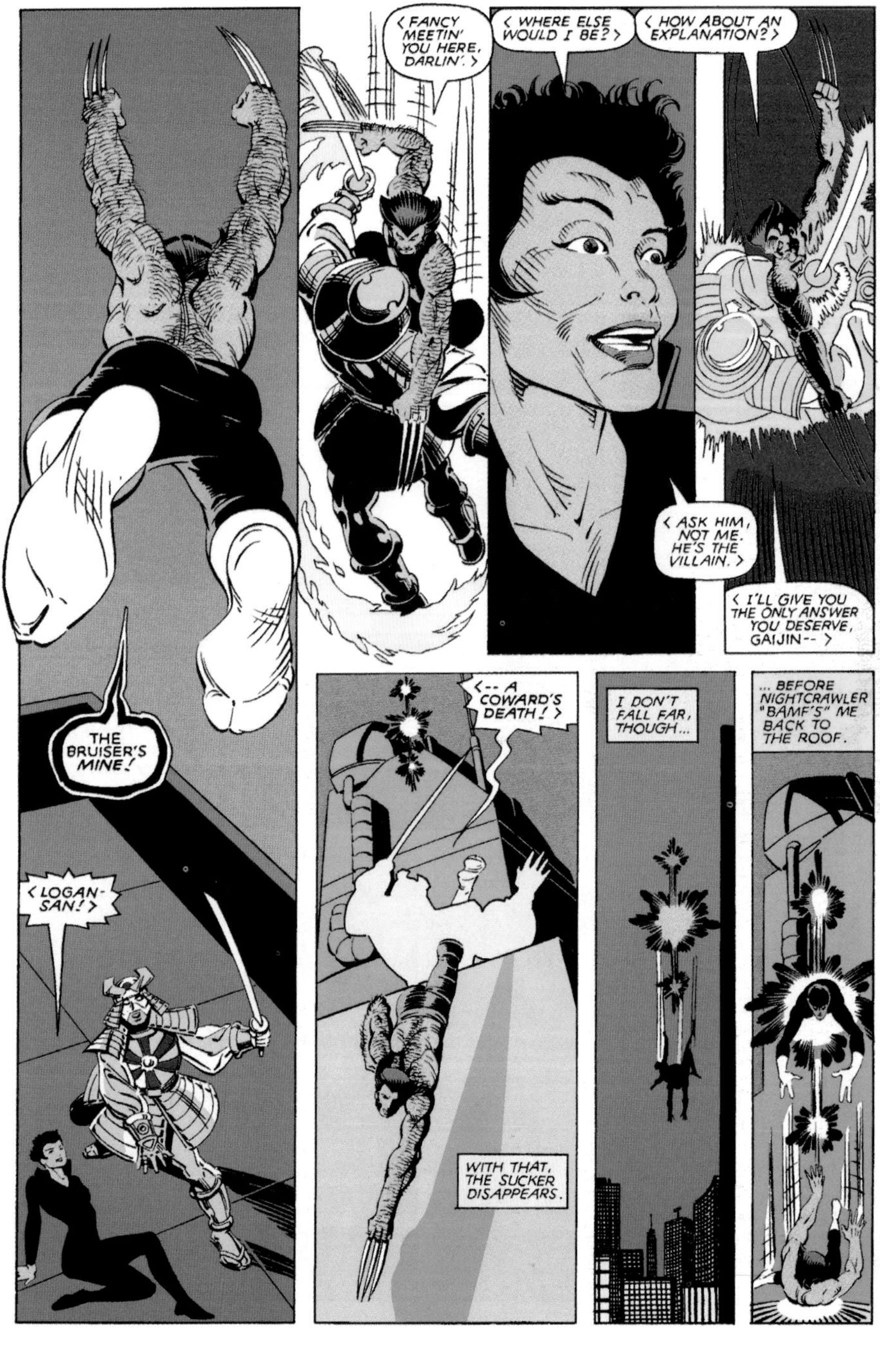

‹ FANCY MEETIN' YOU HERE, DARLIN'. ›
‹ WHERE ELSE WOULD I BE? ›
‹ HOW ABOUT AN EXPLANATION? ›
‹ ASK HIM, NOT ME. HE'S THE VILLAIN. ›
‹ I'LL GIVE YOU THE ONLY ANSWER YOU DESERVE, GAIJIN-- ›
THE BRUISER'S MINE!
‹ LOGAN-SAN! ›
‹-- A COWARD'S DEATH! ›
WITH THAT, THE SUCKER DISAPPEARS.
I DON'T FALL FAR, THOUGH...
... BEFORE NIGHTCRAWLER "BAMF'S" ME BACK TO THE ROOF.

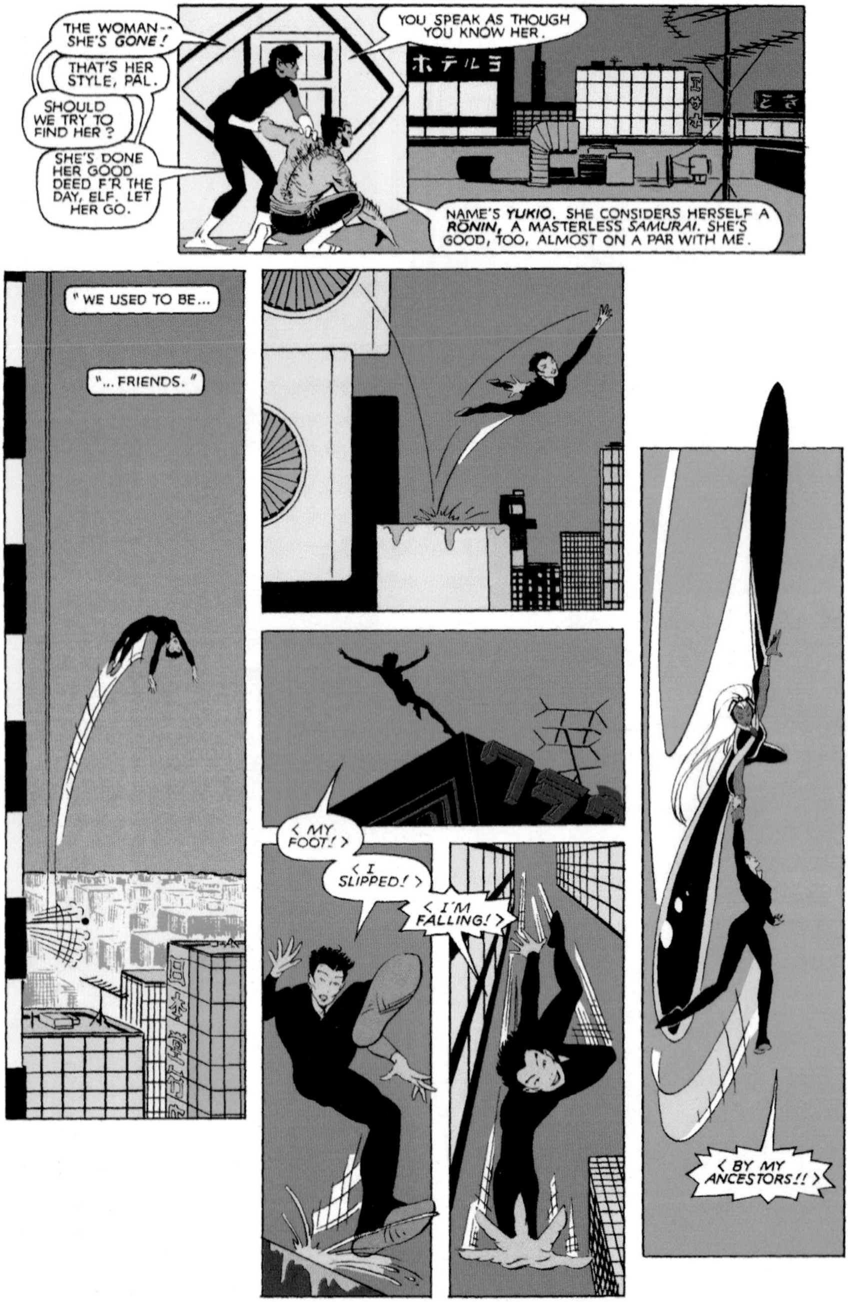
THE WOMAN-- SHE'S GONE!
YOU SPEAK AS THOUGH YOU KNOW HER.
THAT'S HER STYLE, PAL.
SHOULD WE TRY TO FIND HER?
SHE'S DONE HER GOOD DEED F'R THE DAY, ELF. LET HER GO.
NAME'S YUKIO. SHE CONSIDERS HERSELF A RŌNIN, A MASTERLESS SAMURAI. SHE'S GOOD, TOO, ALMOST ON A PAR WITH ME.
"WE USED TO BE...
"...FRIENDS."
< MY FOOT! >
< I SLIPPED! >
< I'M FALLING! >
< BY MY ANCESTORS!! >

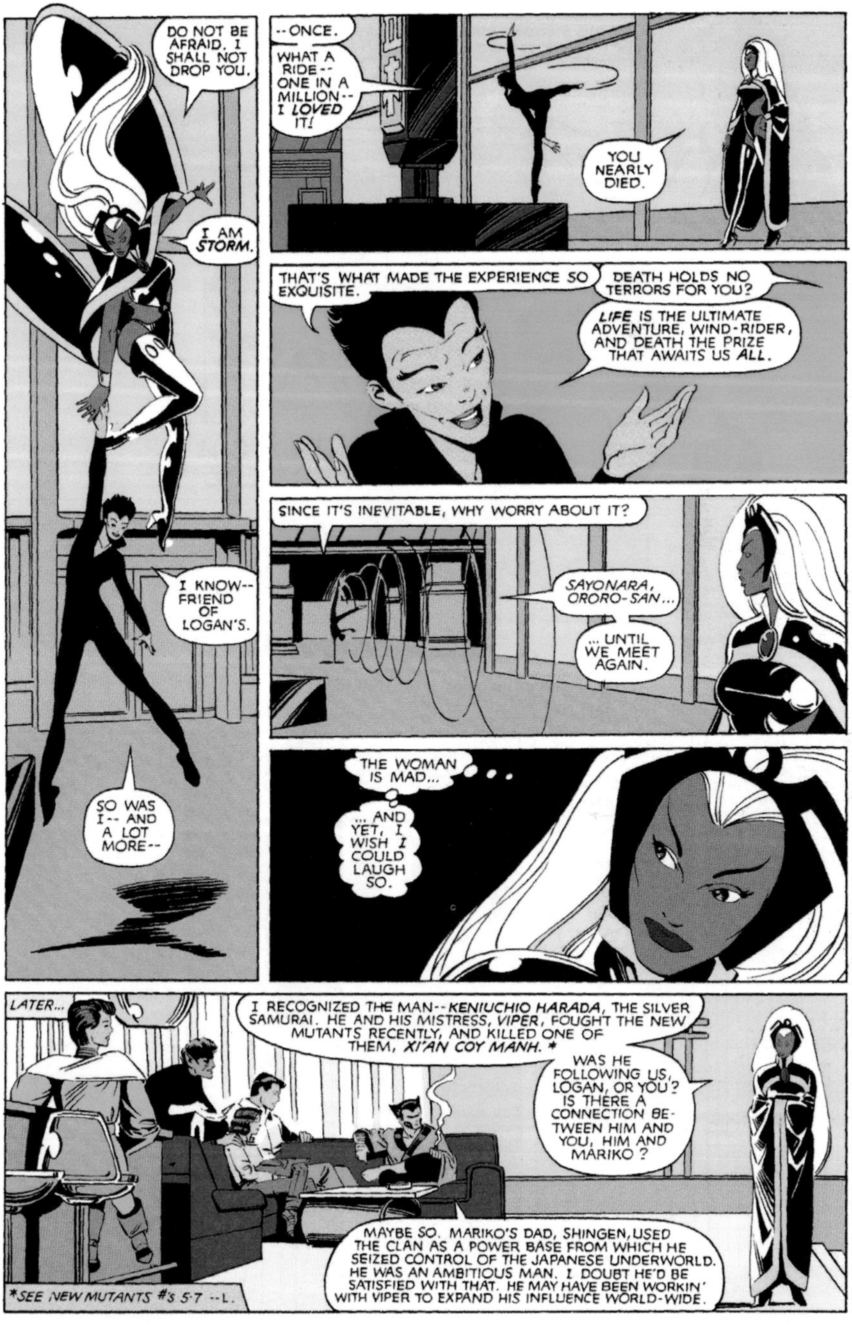
DO NOT BE AFRAID. I SHALL NOT DROP YOU.
I AM STORM.
I KNOW-- FRIEND OF LOGAN'S.
SO WAS I-- AND A LOT MORE--
--ONCE.
WHAT A RIDE-- ONE IN A MILLION-- I LOVED IT!
YOU NEARLY DIED.
THAT'S WHAT MADE THE EXPERIENCE SO EXQUISITE.
DEATH HOLDS NO TERRORS FOR YOU?
LIFE IS THE ULTIMATE ADVENTURE, WIND-RIDER, AND DEATH THE PRIZE THAT AWAITS US ALL.
SINCE IT'S INEVITABLE, WHY WORRY ABOUT IT?
SAYONARA, ORORO-SAN...
... UNTIL WE MEET AGAIN.
THE WOMAN IS MAD...
... AND YET, I WISH I COULD LAUGH SO.
LATER...
I RECOGNIZED THE MAN--KENIUCHIO HARADA, THE SILVER SAMURAI. HE AND HIS MISTRESS, VIPER, FOUGHT THE NEW MUTANTS RECENTLY, AND KILLED ONE OF THEM, XI'AN COY MANH. *
WAS HE FOLLOWING US, LOGAN, OR YOU? IS THERE A CONNECTION BE-TWEEN HIM AND YOU, HIM AND MARIKO?
MAYBE SO. MARIKO'S DAD, SHINGEN, USED THE CLAN AS A POWER BASE FROM WHICH HE SEIZED CONTROL OF THE JAPANESE UNDERWORLD. HE WAS AN AMBITIOUS MAN. I DOUBT HE'D BE SATISFIED WITH THAT. HE MAY HAVE BEEN WORKIN' WITH VIPER TO EXPAND HIS INFLUENCE WORLD-WIDE.
*SEE NEW MUTANTS #'s 5-7 --L.

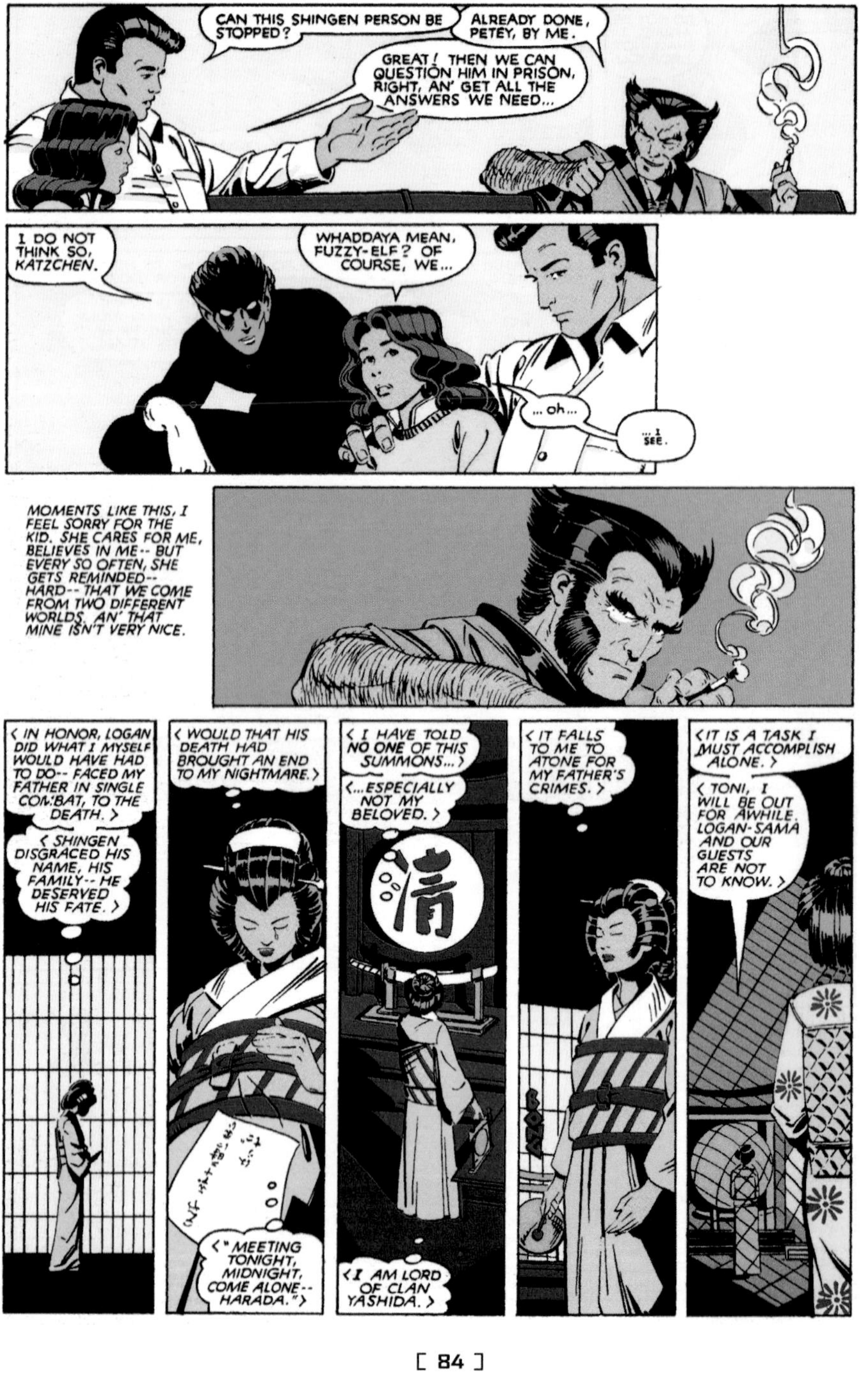
CAN THIS SHINGEN PERSON BE STOPPED?
ALREADY DONE, PETEY, BY ME.
GREAT! THEN WE CAN QUESTION HIM IN PRISON, RIGHT, AN' GET ALL THE ANSWERS WE NEED...
I DO NOT THINK SO, KATZCHEN.
WHADDAYA MEAN, FUZZY-ELF? OF COURSE, WE...
... oh ...
... I SEE.
MOMENTS LIKE THIS, I FEEL SORRY FOR THE KID. SHE CARES FOR ME, BELIEVES IN ME-- BUT EVERY SO OFTEN, SHE GETS REMINDED-- HARD-- THAT WE COME FROM TWO DIFFERENT WORLDS. AN' THAT MINE ISN'T VERY NICE.
< IN HONOR, LOGAN DID WHAT I MYSELF WOULD HAVE HAD TO DO-- FACED MY FATHER IN SINGLE COMBAT, TO THE DEATH. >
< SHINGEN DISGRACED HIS NAME, HIS FAMILY-- HE DESERVED HIS FATE. >
< WOULD THAT HIS DEATH HAD BROUGHT AN END TO MY NIGHTMARE. >
< "MEETING TONIGHT, MIDNIGHT, COME ALONE-- HARADA." >
< I HAVE TOLD NO ONE OF THIS SUMMONS... >
< ...ESPECIALLY NOT MY BELOVED. >
< I AM LORD OF CLAN YASHIDA. >
< IT FALLS TO ME TO ATONE FOR MY FATHER'S CRIMES. >
< IT IS A TASK I MUST ACCOMPLISH ALONE. >
< TONI, I WILL BE OUT FOR AWHILE. LOGAN-SAMA AND OUR GUESTS ARE NOT TO KNOW. >

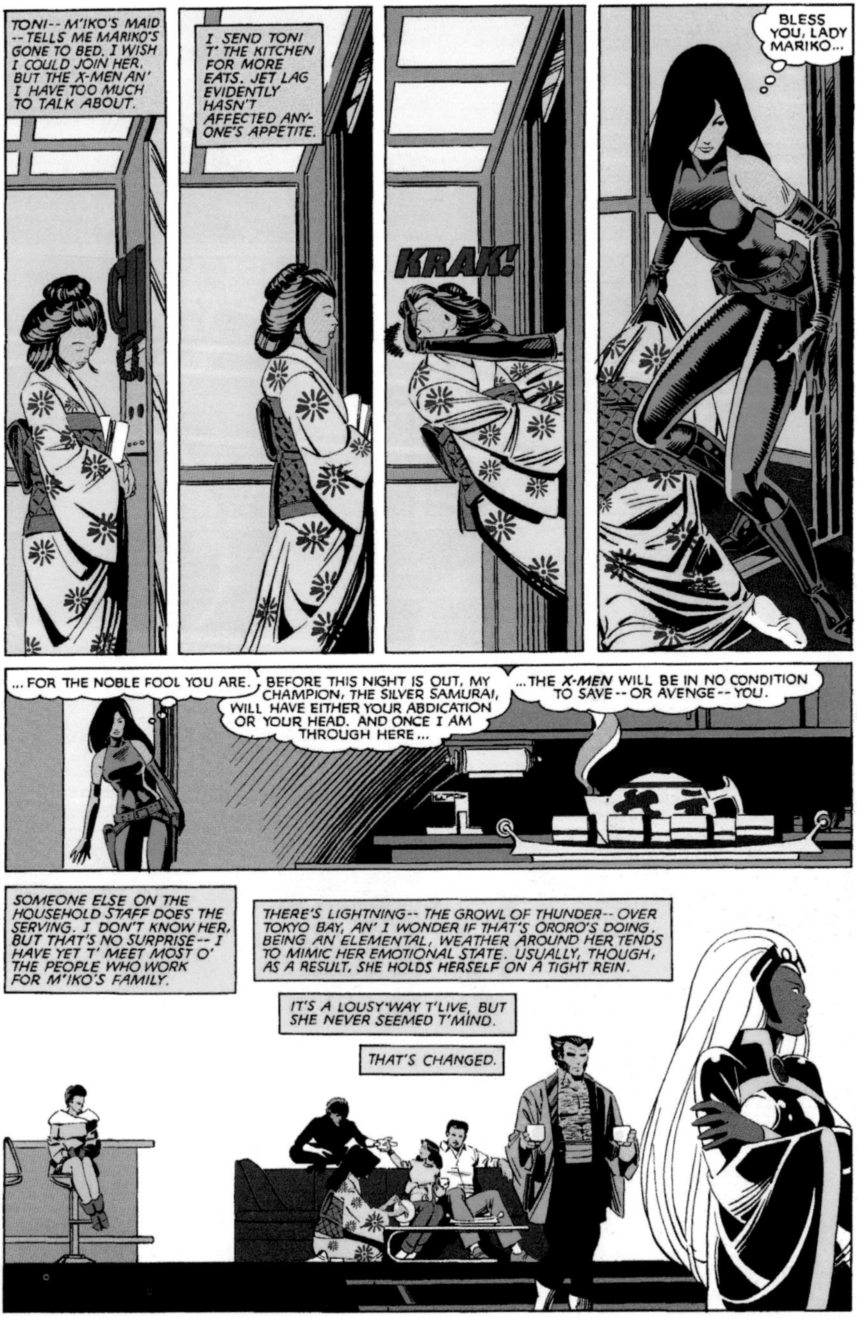
TONI-- M'IKO'S MAID --TELLS ME MARIKO'S GONE TO BED. I WISH I COULD JOIN HER, BUT THE X-MEN AN' I HAVE TOO MUCH TO TALK ABOUT.
I SEND TONI T' THE KITCHEN FOR MORE EATS. JET LAG EVIDENTLY HASN'T AFFECTED ANYONE'S APPETITE.
KRAK!
BLESS YOU, LADY MARIKO...
...FOR THE NOBLE FOOL YOU ARE.
BEFORE THIS NIGHT IS OUT, MY CHAMPION, THE SILVER SAMURAI, WILL HAVE EITHER YOUR ABDICATION OR YOUR HEAD. AND ONCE I AM THROUGH HERE...
...THE X-MEN WILL BE IN NO CONDITION TO SAVE--OR AVENGE--YOU.
SOMEONE ELSE ON THE HOUSEHOLD STAFF DOES THE SERVING. I DON'T KNOW HER, BUT THAT'S NO SURPRISE-- I HAVE YET T' MEET MOST O' THE PEOPLE WHO WORK FOR M'IKO'S FAMILY.
THERE'S LIGHTNING-- THE GROWL OF THUNDER-- OVER TOKYO BAY, AN' I WONDER IF THAT'S ORORO'S DOING. BEING AN ELEMENTAL, WEATHER AROUND HER TENDS TO MIMIC HER EMOTIONAL STATE. USUALLY, THOUGH, AS A RESULT, SHE HOLDS HERSELF ON A TIGHT REIN.
IT'S A LOUSY WAY T'LIVE, BUT SHE NEVER SEEMED T'MIND.
THAT'S CHANGED.

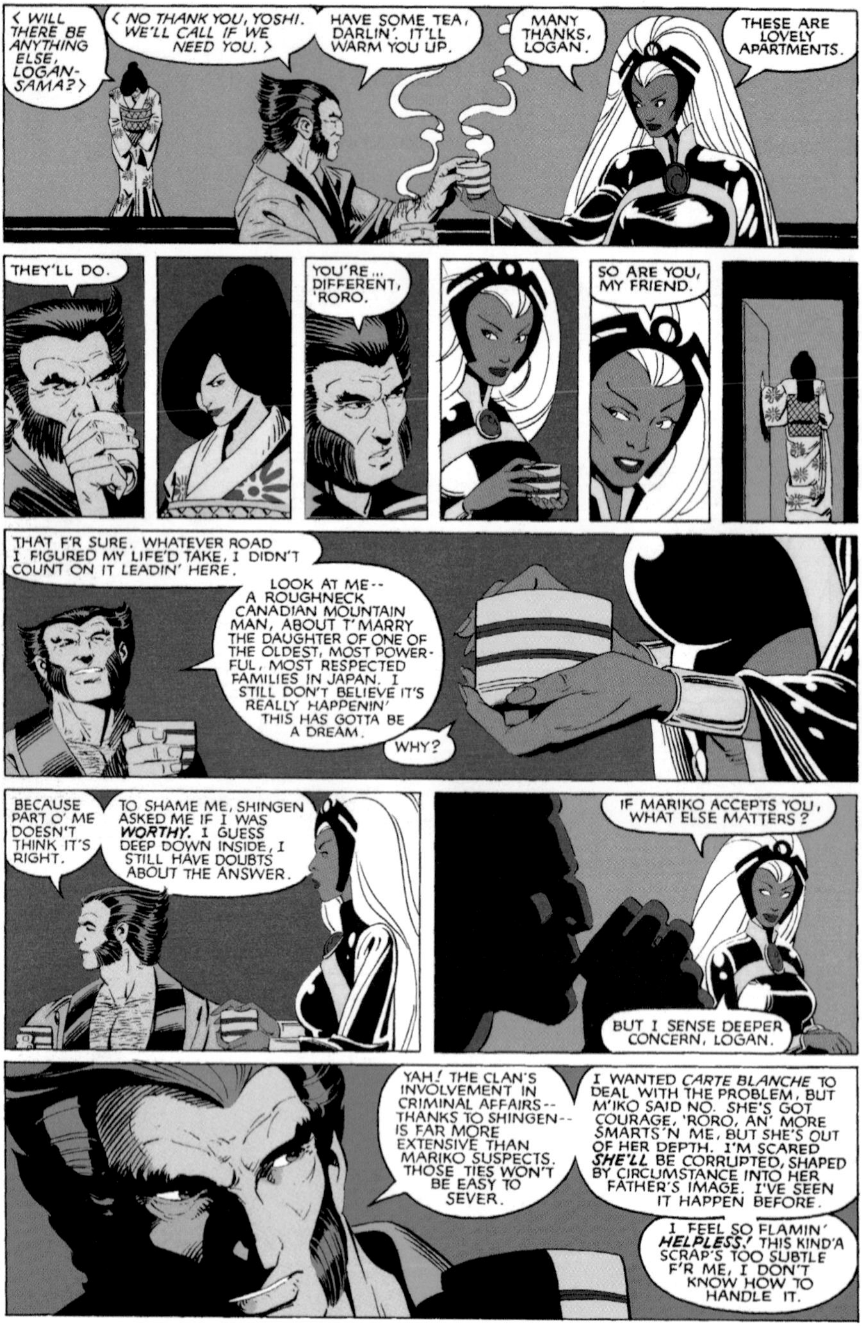
< WILL THERE BE ANYTHING ELSE, LOGAN-SAMA? >
< NO THANK YOU, YOSHI. WE'LL CALL IF WE NEED YOU. >
HAVE SOME TEA, DARLIN'. IT'LL WARM YOU UP.
MANY THANKS, LOGAN.
THESE ARE LOVELY APARTMENTS.
THEY'LL DO.
YOU'RE... DIFFERENT, 'RORO.
SO ARE YOU, MY FRIEND.
THAT F'R SURE. WHATEVER ROAD I FIGURED MY LIFE'D TAKE, I DIDN'T COUNT ON IT LEADIN' HERE.
LOOK AT ME-- A ROUGHNECK CANADIAN MOUNTAIN MAN, ABOUT T'MARRY THE DAUGHTER OF ONE OF THE OLDEST, MOST POWERFUL, MOST RESPECTED FAMILIES IN JAPAN. I STILL DON'T BELIEVE IT'S REALLY HAPPENIN'. THIS HAS GOTTA BE A DREAM.
WHY?
BECAUSE PART O' ME DOESN'T THINK IT'S RIGHT.
TO SHAME ME, SHINGEN ASKED ME IF I WAS *WORTHY*. I GUESS DEEP DOWN INSIDE, I STILL HAVE DOUBTS ABOUT THE ANSWER.
IF MARIKO ACCEPTS YOU, WHAT ELSE MATTERS?
BUT I SENSE DEEPER CONCERN, LOGAN.
YAH! THE CLAN'S INVOLVEMENT IN CRIMINAL AFFAIRS-- THANKS TO SHINGEN-- IS FAR MORE EXTENSIVE THAN MARIKO SUSPECTS. THOSE TIES WON'T BE EASY TO SEVER.
I WANTED *CARTE BLANCHE* TO DEAL WITH THE PROBLEM, BUT M'IKO SAID NO. SHE'S GOT COURAGE, 'RORO, AN' MORE SMARTS 'N ME, BUT SHE'S OUT OF HER DEPTH. I'M SCARED ***SHE'LL*** BE CORRUPTED, SHAPED BY CIRCUMSTANCE INTO HER FATHER'S IMAGE. I'VE SEEN IT HAPPEN BEFORE.
I FEEL SO FLAMIN' ***HELPLESS!*** THIS KIND'A SCRAP'S TOO SUBTLE F'R ME. I DON'T KNOW HOW TO HANDLE IT.

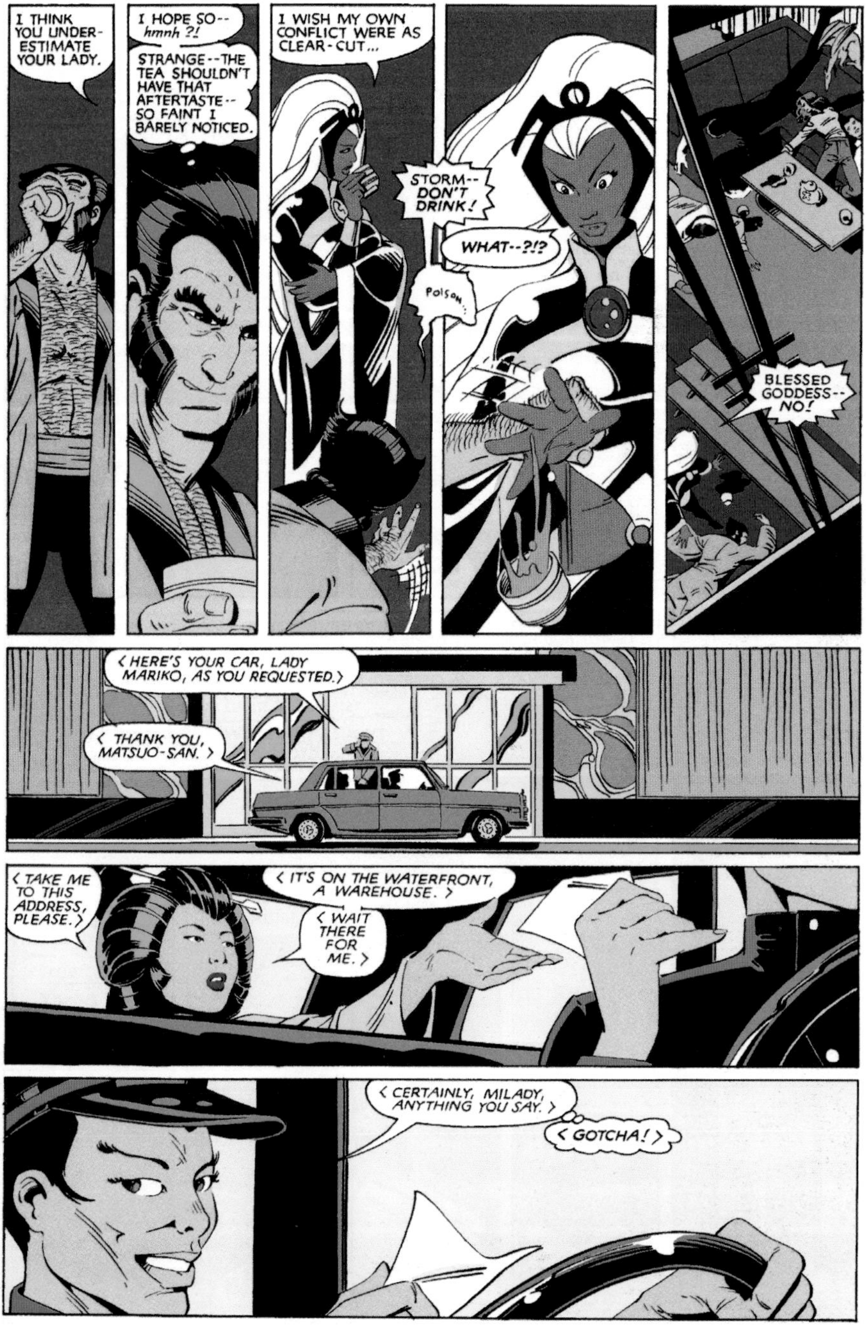
I THINK YOU UNDER-ESTIMATE YOUR LADY.
I HOPE SO-- hmnh ?!
STRANGE--THE TEA SHOULDN'T HAVE THAT AFTERTASTE-- SO FAINT I BARELY NOTICED.
I WISH MY OWN CONFLICT WERE AS CLEAR-CUT...
STORM-- DON'T DRINK!
WHAT--?!?
POISON...
BLESSED GODDESS-- NO!
< HERE'S YOUR CAR, LADY MARIKO, AS YOU REQUESTED. >
< THANK YOU, MATSUO-SAN. >
< TAKE ME TO THIS ADDRESS, PLEASE. >
< IT'S ON THE WATERFRONT, A WAREHOUSE. >
< WAIT THERE FOR ME. >
< CERTAINLY, MILADY, ANYTHING YOU SAY. >
< GOTCHA! >

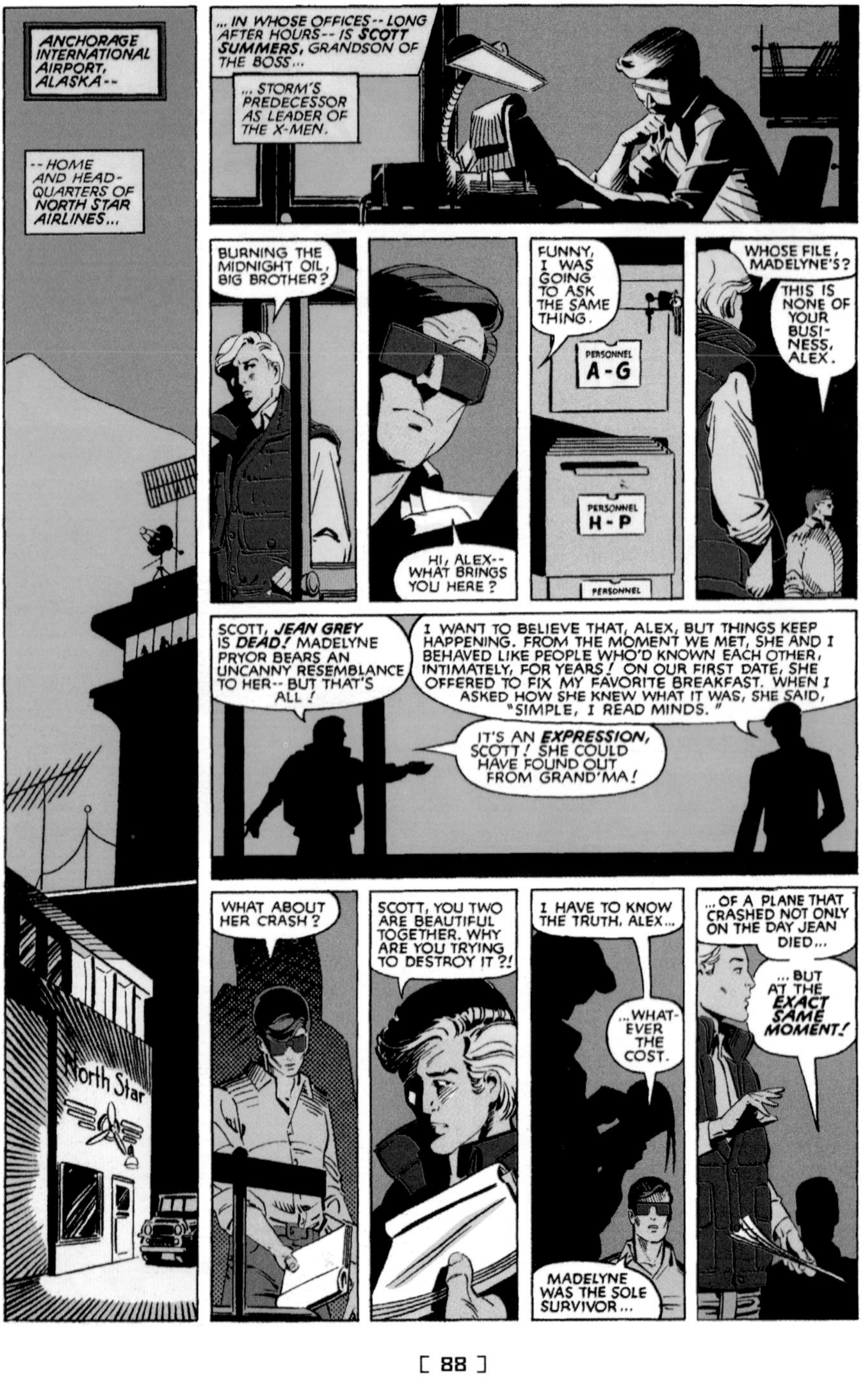
ANCHORAGE INTERNATIONAL AIRPORT, ALASKA--
--HOME AND HEAD-QUARTERS OF NORTH STAR AIRLINES...
North Star
...IN WHOSE OFFICES--LONG AFTER HOURS--IS SCOTT SUMMERS, GRANDSON OF THE BOSS...
...STORM'S PREDECESSOR AS LEADER OF THE X-MEN.
BURNING THE MIDNIGHT OIL, BIG BROTHER?
HI, ALEX--WHAT BRINGS YOU HERE?
FUNNY, I WAS GOING TO ASK THE SAME THING.
PERSONNEL A-G
PERSONNEL H-P
PERSONNEL
WHOSE FILE, MADELYNE'S?
THIS IS NONE OF YOUR BUSINESS, ALEX.
SCOTT, JEAN GREY IS DEAD! MADELYNE PRYOR BEARS AN UNCANNY RESEMBLANCE TO HER--BUT THAT'S ALL!
I WANT TO BELIEVE THAT, ALEX, BUT THINGS KEEP HAPPENING. FROM THE MOMENT WE MET, SHE AND I BEHAVED LIKE PEOPLE WHO'D KNOWN EACH OTHER, INTIMATELY, FOR YEARS! ON OUR FIRST DATE, SHE OFFERED TO FIX MY FAVORITE BREAKFAST. WHEN I ASKED HOW SHE KNEW WHAT IT WAS, SHE SAID, "SIMPLE, I READ MINDS."
IT'S AN EXPRESSION, SCOTT! SHE COULD HAVE FOUND OUT FROM GRAND'MA!
WHAT ABOUT HER CRASH?
SCOTT, YOU TWO ARE BEAUTIFUL TOGETHER. WHY ARE YOU TRYING TO DESTROY IT?!
I HAVE TO KNOW THE TRUTH, ALEX...
...WHATEVER THE COST.
MADELYNE WAS THE SOLE SURVIVOR...
...OF A PLANE THAT CRASHED NOT ONLY ON THE DAY JEAN DIED...
...BUT AT THE EXACT SAME MOMENT!

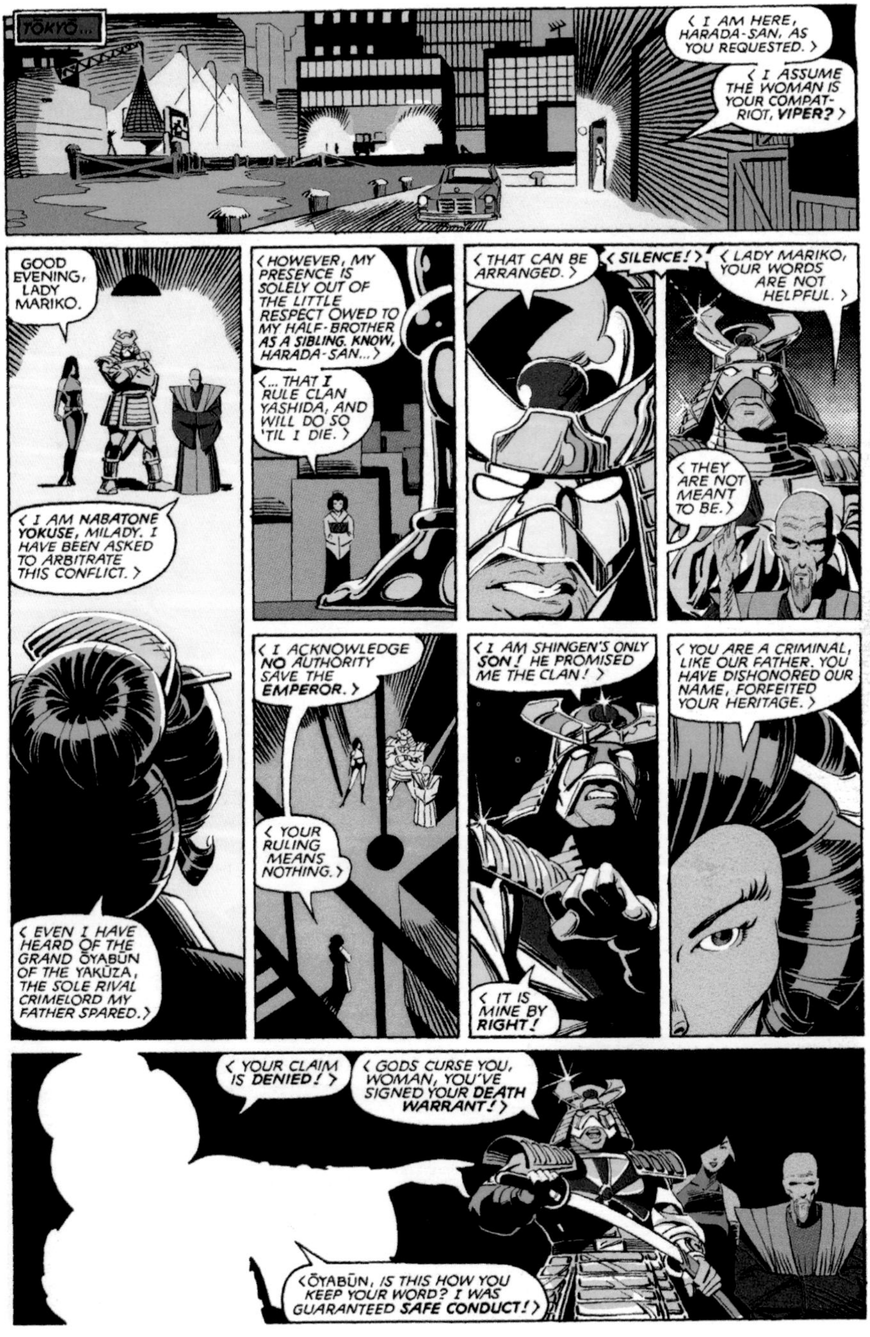
TOKYO...
< I AM HERE, HARADA-SAN, AS YOU REQUESTED. >
< I ASSUME THE WOMAN IS YOUR COMPATRIOT, VIPER? >
GOOD EVENING, LADY MARIKO.
< I AM NABATONE YOKUSE, MILADY. I HAVE BEEN ASKED TO ARBITRATE THIS CONFLICT. >
< HOWEVER, MY PRESENCE IS SOLELY OUT OF THE LITTLE RESPECT OWED TO MY HALF-BROTHER AS A SIBLING. KNOW, HARADA-SAN... >
<... THAT I RULE CLAN YASHIDA, AND WILL DO SO 'TIL I DIE. >
< THAT CAN BE ARRANGED. >
< SILENCE! >
< LADY MARIKO, YOUR WORDS ARE NOT HELPFUL. >
< THEY ARE NOT MEANT TO BE. >
< EVEN I HAVE HEARD OF THE GRAND ŌYABŪN OF THE YAKŪZA, THE SOLE RIVAL CRIMELORD MY FATHER SPARED. >
< I ACKNOWLEDGE NO AUTHORITY SAVE THE EMPEROR. >
< YOUR RULING MEANS NOTHING. >
< I AM SHINGEN'S ONLY SON! HE PROMISED ME THE CLAN! >
< IT IS MINE BY RIGHT! >
< YOU ARE A CRIMINAL, LIKE OUR FATHER. YOU HAVE DISHONORED OUR NAME, FORFEITED YOUR HERITAGE. >
< YOUR CLAIM IS DENIED! >
< GODS CURSE YOU, WOMAN, YOU'VE SIGNED YOUR DEATH WARRANT! >
<ŌYABŪN, IS THIS HOW YOU KEEP YOUR WORD? I WAS GUARANTEED SAFE CONDUCT! >

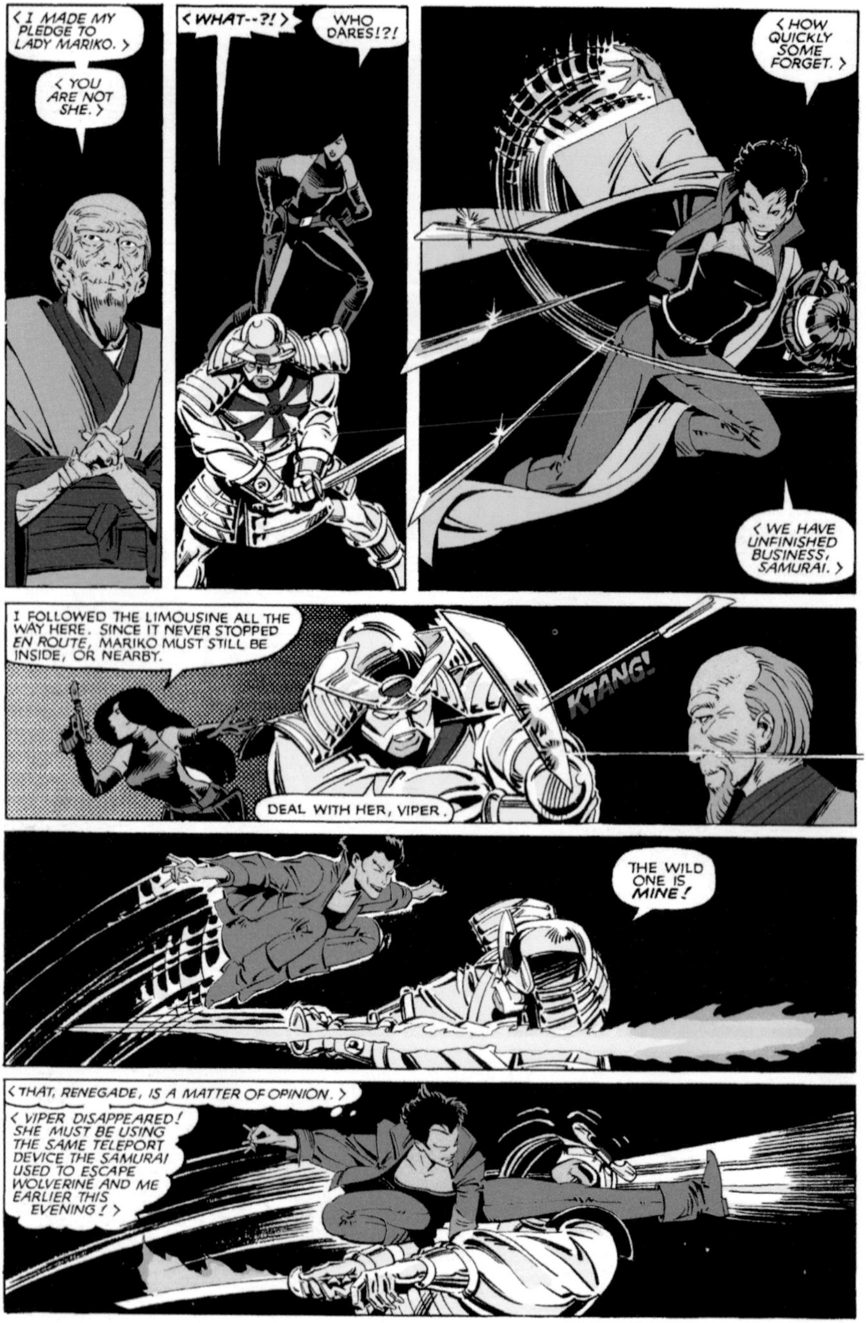
< I MADE MY PLEDGE TO LADY MARIKO. >
< YOU ARE NOT SHE. >
< WHAT--?! >
WHO DARES!?!
< HOW QUICKLY SOME FORGET. >
< WE HAVE UNFINISHED BUSINESS, SAMURAI. >
I FOLLOWED THE LIMOUSINE ALL THE WAY HERE. SINCE IT NEVER STOPPED EN ROUTE, MARIKO MUST STILL BE INSIDE, OR NEARBY.
KTANG!
DEAL WITH HER, VIPER.
THE WILD ONE IS MINE!
< THAT, RENEGADE, IS A MATTER OF OPINION. >
< VIPER DISAPPEARED! SHE MUST BE USING THE SAME TELEPORT DEVICE THE SAMURAI USED TO ESCAPE WOLVERINE AND ME EARLIER THIS EVENING! >

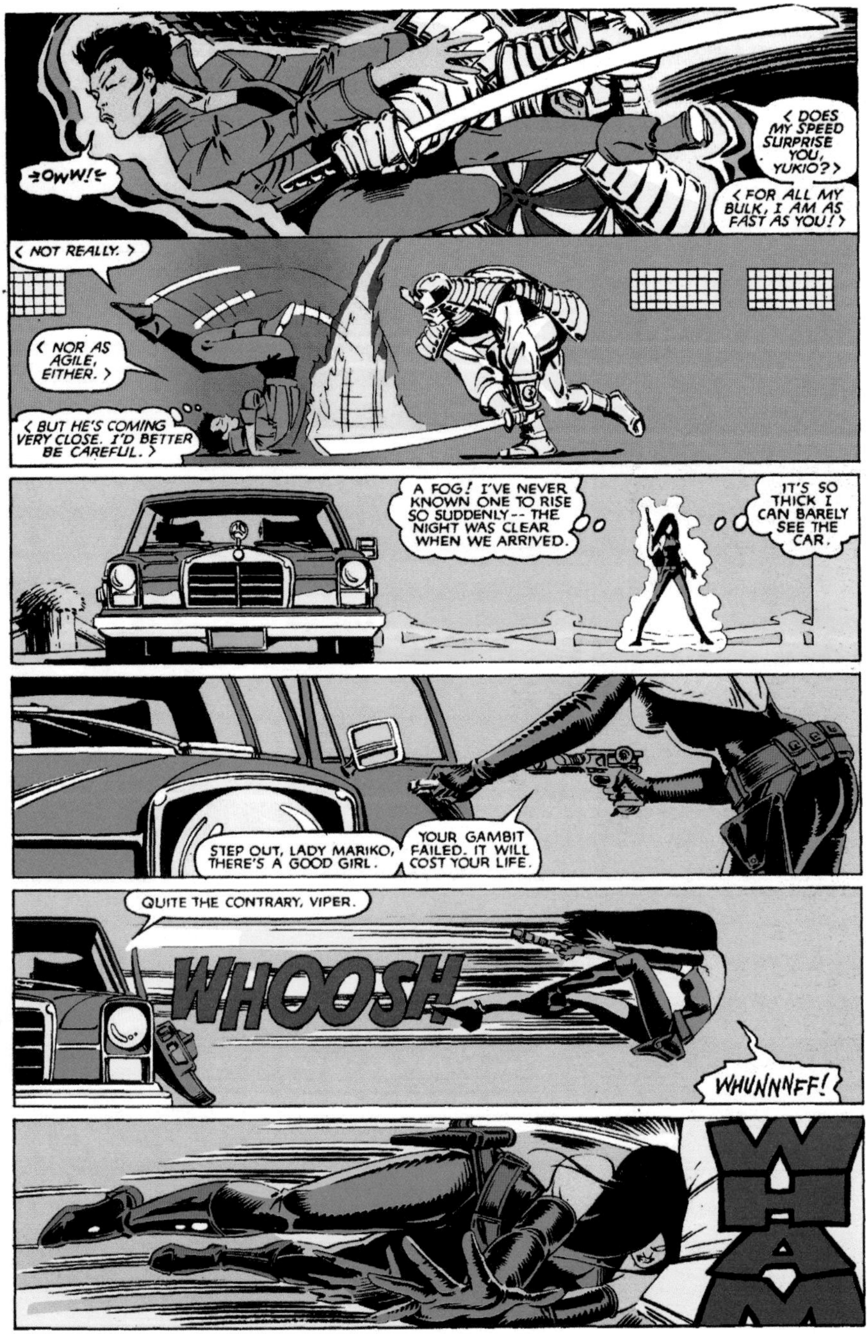

OWW!
< DOES MY SPEED SURPRISE YOU, YUKIO? >
< FOR ALL MY BULK, I AM AS FAST AS YOU! >
< NOT REALLY. >
< NOR AS AGILE, EITHER. >
< BUT HE'S COMING VERY CLOSE. I'D BETTER BE CAREFUL. >
A FOG! I'VE NEVER KNOWN ONE TO RISE SO SUDDENLY-- THE NIGHT WAS CLEAR WHEN WE ARRIVED.
IT'S SO THICK I CAN BARELY SEE THE CAR.
STEP OUT, LADY MARIKO, THERE'S A GOOD GIRL.
YOUR GAMBIT FAILED. IT WILL COST YOUR LIFE.
QUITE THE CONTRARY, VIPER.
WHOOSH
WHUNNNFF!
WHAM

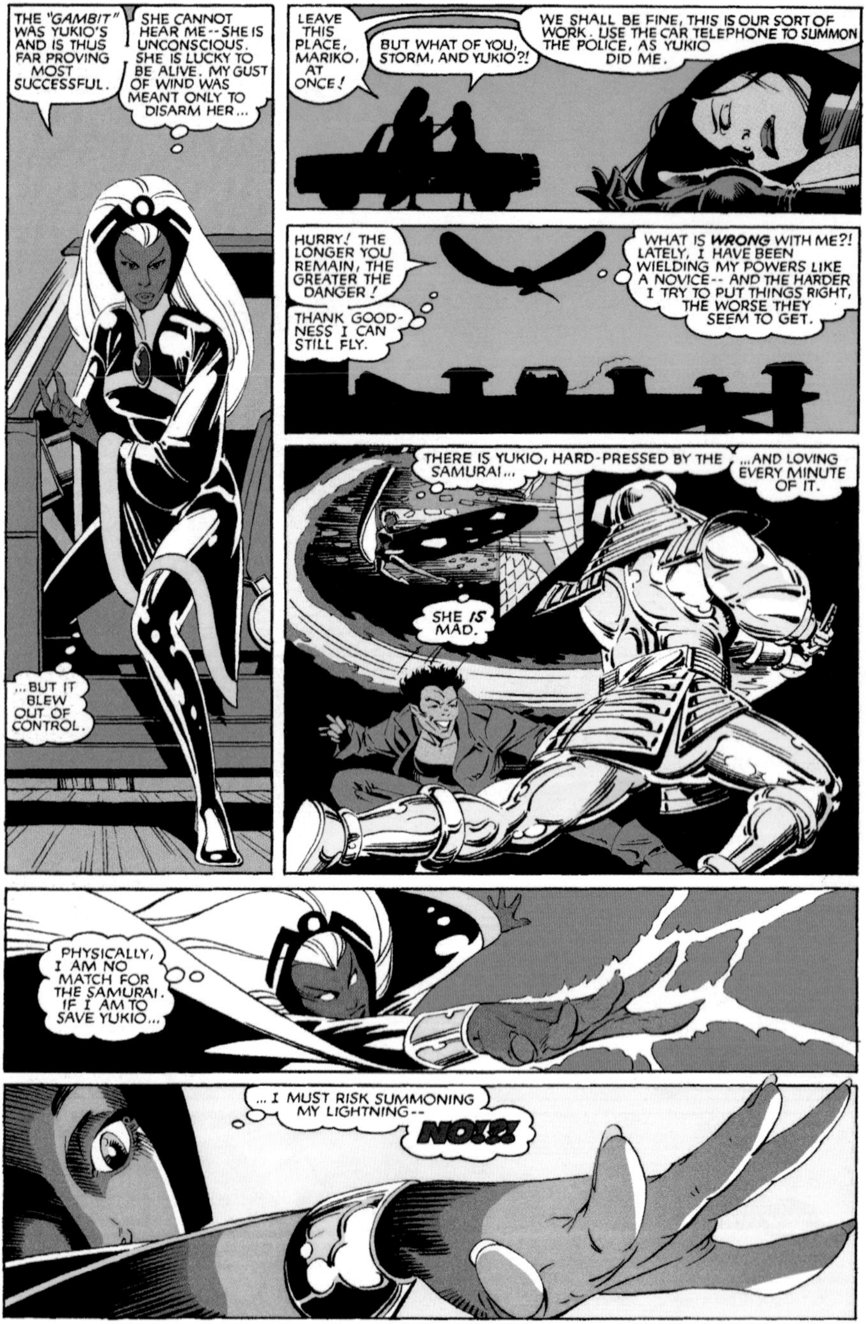
THE "GAMBIT" WAS YUKIO'S AND IS THUS FAR PROVING MOST SUCCESSFUL.
SHE CANNOT HEAR ME--SHE IS UNCONSCIOUS. SHE IS LUCKY TO BE ALIVE. MY GUST OF WIND WAS MEANT ONLY TO DISARM HER...
...BUT IT BLEW OUT OF CONTROL.
LEAVE THIS PLACE, MARIKO, AT ONCE!
BUT WHAT OF YOU, STORM, AND YUKIO?!
WE SHALL BE FINE, THIS IS OUR SORT OF WORK. USE THE CAR TELEPHONE TO SUMMON THE POLICE, AS YUKIO DID ME.
HURRY! THE LONGER YOU REMAIN, THE GREATER THE DANGER!
THANK GOODNESS I CAN STILL FLY.
WHAT IS WRONG WITH ME?! LATELY, I HAVE BEEN WIELDING MY POWERS LIKE A NOVICE-- AND THE HARDER I TRY TO PUT THINGS RIGHT, THE WORSE THEY SEEM TO GET.
THERE IS YUKIO, HARD-PRESSED BY THE SAMURAI...
...AND LOVING EVERY MINUTE OF IT.
SHE IS MAD.
PHYSICALLY, I AM NO MATCH FOR THE SAMURAI. IF I AM TO SAVE YUKIO...
...I MUST RISK SUMMONING MY LIGHTNING--
NO!?!

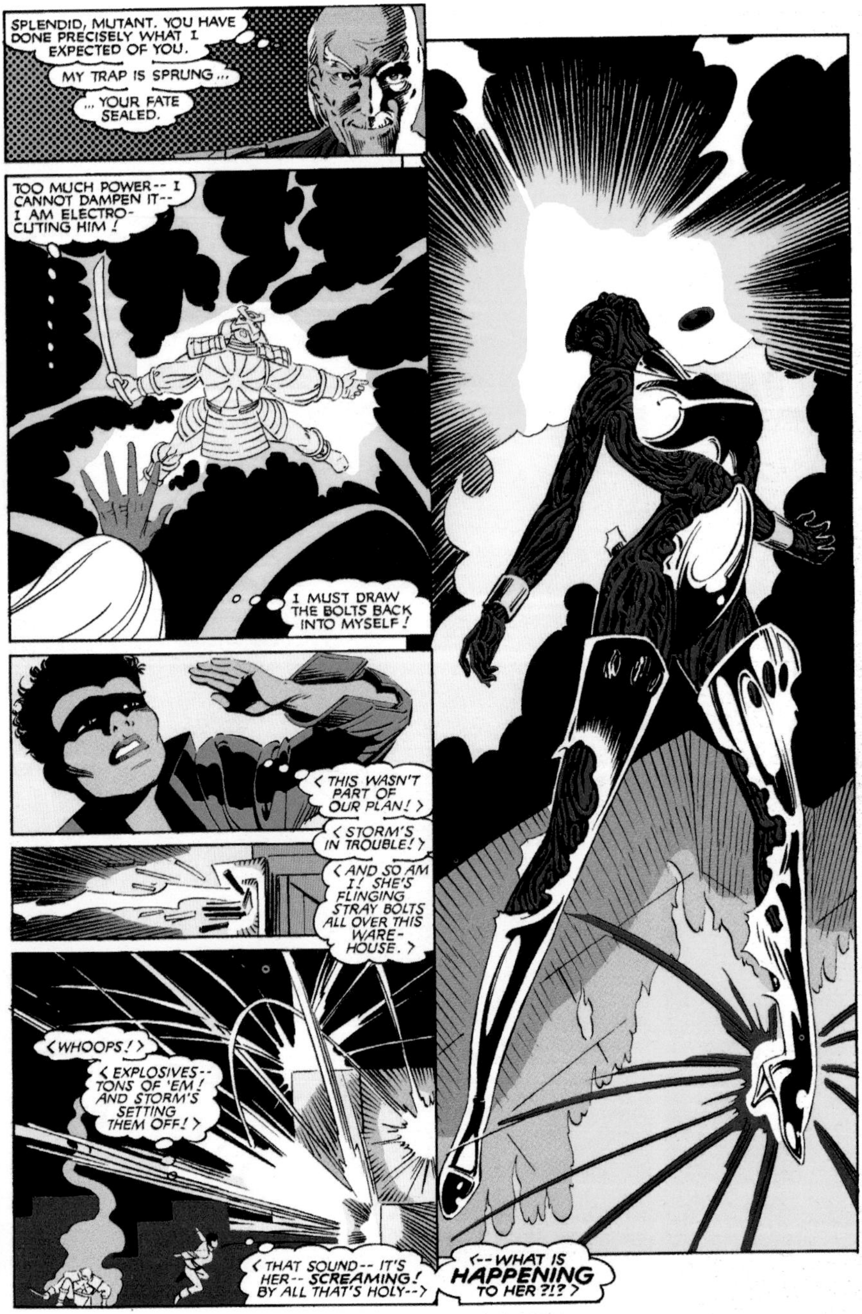
SPLENDID, MUTANT. YOU HAVE DONE PRECISELY WHAT I EXPECTED OF YOU.
MY TRAP IS SPRUNG...
...YOUR FATE SEALED.
TOO MUCH POWER-- I CANNOT DAMPEN IT-- I AM ELECTRO-CUTING HIM!
I MUST DRAW THE BOLTS BACK INTO MYSELF!
<THIS WASN'T PART OF OUR PLAN!>
<STORM'S IN TROUBLE!>
<AND SO AM I! SHE'S FLINGING STRAY BOLTS ALL OVER THIS WARE-HOUSE.>
<WHOOPS!>
<EXPLOSIVES-- TONS OF 'EM! AND STORM'S SETTING THEM OFF!>
<THAT SOUND-- IT'S HER-- SCREAMING! BY ALL THAT'S HOLY-->
<--WHAT IS HAPPENING TO HER?!?>

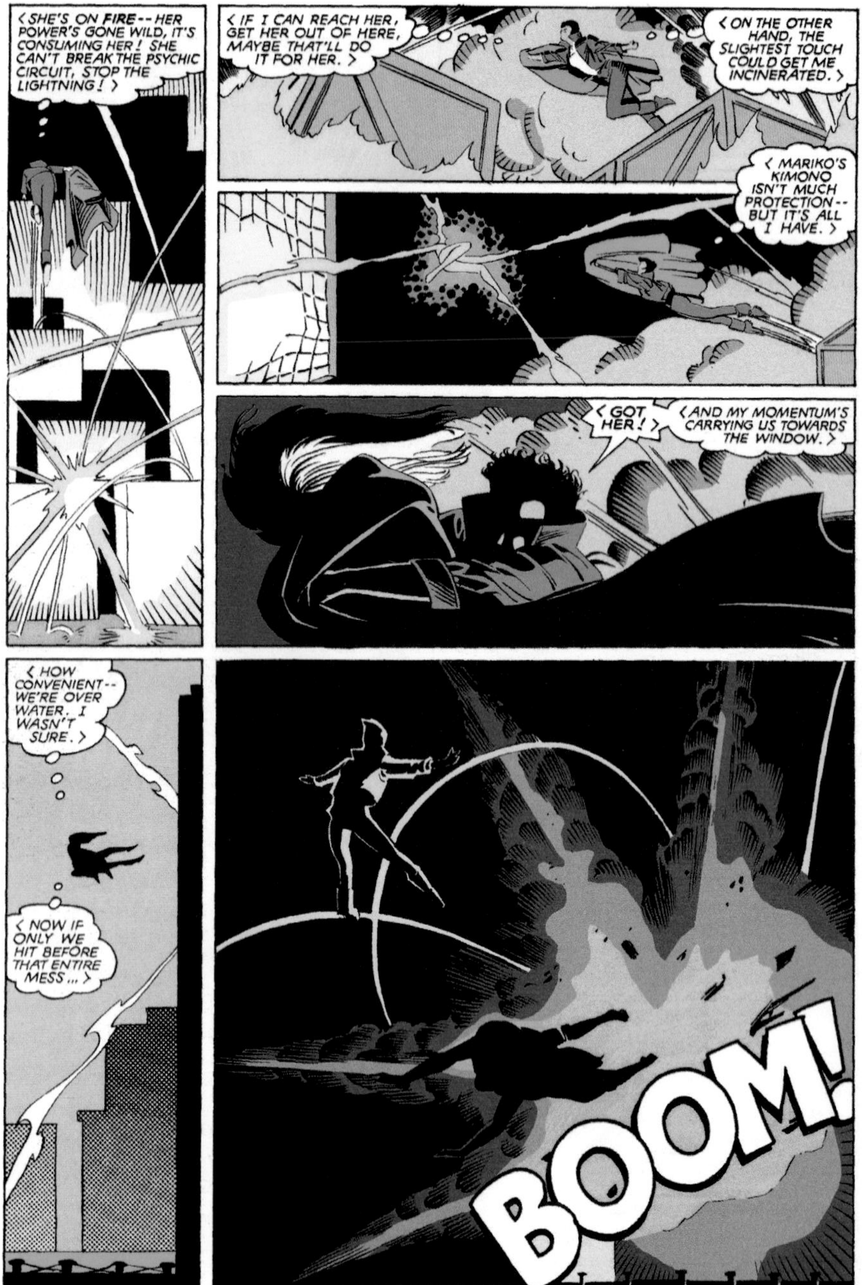

< SHE'S ON FIRE -- HER POWER'S GONE WILD, IT'S CONSUMING HER! SHE CAN'T BREAK THE PSYCHIC CIRCUIT, STOP THE LIGHTNING! >
< IF I CAN REACH HER, GET HER OUT OF HERE, MAYBE THAT'LL DO IT FOR HER. >
< ON THE OTHER HAND, THE SLIGHTEST TOUCH COULD GET ME INCINERATED. >
< MARIKO'S KIMONO ISN'T MUCH PROTECTION -- BUT IT'S ALL I HAVE. >
< GOT HER! >
< AND MY MOMENTUM'S CARRYING US TOWARDS THE WINDOW. >
< HOW CONVENIENT -- WE'RE OVER WATER. I WASN'T SURE. >
< NOW IF ONLY WE HIT BEFORE THAT ENTIRE MESS ... >
BOOM!

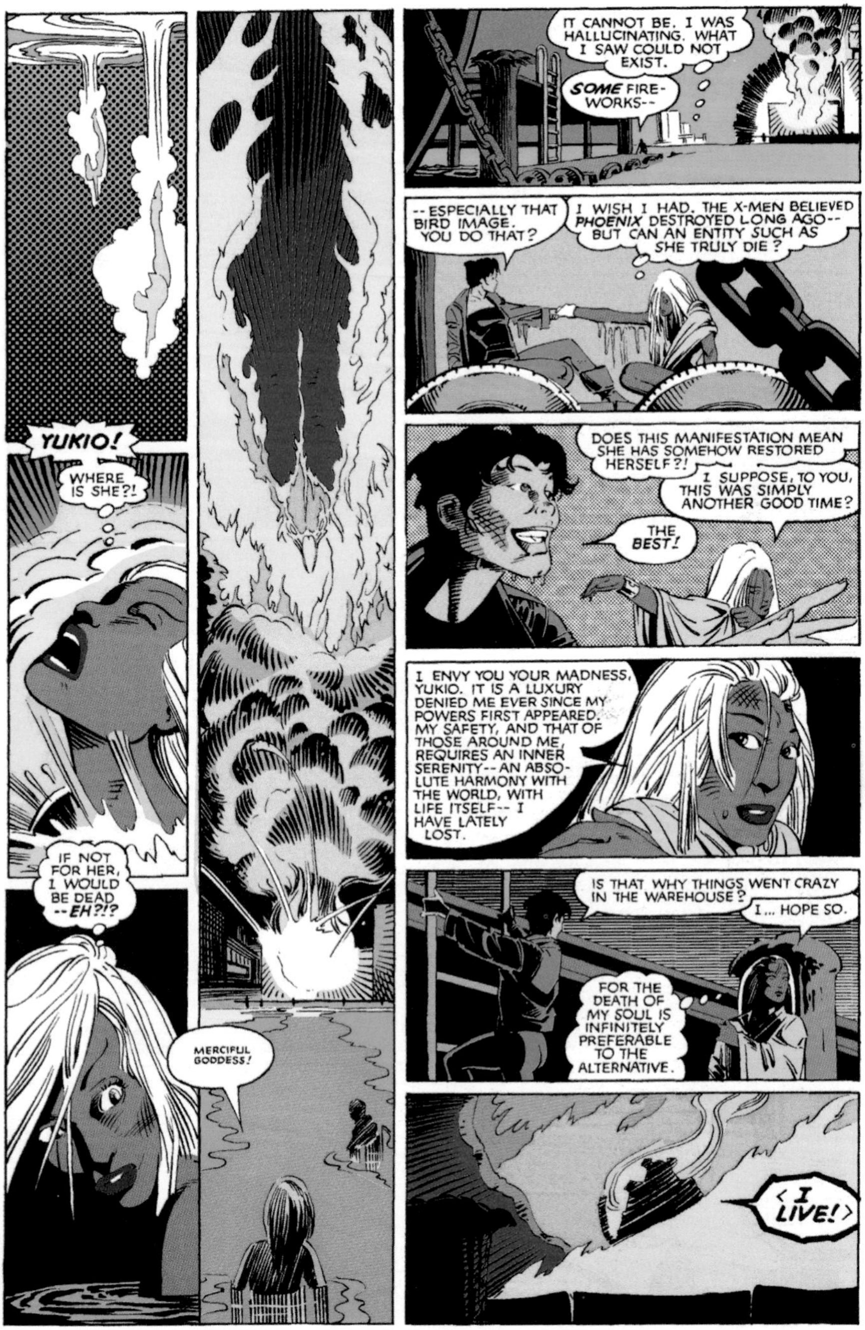

YUKIO!
WHERE IS SHE?!
IF NOT FOR HER, I WOULD BE DEAD --EH?!?
MERCIFUL GODDESS!
IT CANNOT BE. I WAS HALLUCINATING. WHAT I SAW COULD NOT EXIST.
SOME FIRE-WORKS--
-- ESPECIALLY THAT BIRD IMAGE. YOU DO THAT?
I WISH I HAD. THE X-MEN BELIEVED PHOENIX DESTROYED LONG AGO-- BUT CAN AN ENTITY SUCH AS SHE TRULY DIE?
DOES THIS MANIFESTATION MEAN SHE HAS SOMEHOW RESTORED HERSELF?!
I SUPPOSE, TO YOU, THIS WAS SIMPLY ANOTHER GOOD TIME?
THE BEST!
I ENVY YOU YOUR MADNESS, YUKIO. IT IS A LUXURY DENIED ME EVER SINCE MY POWERS FIRST APPEARED. MY SAFETY, AND THAT OF THOSE AROUND ME, REQUIRES AN INNER SERENITY-- AN ABSOLUTE HARMONY WITH THE WORLD, WITH LIFE ITSELF-- I HAVE LATELY LOST.
IS THAT WHY THINGS WENT CRAZY IN THE WAREHOUSE?
I... HOPE SO.
FOR THE DEATH OF MY SOUL IS INFINITELY PREFERABLE TO THE ALTERNATIVE.
<I LIVE!>

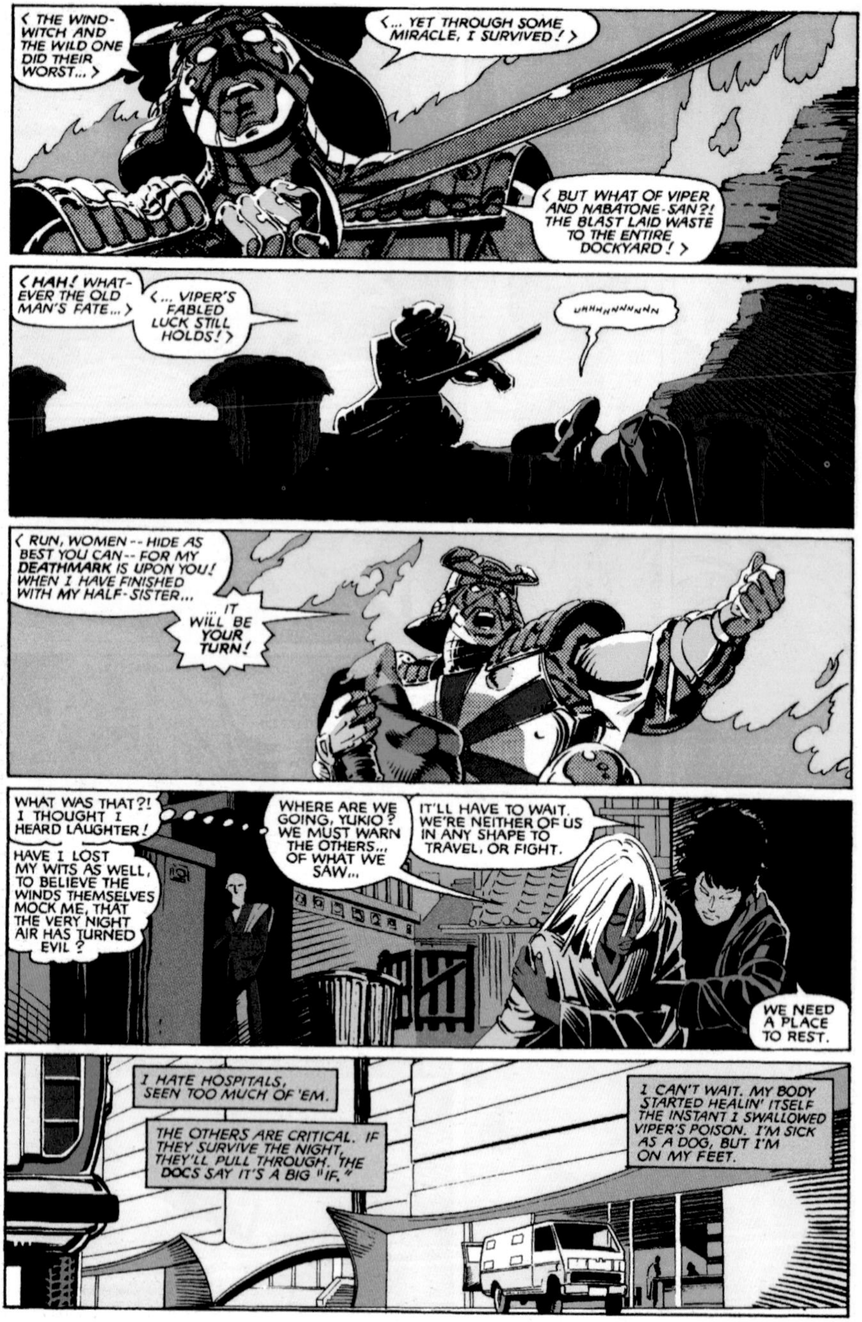

< THE WIND-WITCH AND THE WILD ONE DID THEIR WORST... >
<... YET THROUGH SOME MIRACLE, I SURVIVED! >
< BUT WHAT OF VIPER AND NABATONE-SAN?! THE BLAST LAID WASTE TO THE ENTIRE DOCKYARD! >
< HAH! WHATEVER THE OLD MAN'S FATE... >
<... VIPER'S FABLED LUCK STILL HOLDS! >
UHHHHNNNNNN
< RUN, WOMEN -- HIDE AS BEST YOU CAN -- FOR MY DEATHMARK IS UPON YOU! WHEN I HAVE FINISHED WITH MY HALF-SISTER...
... IT WILL BE YOUR TURN! >
WHAT WAS THAT?! I THOUGHT I HEARD LAUGHTER!
HAVE I LOST MY WITS AS WELL, TO BELIEVE THE WINDS THEMSELVES MOCK ME, THAT THE VERY NIGHT AIR HAS TURNED EVIL?
WHERE ARE WE GOING, YUKIO? WE MUST WARN THE OTHERS... OF WHAT WE SAW...
IT'LL HAVE TO WAIT. WE'RE NEITHER OF US IN ANY SHAPE TO TRAVEL, OR FIGHT.
WE NEED A PLACE TO REST.
I HATE HOSPITALS, SEEN TOO MUCH OF 'EM.
THE OTHERS ARE CRITICAL. IF THEY SURVIVE THE NIGHT, THEY'LL PULL THROUGH. THE DOCS SAY IT'S A BIG "IF."
I CAN'T WAIT. MY BODY STARTED HEALIN' ITSELF THE INSTANT I SWALLOWED VIPER'S POISON. I'M SICK AS A DOG, BUT I'M ON MY FEET.

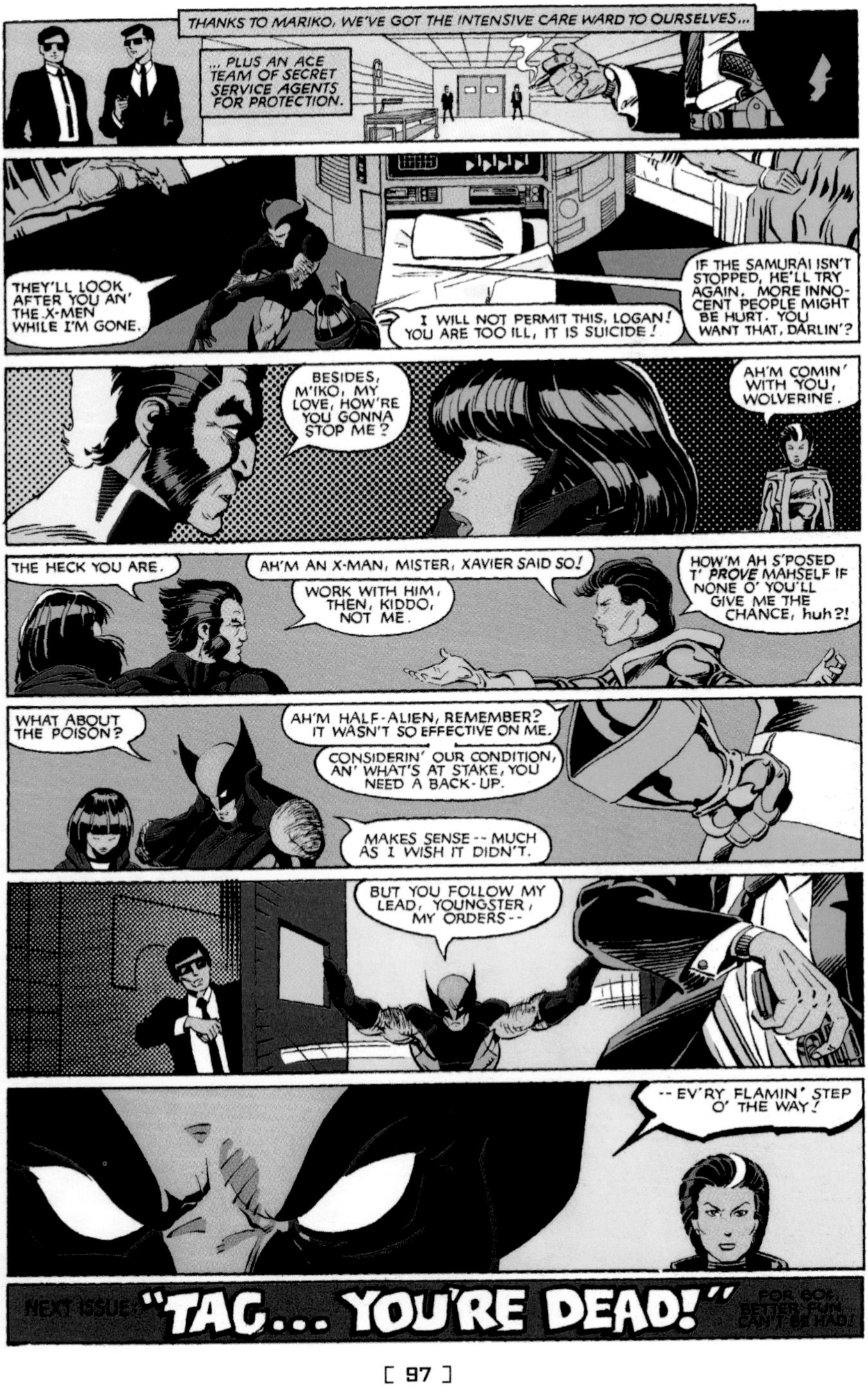
THANKS TO MARIKO, WE'VE GOT THE INTENSIVE CARE WARD TO OURSELVES...
...PLUS AN ACE TEAM OF SECRET SERVICE AGENTS FOR PROTECTION.
THEY'LL LOOK AFTER YOU AN' THE X-MEN WHILE I'M GONE.
I WILL NOT PERMIT THIS, LOGAN! YOU ARE TOO ILL, IT IS SUICIDE!
IF THE SAMURAI ISN'T STOPPED, HE'LL TRY AGAIN. MORE INNOCENT PEOPLE MIGHT BE HURT. YOU WANT THAT, DARLIN'?
BESIDES, M'IKO, MY LOVE, HOW'RE YOU GONNA STOP ME?
AH'M COMIN' WITH YOU, WOLVERINE.
THE HECK YOU ARE.
AH'M AN X-MAN, MISTER, XAVIER SAID SO!
WORK WITH HIM, THEN, KIDDO, NOT ME.
HOW'M AH S'POSED T' PROVE MAHSELF IF NONE O' YOU'LL GIVE ME THE CHANCE, huh?!
WHAT ABOUT THE POISON?
AH'M HALF-ALIEN, REMEMBER? IT WASN'T SO EFFECTIVE ON ME.
CONSIDERIN' OUR CONDITION, AN' WHAT'S AT STAKE, YOU NEED A BACK-UP.
MAKES SENSE -- MUCH AS I WISH IT DIDN'T.
BUT YOU FOLLOW MY LEAD, YOUNGSTER, MY ORDERS --
-- EV'RY FLAMIN' STEP O' THE WAY!
NEXT ISSUE: "TAG... YOU'RE DEAD!"
FOR 60¢, BETTER FUN CAN'T BE HAD!

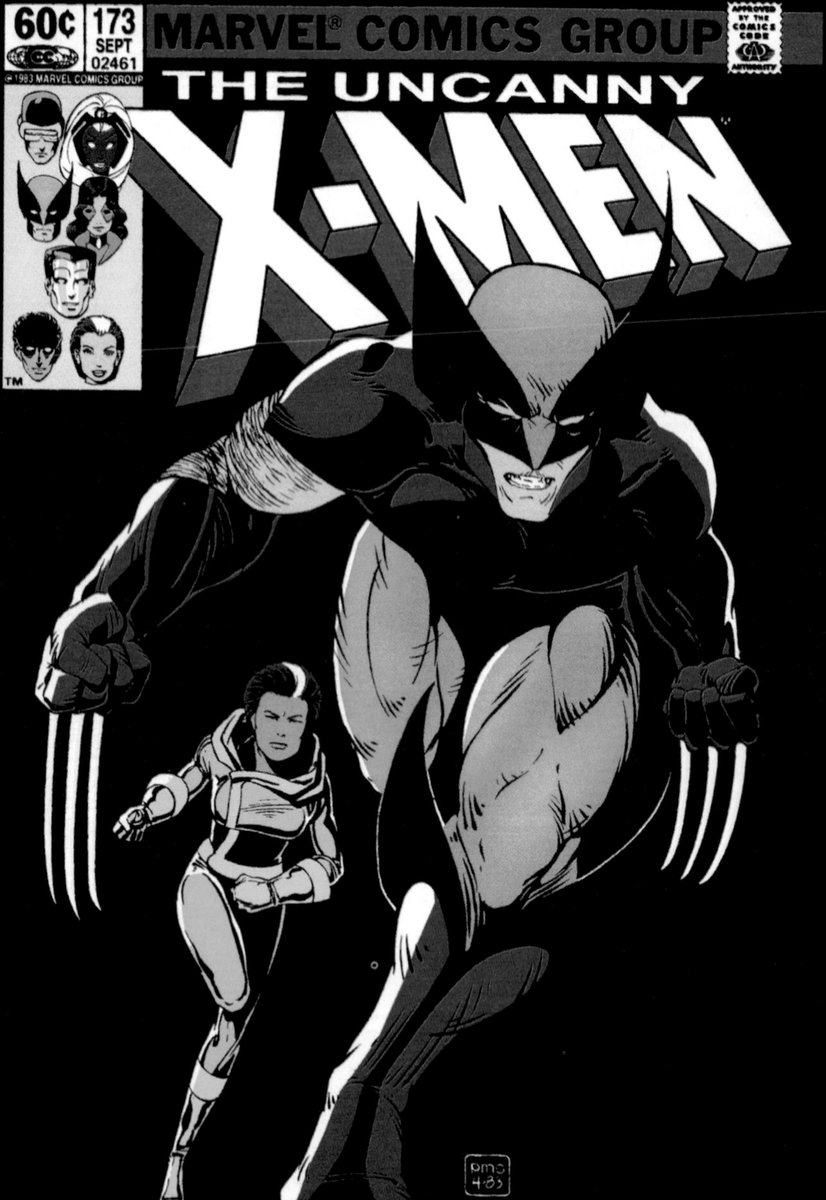
60¢
173
SEPT
02461
© 1983 MARVEL COMICS GROUP
MARVEL® COMICS GROUP
APPROVED BY THE COMICS CODE AUTHORITY
THE UNCANNY
X-MEN
TM
pmc
4-83

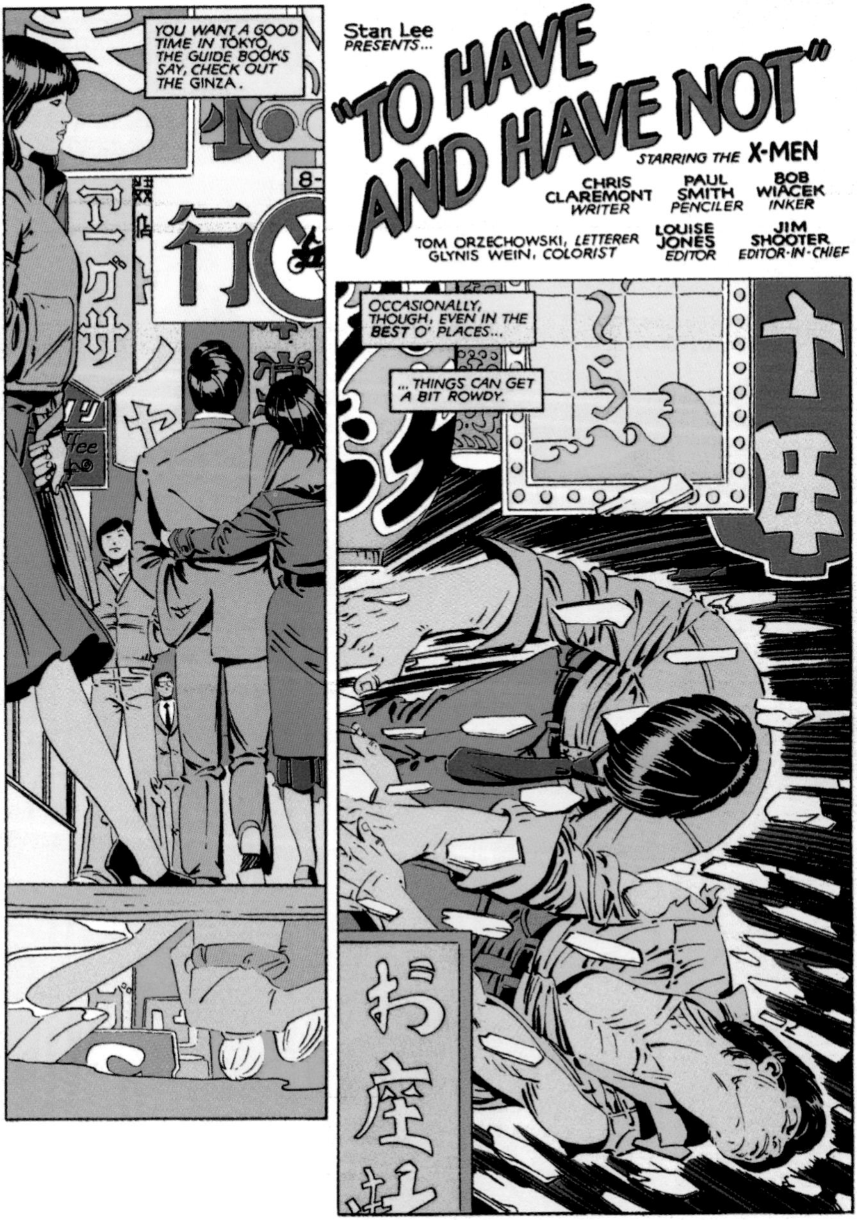
YOU WANT A GOOD TIME IN TOKYO, THE GUIDE BOOKS SAY, CHECK OUT THE GINZA.
Stan Lee PRESENTS...
"TO HAVE AND HAVE NOT"
STARRING THE X-MEN
CHRIS CLAREMONT WRITER
PAUL SMITH PENCILER
BOB WIACEK INKER
TOM ORZECHOWSKI, LETTERER
GLYNIS WEIN, COLORIST
LOUISE JONES EDITOR
JIM SHOOTER EDITOR-IN-CHIEF
OCCASIONALLY, THOUGH, EVEN IN THE BEST O' PLACES...
...THINGS CAN GET A BIT ROWDY.

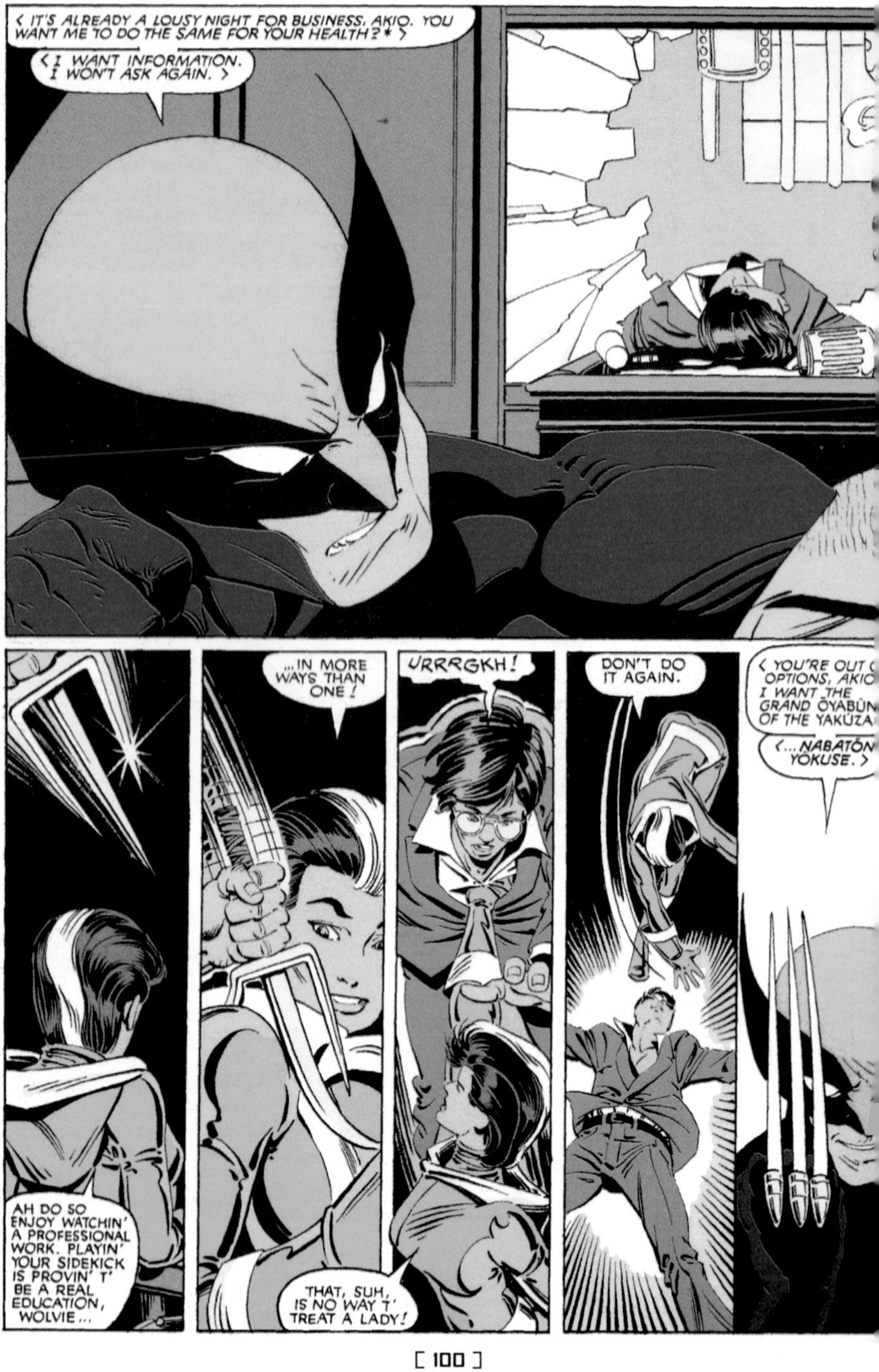

< IT'S ALREADY A LOUSY NIGHT FOR BUSINESS, AKIO. YOU WANT ME TO DO THE SAME FOR YOUR HEALTH? * >
< I WANT INFORMATION. I WON'T ASK AGAIN. >
AH DO SO ENJOY WATCHIN' A PROFESSIONAL WORK. PLAYIN' YOUR SIDEKICK IS PROVIN' T' BE A REAL EDUCATION, WOLVIE...
...IN MORE WAYS THAN ONE!
THAT, SUH, IS NO WAY T' TREAT A LADY!
URRRGKH!
DON'T DO IT AGAIN.
< YOU'RE OUT OF OPTIONS, AKIO. I WANT THE GRAND ŌYABŪN OF THE YAKŪZA
< ...NABATŌN YŌKUSE. >

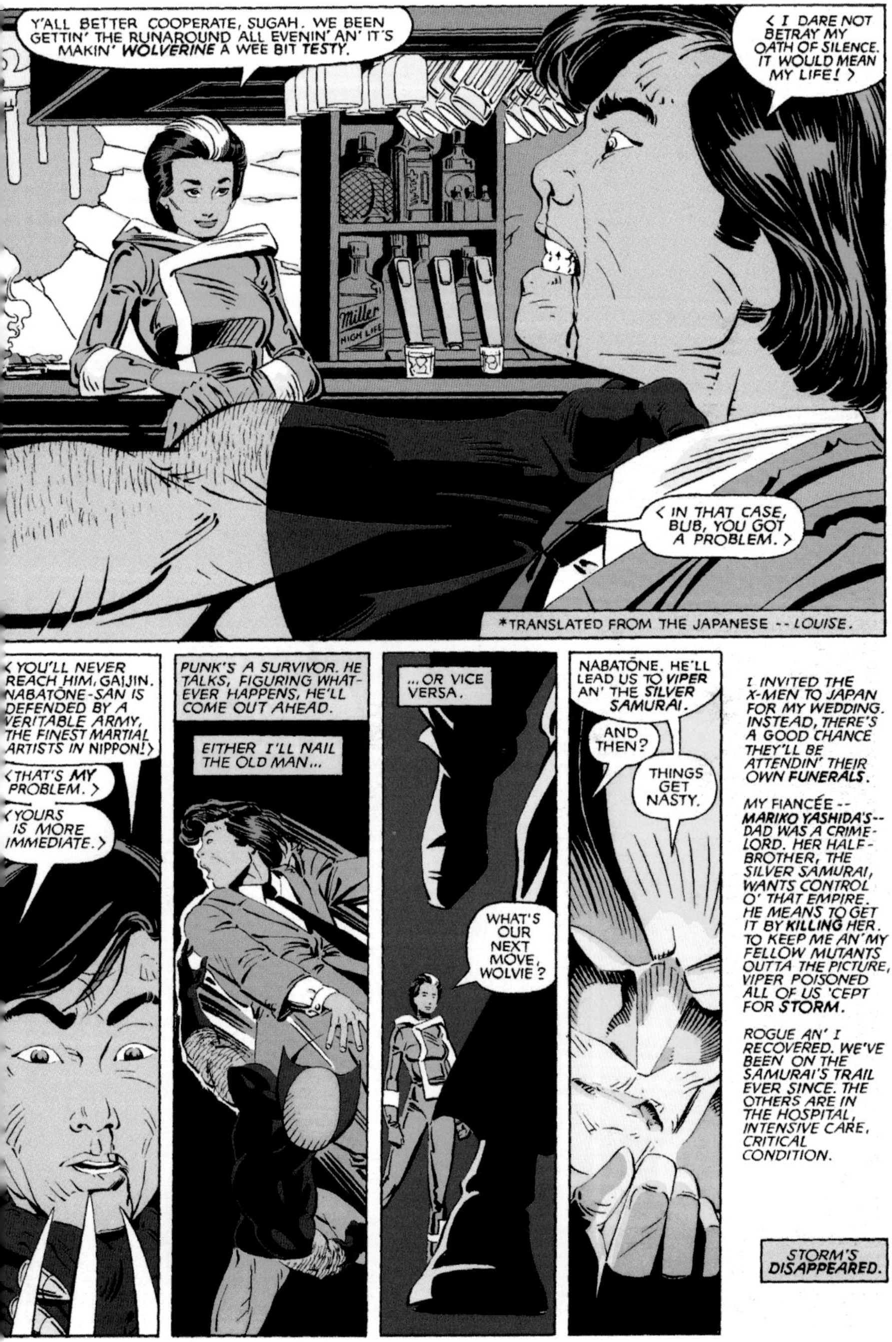

Y'ALL BETTER COOPERATE, SUGAH. WE BEEN GETTIN' THE RUNAROUND ALL EVENIN' AN' IT'S MAKIN' WOLVERINE A WEE BIT TESTY.
< I DARE NOT BETRAY MY OATH OF SILENCE. IT WOULD MEAN MY LIFE! >
< IN THAT CASE, BUB, YOU GOT A PROBLEM. >
*TRANSLATED FROM THE JAPANESE -- LOUISE.
< YOU'LL NEVER REACH HIM, GAIJIN. NABATŌNE-SAN IS DEFENDED BY A VERITABLE ARMY, THE FINEST MARTIAL ARTISTS IN NIPPON! >
< THAT'S MY PROBLEM. >
< YOURS IS MORE IMMEDIATE. >
PUNK'S A SURVIVOR. HE TALKS, FIGURING WHATEVER HAPPENS, HE'LL COME OUT AHEAD.
EITHER I'LL NAIL THE OLD MAN...
...OR VICE VERSA.
WHAT'S OUR NEXT MOVE, WOLVIE?
NABATŌNE. HE'LL LEAD US TO VIPER AN' THE SILVER SAMURAI.
AND THEN?
THINGS GET NASTY.
I INVITED THE X-MEN TO JAPAN FOR MY WEDDING. INSTEAD, THERE'S A GOOD CHANCE THEY'LL BE ATTENDIN' THEIR OWN FUNERALS.
MY FIANCÉE -- MARIKO YASHIDA'S -- DAD WAS A CRIMELORD. HER HALF-BROTHER, THE SILVER SAMURAI, WANTS CONTROL O' THAT EMPIRE. HE MEANS TO GET IT BY KILLING HER. TO KEEP ME AN' MY FELLOW MUTANTS OUTTA THE PICTURE, VIPER POISONED ALL OF US 'CEPT FOR STORM.
ROGUE AN' I RECOVERED. WE'VE BEEN ON THE SAMURAI'S TRAIL EVER SINCE. THE OTHERS ARE IN THE HOSPITAL, INTENSIVE CARE, CRITICAL CONDITION.
STORM'S DISAPPEARED.

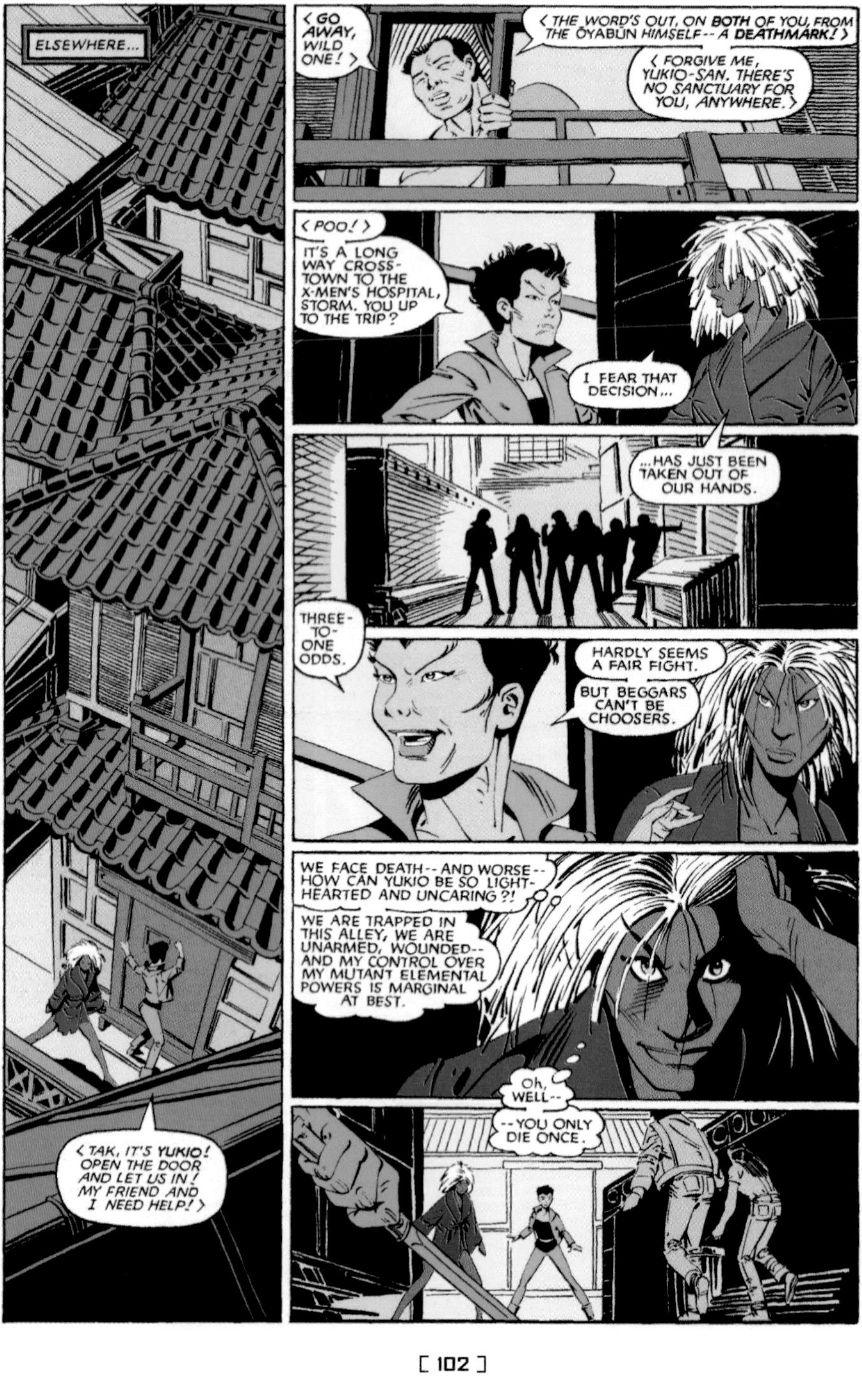

ELSEWHERE...
< TAK, IT'S YUKIO! OPEN THE DOOR AND LET US IN! MY FRIEND AND I NEED HELP! >
< GO AWAY, WILD ONE! >
< THE WORD'S OUT, ON BOTH OF YOU, FROM THE ŌYABŪN HIMSELF-- A DEATHMARK! >
< FORGIVE ME, YUKIO-SAN. THERE'S NO SANCTUARY FOR YOU, ANYWHERE. >
< POO! >
IT'S A LONG WAY CROSS-TOWN TO THE X-MEN'S HOSPITAL, STORM. YOU UP TO THE TRIP?
I FEAR THAT DECISION...
...HAS JUST BEEN TAKEN OUT OF OUR HANDS.
THREE-TO-ONE ODDS.
HARDLY SEEMS A FAIR FIGHT.
BUT BEGGARS CAN'T BE CHOOSERS.
WE FACE DEATH-- AND WORSE-- HOW CAN YUKIO BE SO LIGHT-HEARTED AND UNCARING?!
WE ARE TRAPPED IN THIS ALLEY, WE ARE UNARMED, WOUNDED-- AND MY CONTROL OVER MY MUTANT ELEMENTAL POWERS IS MARGINAL AT BEST.
Oh, WELL--
--YOU ONLY DIE ONCE.

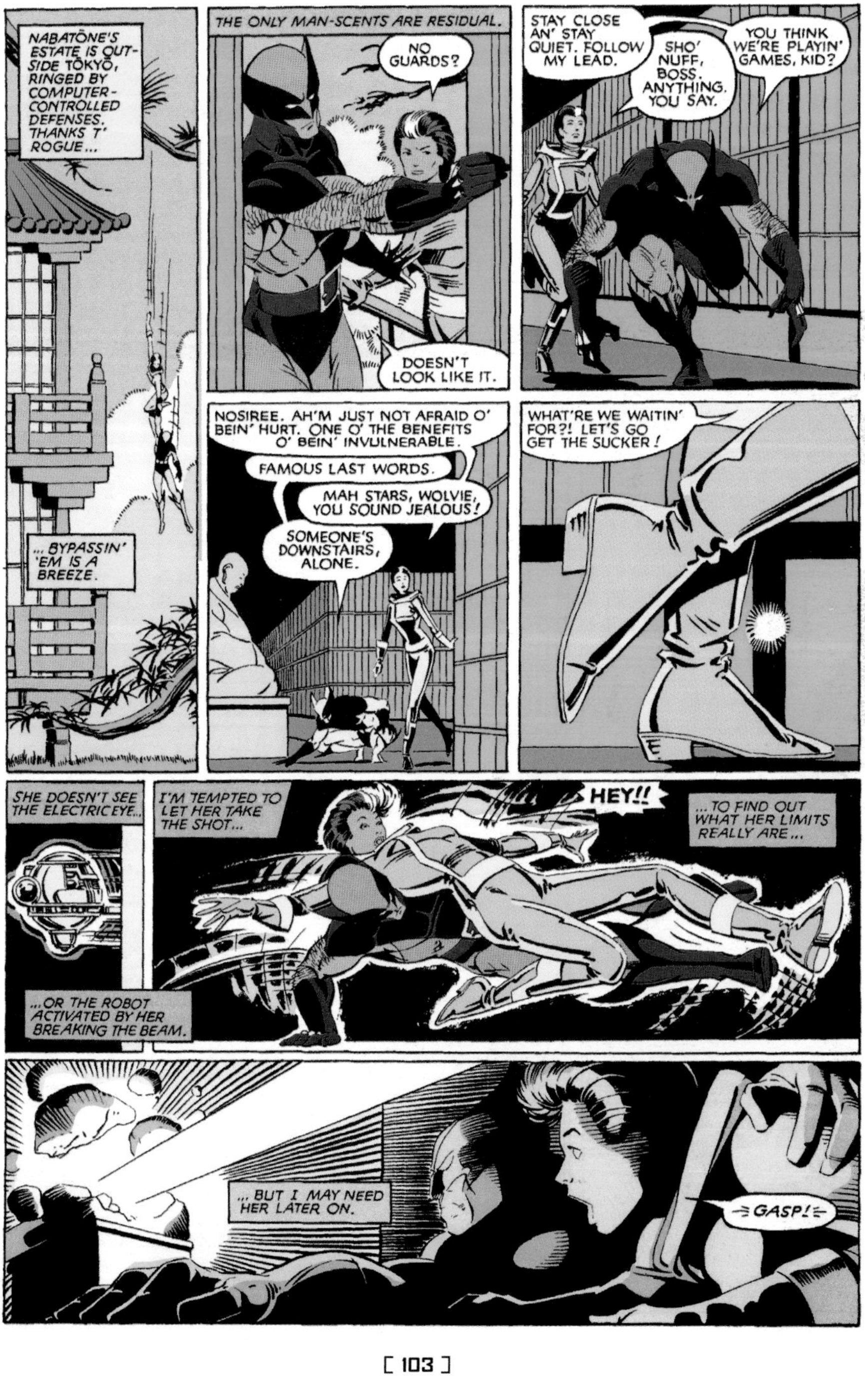

NABATŌNE'S ESTATE IS OUTSIDE TŌKYŌ, RINGED BY COMPUTER-CONTROLLED DEFENSES. THANKS T' ROGUE...
...BYPASSIN' 'EM IS A BREEZE.
THE ONLY MAN-SCENTS ARE RESIDUAL.
NO GUARDS?
DOESN'T LOOK LIKE IT.
STAY CLOSE AN' STAY QUIET. FOLLOW MY LEAD.
SHO' NUFF, BOSS. ANYTHING YOU SAY.
YOU THINK WE'RE PLAYIN' GAMES, KID?
NOSIREE. AH'M JUST NOT AFRAID O' BEIN' HURT. ONE O' THE BENEFITS O' BEIN' INVULNERABLE.
FAMOUS LAST WORDS.
MAH STARS, WOLVIE, YOU SOUND JEALOUS!
SOMEONE'S DOWNSTAIRS, ALONE.
WHAT'RE WE WAITIN' FOR?! LET'S GO GET THE SUCKER!
SHE DOESN'T SEE THE ELECTRIC EYE...
...OR THE ROBOT ACTIVATED BY HER BREAKING THE BEAM.
I'M TEMPTED TO LET HER TAKE THE SHOT...
HEY!!
...TO FIND OUT WHAT HER LIMITS REALLY ARE...
...BUT I MAY NEED HER LATER ON.
GASP!

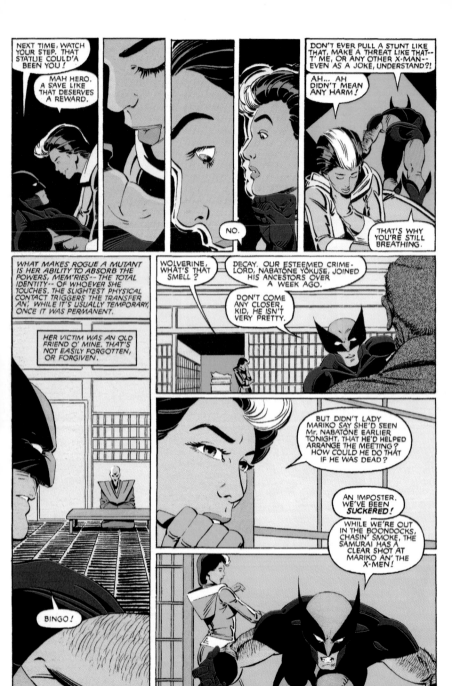

NEXT TIME, WATCH YOUR STEP. THAT STATUE COULD'A BEEN YOU!

MAH HERO. A SAVE LIKE THAT DESERVES A REWARD.

DON'T EVER PULL A STUNT LIKE THAT, MAKE A THREAT LIKE THAT-- T' ME, OR ANY OTHER X-MAN-- EVEN AS A JOKE, UNDERSTAND?!

AH... AH DIDN'T MEAN ANY HARM!

NO.

THAT'S WHY YOU'RE STILL BREATHING.

WHAT MAKES ROGUE A MUTANT IS HER ABILITY TO ABSORB THE POWERS, MEM'RIES-- THE TOTAL IDENTITY-- OF WHOEVER SHE TOUCHES. THE SLIGHTEST PHYSICAL CONTACT TRIGGERS THE TRANSFER AN; WHILE IT'S USUALLY TEMPORARY, ONCE IT WAS PERMANENT.

HER VICTIM WAS AN OLD FRIEND O' MINE. THAT'S NOT EASILY FORGOTTEN, OR FORGIVEN.

WOLVERINE, WHAT'S THAT SMELL?

DECAY. OUR ESTEEMED CRIME-LORD, NABATŌNE YŌKUSE, JOINED HIS ANCESTORS OVER A WEEK AGO.

DON'T COME ANY CLOSER, KID, HE ISN'T VERY PRETTY.

BUT DIDN'T LADY MARIKO SAY SHE'D SEEN Mr. NABATŌNE EARLIER TONIGHT, THAT HE'D HELPED ARRANGE THE MEETING? HOW COULD HE DO THAT IF HE WAS DEAD?

AN IMPOSTER. WE'VE BEEN SUCKERED!

WHILE WE'RE OUT IN THE BOONDOCKS, CHASIN' SMOKE, THE SAMURAI HAS A CLEAR SHOT AT MARIKO AN' THE X-MEN!

BINGO!

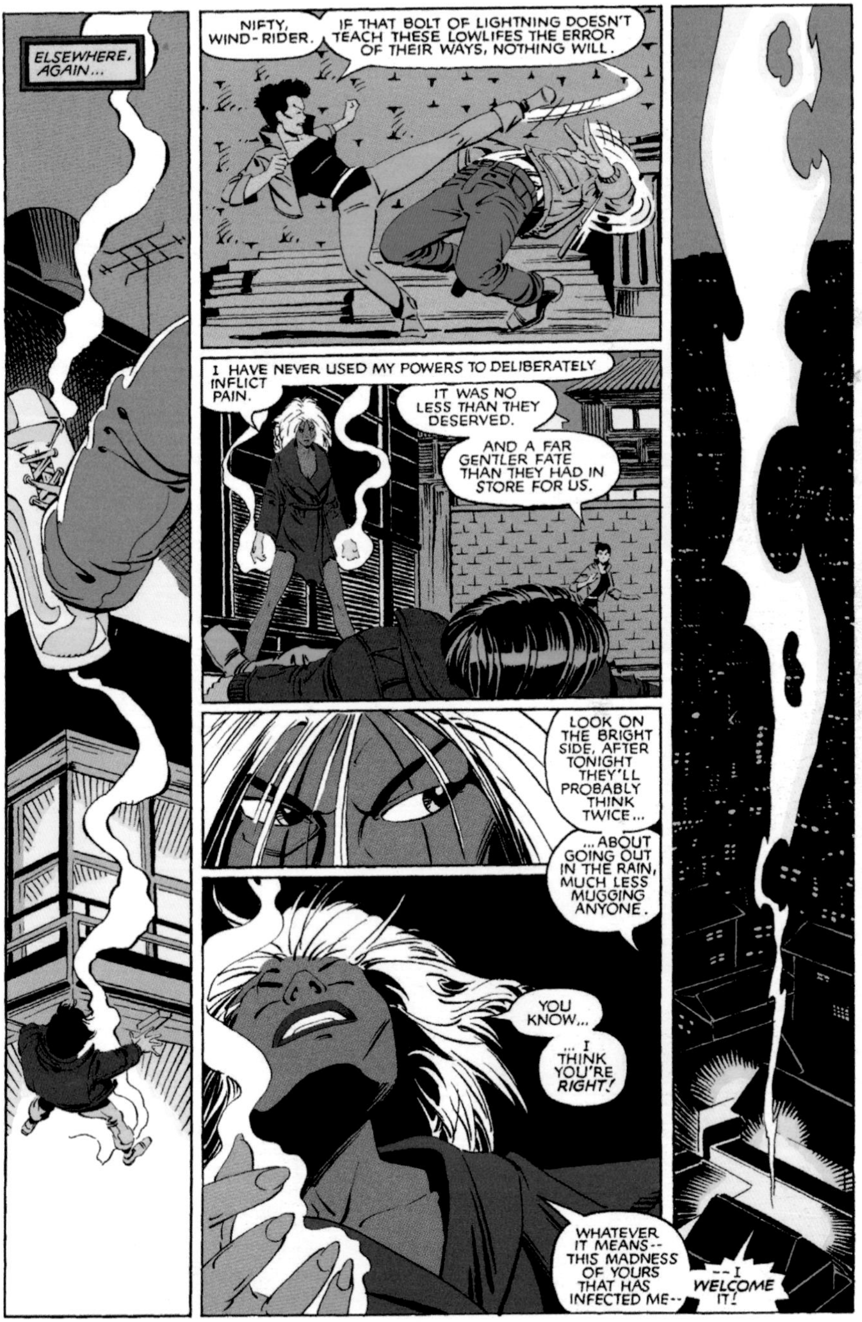
ELSEWHERE, AGAIN...
NIFTY, WIND-RIDER.
IF THAT BOLT OF LIGHTNING DOESN'T TEACH THESE LOWLIFES THE ERROR OF THEIR WAYS, NOTHING WILL.
I HAVE NEVER USED MY POWERS TO DELIBERATELY INFLICT PAIN.
IT WAS NO LESS THAN THEY DESERVED.
AND A FAR GENTLER FATE THAN THEY HAD IN STORE FOR US.
LOOK ON THE BRIGHT SIDE, AFTER TONIGHT THEY'LL PROBABLY THINK TWICE...
...ABOUT GOING OUT IN THE RAIN, MUCH LESS MUGGING ANYONE.
YOU KNOW...
...I THINK YOU'RE RIGHT!
WHATEVER IT MEANS-- THIS MADNESS OF YOURS THAT HAS INFECTED ME--
--I WELCOME IT!

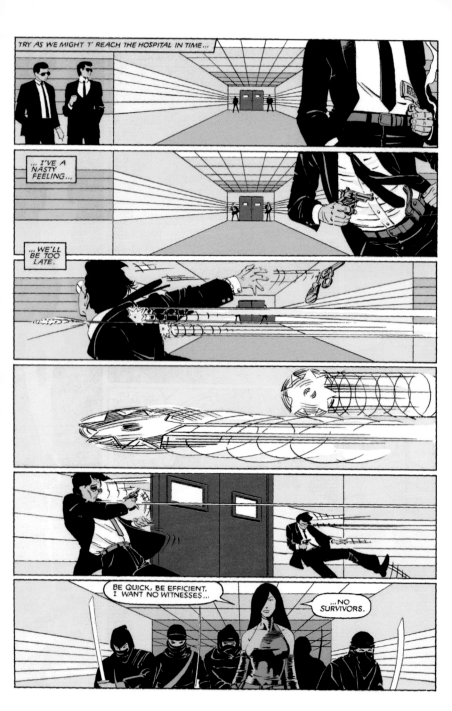

TRY AS WE MIGHT T' REACH THE HOSPITAL IN TIME...

... I'VE A NASTY FEELING...

... WE'LL BE TOO LATE.

BE QUICK, BE EFFICIENT. I WANT NO WITNESSES...

...NO SURVIVORS.

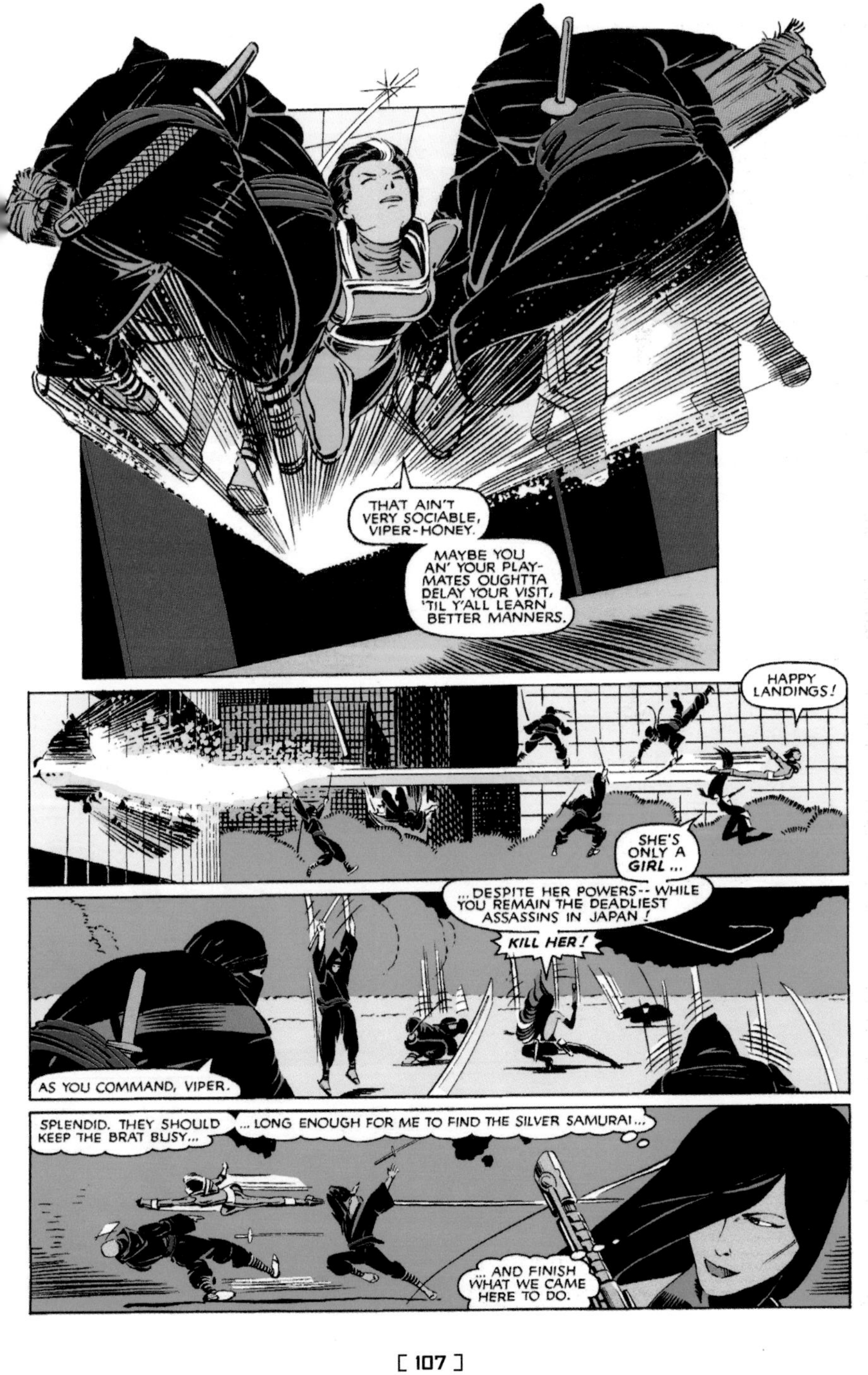
THAT AIN'T VERY SOCIABLE, VIPER-HONEY.
MAYBE YOU AN' YOUR PLAY-MATES OUGHTTA DELAY YOUR VISIT, 'TIL Y'ALL LEARN BETTER MANNERS.
HAPPY LANDINGS!
SHE'S ONLY A GIRL ...
... DESPITE HER POWERS-- WHILE YOU REMAIN THE DEADLIEST ASSASSINS IN JAPAN!
KILL HER!
AS YOU COMMAND, VIPER.
SPLENDID. THEY SHOULD KEEP THE BRAT BUSY...
... LONG ENOUGH FOR ME TO FIND THE SILVER SAMURAI...
... AND FINISH WHAT WE CAME HERE TO DO.

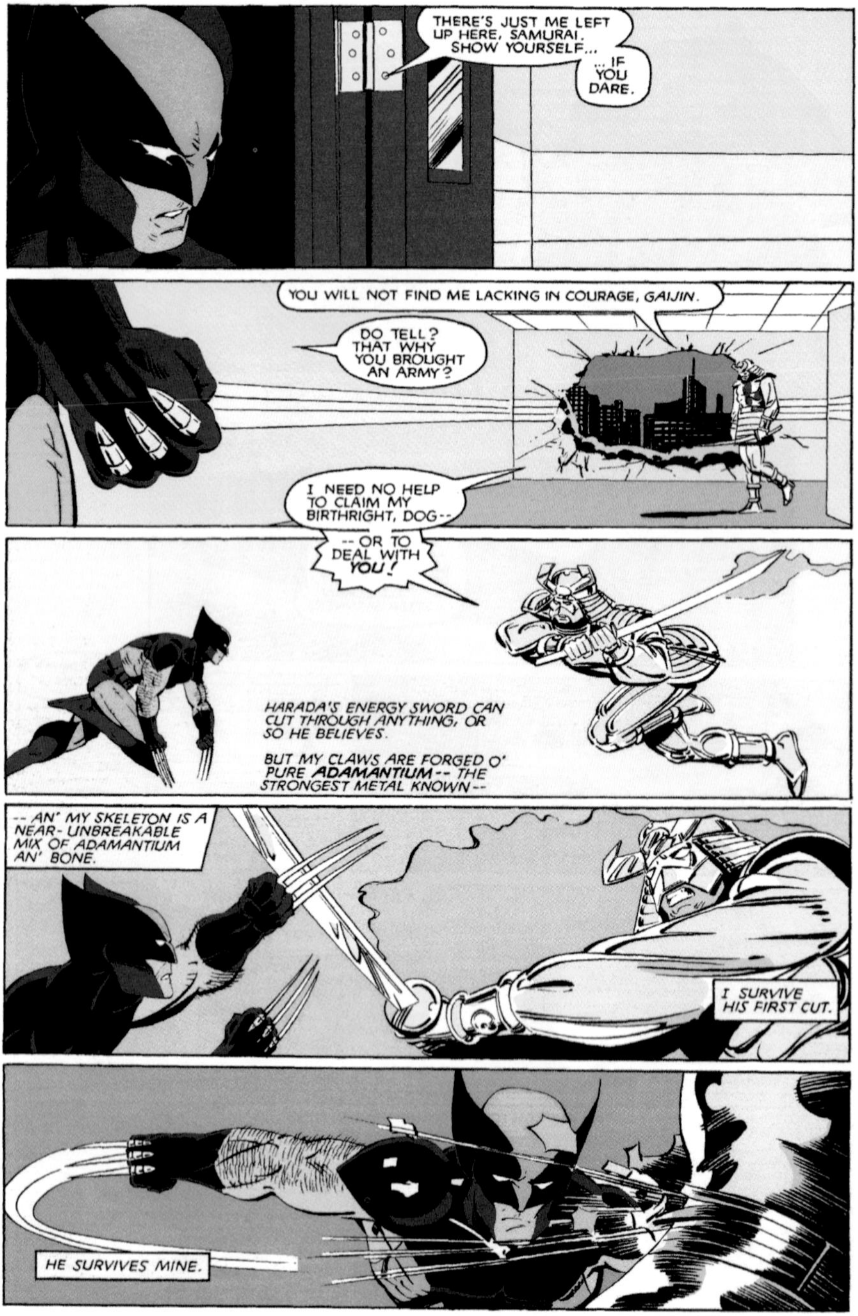

THERE'S JUST ME LEFT UP HERE, SAMURAI. SHOW YOURSELF...
... IF YOU DARE.
YOU WILL NOT FIND ME LACKING IN COURAGE, GAIJIN.
DO TELL? THAT WHY YOU BROUGHT AN ARMY?
I NEED NO HELP TO CLAIM MY BIRTHRIGHT, DOG--
-- OR TO DEAL WITH YOU!
HARADA'S ENERGY SWORD CAN CUT THROUGH ANYTHING, OR SO HE BELIEVES.
BUT MY CLAWS ARE FORGED O' PURE ADAMANTIUM -- THE STRONGEST METAL KNOWN--
-- AN' MY SKELETON IS A NEAR-UNBREAKABLE MIX OF ADAMANTIUM AN' BONE.
I SURVIVE HIS FIRST CUT.
HE SURVIVES MINE.

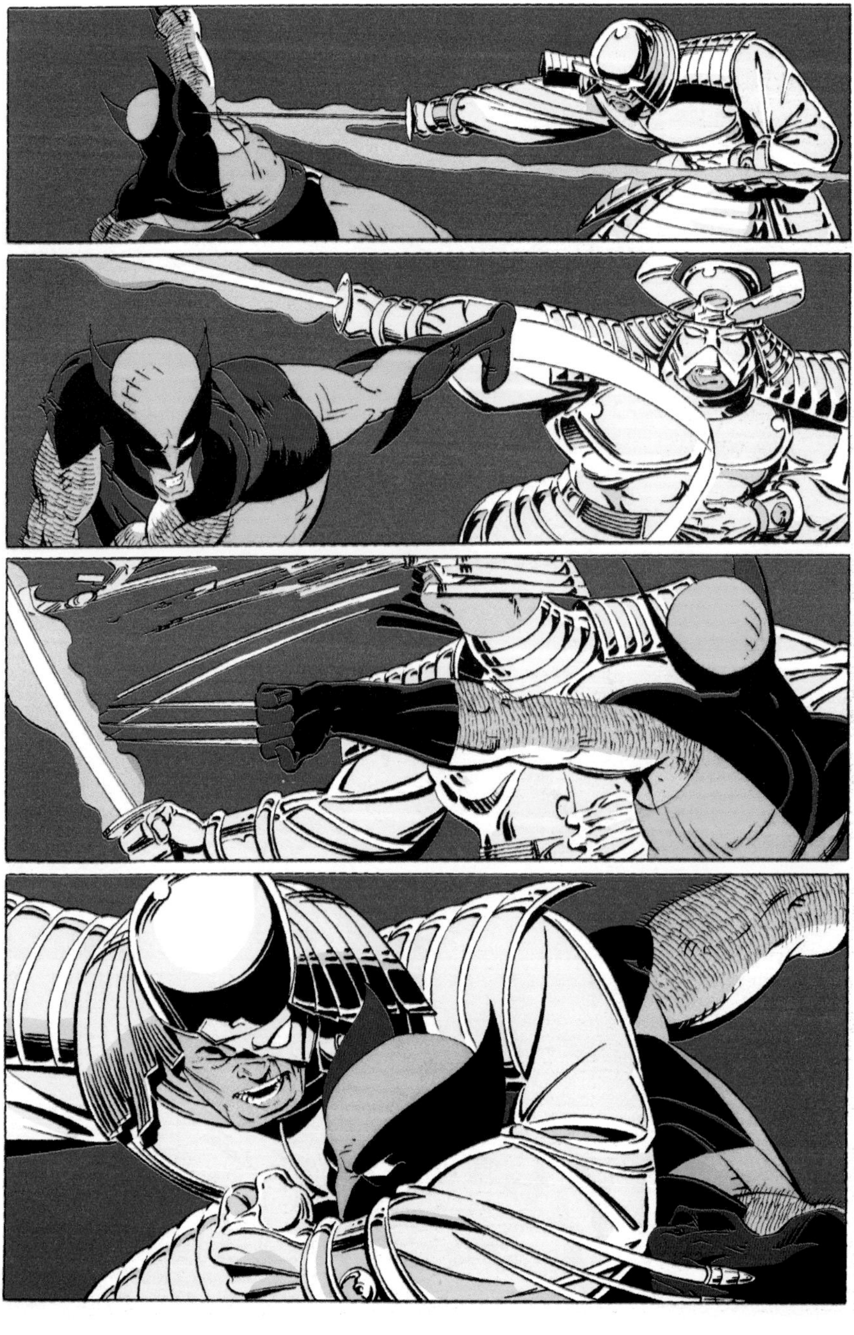

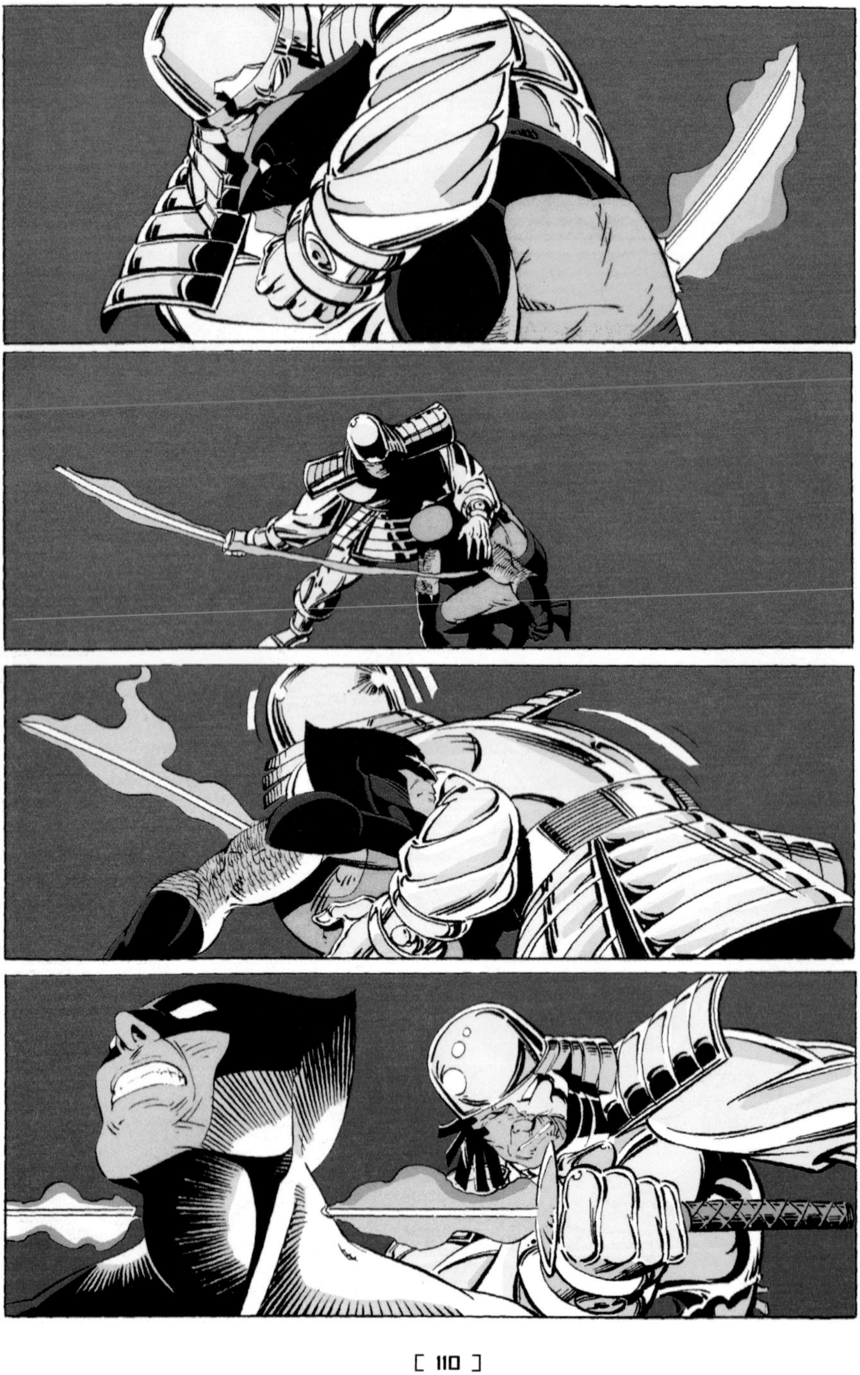

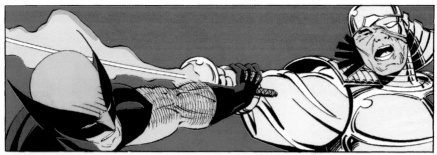

SNAP!

IIE, LOGAN-SAN-- NO!!

ENOUGH BLOOD HAS BEEN SPILLED, BELOVED. LET THIS BE AN END TO IT!

MY HALF-BROTHER HAS LOST. GRANT HIM HIS LIFE!

I DO THAT, M'IKO, THIS'LL **NEVER** BE OVER. HE'LL KEEP COMIN' BACK, 'TIL ONE OF YOU IS **DEAD!**

HAVE NO FEAR, WOLVERINE. YOUR DILEMMA IS ABOUT TO BE RESOLVED.

STAND AWAY FROM THE SAMURAI-- AND NO FALSE MOVES, OR I'LL FIRE.

SHE'LL FIRE ANYWAY, SOON AS HARADA'S CLEAR...

... BUT FOR NOW, I PLAY THINGS HER WAY. NO REAL ALTERNATIVE. IN THE SHAPE I'M IN, VIPER COULD CUT ME DOWN LONG BEFORE I REACHED HER.

INSTEAD, I EDGE MARIKO TOWARDS THE DOOR, FIGURIN' TO SHOVE HER THROUGH TO SAFETY IF VIPER GIVES ME HALF A CHANCE. THERE'S NO SIGN OR SOUND O' ROGUE. DUMB KID PROB'LY GOT OVER-CONFIDENT AGAIN AN' LET HERSELF GET NAILED.

VIPER... MISTRESS-- FORGIVE YOUR HUMBLE SERVANT...

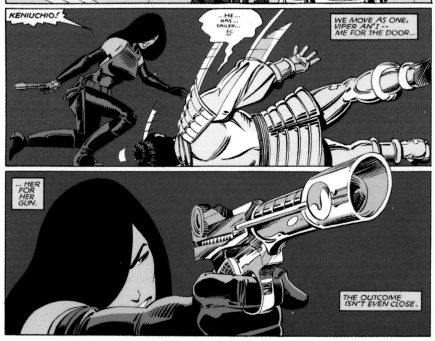

KENIUCHIO!

...HE... HAS... FAILED...

WE MOVE AS ONE, VIPER AN' I -- ME FOR THE DOOR...

... HER FOR HER GUN.

THE OUTCOME ISN'T EVEN CLOSE.

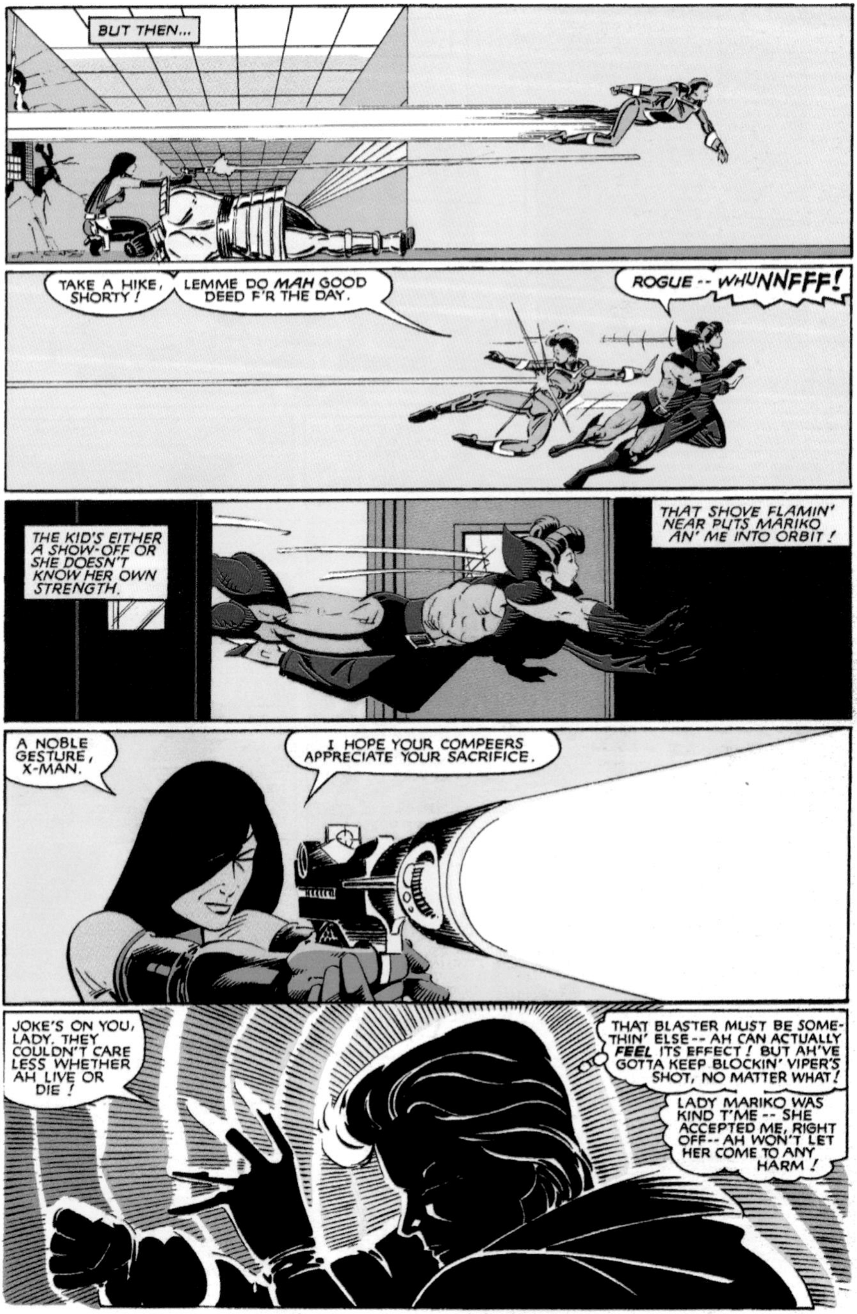
BUT THEN...
TAKE A HIKE, SHORTY!
LEMME DO MAH GOOD DEED F'R THE DAY.
ROGUE -- WHUNNFFF!
THE KID'S EITHER A SHOW-OFF OR SHE DOESN'T KNOW HER OWN STRENGTH.
THAT SHOVE FLAMIN' NEAR PUTS MARIKO AN' ME INTO ORBIT!
A NOBLE GESTURE, X-MAN.
I HOPE YOUR COMPEERS APPRECIATE YOUR SACRIFICE.
JOKE'S ON YOU, LADY. THEY COULDN'T CARE LESS WHETHER AH LIVE OR DIE!
THAT BLASTER MUST BE SOMETHIN' ELSE -- AH CAN ACTUALLY FEEL ITS EFFECT! BUT AH'VE GOTTA KEEP BLOCKIN' VIPER'S SHOT, NO MATTER WHAT!
LADY MARIKO WAS KIND T'ME -- SHE ACCEPTED ME, RIGHT OFF -- AH WON'T LET HER COME TO ANY HARM!

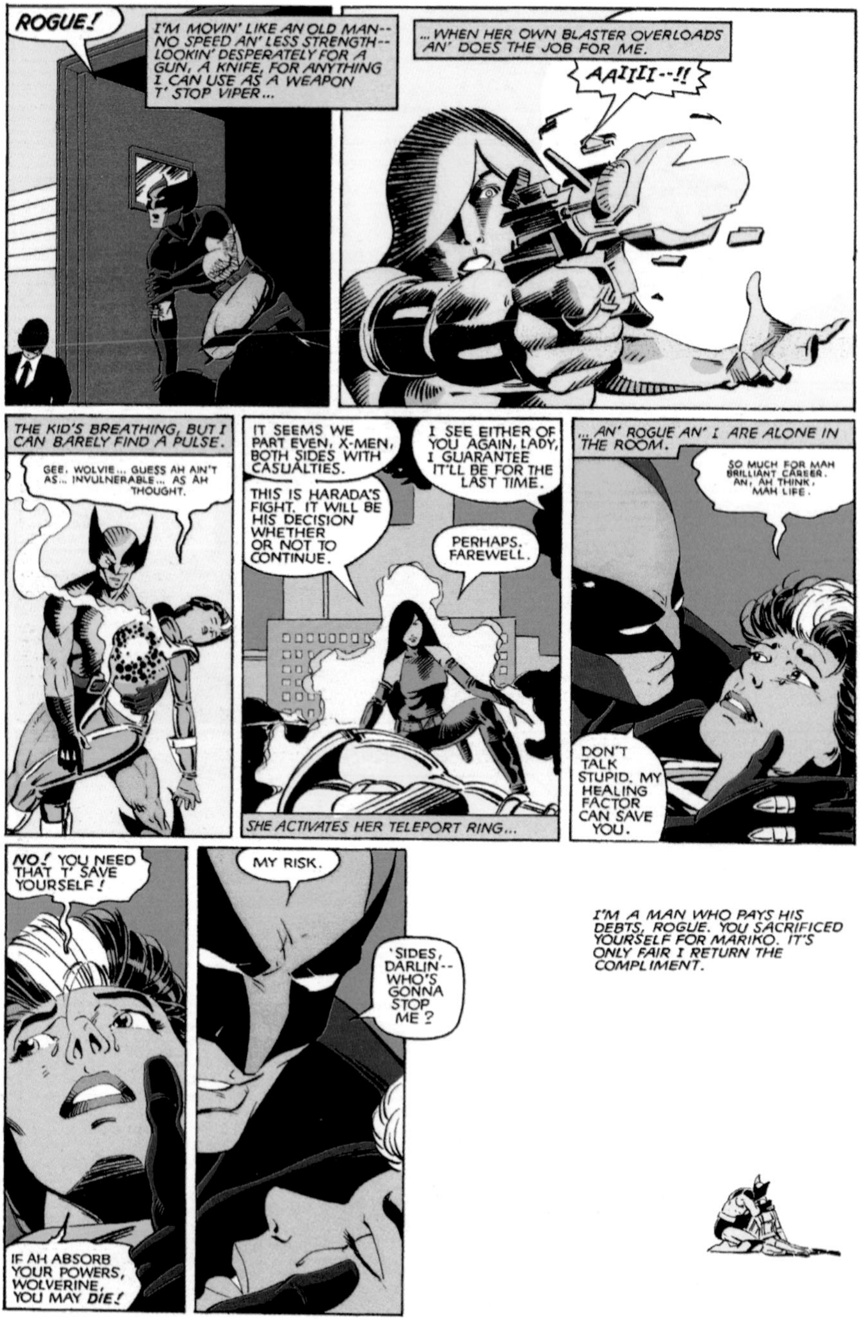

ROGUE!
I'M MOVIN' LIKE AN OLD MAN-- NO SPEED AN' LESS STRENGTH-- LOOKIN' DESPERATELY FOR A GUN, A KNIFE, FOR ANYTHING I CAN USE AS A WEAPON T' STOP VIPER...
...WHEN HER OWN BLASTER OVERLOADS AN' DOES THE JOB FOR ME.
AAIIII--!!
THE KID'S BREATHING, BUT I CAN BARELY FIND A PULSE.
GEE, WOLVIE... GUESS AH AIN'T AS... INVULNERABLE... AS AH THOUGHT.
IT SEEMS WE PART EVEN, X-MEN. BOTH SIDES WITH CASUALTIES.
THIS IS HARADA'S FIGHT. IT WILL BE HIS DECISION WHETHER OR NOT TO CONTINUE.
I SEE EITHER OF YOU AGAIN, LADY, I GUARANTEE IT'LL BE FOR THE LAST TIME.
PERHAPS. FAREWELL.
SHE ACTIVATES HER TELEPORT RING...
...AN' ROGUE AN' I ARE ALONE IN THE ROOM.
SO MUCH FOR MAH BRILLIANT CAREER. AN, AH THINK, MAH LIFE.
DON'T TALK STUPID. MY HEALING FACTOR CAN SAVE YOU.
NO! YOU NEED THAT T' SAVE YOURSELF!
IF AH ABSORB YOUR POWERS, WOLVERINE, YOU MAY DIE!
MY RISK.
'SIDES, DARLIN-- WHO'S GONNA STOP ME?
I'M A MAN WHO PAYS HIS DEBTS, ROGUE. YOU SACRIFICED YOURSELF FOR MARIKO. IT'S ONLY FAIR I RETURN THE COMPLIMENT.

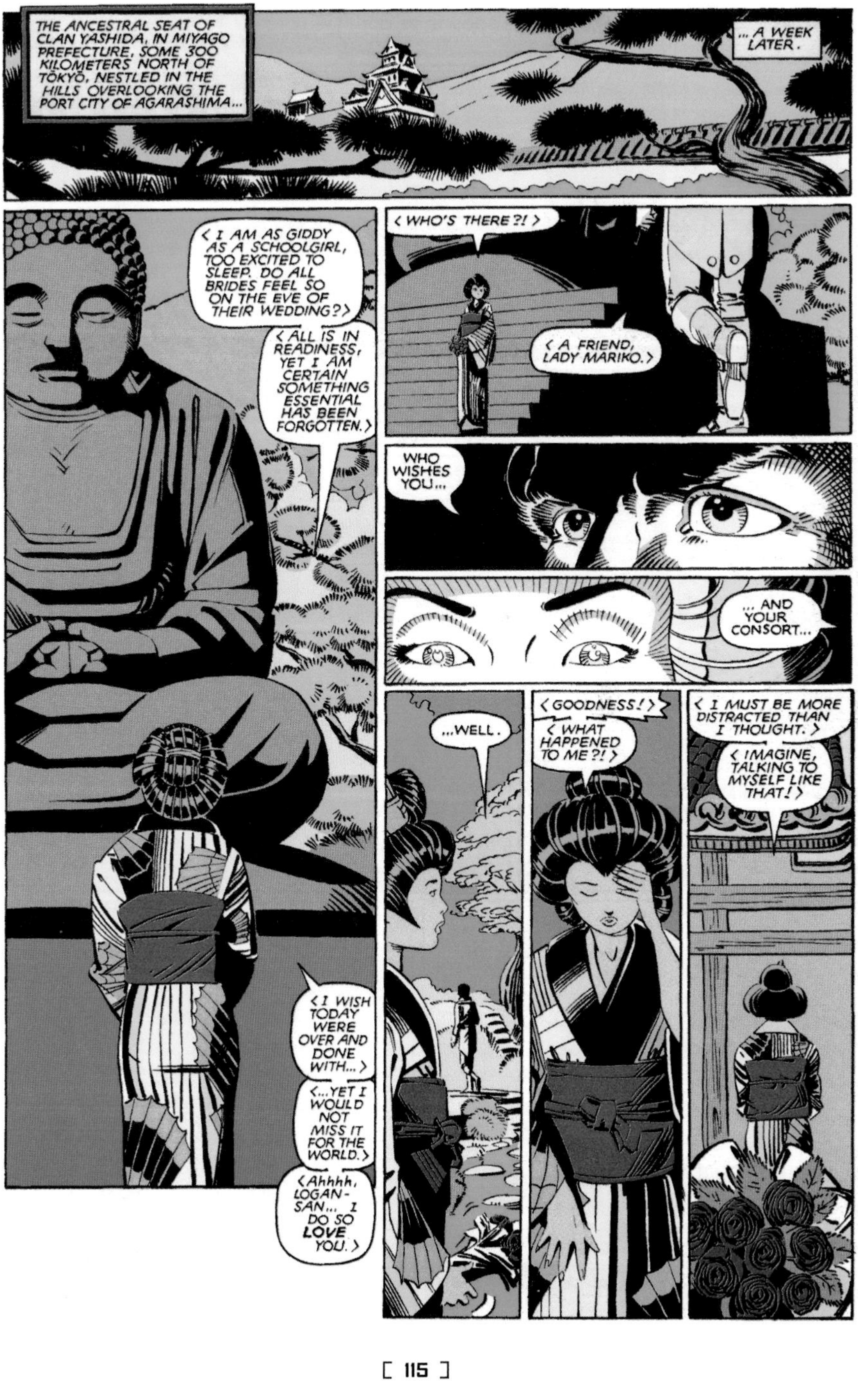
THE ANCESTRAL SEAT OF CLAN YASHIDA, IN MIYAGO PREFECTURE, SOME 300 KILOMETERS NORTH OF TŌKYŌ, NESTLED IN THE HILLS OVERLOOKING THE PORT CITY OF AGARASHIMA...
...A WEEK LATER.
< I AM AS GIDDY AS A SCHOOLGIRL, TOO EXCITED TO SLEEP. DO ALL BRIDES FEEL SO ON THE EVE OF THEIR WEDDING?>
< ALL IS IN READINESS, YET I AM CERTAIN SOMETHING ESSENTIAL HAS BEEN FORGOTTEN.>
< I WISH TODAY WERE OVER AND DONE WITH...>
<...YET I WOULD NOT MISS IT FOR THE WORLD.>
<Ahhhh, LOGAN-SAN... I DO SO LOVE YOU.>
< WHO'S THERE?! >
< A FRIEND, LADY MARIKO.>
WHO WISHES YOU...
... AND YOUR CONSORT...
...WELL.
< GOODNESS! >
< WHAT HAPPENED TO ME?! >
< I MUST BE MORE DISTRACTED THAN I THOUGHT. >
< IMAGINE, TALKING TO MYSELF LIKE THAT! >

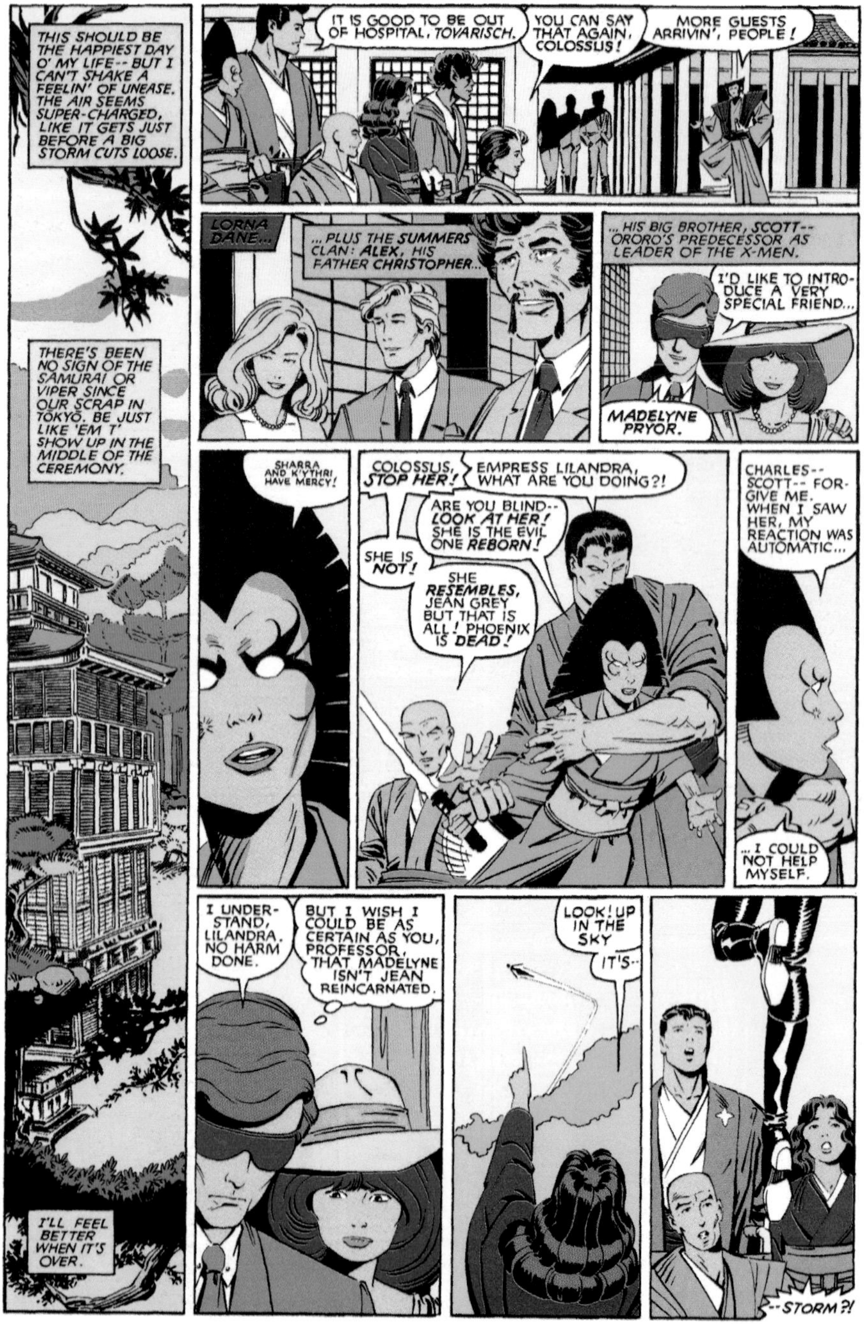
THIS SHOULD BE THE HAPPIEST DAY O' MY LIFE-- BUT I CAN'T SHAKE A FEELIN' OF UNEASE. THE AIR SEEMS SUPER-CHARGED, LIKE IT GETS JUST BEFORE A BIG STORM CUTS LOOSE.
IT IS GOOD TO BE OUT OF HOSPITAL, TOVARISCH.
YOU CAN SAY THAT AGAIN, COLOSSUS!
MORE GUESTS ARRIVIN', PEOPLE!
LORNA DANE...
...PLUS THE SUMMERS CLAN: ALEX, HIS FATHER CHRISTOPHER...
...HIS BIG BROTHER, SCOTT-- ORORO'S PREDECESSOR AS LEADER OF THE X-MEN.
I'D LIKE TO INTRODUCE A VERY SPECIAL FRIEND...
MADELYNE PRYOR.
THERE'S BEEN NO SIGN OF THE SAMURAI OR VIPER SINCE OUR SCRAP IN TŌKYŌ. BE JUST LIKE 'EM T' SHOW UP IN THE MIDDLE OF THE CEREMONY.
SHARRA AND K'YTHRI HAVE MERCY!
COLOSSUS, STOP HER!
EMPRESS LILANDRA, WHAT ARE YOU DOING?!
ARE YOU BLIND-- LOOK AT HER! SHE IS THE EVIL ONE REBORN!
SHE IS NOT!
SHE RESEMBLES, JEAN GREY BUT THAT IS ALL! PHOENIX IS DEAD!
CHARLES-- SCOTT-- FORGIVE ME. WHEN I SAW HER, MY REACTION WAS AUTOMATIC...
...I COULD NOT HELP MYSELF.
I UNDERSTAND, LILANDRA. NO HARM DONE.
BUT I WISH I COULD BE AS CERTAIN AS YOU, PROFESSOR, THAT MADELYNE ISN'T JEAN REINCARNATED.
LOOK! UP IN THE SKY
IT'S--
--STORM?!
I'LL FEEL BETTER WHEN IT'S OVER.

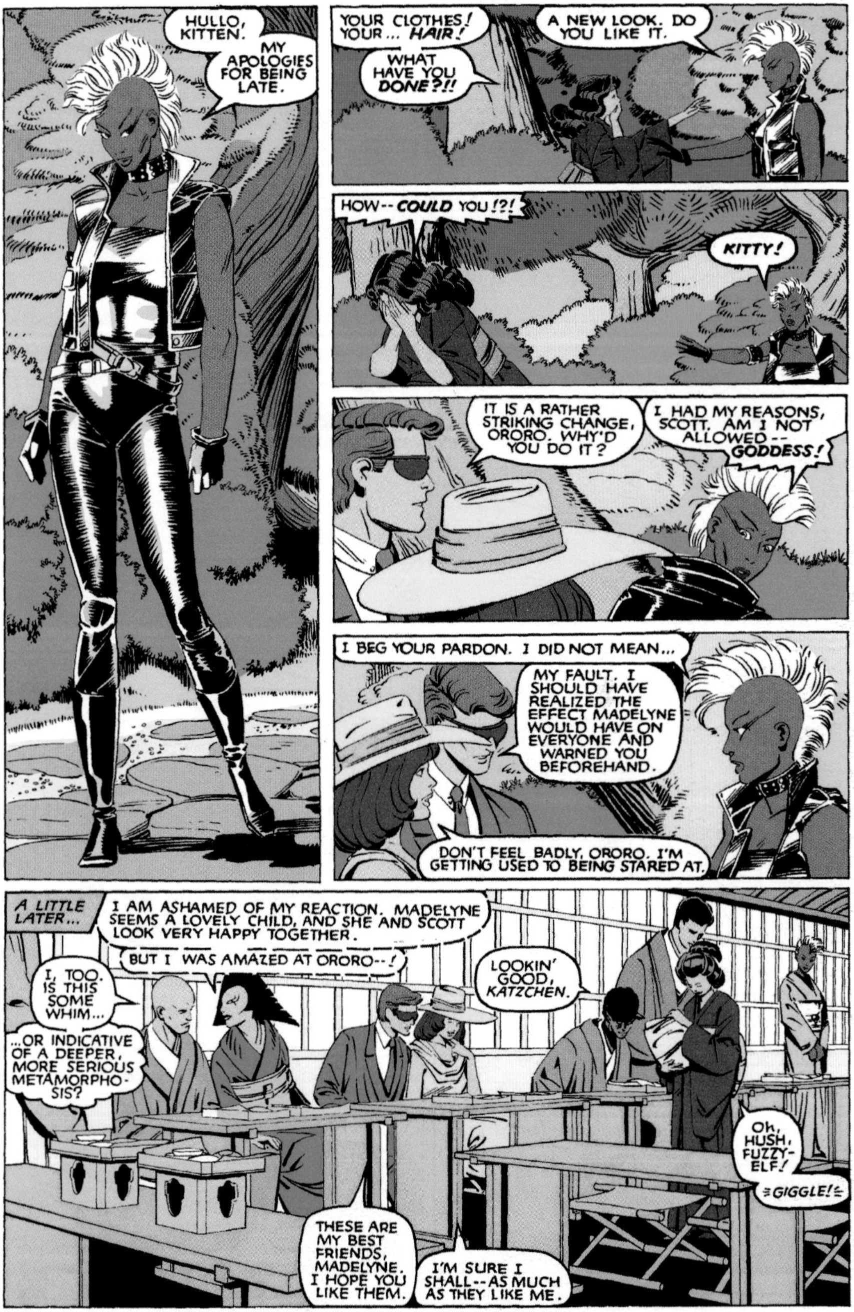
HULLO, KITTEN.
MY APOLOGIES FOR BEING LATE.
YOUR CLOTHES! YOUR... HAIR!
WHAT HAVE YOU DONE?!!
A NEW LOOK. DO YOU LIKE IT.
HOW--COULD YOU!?!
KITTY!
IT IS A RATHER STRIKING CHANGE, ORORO. WHY'D YOU DO IT?
I HAD MY REASONS, SCOTT. AM I NOT ALLOWED--
GODDESS!
I BEG YOUR PARDON. I DID NOT MEAN...
MY FAULT. I SHOULD HAVE REALIZED THE EFFECT MADELYNE WOULD HAVE ON EVERYONE AND WARNED YOU BEFOREHAND.
DON'T FEEL BADLY, ORORO. I'M GETTING USED TO BEING STARED AT.
A LITTLE LATER...
I AM ASHAMED OF MY REACTION. MADELYNE SEEMS A LOVELY CHILD, AND SHE AND SCOTT LOOK VERY HAPPY TOGETHER.
BUT I WAS AMAZED AT ORORO--!
I, TOO. IS THIS SOME WHIM...
...OR INDICATIVE OF A DEEPER, MORE SERIOUS METAMORPHOSIS?
LOOKIN' GOOD, KATZCHEN.
Oh, HUSH, FUZZY-ELF!
GIGGLE!
THESE ARE MY BEST FRIENDS, MADELYNE. I HOPE YOU LIKE THEM.
I'M SURE I SHALL--AS MUCH AS THEY LIKE ME.

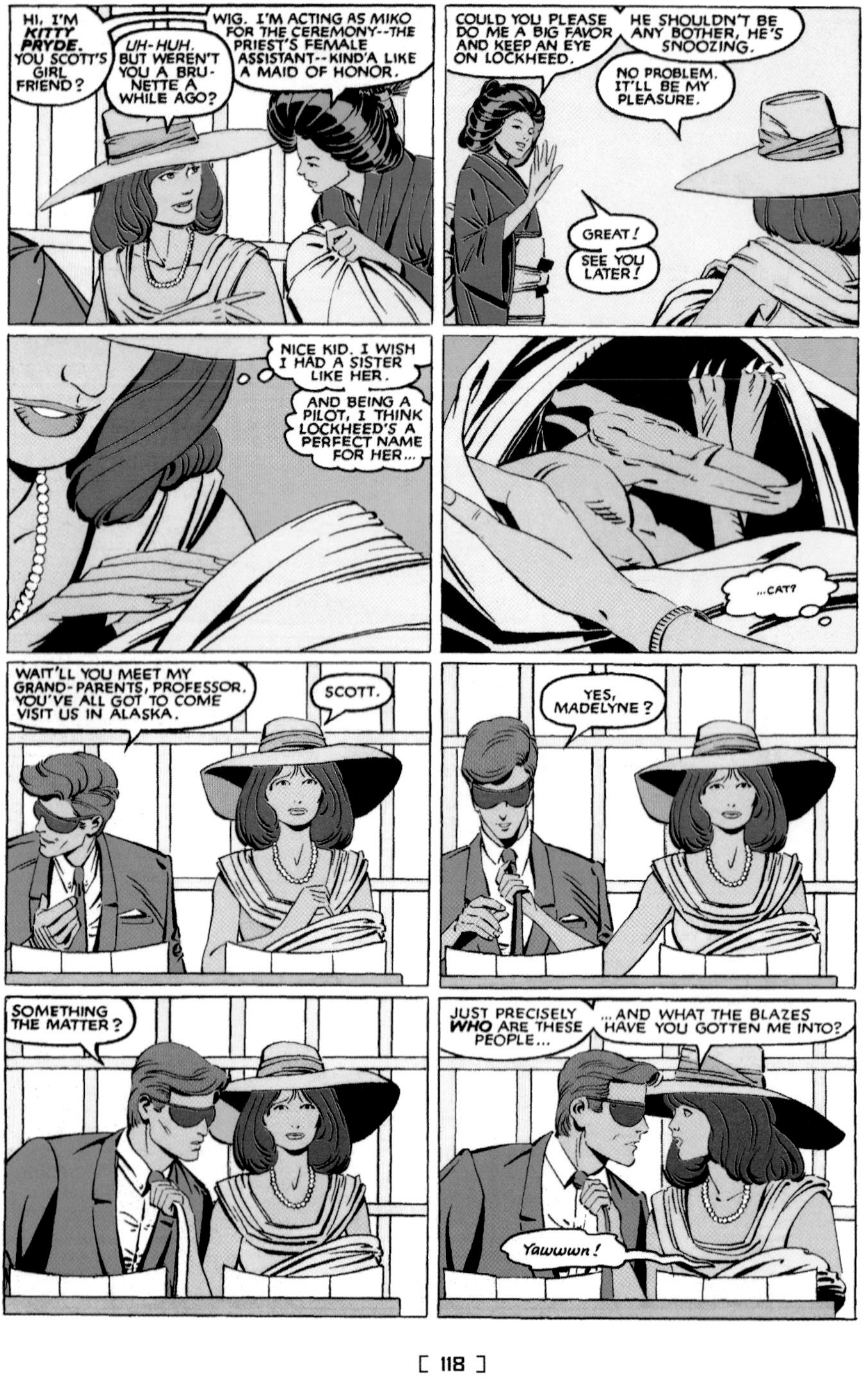
HI, I'M KITTY PRYDE. YOU SCOTT'S GIRL FRIEND?
UH-HUH. BUT WEREN'T YOU A BRU-NETTE A WHILE AGO?
WIG. I'M ACTING AS MIKO FOR THE CEREMONY--THE PRIEST'S FEMALE ASSISTANT--KIND'A LIKE A MAID OF HONOR.
COULD YOU PLEASE DO ME A BIG FAVOR AND KEEP AN EYE ON LOCKHEED.
HE SHOULDN'T BE ANY BOTHER, HE'S SNOOZING.
NO PROBLEM. IT'LL BE MY PLEASURE.
GREAT!
SEE YOU LATER!
NICE KID. I WISH I HAD A SISTER LIKE HER.
AND BEING A PILOT, I THINK LOCKHEED'S A PERFECT NAME FOR HER...
...CAT?
WAIT'LL YOU MEET MY GRAND-PARENTS, PROFESSOR. YOU'VE ALL GOT TO COME VISIT US IN ALASKA.
SCOTT.
YES, MADELYNE?
SOMETHING THE MATTER?
JUST PRECISELY WHO ARE THESE PEOPLE...
...AND WHAT THE BLAZES HAVE YOU GOTTEN ME INTO?
Yawwwn!

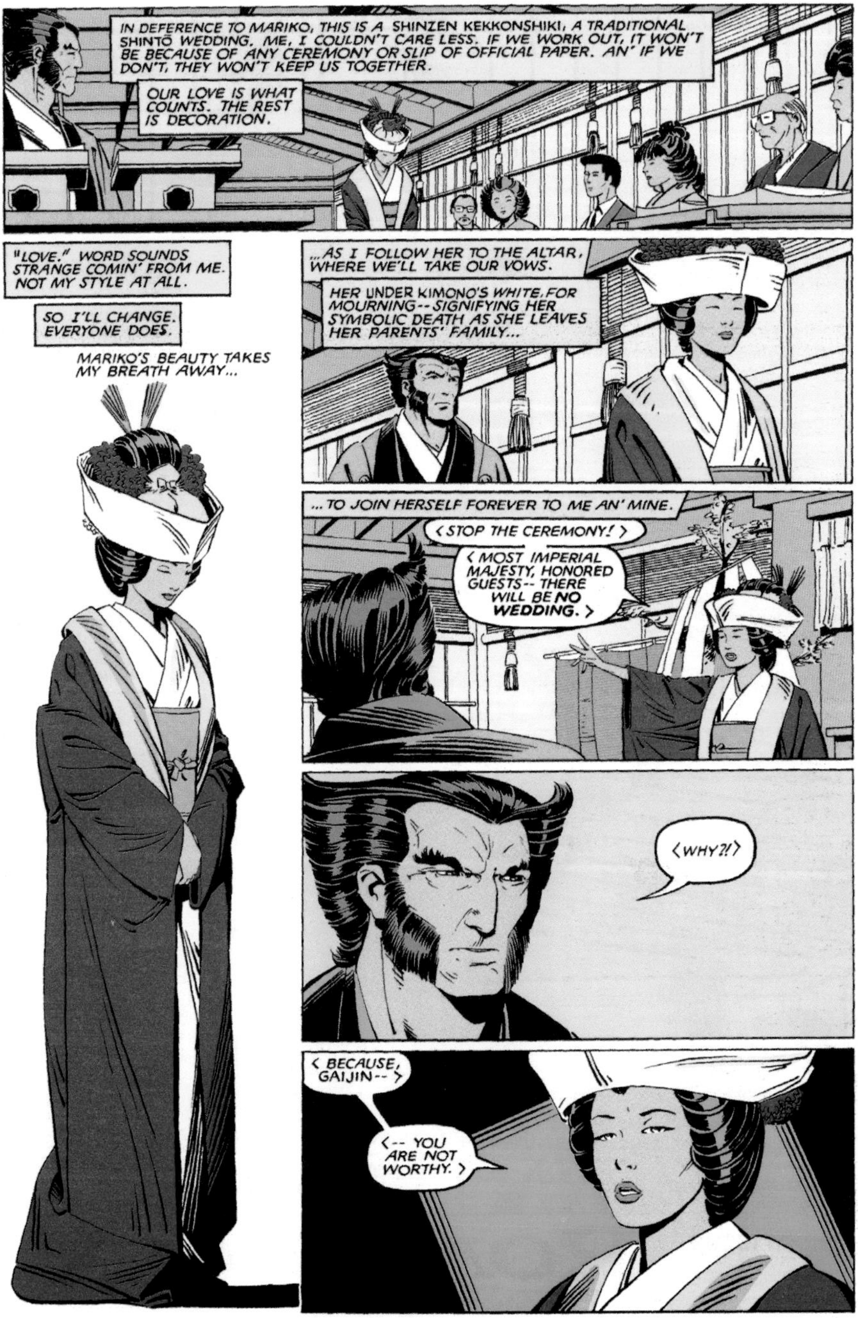
IN DEFERENCE TO MARIKO, THIS IS A SHINZEN KEKKONSHIKI, A TRADITIONAL SHINTŌ WEDDING. ME, I COULDN'T CARE LESS. IF WE WORK OUT, IT WON'T BE BECAUSE OF ANY CEREMONY OR SLIP OF OFFICIAL PAPER. AN' IF WE DON'T, THEY WON'T KEEP US TOGETHER.
OUR LOVE IS WHAT COUNTS. THE REST IS DECORATION.
"LOVE." WORD SOUNDS STRANGE COMIN' FROM ME. NOT MY STYLE AT ALL.
SO I'LL CHANGE. EVERYONE DOES.
MARIKO'S BEAUTY TAKES MY BREATH AWAY...
...AS I FOLLOW HER TO THE ALTAR, WHERE WE'LL TAKE OUR VOWS.
HER UNDER KIMONO'S WHITE, FOR MOURNING -- SIGNIFYING HER SYMBOLIC DEATH AS SHE LEAVES HER PARENTS' FAMILY...
...TO JOIN HERSELF FOREVER TO ME AN' MINE.
‹ STOP THE CEREMONY! ›
‹ MOST IMPERIAL MAJESTY, HONORED GUESTS -- THERE WILL BE NO WEDDING. ›
‹ WHY?! ›
‹ BECAUSE, GAIJIN -- ›
‹ -- YOU ARE NOT WORTHY. ›

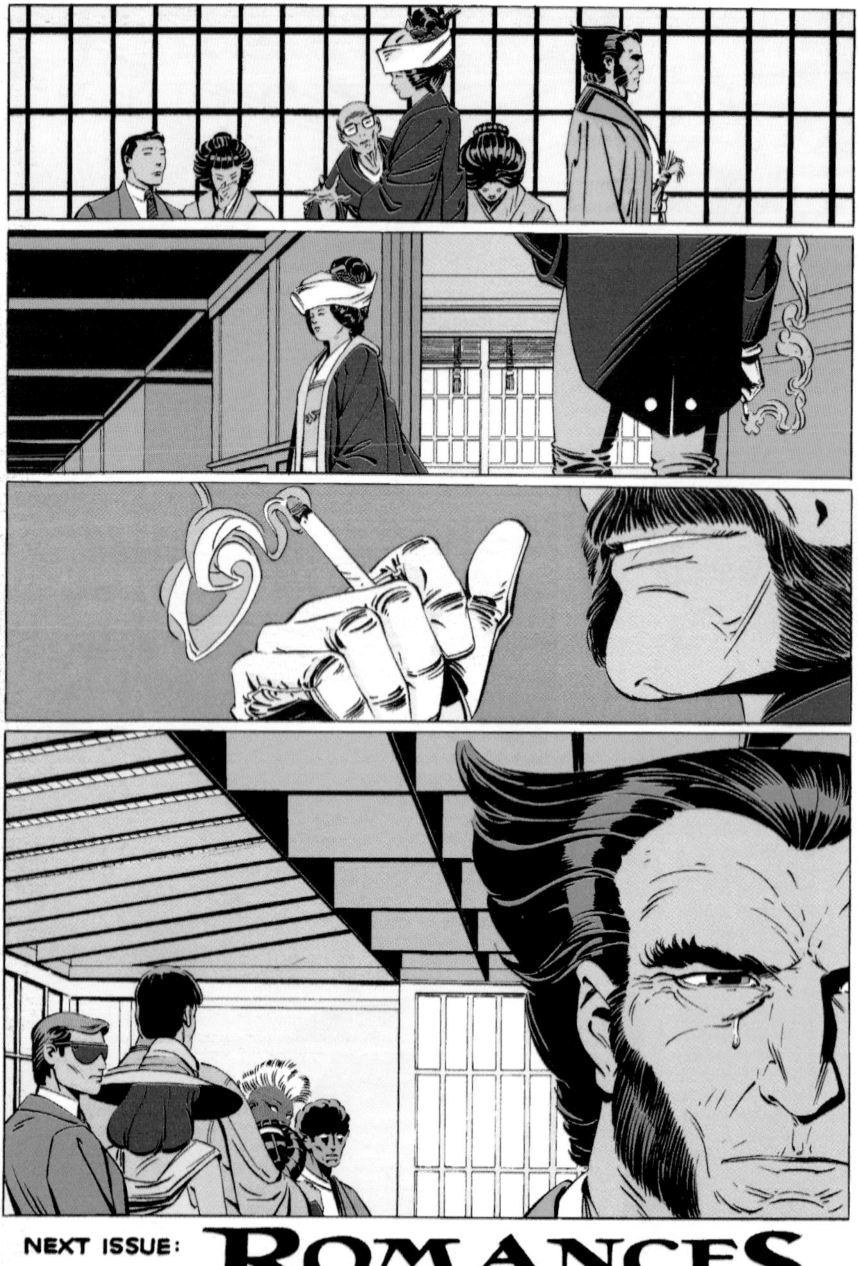

NEXT ISSUE: **ROMANCES**

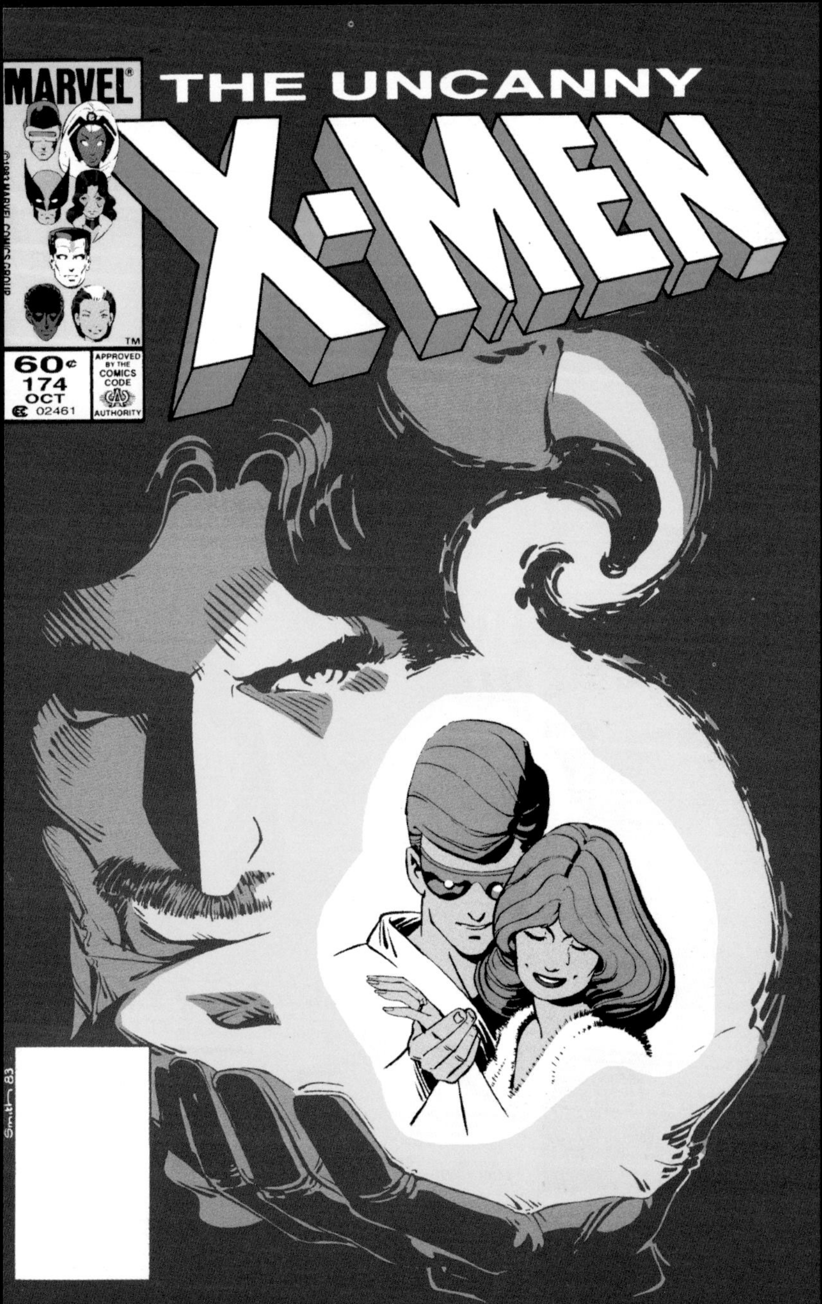
MARVEL®
THE UNCANNY
X-MEN
TM
©1983 MARVEL COMICS GROUP
60¢
174
OCT
02461
APPROVED BY THE COMICS CODE AUTHORITY
Smith 83

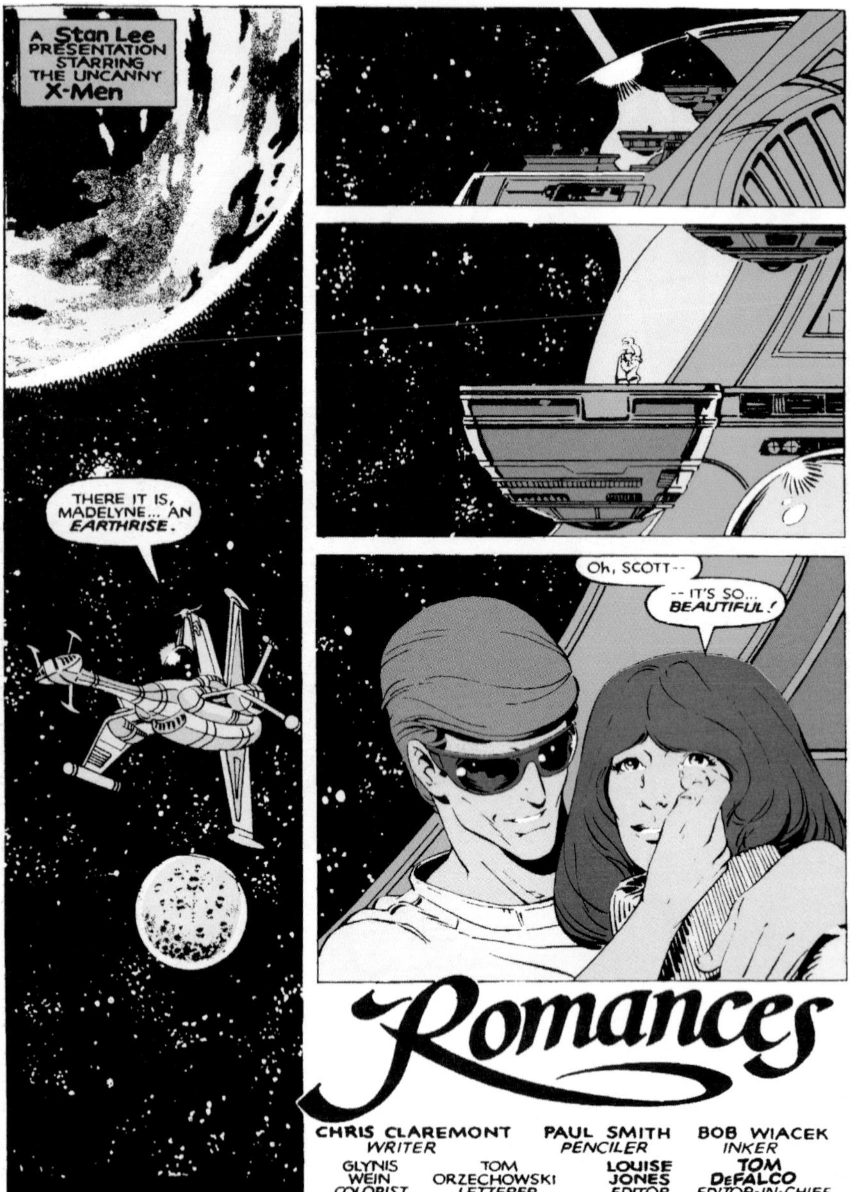

A Stan Lee
PRESENTATION
STARRING
THE UNCANNY
X-Men
THERE IT IS, MADELYNE... AN EARTHRISE.
Oh, SCOTT--
-- IT'S SO... BEAUTIFUL!
Romances
CHRIS CLAREMONT WRITER
PAUL SMITH PENCILER
BOB WIACEK INKER
GLYNIS WEIN COLORIST
TOM ORZECHOWSKI LETTERER
LOUISE JONES EDITOR
TOM DeFALCO EDITOR-IN-CHIEF

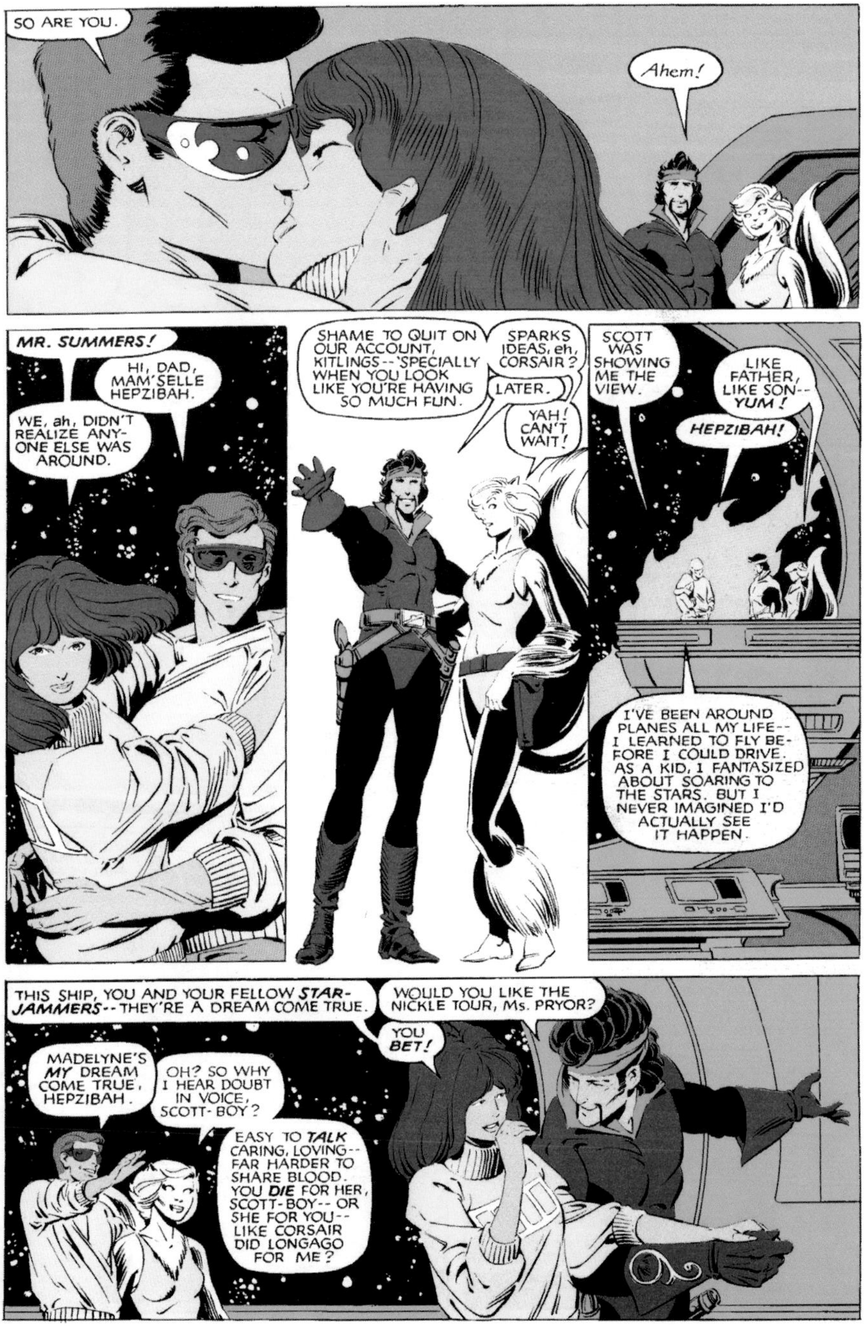
SO ARE YOU.
Ahem!
MR. SUMMERS!
HI, DAD, MAM'SELLE HEPZIBAH.
WE, ah, DIDN'T REALIZE ANYONE ELSE WAS AROUND.
SHAME TO QUIT ON OUR ACCOUNT, KITLINGS--'SPECIALLY WHEN YOU LOOK LIKE YOU'RE HAVING SO MUCH FUN.
SPARKS IDEAS, eh, CORSAIR?
LATER.
YAH! CAN'T WAIT!
SCOTT WAS SHOWING ME THE VIEW.
LIKE FATHER, LIKE SON--YUM!
HEPZIBAH!
I'VE BEEN AROUND PLANES ALL MY LIFE--I LEARNED TO FLY BEFORE I COULD DRIVE. AS A KID, I FANTASIZED ABOUT SOARING TO THE STARS. BUT I NEVER IMAGINED I'D ACTUALLY SEE IT HAPPEN.
THIS SHIP, YOU AND YOUR FELLOW STAR-JAMMERS--THEY'RE A DREAM COME TRUE.
MADELYNE'S MY DREAM COME TRUE, HEPZIBAH.
OH? SO WHY I HEAR DOUBT IN VOICE, SCOTT-BOY?
EASY TO TALK CARING, LOVING--FAR HARDER TO SHARE BLOOD. YOU DIE FOR HER, SCOTT-BOY--OR SHE FOR YOU--LIKE CORSAIR DID LONGAGO FOR ME?
WOULD YOU LIKE THE NICKLE TOUR, Ms. PRYOR?
YOU BET!

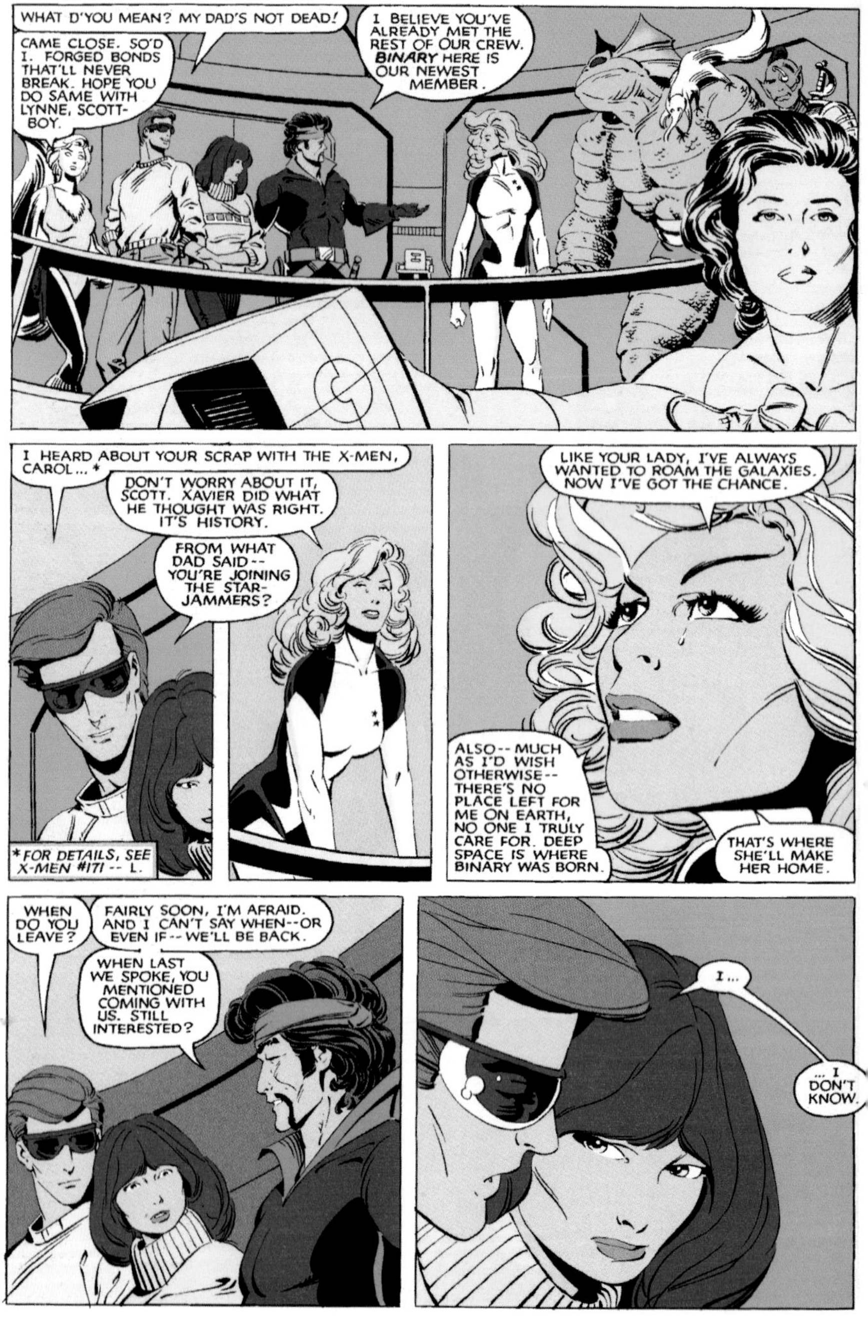
WHAT D'YOU MEAN? MY DAD'S NOT DEAD!
CAME CLOSE. SO'D I. FORGED BONDS THAT'LL NEVER BREAK. HOPE YOU DO SAME WITH LYNNE, SCOTT-BOY.
I BELIEVE YOU'VE ALREADY MET THE REST OF OUR CREW. BINARY HERE IS OUR NEWEST MEMBER.
I HEARD ABOUT YOUR SCRAP WITH THE X-MEN, CAROL... *
DON'T WORRY ABOUT IT, SCOTT. XAVIER DID WHAT HE THOUGHT WAS RIGHT. IT'S HISTORY.
FROM WHAT DAD SAID -- YOU'RE JOINING THE STAR-JAMMERS?
* FOR DETAILS, SEE X-MEN #171 -- L.
LIKE YOUR LADY, I'VE ALWAYS WANTED TO ROAM THE GALAXIES. NOW I'VE GOT THE CHANCE.
ALSO -- MUCH AS I'D WISH OTHERWISE -- THERE'S NO PLACE LEFT FOR ME ON EARTH, NO ONE I TRULY CARE FOR. DEEP SPACE IS WHERE BINARY WAS BORN.
THAT'S WHERE SHE'LL MAKE HER HOME.
WHEN DO YOU LEAVE?
FAIRLY SOON, I'M AFRAID. AND I CAN'T SAY WHEN -- OR EVEN IF -- WE'LL BE BACK.
WHEN LAST WE SPOKE, YOU MENTIONED COMING WITH US. STILL INTERESTED?
I...
... I DON'T KNOW.

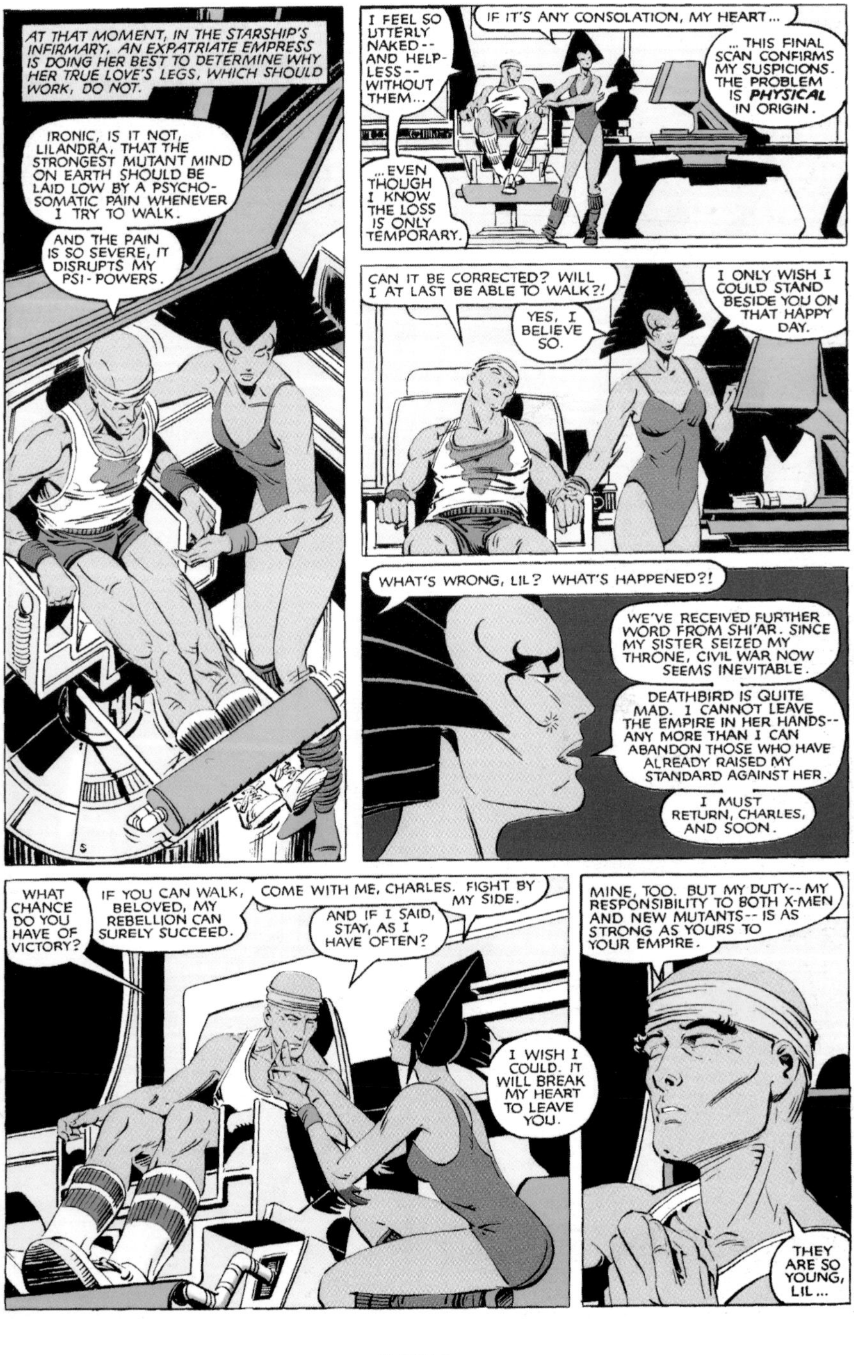
AT THAT MOMENT, IN THE STARSHIP'S INFIRMARY, AN EXPATRIATE EMPRESS IS DOING HER BEST TO DETERMINE WHY HER TRUE LOVE'S LEGS, WHICH SHOULD WORK, DO NOT.
IRONIC, IS IT NOT, LILANDRA, THAT THE STRONGEST MUTANT MIND ON EARTH SHOULD BE LAID LOW BY A PSYCHO-SOMATIC PAIN WHENEVER I TRY TO WALK.
AND THE PAIN IS SO SEVERE, IT DISRUPTS MY PSI-POWERS.
I FEEL SO UTTERLY NAKED--AND HELP-LESS--WITHOUT THEM...
...EVEN THOUGH I KNOW THE LOSS IS ONLY TEMPORARY.
IF IT'S ANY CONSOLATION, MY HEART...
... THIS FINAL SCAN CONFIRMS MY SUSPICIONS. THE PROBLEM IS PHYSICAL IN ORIGIN.
CAN IT BE CORRECTED? WILL I AT LAST BE ABLE TO WALK?!
YES, I BELIEVE SO.
I ONLY WISH I COULD STAND BESIDE YOU ON THAT HAPPY DAY.
WHAT'S WRONG, LIL? WHAT'S HAPPENED?!
WE'VE RECEIVED FURTHER WORD FROM SHI'AR. SINCE MY SISTER SEIZED MY THRONE, CIVIL WAR NOW SEEMS INEVITABLE.
DEATHBIRD IS QUITE MAD. I CANNOT LEAVE THE EMPIRE IN HER HANDS--ANY MORE THAN I CAN ABANDON THOSE WHO HAVE ALREADY RAISED MY STANDARD AGAINST HER.
I MUST RETURN, CHARLES, AND SOON.
WHAT CHANCE DO YOU HAVE OF VICTORY?
IF YOU CAN WALK, BELOVED, MY REBELLION CAN SURELY SUCCEED.
COME WITH ME, CHARLES. FIGHT BY MY SIDE.
AND IF I SAID, STAY, AS I HAVE OFTEN?
I WISH I COULD. IT WILL BREAK MY HEART TO LEAVE YOU.
MINE, TOO. BUT MY DUTY--MY RESPONSIBILITY TO BOTH X-MEN AND NEW MUTANTS--IS AS STRONG AS YOURS TO YOUR EMPIRE.
THEY ARE SO YOUNG, LIL...

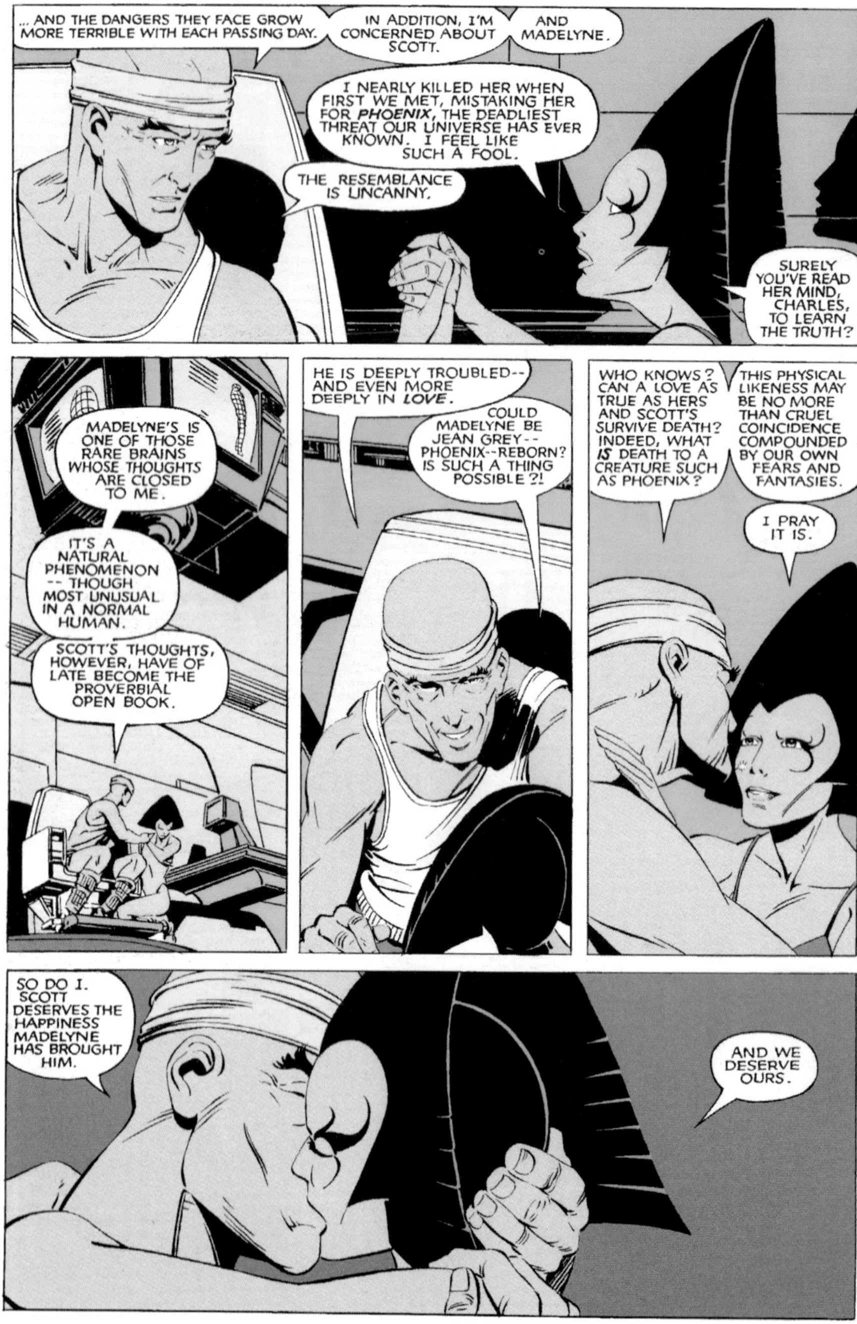

... AND THE DANGERS THEY FACE GROW MORE TERRIBLE WITH EACH PASSING DAY.
IN ADDITION, I'M CONCERNED ABOUT SCOTT.
AND MADELYNE.
I NEARLY KILLED HER WHEN FIRST WE MET, MISTAKING HER FOR PHOENIX, THE DEADLIEST THREAT OUR UNIVERSE HAS EVER KNOWN. I FEEL LIKE SUCH A FOOL.
THE RESEMBLANCE IS UNCANNY.
SURELY YOU'VE READ HER MIND, CHARLES, TO LEARN THE TRUTH?
MADELYNE'S IS ONE OF THOSE RARE BRAINS WHOSE THOUGHTS ARE CLOSED TO ME.
IT'S A NATURAL PHENOMENON -- THOUGH MOST UNUSUAL IN A NORMAL HUMAN.
SCOTT'S THOUGHTS, HOWEVER, HAVE OF LATE BECOME THE PROVERBIAL OPEN BOOK.
HE IS DEEPLY TROUBLED-- AND EVEN MORE DEEPLY IN LOVE.
COULD MADELYNE BE JEAN GREY-- PHOENIX--REBORN? IS SUCH A THING POSSIBLE?!
WHO KNOWS? CAN A LOVE AS TRUE AS HERS AND SCOTT'S SURVIVE DEATH? INDEED, WHAT IS DEATH TO A CREATURE SUCH AS PHOENIX?
THIS PHYSICAL LIKENESS MAY BE NO MORE THAN CRUEL COINCIDENCE COMPOUNDED BY OUR OWN FEARS AND FANTASIES.
I PRAY IT IS.
SO DO I. SCOTT DESERVES THE HAPPINESS MADELYNE HAS BROUGHT HIM.
AND WE DESERVE OURS.

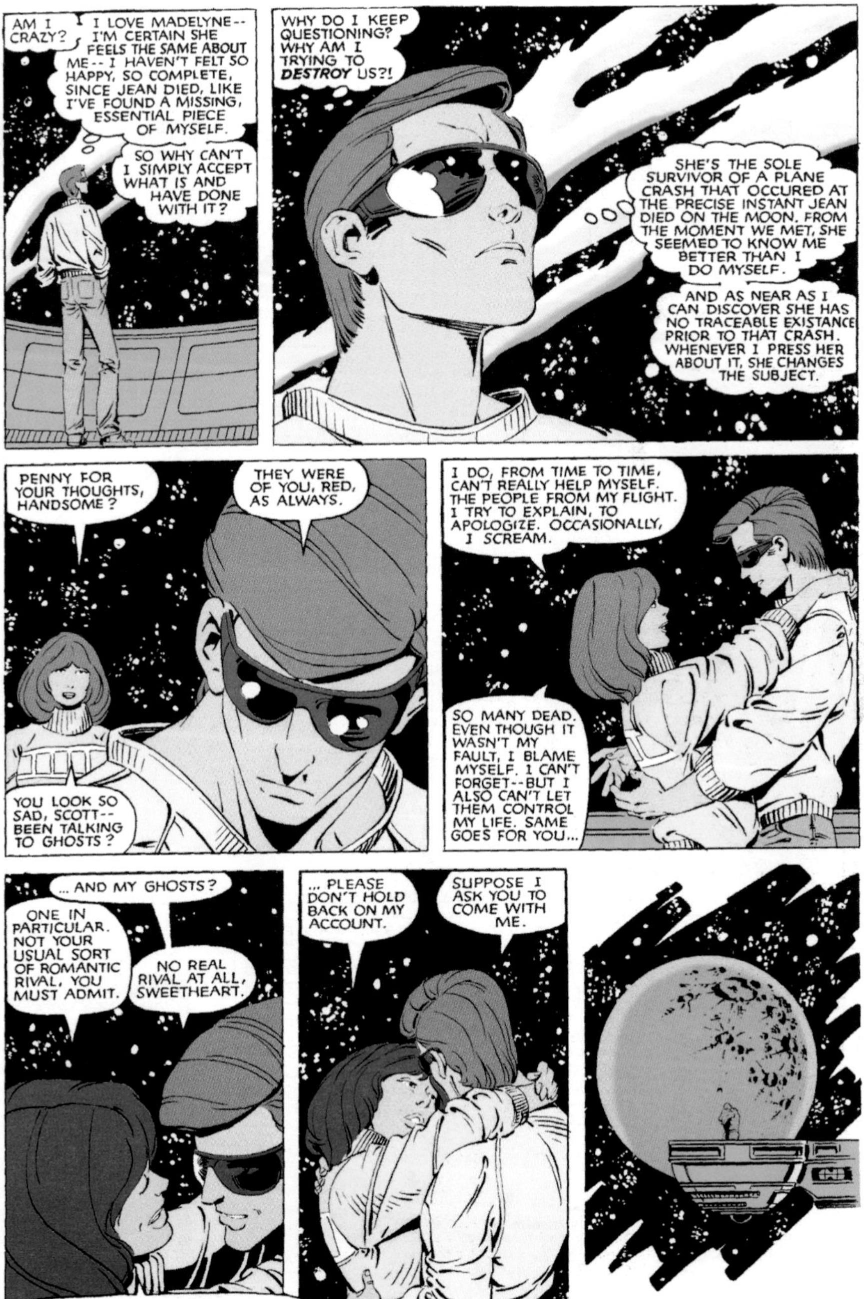
AM I CRAZY?
I LOVE MADELYNE-- I'M CERTAIN SHE FEELS THE SAME ABOUT ME-- I HAVEN'T FELT SO HAPPY, SO COMPLETE, SINCE JEAN DIED, LIKE I'VE FOUND A MISSING, ESSENTIAL PIECE OF MYSELF.
SO WHY CAN'T I SIMPLY ACCEPT WHAT IS AND HAVE DONE WITH IT?
WHY DO I KEEP QUESTIONING? WHY AM I TRYING TO DESTROY US?!
SHE'S THE SOLE SURVIVOR OF A PLANE CRASH THAT OCCURED AT THE PRECISE INSTANT JEAN DIED ON THE MOON. FROM THE MOMENT WE MET, SHE SEEMED TO KNOW ME BETTER THAN I DO MYSELF.
AND AS NEAR AS I CAN DISCOVER SHE HAS NO TRACEABLE EXISTANCE PRIOR TO THAT CRASH. WHENEVER I PRESS HER ABOUT IT, SHE CHANGES THE SUBJECT.
PENNY FOR YOUR THOUGHTS, HANDSOME?
THEY WERE OF YOU, RED, AS ALWAYS.
YOU LOOK SO SAD, SCOTT-- BEEN TALKING TO GHOSTS?
I DO, FROM TIME TO TIME, CAN'T REALLY HELP MYSELF. THE PEOPLE FROM MY FLIGHT. I TRY TO EXPLAIN, TO APOLOGIZE. OCCASIONALLY, I SCREAM.
SO MANY DEAD. EVEN THOUGH IT WASN'T MY FAULT, I BLAME MYSELF. I CAN'T FORGET--BUT I ALSO CAN'T LET THEM CONTROL MY LIFE. SAME GOES FOR YOU...
... AND MY GHOSTS?
ONE IN PARTICULAR. NOT YOUR USUAL SORT OF ROMANTIC RIVAL, YOU MUST ADMIT.
NO REAL RIVAL AT ALL, SWEETHEART.
SCOTT, ABOUT YOUR DAD'S OFFER...
... PLEASE DON'T HOLD BACK ON MY ACCOUNT.
SUPPOSE I ASK YOU TO COME WITH ME.

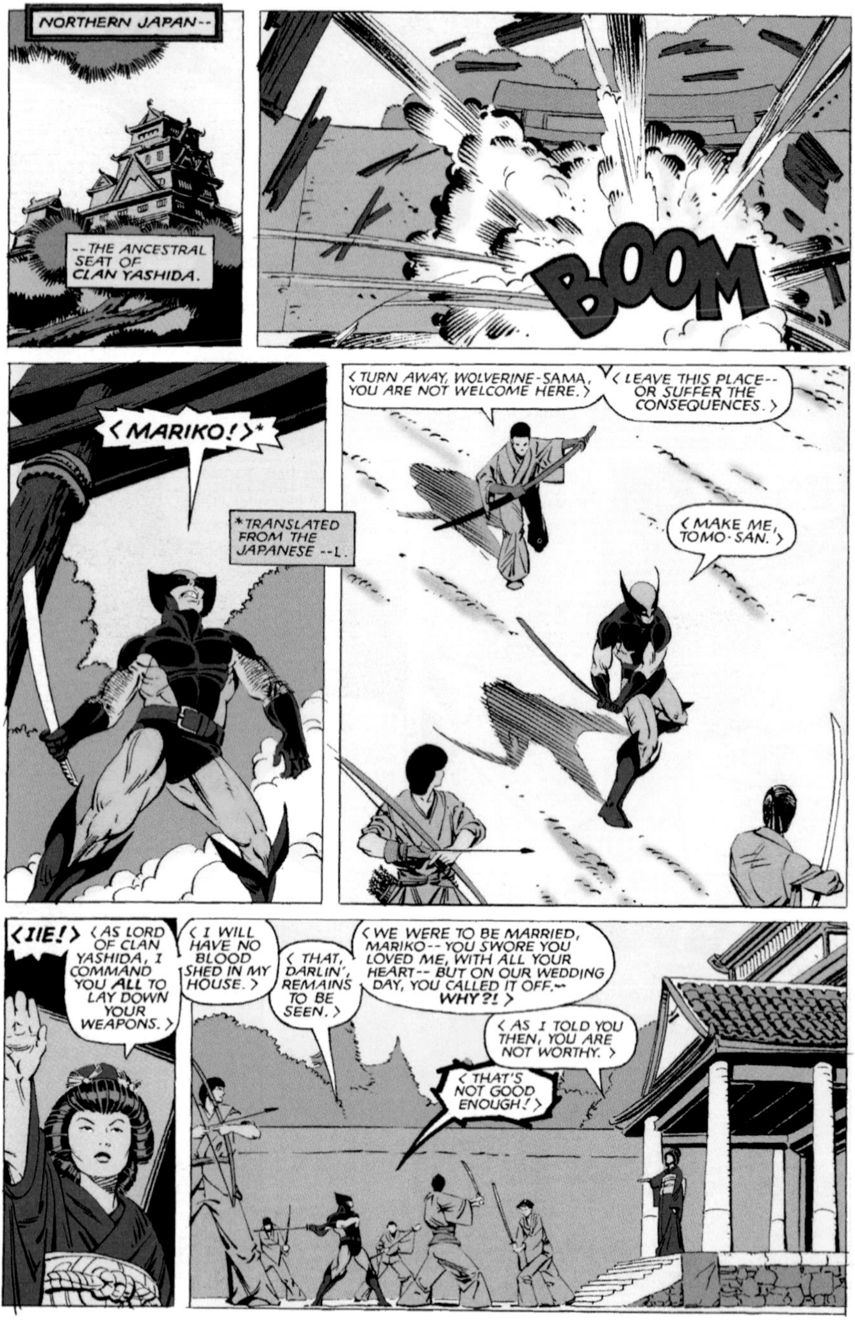
NORTHERN JAPAN--
--THE ANCESTRAL SEAT OF CLAN YASHIDA.
BOOM
⟨MARIKO!⟩*
*TRANSLATED FROM THE JAPANESE --L.
⟨TURN AWAY, WOLVERINE-SAMA, YOU ARE NOT WELCOME HERE.⟩
⟨LEAVE THIS PLACE-- OR SUFFER THE CONSEQUENCES.⟩
⟨MAKE ME, TOMO-SAN.⟩
⟨IIE!⟩
⟨AS LORD OF CLAN YASHIDA, I COMMAND YOU ALL TO LAY DOWN YOUR WEAPONS.⟩
⟨I WILL HAVE NO BLOOD SHED IN MY HOUSE.⟩
⟨THAT, DARLIN', REMAINS TO BE SEEN.⟩
⟨WE WERE TO BE MARRIED, MARIKO-- YOU SWORE YOU LOVED ME, WITH ALL YOUR HEART-- BUT ON OUR WEDDING DAY, YOU CALLED IT OFF.-- WHY?!⟩
⟨AS I TOLD YOU THEN, YOU ARE NOT WORTHY.⟩
⟨THAT'S NOT GOOD ENOUGH!⟩

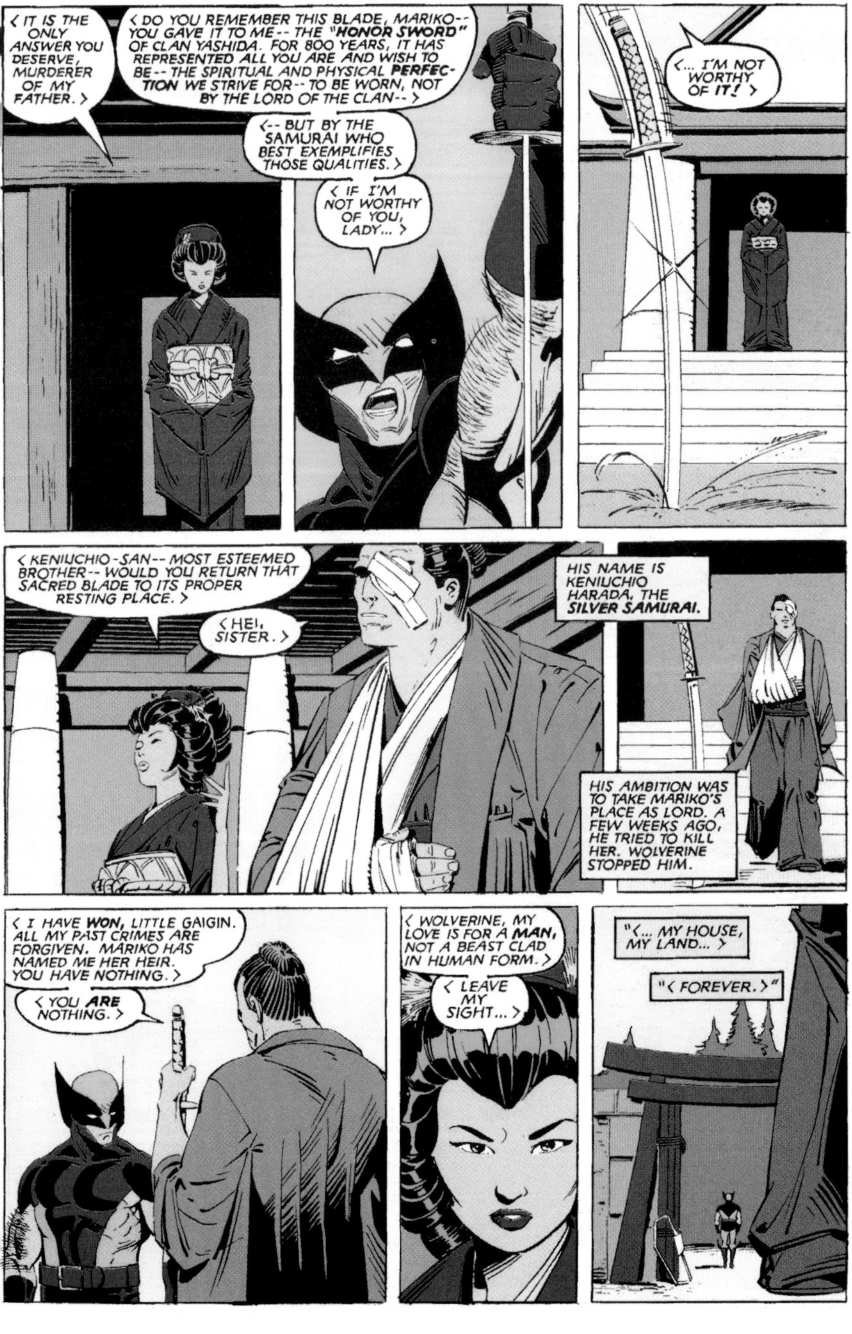

< IT IS THE ONLY ANSWER YOU DESERVE, MURDERER OF MY FATHER. >
< DO YOU REMEMBER THIS BLADE, MARIKO-- YOU GAVE IT TO ME-- THE "HONOR SWORD" OF CLAN YASHIDA. FOR 800 YEARS, IT HAS REPRESENTED ALL YOU ARE AND WISH TO BE-- THE SPIRITUAL AND PHYSICAL PERFECTION WE STRIVE FOR-- TO BE WORN, NOT BY THE LORD OF THE CLAN-- >
<-- BUT BY THE SAMURAI WHO BEST EXEMPLIFIES THOSE QUALITIES. >
< IF I'M NOT WORTHY OF YOU, LADY... >
<... I'M NOT WORTHY OF IT! >
< KENIUCHIO-SAN-- MOST ESTEEMED BROTHER-- WOULD YOU RETURN THAT SACRED BLADE TO ITS PROPER RESTING PLACE. >
< HEI, SISTER. >
HIS NAME IS KENIUCHIO HARADA, THE SILVER SAMURAI.
HIS AMBITION WAS TO TAKE MARIKO'S PLACE AS LORD. A FEW WEEKS AGO, HE TRIED TO KILL HER. WOLVERINE STOPPED HIM.
< I HAVE WON, LITTLE GAIGIN. ALL MY PAST CRIMES ARE FORGIVEN. MARIKO HAS NAMED ME HER HEIR. YOU HAVE NOTHING. >
< YOU ARE NOTHING. >
< WOLVERINE, MY LOVE IS FOR A MAN, NOT A BEAST CLAD IN HUMAN FORM. >
< LEAVE MY SIGHT... >
"<... MY HOUSE, MY LAND... >
"< FOREVER. >"

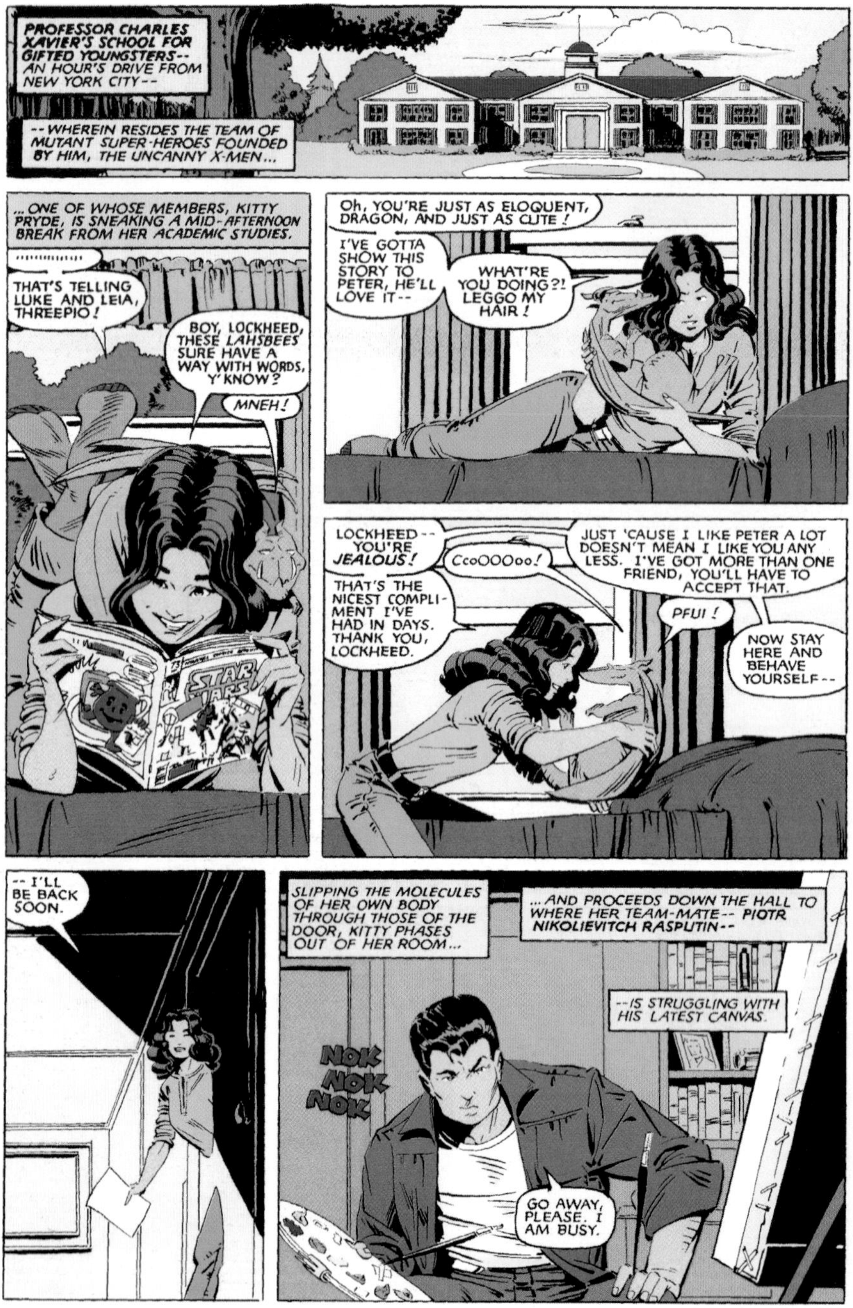

PROFESSOR CHARLES XAVIER'S SCHOOL FOR GIFTED YOUNGSTERS-- AN HOUR'S DRIVE FROM NEW YORK CITY--
--WHEREIN RESIDES THE TEAM OF MUTANT SUPER-HEROES FOUNDED BY HIM, THE UNCANNY X-MEN...
...ONE OF WHOSE MEMBERS, KITTY PRYDE, IS SNEAKING A MID-AFTERNOON BREAK FROM HER ACADEMIC STUDIES.
THAT'S TELLING LUKE AND LEIA, THREEPIO!
BOY, LOCKHEED, THESE LAHSBEES SURE HAVE A WAY WITH WORDS, Y'KNOW?
MNEH!
STAR WARS
Oh, YOU'RE JUST AS ELOQUENT, DRAGON, AND JUST AS CUTE!
I'VE GOTTA SHOW THIS STORY TO PETER, HE'LL LOVE IT--
WHAT'RE YOU DOING?! LEGGO MY HAIR!
LOCKHEED-- YOU'RE JEALOUS!
THAT'S THE NICEST COMPLIMENT I'VE HAD IN DAYS. THANK YOU, LOCKHEED.
CcoOOOoo!
JUST 'CAUSE I LIKE PETER A LOT DOESN'T MEAN I LIKE YOU ANY LESS. I'VE GOT MORE THAN ONE FRIEND, YOU'LL HAVE TO ACCEPT THAT.
PFUI!
NOW STAY HERE AND BEHAVE YOURSELF--
--I'LL BE BACK SOON.
SLIPPING THE MOLECULES OF HER OWN BODY THROUGH THOSE OF THE DOOR, KITTY PHASES OUT OF HER ROOM...
...AND PROCEEDS DOWN THE HALL TO WHERE HER TEAM-MATE-- PIOTR NIKOLIEVITCH RASPUTIN--
--IS STRUGGLING WITH HIS LATEST CANVAS.
NOK NOK NOK
GO AWAY, PLEASE. I AM BUSY.

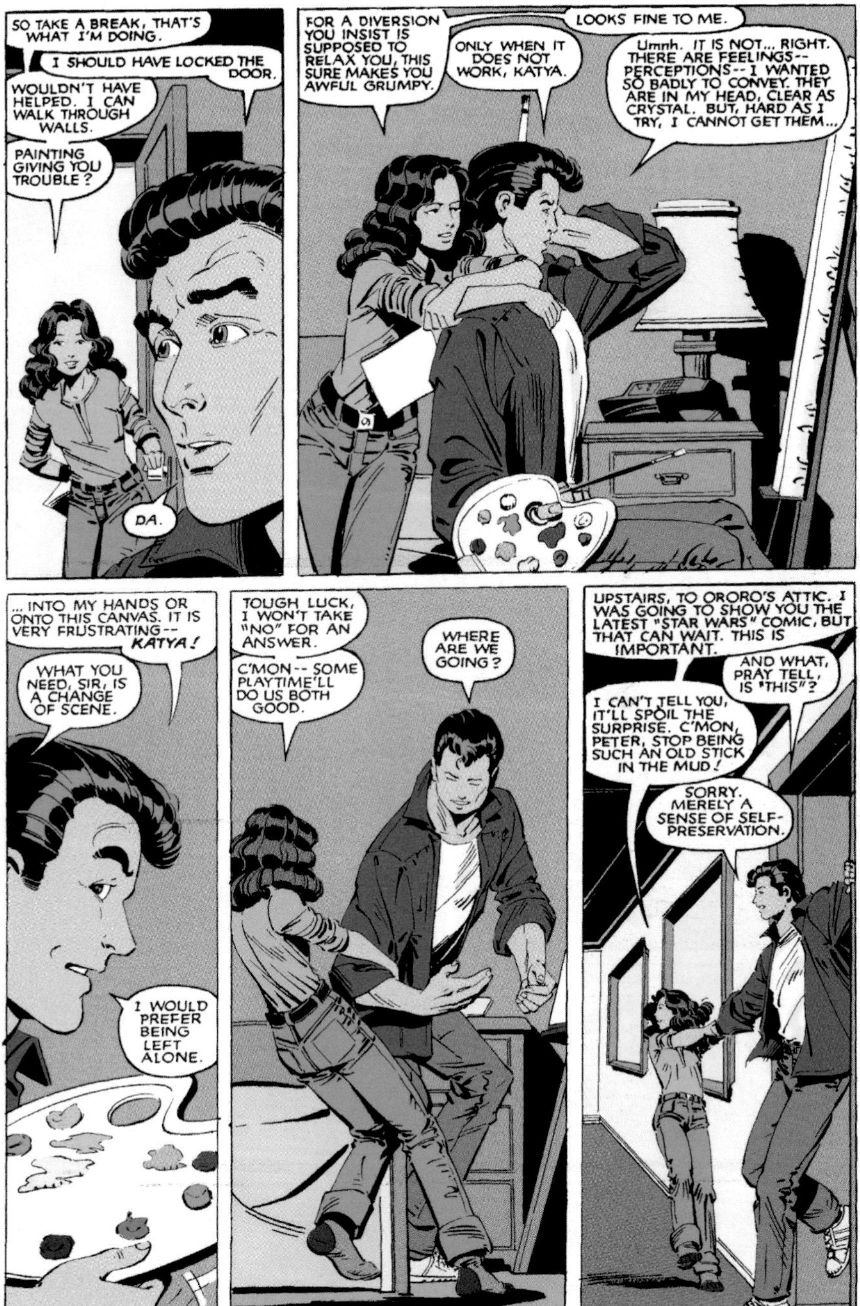
SO TAKE A BREAK, THAT'S WHAT I'M DOING.
I SHOULD HAVE LOCKED THE DOOR.
WOULDN'T HAVE HELPED. I CAN WALK THROUGH WALLS.
PAINTING GIVING YOU TROUBLE?
DA.
FOR A DIVERSION YOU INSIST IS SUPPOSED TO RELAX YOU, THIS SURE MAKES YOU AWFUL GRUMPY.
ONLY WHEN IT DOES NOT WORK, KATYA.
LOOKS FINE TO ME.
Umnh. IT IS NOT... RIGHT. THERE ARE FEELINGS-- PERCEPTIONS-- I WANTED SO BADLY TO CONVEY. THEY ARE IN MY HEAD, CLEAR AS CRYSTAL. BUT, HARD AS I TRY, I CANNOT GET THEM...
... INTO MY HANDS OR ONTO THIS CANVAS. IT IS VERY FRUSTRATING-- KATYA!
WHAT YOU NEED, SIR, IS A CHANGE OF SCENE.
I WOULD PREFER BEING LEFT ALONE.
TOUGH LUCK, I WON'T TAKE "NO" FOR AN ANSWER.
C'MON-- SOME PLAYTIME'LL DO US BOTH GOOD.
WHERE ARE WE GOING?
UPSTAIRS, TO ORORO'S ATTIC. I WAS GOING TO SHOW YOU THE LATEST "STAR WARS" COMIC, BUT THAT CAN WAIT. THIS IS IMPORTANT.
AND WHAT, PRAY TELL, IS "THIS"?
I CAN'T TELL YOU, IT'LL SPOIL THE SURPRISE. C'MON, PETER, STOP BEING SUCH AN OLD STICK IN THE MUD!
SORRY. MERELY A SENSE OF SELF-PRESERVATION.

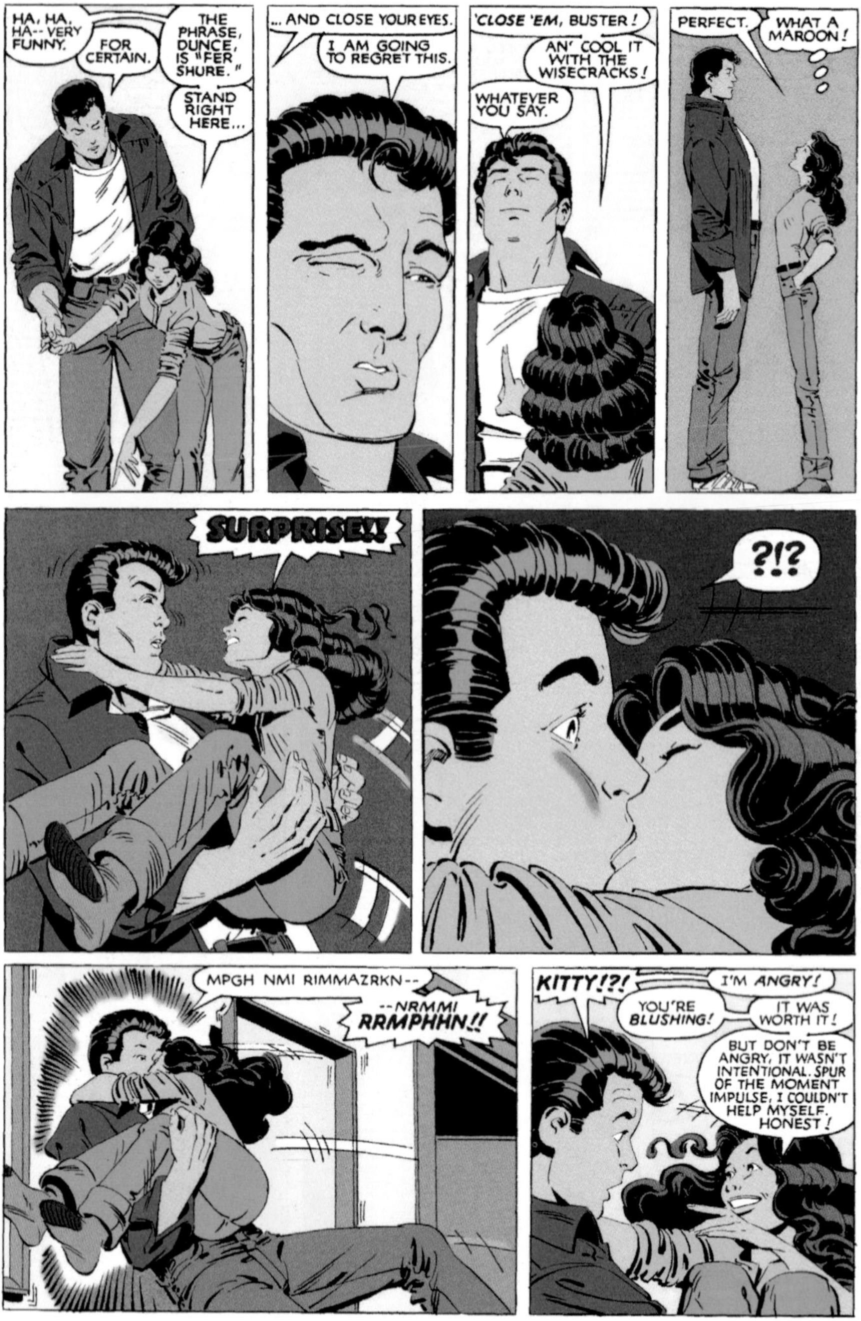
HA, HA, HA-- VERY FUNNY.
FOR CERTAIN.
THE PHRASE, DUNCE, IS "FER SHURE."
STAND RIGHT HERE...
... AND CLOSE YOUR EYES.
I AM GOING TO REGRET THIS.
'CLOSE 'EM, BUSTER!
AN' COOL IT WITH THE WISECRACKS!
WHATEVER YOU SAY.
PERFECT.
WHAT A MAROON!
SURPRISE!!
?!?
MPGH NMI RIMMAZRKN--
--NRMMI RRMPHHN!!
KITTY!?!
I'M ANGRY!
YOU'RE BLUSHING!
IT WAS WORTH IT!
BUT DON'T BE ANGRY. IT WASN'T INTENTIONAL. SPUR OF THE MOMENT IMPULSE; I COULDN'T HELP MYSELF. HONEST!

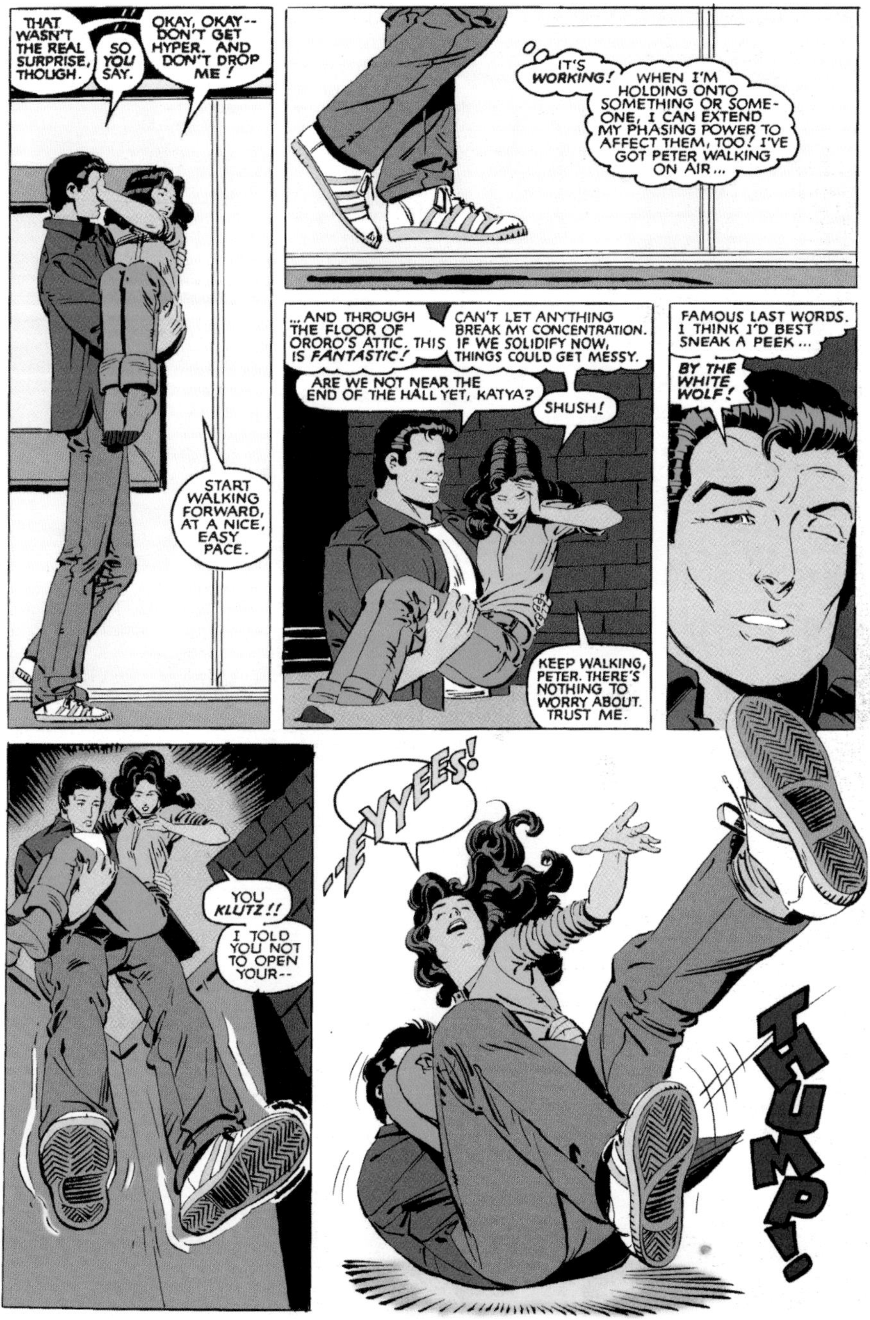
THAT WASN'T THE REAL SURPRISE, THOUGH.
SO YOU SAY.
OKAY, OKAY-- DON'T GET HYPER. AND DON'T DROP ME!
START WALKING FORWARD, AT A NICE, EASY PACE.
IT'S WORKING! WHEN I'M HOLDING ONTO SOMETHING OR SOMEONE, I CAN EXTEND MY PHASING POWER TO AFFECT THEM, TOO! I'VE GOT PETER WALKING ON AIR...
...AND THROUGH THE FLOOR OF ORORO'S ATTIC. THIS IS FANTASTIC!
CAN'T LET ANYTHING BREAK MY CONCENTRATION. IF WE SOLIDIFY NOW, THINGS COULD GET MESSY.
ARE WE NOT NEAR THE END OF THE HALL YET, KATYA?
SHUSH!
KEEP WALKING, PETER. THERE'S NOTHING TO WORRY ABOUT. TRUST ME.
FAMOUS LAST WORDS. I THINK I'D BEST SNEAK A PEEK...
BY THE WHITE WOLF!
YOU KLUTZ!!
I TOLD YOU NOT TO OPEN YOUR--
--EYYEES!
THUMP!

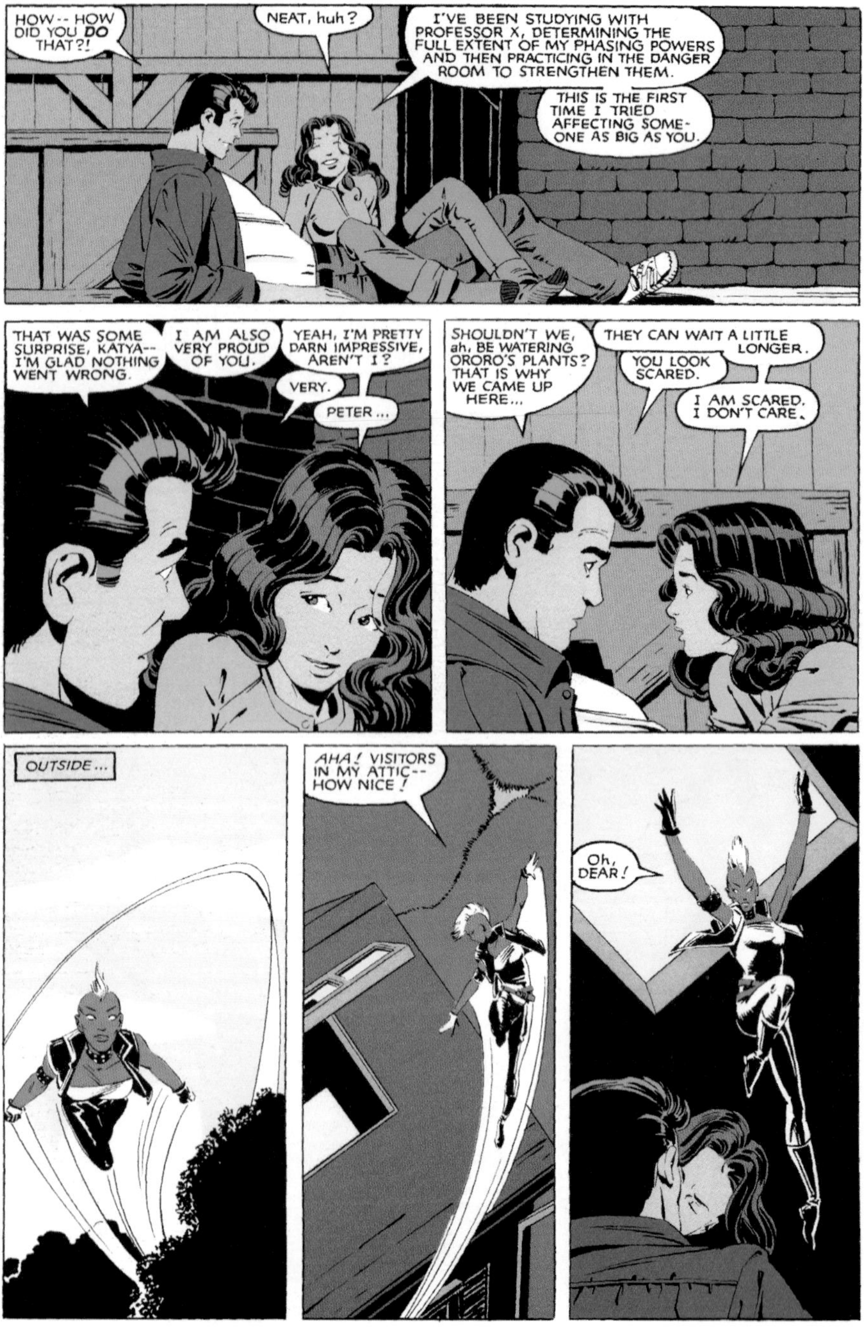
HOW-- HOW DID YOU DO THAT?!
NEAT, huh?
I'VE BEEN STUDYING WITH PROFESSOR X, DETERMINING THE FULL EXTENT OF MY PHASING POWERS AND THEN PRACTICING IN THE DANGER ROOM TO STRENGTHEN THEM.
THIS IS THE FIRST TIME I TRIED AFFECTING SOME-ONE AS BIG AS YOU.
THAT WAS SOME SURPRISE, KATYA-- I'M GLAD NOTHING WENT WRONG.
I AM ALSO VERY PROUD OF YOU.
YEAH, I'M PRETTY DARN IMPRESSIVE, AREN'T I?
VERY.
PETER...
SHOULDN'T WE, ah, BE WATERING ORORO'S PLANTS? THAT IS WHY WE CAME UP HERE...
THEY CAN WAIT A LITTLE LONGER.
YOU LOOK SCARED.
I AM SCARED. I DON'T CARE.
OUTSIDE...
AHA! VISITORS IN MY ATTIC-- HOW NICE!
Oh, DEAR!

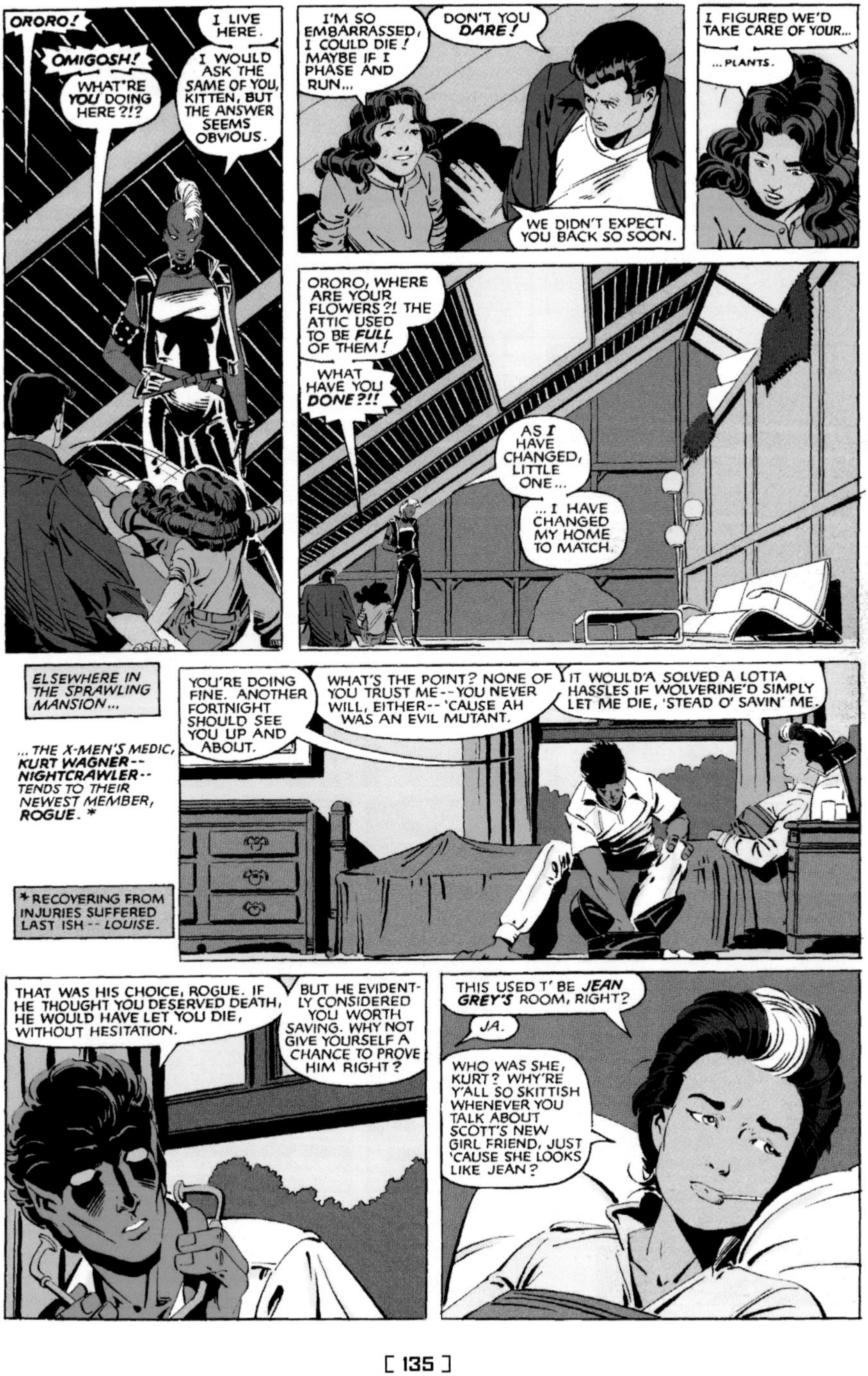
ORORO!
OMIGOSH!
WHAT'RE YOU DOING HERE?!?
I LIVE HERE.
I WOULD ASK THE SAME OF YOU, KITTEN, BUT THE ANSWER SEEMS OBVIOUS.
I'M SO EMBARRASSED, I COULD DIE! MAYBE IF I PHASE AND RUN...
DON'T YOU DARE!
WE DIDN'T EXPECT YOU BACK SO SOON.
I FIGURED WE'D TAKE CARE OF YOUR...
...PLANTS.
ORORO, WHERE ARE YOUR FLOWERS?! THE ATTIC USED TO BE FULL OF THEM!
WHAT HAVE YOU DONE?!!
AS I HAVE CHANGED, LITTLE ONE...
...I HAVE CHANGED MY HOME TO MATCH.
ELSEWHERE IN THE SPRAWLING MANSION...
...THE X-MEN'S MEDIC, KURT WAGNER-- NIGHTCRAWLER-- TENDS TO THEIR NEWEST MEMBER, ROGUE. *
* RECOVERING FROM INJURIES SUFFERED LAST ISH -- LOUISE.
YOU'RE DOING FINE. ANOTHER FORTNIGHT SHOULD SEE YOU UP AND ABOUT.
WHAT'S THE POINT? NONE OF YOU TRUST ME--YOU NEVER WILL, EITHER-- 'CAUSE AH WAS AN EVIL MUTANT.
IT WOULD'A SOLVED A LOTTA HASSLES IF WOLVERINE'D SIMPLY LET ME DIE, 'STEAD O' SAVIN' ME.
THAT WAS HIS CHOICE, ROGUE. IF HE THOUGHT YOU DESERVED DEATH, HE WOULD HAVE LET YOU DIE, WITHOUT HESITATION.
BUT HE EVIDENTLY CONSIDERED YOU WORTH SAVING. WHY NOT GIVE YOURSELF A CHANCE TO PROVE HIM RIGHT?
THIS USED T' BE JEAN GREY'S ROOM, RIGHT?
JA.
WHO WAS SHE, KURT? WHY'RE Y'ALL SO SKITTISH WHENEVER YOU TALK ABOUT SCOTT'S NEW GIRL FRIEND, JUST 'CAUSE SHE LOOKS LIKE JEAN?

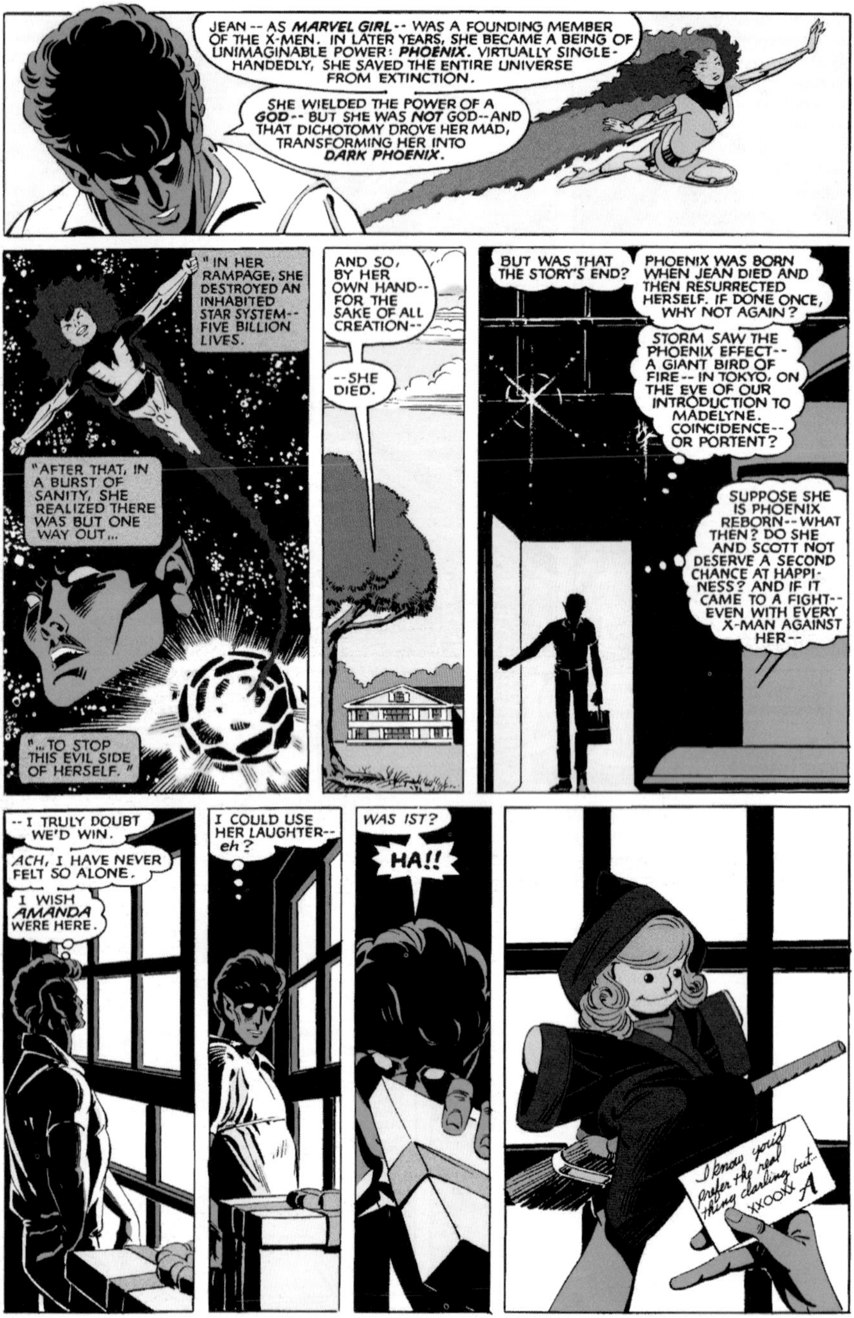

JEAN -- AS MARVEL GIRL -- WAS A FOUNDING MEMBER OF THE X-MEN. IN LATER YEARS, SHE BECAME A BEING OF UNIMAGINABLE POWER: PHOENIX. VIRTUALLY SINGLE-HANDEDLY, SHE SAVED THE ENTIRE UNIVERSE FROM EXTINCTION.
SHE WIELDED THE POWER OF A GOD -- BUT SHE WAS NOT GOD--AND THAT DICHOTOMY DROVE HER MAD, TRANSFORMING HER INTO DARK PHOENIX.
"IN HER RAMPAGE, SHE DESTROYED AN INHABITED STAR SYSTEM-- FIVE BILLION LIVES.
"AFTER THAT, IN A BURST OF SANITY, SHE REALIZED THERE WAS BUT ONE WAY OUT...
"...TO STOP THIS EVIL SIDE OF HERSELF."
AND SO, BY HER OWN HAND-- FOR THE SAKE OF ALL CREATION--
--SHE DIED.
BUT WAS THAT THE STORY'S END?
PHOENIX WAS BORN WHEN JEAN DIED AND THEN RESURRECTED HERSELF. IF DONE ONCE, WHY NOT AGAIN?
STORM SAW THE PHOENIX EFFECT-- A GIANT BIRD OF FIRE-- IN TOKYO, ON THE EVE OF OUR INTRODUCTION TO MADELYNE. COINCIDENCE-- OR PORTENT?
SUPPOSE SHE IS PHOENIX REBORN--WHAT THEN? DO SHE AND SCOTT NOT DESERVE A SECOND CHANCE AT HAPPINESS? AND IF IT CAME TO A FIGHT-- EVEN WITH EVERY X-MAN AGAINST HER--
-- I TRULY DOUBT WE'D WIN.
ACH, I HAVE NEVER FELT SO ALONE.
I WISH AMANDA WERE HERE.
I COULD USE HER LAUGHTER-- eh?
WAS IST?
HA!!
I know you'd prefer the real thing darling but... XXOOXX A

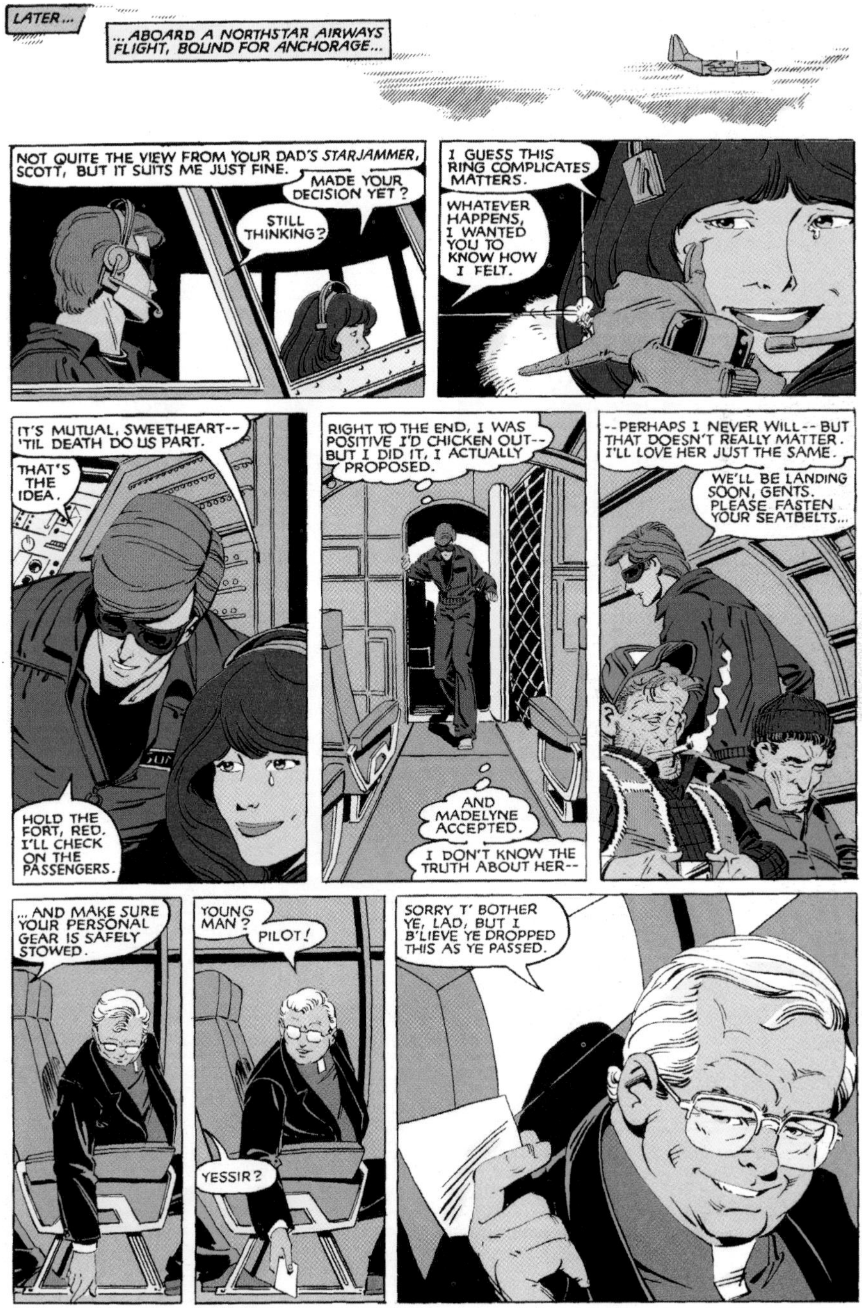
LATER...
...ABOARD A NORTHSTAR AIRWAYS FLIGHT, BOUND FOR ANCHORAGE...
NOT QUITE THE VIEW FROM YOUR DAD'S STARJAMMER, SCOTT, BUT IT SUITS ME JUST FINE.
MADE YOUR DECISION YET?
STILL THINKING?
I GUESS THIS RING COMPLICATES MATTERS.
WHATEVER HAPPENS, I WANTED YOU TO KNOW HOW I FELT.
IT'S MUTUAL, SWEETHEART-- 'TIL DEATH DO US PART.
THAT'S THE IDEA.
HOLD THE FORT, RED. I'LL CHECK ON THE PASSENGERS.
RIGHT TO THE END, I WAS POSITIVE I'D CHICKEN OUT-- BUT I DID IT, I ACTUALLY PROPOSED.
AND MADELYNE ACCEPTED.
I DON'T KNOW THE TRUTH ABOUT HER--
--PERHAPS I NEVER WILL-- BUT THAT DOESN'T REALLY MATTER. I'LL LOVE HER JUST THE SAME.
WE'LL BE LANDING SOON, GENTS. PLEASE FASTEN YOUR SEATBELTS...
...AND MAKE SURE YOUR PERSONAL GEAR IS SAFELY STOWED.
YOUNG MAN?
PILOT!
YESSIR?
SORRY T' BOTHER YE, LAD, BUT I B'LIEVE YE DROPPED THIS AS YE PASSED.

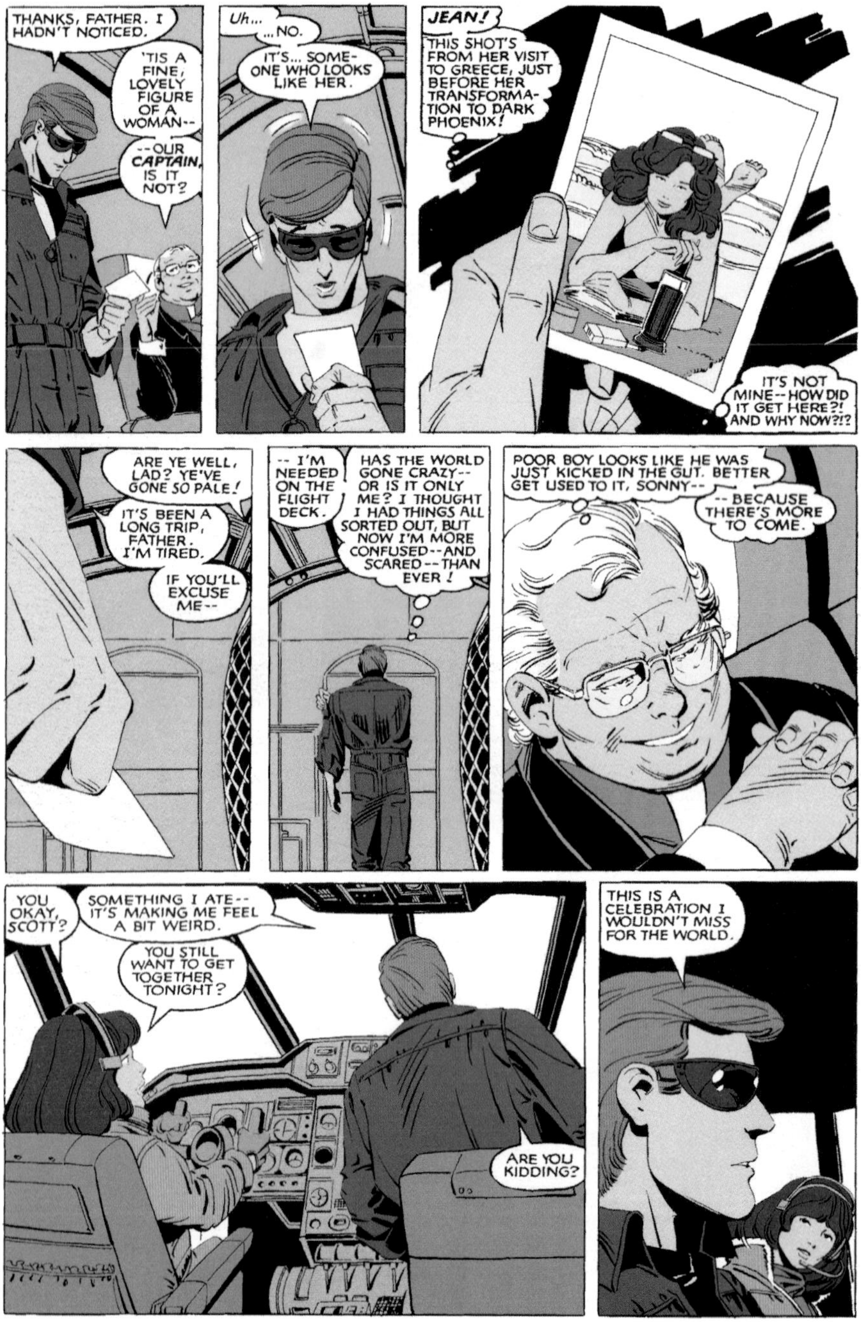
THANKS, FATHER. I HADN'T NOTICED.
'TIS A FINE, LOVELY FIGURE OF A WOMAN--
--OUR CAPTAIN, IS IT NOT?
Uh...
...NO.
IT'S... SOME-ONE WHO LOOKS LIKE HER.
JEAN!
THIS SHOT'S FROM HER VISIT TO GREECE, JUST BEFORE HER TRANSFORMA-TION TO DARK PHOENIX!
IT'S NOT MINE--HOW DID IT GET HERE?! AND WHY NOW?!?
ARE YE WELL, LAD? YE'VE GONE SO PALE!
IT'S BEEN A LONG TRIP, FATHER. I'M TIRED.
IF YOU'LL EXCUSE ME--
-- I'M NEEDED ON THE FLIGHT DECK.
HAS THE WORLD GONE CRAZY-- OR IS IT ONLY ME? I THOUGHT I HAD THINGS ALL SORTED OUT, BUT NOW I'M MORE CONFUSED--AND SCARED--THAN EVER!
POOR BOY LOOKS LIKE HE WAS JUST KICKED IN THE GUT. BETTER GET USED TO IT, SONNY--
--BECAUSE THERE'S MORE TO COME.
YOU OKAY, SCOTT?
SOMETHING I ATE-- IT'S MAKING ME FEEL A BIT WEIRD.
YOU STILL WANT TO GET TOGETHER TONIGHT?
ARE YOU KIDDING?
THIS IS A CELEBRATION I WOULDN'T MISS FOR THE WORLD.

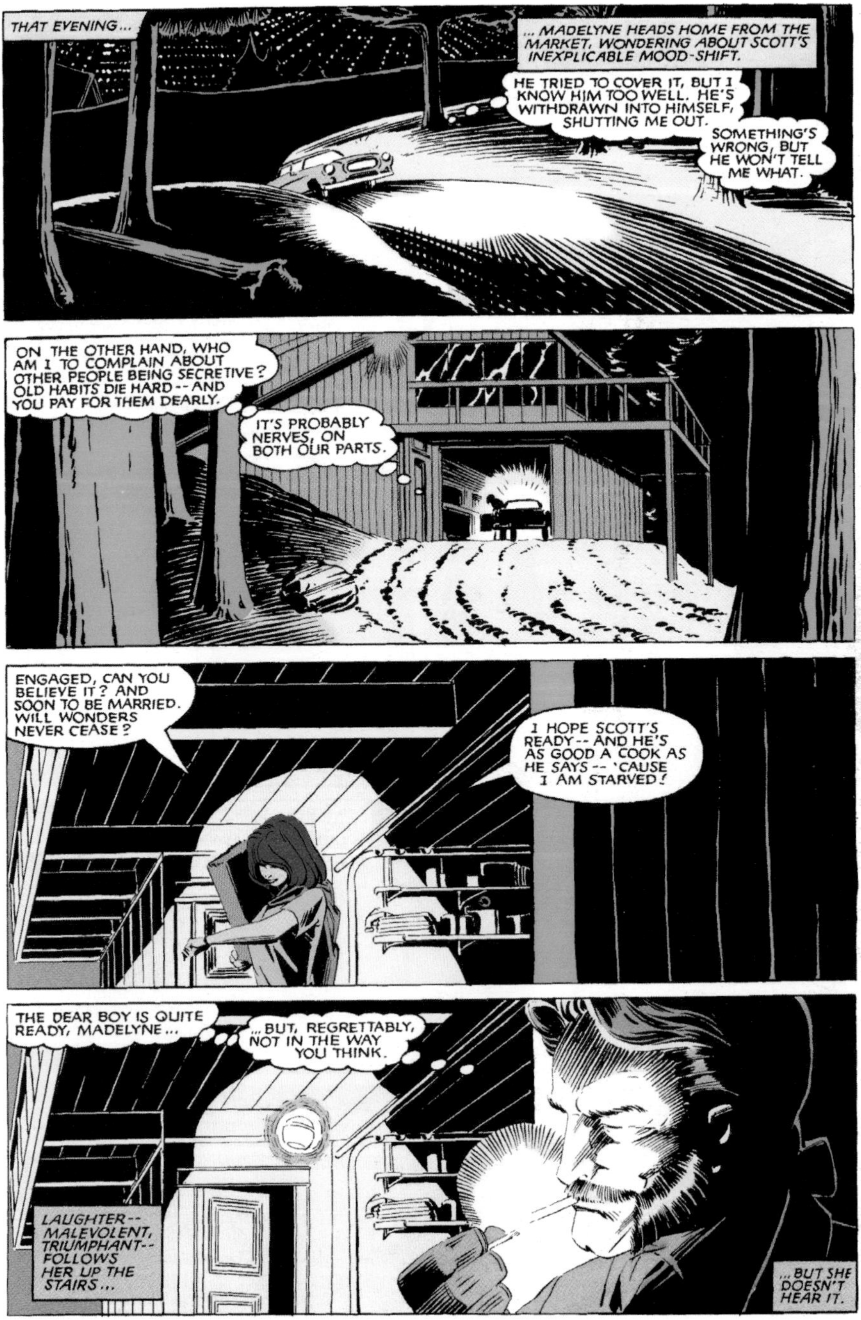
THAT EVENING...
...MADELYNE HEADS HOME FROM THE MARKET, WONDERING ABOUT SCOTT'S INEXPLICABLE MOOD-SHIFT.
HE TRIED TO COVER IT, BUT I KNOW HIM TOO WELL. HE'S WITHDRAWN INTO HIMSELF, SHUTTING ME OUT.
SOMETHING'S WRONG, BUT HE WON'T TELL ME WHAT.
ON THE OTHER HAND, WHO AM I TO COMPLAIN ABOUT OTHER PEOPLE BEING SECRETIVE? OLD HABITS DIE HARD -- AND YOU PAY FOR THEM DEARLY.
IT'S PROBABLY NERVES, ON BOTH OUR PARTS.
ENGAGED, CAN YOU BELIEVE IT? AND SOON TO BE MARRIED. WILL WONDERS NEVER CEASE?
I HOPE SCOTT'S READY -- AND HE'S AS GOOD A COOK AS HE SAYS -- 'CAUSE I AM STARVED!
THE DEAR BOY IS QUITE READY, MADELYNE...
...BUT, REGRETTABLY, NOT IN THE WAY YOU THINK.
LAUGHTER -- MALEVOLENT, TRIUMPHANT -- FOLLOWS HER UP THE STAIRS...
...BUT SHE DOESN'T HEAR IT.

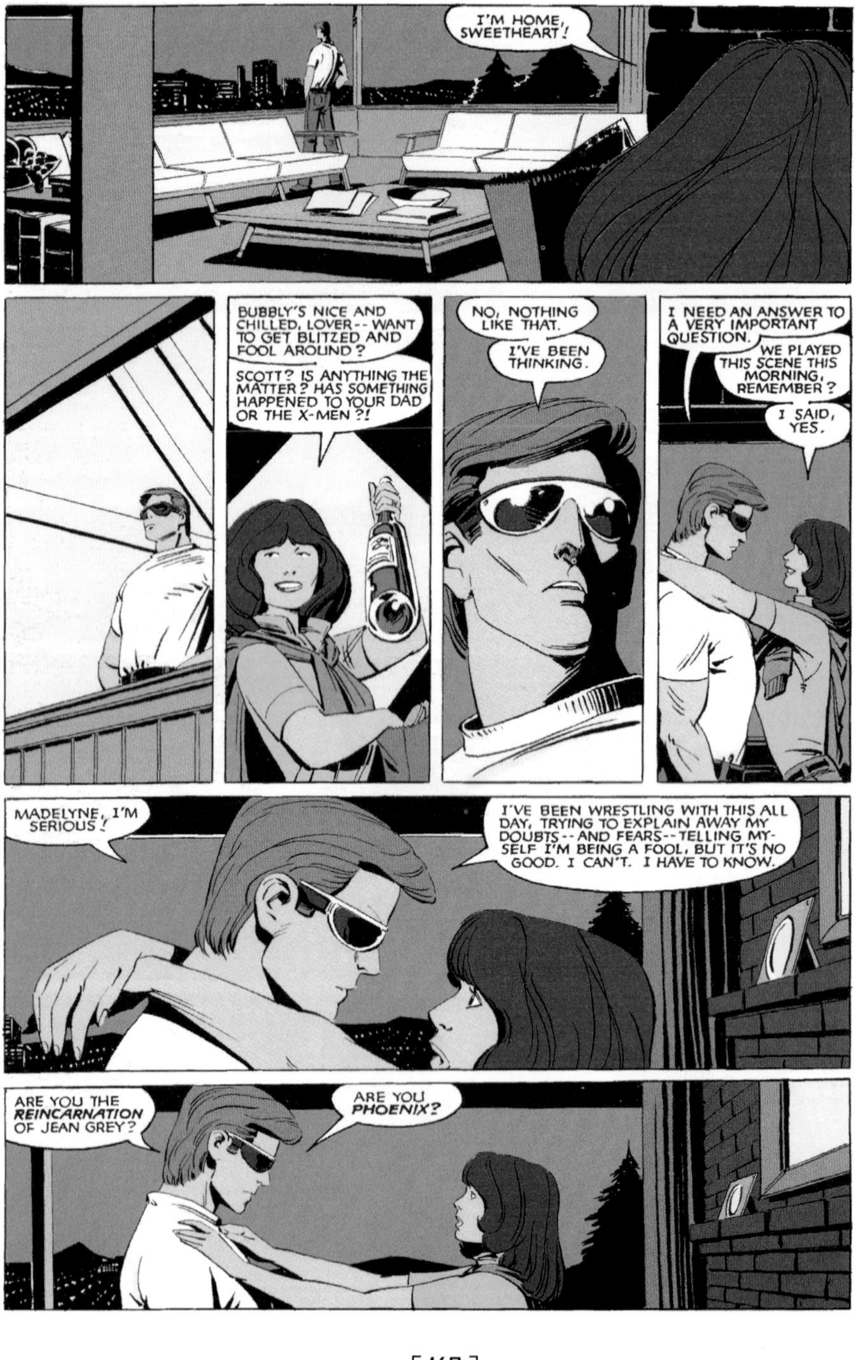
I'M HOME, SWEETHEART!
BUBBLY'S NICE AND CHILLED, LOVER-- WANT TO GET BLITZED AND FOOL AROUND?
SCOTT? IS ANYTHING THE MATTER? HAS SOMETHING HAPPENED TO YOUR DAD OR THE X-MEN?!
NO, NOTHING LIKE THAT.
I'VE BEEN THINKING.
I NEED AN ANSWER TO A VERY IMPORTANT QUESTION.
WE PLAYED THIS SCENE THIS MORNING, REMEMBER?
I SAID, YES.
MADELYNE, I'M SERIOUS!
I'VE BEEN WRESTLING WITH THIS ALL DAY, TRYING TO EXPLAIN AWAY MY DOUBTS--AND FEARS--TELLING MY-SELF I'M BEING A FOOL, BUT IT'S NO GOOD. I CAN'T. I HAVE TO KNOW.
ARE YOU THE REINCARNATION OF JEAN GREY?
ARE YOU PHOENIX?

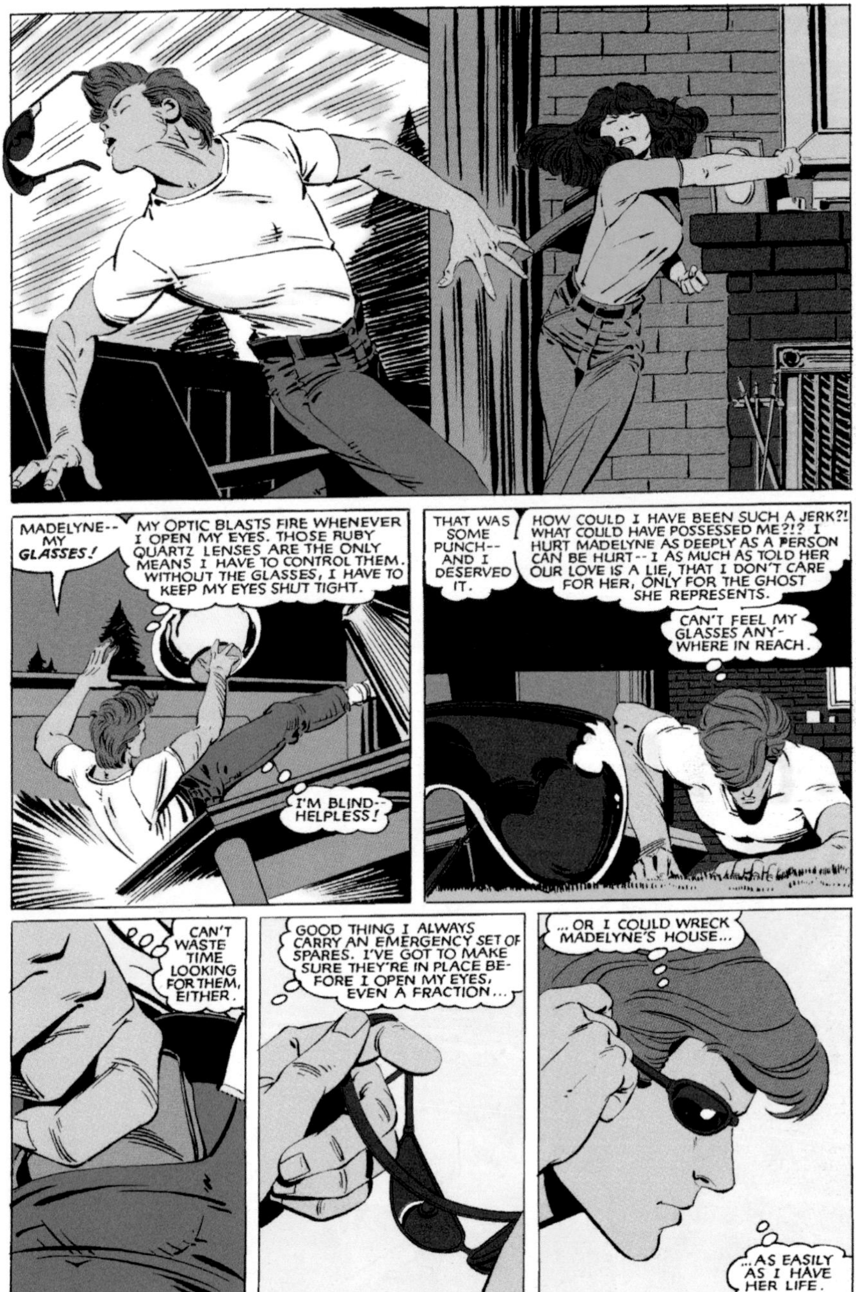

MADELYNE-- MY GLASSES!
MY OPTIC BLASTS FIRE WHENEVER I OPEN MY EYES. THOSE RUBY QUARTZ LENSES ARE THE ONLY MEANS I HAVE TO CONTROL THEM. WITHOUT THE GLASSES, I HAVE TO KEEP MY EYES SHUT TIGHT.
I'M BLIND-- HELPLESS!
THAT WAS SOME PUNCH-- AND I DESERVED IT.
HOW COULD I HAVE BEEN SUCH A JERK?! WHAT COULD HAVE POSSESSED ME?!? I HURT MADELYNE AS DEEPLY AS A PERSON CAN BE HURT-- I AS MUCH AS TOLD HER OUR LOVE IS A LIE, THAT I DON'T CARE FOR HER, ONLY FOR THE GHOST SHE REPRESENTS.
CAN'T FEEL MY GLASSES ANY-WHERE IN REACH.
CAN'T WASTE TIME LOOKING FOR THEM, EITHER.
GOOD THING I ALWAYS CARRY AN EMERGENCY SET OF SPARES. I'VE GOT TO MAKE SURE THEY'RE IN PLACE BE-FORE I OPEN MY EYES, EVEN A FRACTION...
...OR I COULD WRECK MADELYNE'S HOUSE...
...AS EASILY AS I HAVE HER LIFE.

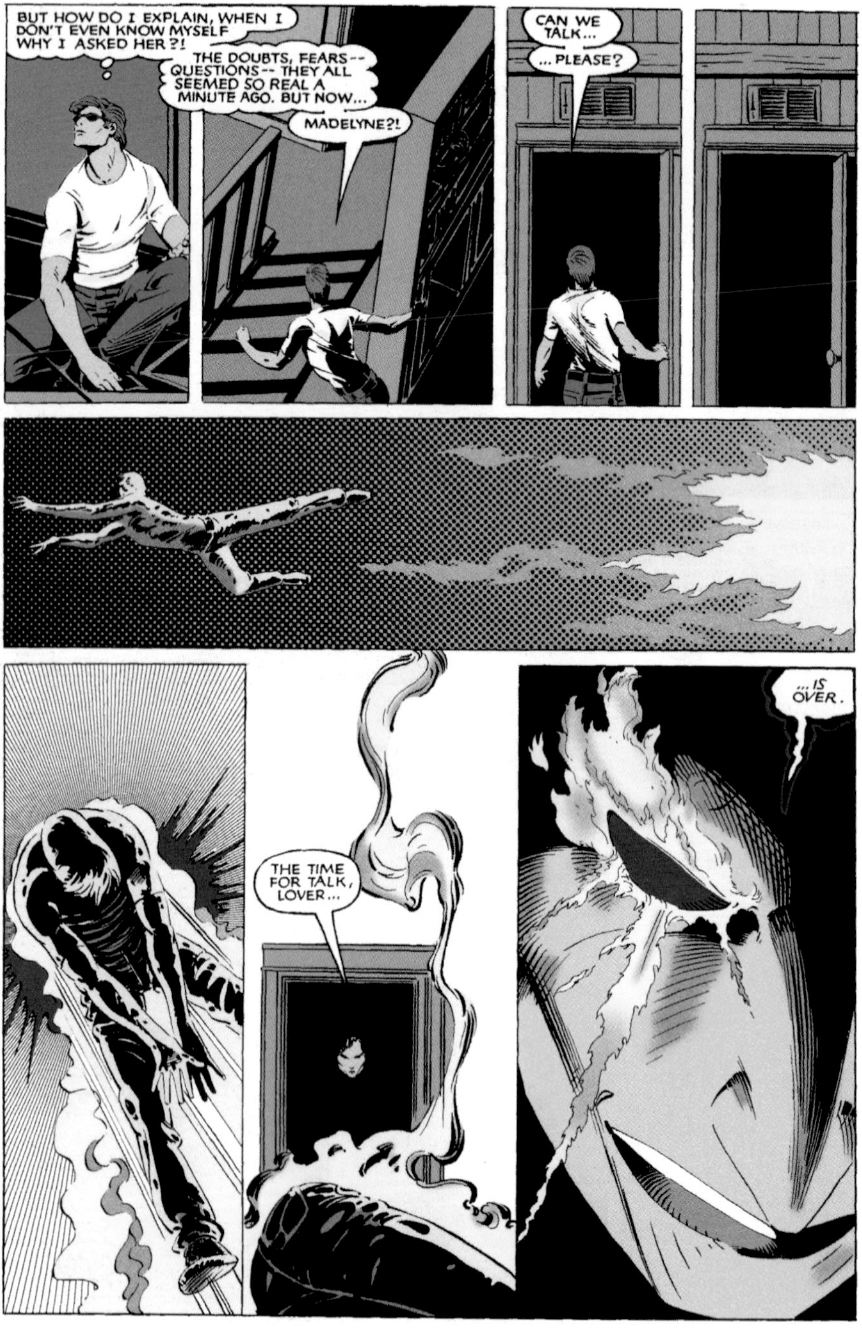
BUT HOW DO I EXPLAIN, WHEN I DON'T EVEN KNOW MYSELF WHY I ASKED HER?!
THE DOUBTS, FEARS-- QUESTIONS-- THEY ALL SEEMED SO REAL A MINUTE AGO. BUT NOW...
MADELYNE?!
CAN WE TALK...
... PLEASE?
THE TIME FOR TALK, LOVER...
...IS OVER.

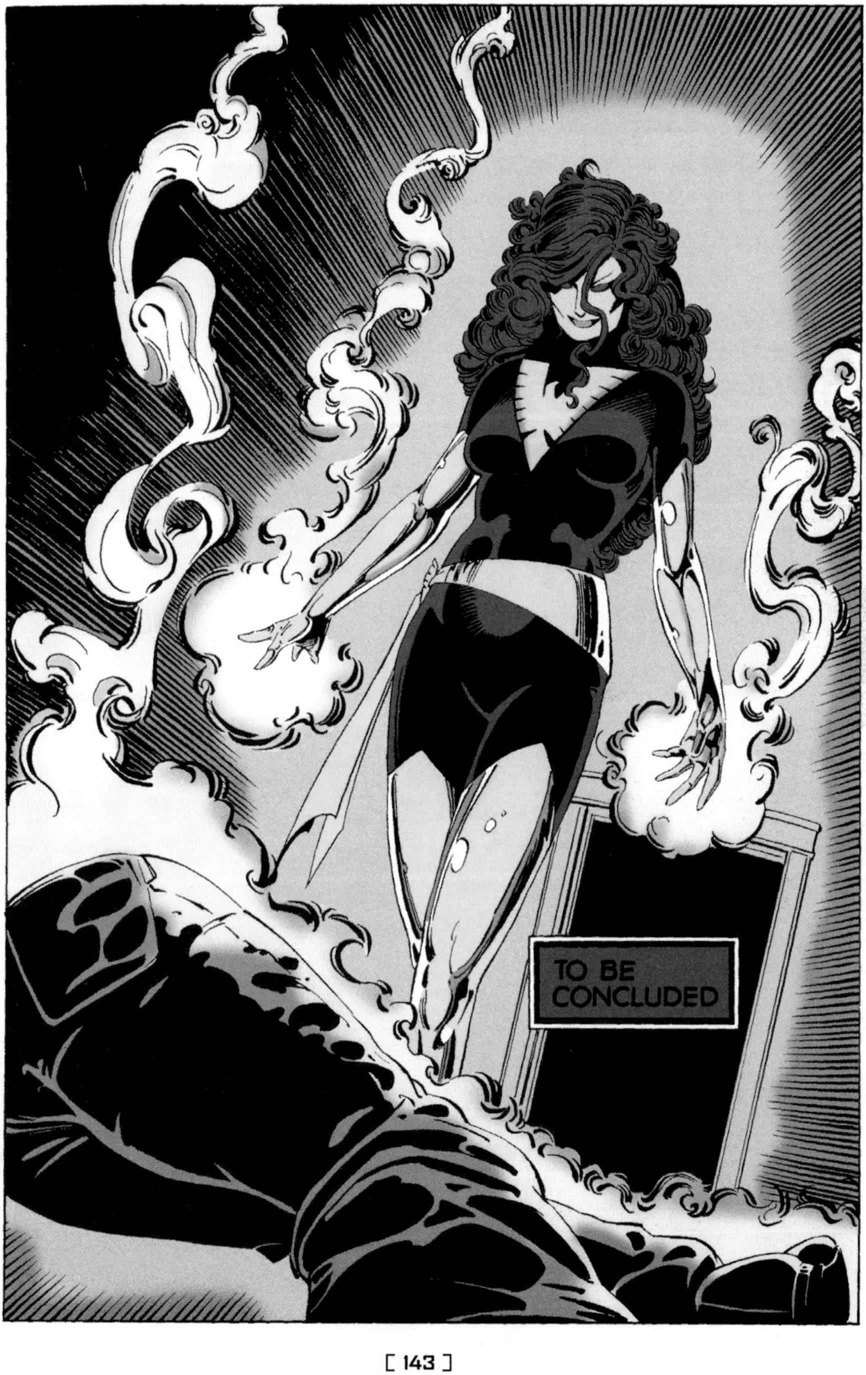
TO BE
CONCLUDED

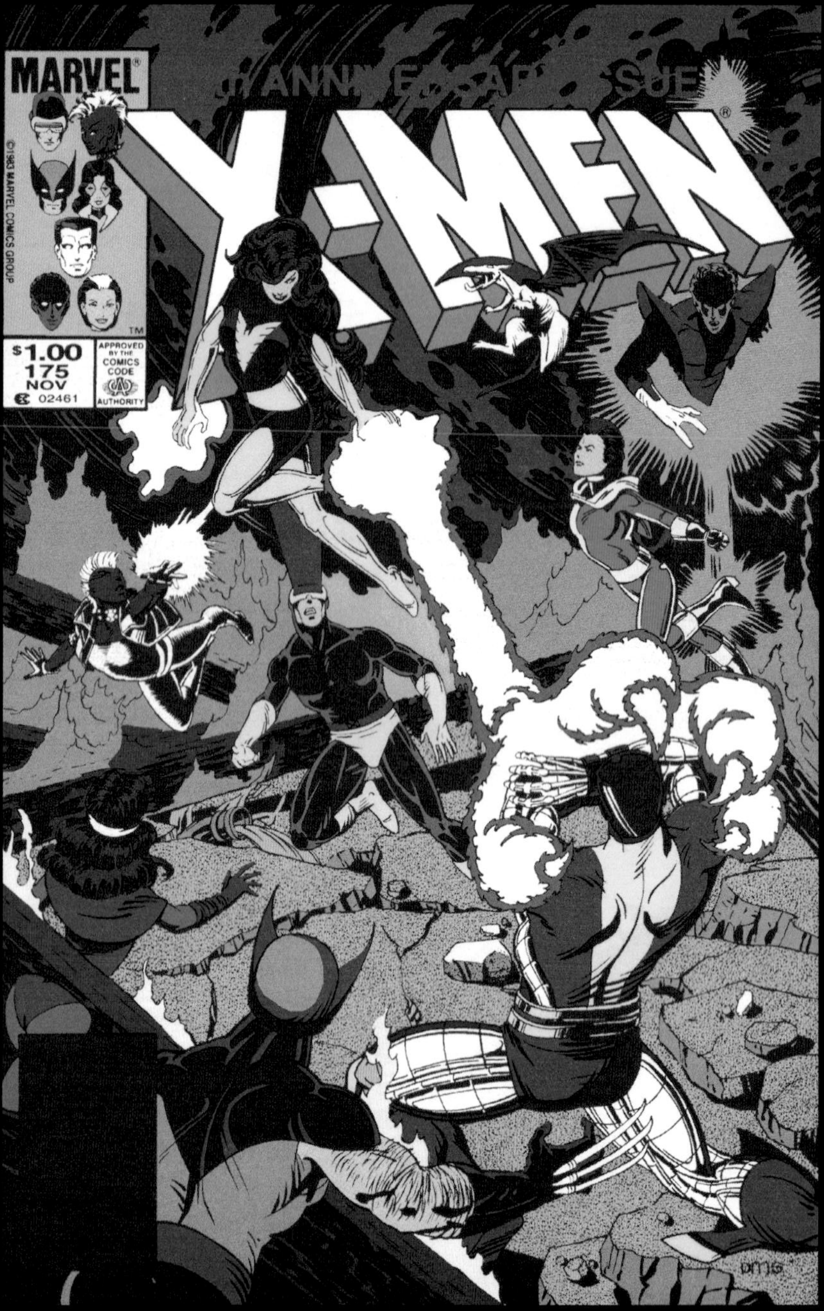
MARVEL®
©1983 MARVEL COMICS GROUP
TM
$1.00
175
NOV
02461
APPROVED BY THE COMICS CODE AUTHORITY
X-MEN®

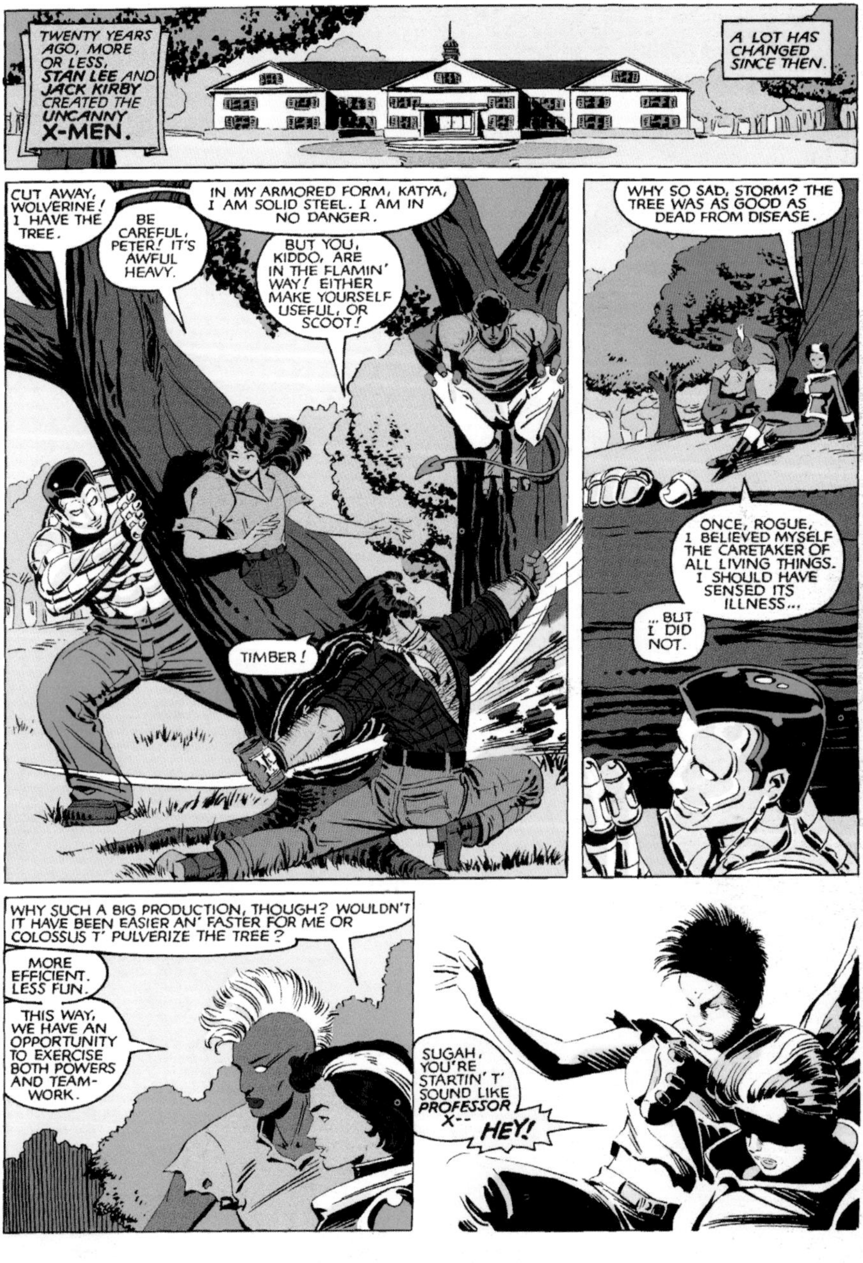
TWENTY YEARS AGO, MORE OR LESS, STAN LEE AND JACK KIRBY CREATED THE UNCANNY X-MEN.
A LOT HAS CHANGED SINCE THEN.
CUT AWAY, WOLVERINE! I HAVE THE TREE.
BE CAREFUL, PETER! IT'S AWFUL HEAVY.
IN MY ARMORED FORM, KATYA, I AM SOLID STEEL. I AM IN NO DANGER.
BUT YOU, KIDDO, ARE IN THE FLAMIN' WAY! EITHER MAKE YOURSELF USEFUL, OR SCOOT!
TIMBER!
WHY SO SAD, STORM? THE TREE WAS AS GOOD AS DEAD FROM DISEASE.
ONCE, ROGUE, I BELIEVED MYSELF THE CARETAKER OF ALL LIVING THINGS. I SHOULD HAVE SENSED ITS ILLNESS...
...BUT I DID NOT.
WHY SUCH A BIG PRODUCTION, THOUGH? WOULDN'T IT HAVE BEEN EASIER AN' FASTER FOR ME OR COLOSSUS T' PULVERIZE THE TREE?
MORE EFFICIENT. LESS FUN.
THIS WAY, WE HAVE AN OPPORTUNITY TO EXERCISE BOTH POWERS AND TEAM-WORK.
SUGAH, YOU'RE STARTIN' T' SOUND LIKE PROFESSOR X--
HEY!

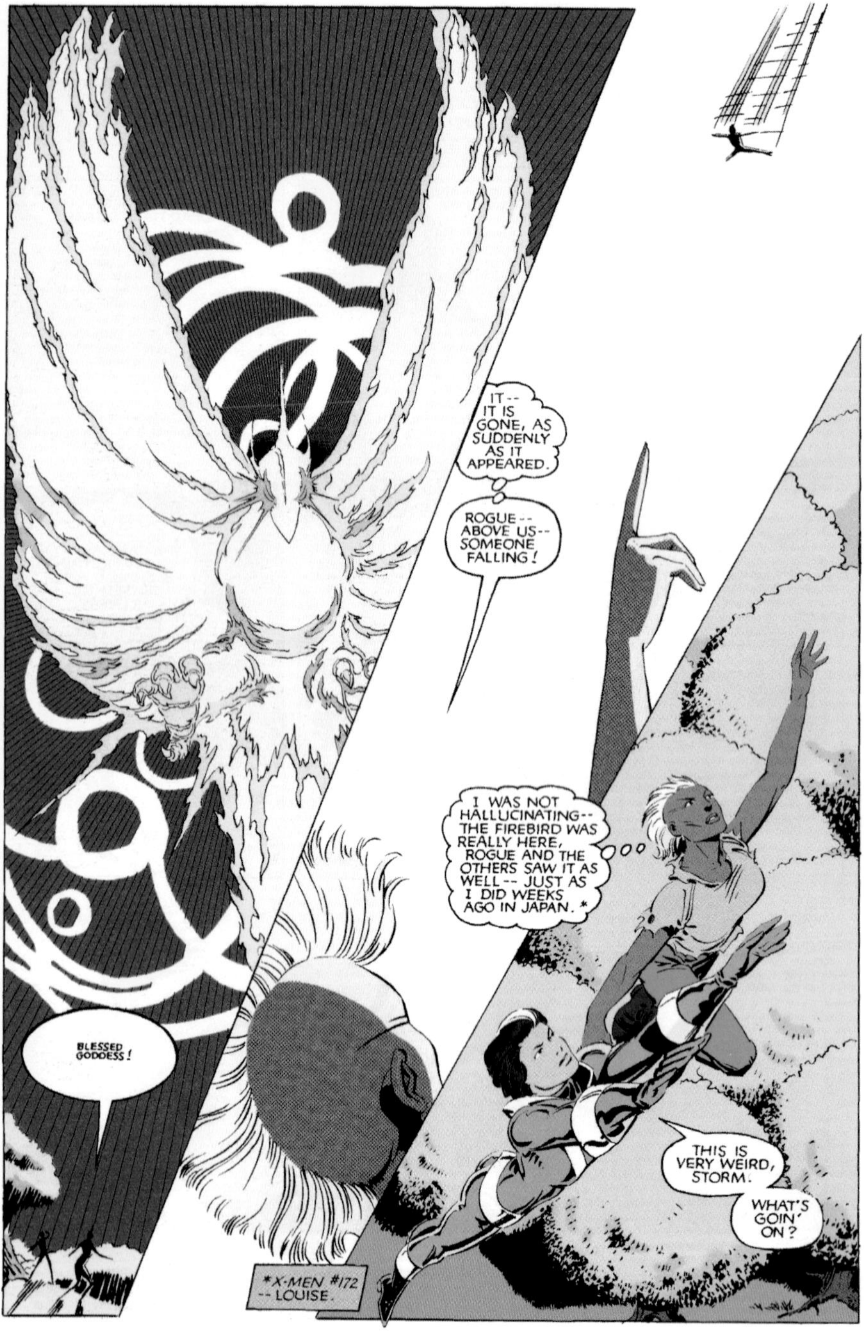
IT-- IT IS GONE, AS SUDDENLY AS IT APPEARED.
ROGUE-- ABOVE US-- SOMEONE FALLING!
I WAS NOT HALLUCINATING-- THE FIREBIRD WAS REALLY HERE, ROGUE AND THE OTHERS SAW IT AS WELL-- JUST AS I DID WEEKS AGO IN JAPAN.*
BLESSED GODDESS!
THIS IS VERY WEIRD, STORM.
WHAT'S GOIN' ON?
*X-MEN #172 --LOUISE.

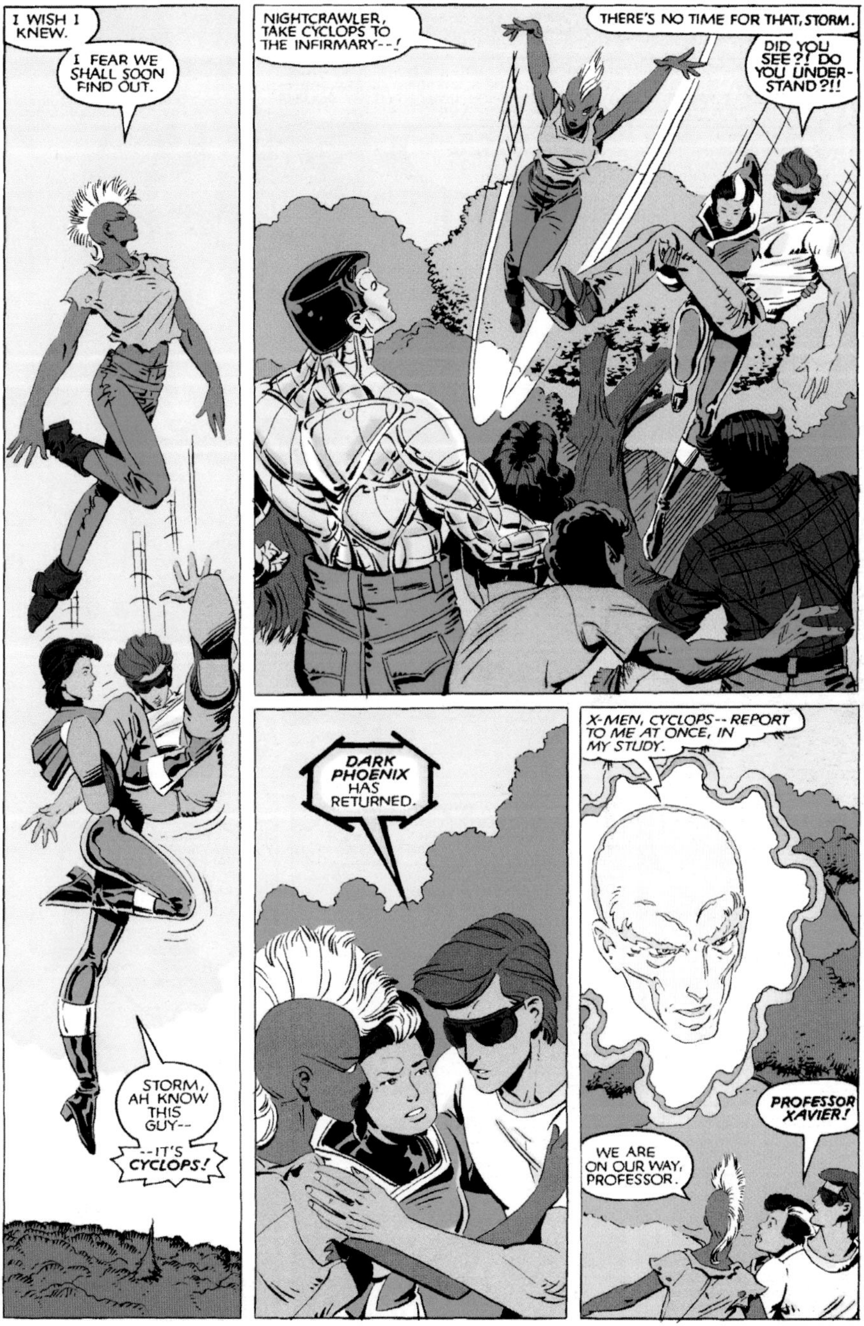
I WISH I KNEW.
I FEAR WE SHALL SOON FIND OUT.
STORM, AH KNOW THIS GUY--
--IT'S CYCLOPS!
NIGHTCRAWLER, TAKE CYCLOPS TO THE INFIRMARY--!
THERE'S NO TIME FOR THAT, STORM.
DID YOU SEE?! DO YOU UNDERSTAND?!!
DARK PHOENIX HAS RETURNED.
X-MEN, CYCLOPS--REPORT TO ME AT ONCE, IN MY STUDY.
PROFESSOR XAVIER!
WE ARE ON OUR WAY, PROFESSOR.

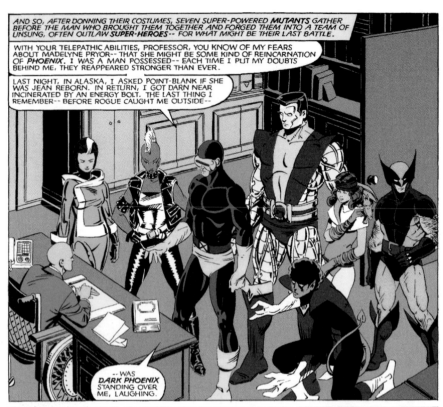

AND SO, AFTER DONNING THEIR COSTUMES, SEVEN SUPER-POWERED **MUTANTS** GATHER BEFORE THE MAN WHO BROUGHT THEM TOGETHER AND FORGED THEM INTO A TEAM OF UNSUNG, OFTEN OUTLAW **SUPER-HEROES**-- FOR WHAT MIGHT BE THEIR LAST BATTLE.

WITH YOUR TELEPATHIC ABILITIES, PROFESSOR, YOU KNOW OF MY FEARS ABOUT MADELYNE PRYOR-- THAT SHE MIGHT BE SOME KIND OF REINCARNATION OF **PHOENIX**. I WAS A MAN POSSESSED-- EACH TIME I PUT MY DOUBTS BEHIND ME, THEY REAPPEARED STRONGER THAN EVER.

LAST NIGHT, IN ALASKA, I ASKED POINT-BLANK IF SHE WAS JEAN REBORN. IN RETURN, I GOT DARN NEAR INCINERATED BY AN ENERGY BOLT. THE LAST THING I REMEMBER-- BEFORE ROGUE CAUGHT ME OUTSIDE--

-- WAS **DARK PHOENIX** STANDING OVER ME, LAUGHING.

JEAN--PHOENIX--**LOVED** YOU, SCOTT. WHY, THEN, DID SHE ATTACK? WHY **HEAL** YOUR WOUNDS-- WHICH THE IMAGES IN YOUR MIND TELL ME WERE AGONIZING AND FATAL?

OUR FIRST STEP MUST BE TO FIND HER AND LEARN HER INTENTIONS-- AND FROM THERE, DEAL WITH THEM.

WE ARE FACING A **COSMIC** ENTITY, PROFESSOR-- PHOENIX CONSUMED ENTIRE STAR SYSTEMS. WOULD IT NOT BE WISE TO SUMMON REENFORCEMENTS?

WHEN I'M CONVINCED OF THE THREAT, STORM. I SENSED JEAN'S DEATH, YEARS AGO...

... BUT NOT THIS MIRACULOUS REBIRTH...

... AND I SHOULD HAVE.

CEREBRO WILL AMPLIFY MY PSI-TALENT A HUNDRED-FOLD. IF PHOENIX EXISTS, THIS WILL ENABLE ME TO FIND HER.

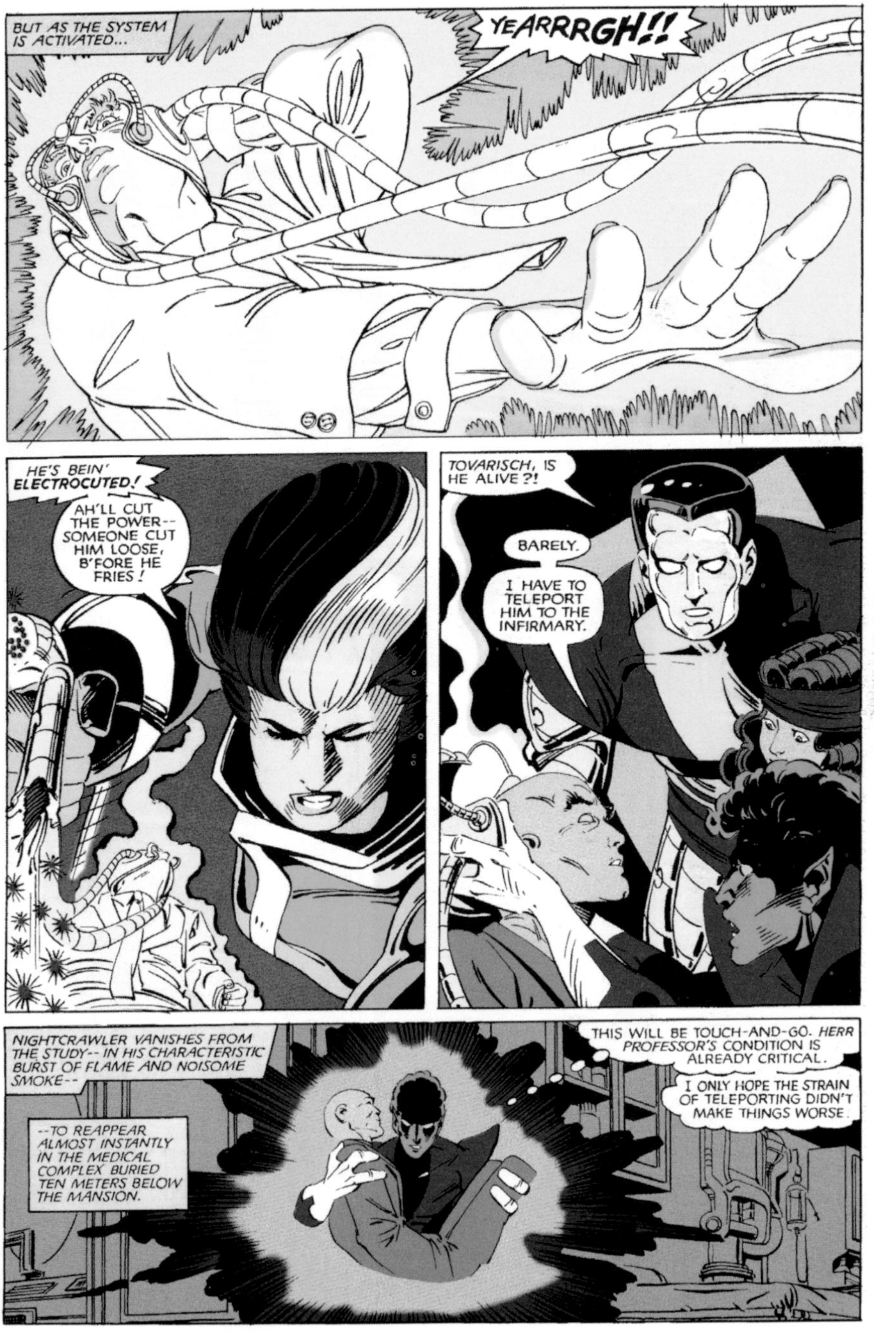
BUT AS THE SYSTEM IS ACTIVATED...
YEARRRGH!!
HE'S BEIN' ELECTROCUTED!
AH'LL CUT THE POWER-- SOMEONE CUT HIM LOOSE, B'FORE HE FRIES!
TOVARISCH, IS HE ALIVE?!
BARELY.
I HAVE TO TELEPORT HIM TO THE INFIRMARY.
NIGHTCRAWLER VANISHES FROM THE STUDY-- IN HIS CHARACTERISTIC BURST OF FLAME AND NOISOME SMOKE--
--TO REAPPEAR ALMOST INSTANTLY IN THE MEDICAL COMPLEX BURIED TEN METERS BELOW THE MANSION.
THIS WILL BE TOUCH-AND-GO. HERR PROFESSOR'S CONDITION IS ALREADY CRITICAL.
I ONLY HOPE THE STRAIN OF TELEPORTING DIDN'T MAKE THINGS WORSE.

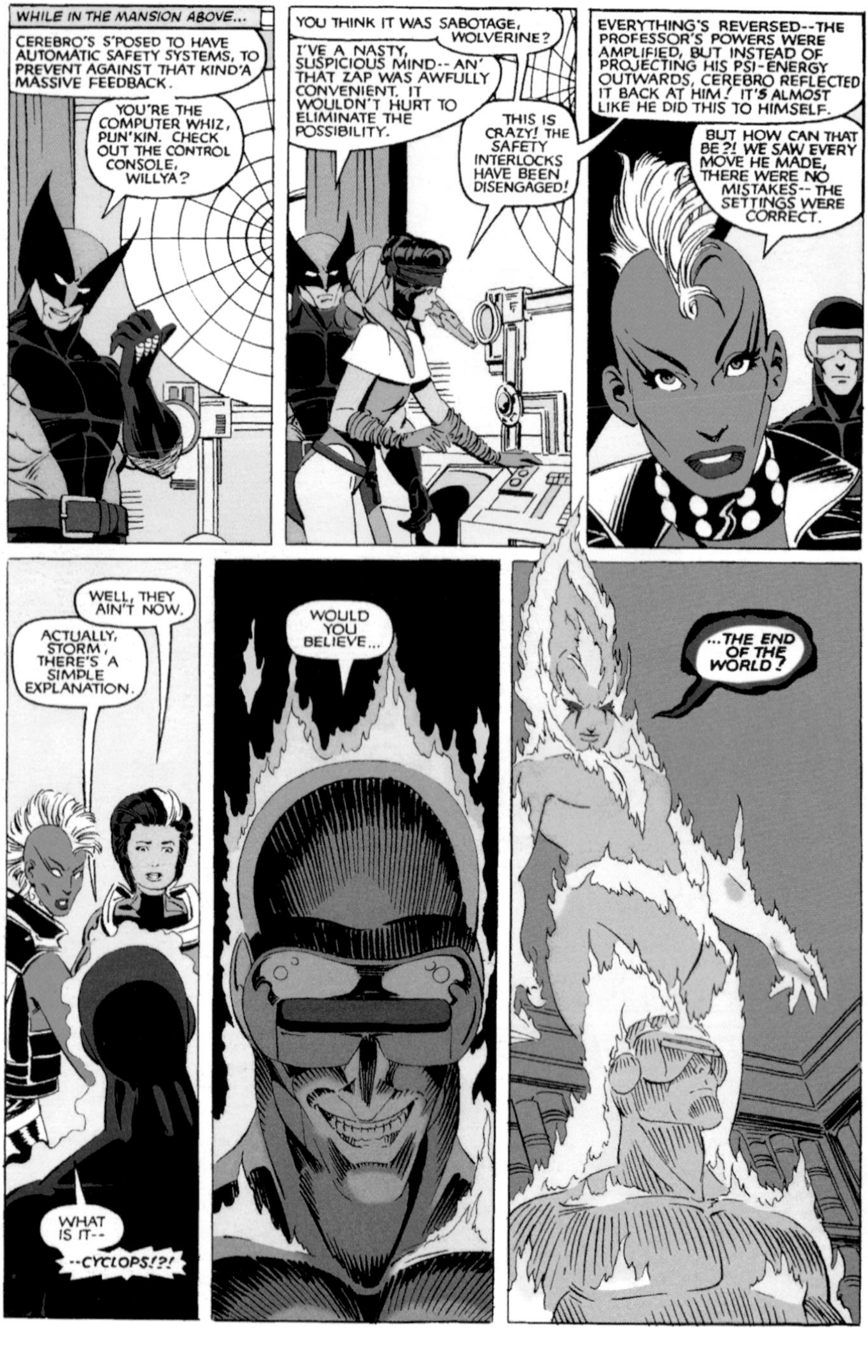

WHILE IN THE MANSION ABOVE...
CEREBRO'S S'POSED TO HAVE AUTOMATIC SAFETY SYSTEMS, TO PREVENT AGAINST THAT KIND'A MASSIVE FEEDBACK.
YOU'RE THE COMPUTER WHIZ, PUN'KIN. CHECK OUT THE CONTROL CONSOLE, WILLYA?
YOU THINK IT WAS SABOTAGE, WOLVERINE?
I'VE A NASTY, SUSPICIOUS MIND-- AN' THAT ZAP WAS AWFULLY CONVENIENT. IT WOULDN'T HURT TO ELIMINATE THE POSSIBILITY.
THIS IS CRAZY! THE SAFETY INTERLOCKS HAVE BEEN DISENGAGED!
EVERYTHING'S REVERSED--THE PROFESSOR'S POWERS WERE AMPLIFIED, BUT INSTEAD OF PROJECTING HIS PSI-ENERGY OUTWARDS, CEREBRO REFLECTED IT BACK AT HIM! IT'S ALMOST LIKE HE DID THIS TO HIMSELF.
BUT HOW CAN THAT BE?! WE SAW EVERY MOVE HE MADE, THERE WERE NO MISTAKES-- THE SETTINGS WERE CORRECT.
WELL, THEY AIN'T NOW.
ACTUALLY, STORM, THERE'S A SIMPLE EXPLANATION.
WHAT IS IT--
--CYCLOPS!?!
WOULD YOU BELIEVE...
...THE END OF THE WORLD?

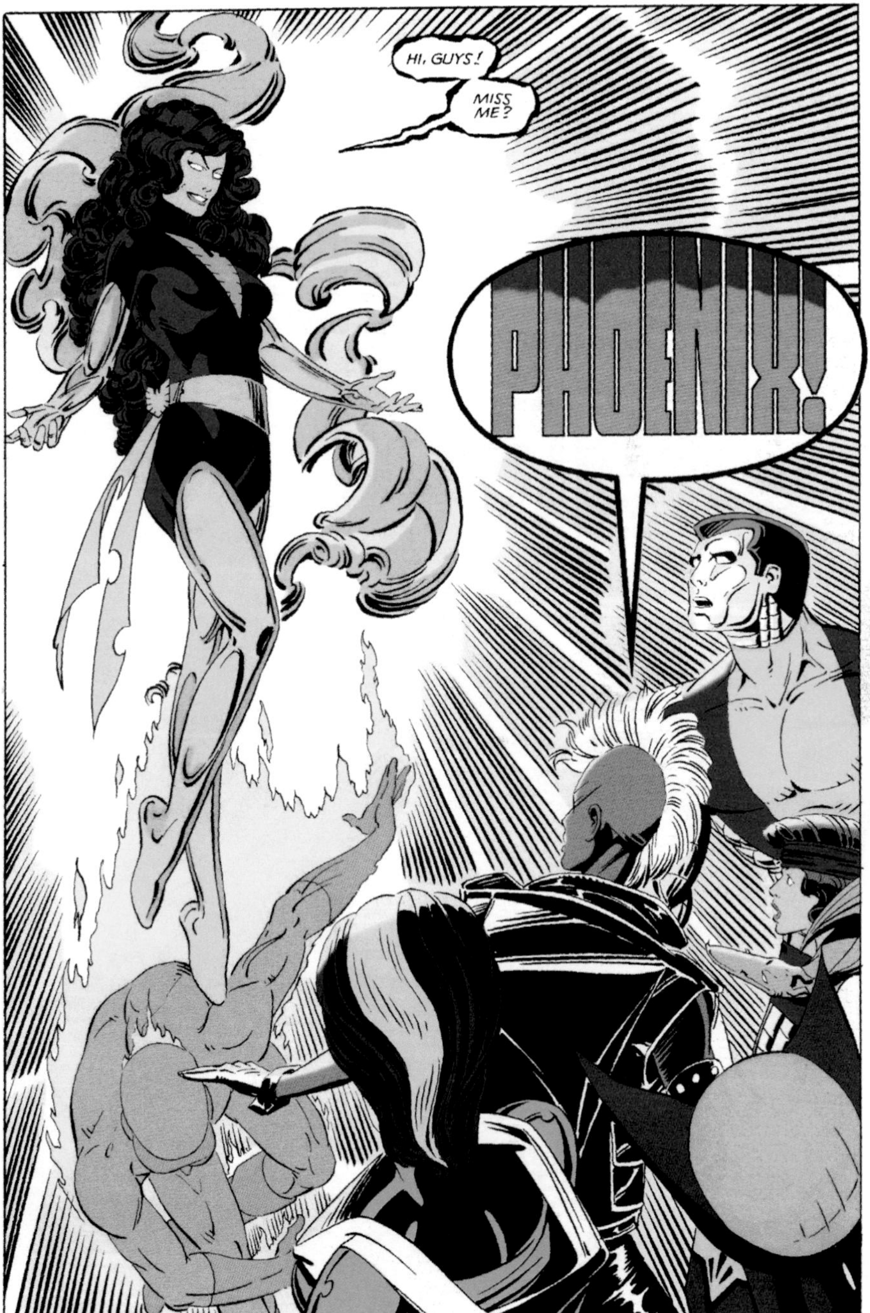
HI, GUYS!
MISS ME?
PHOENIX!

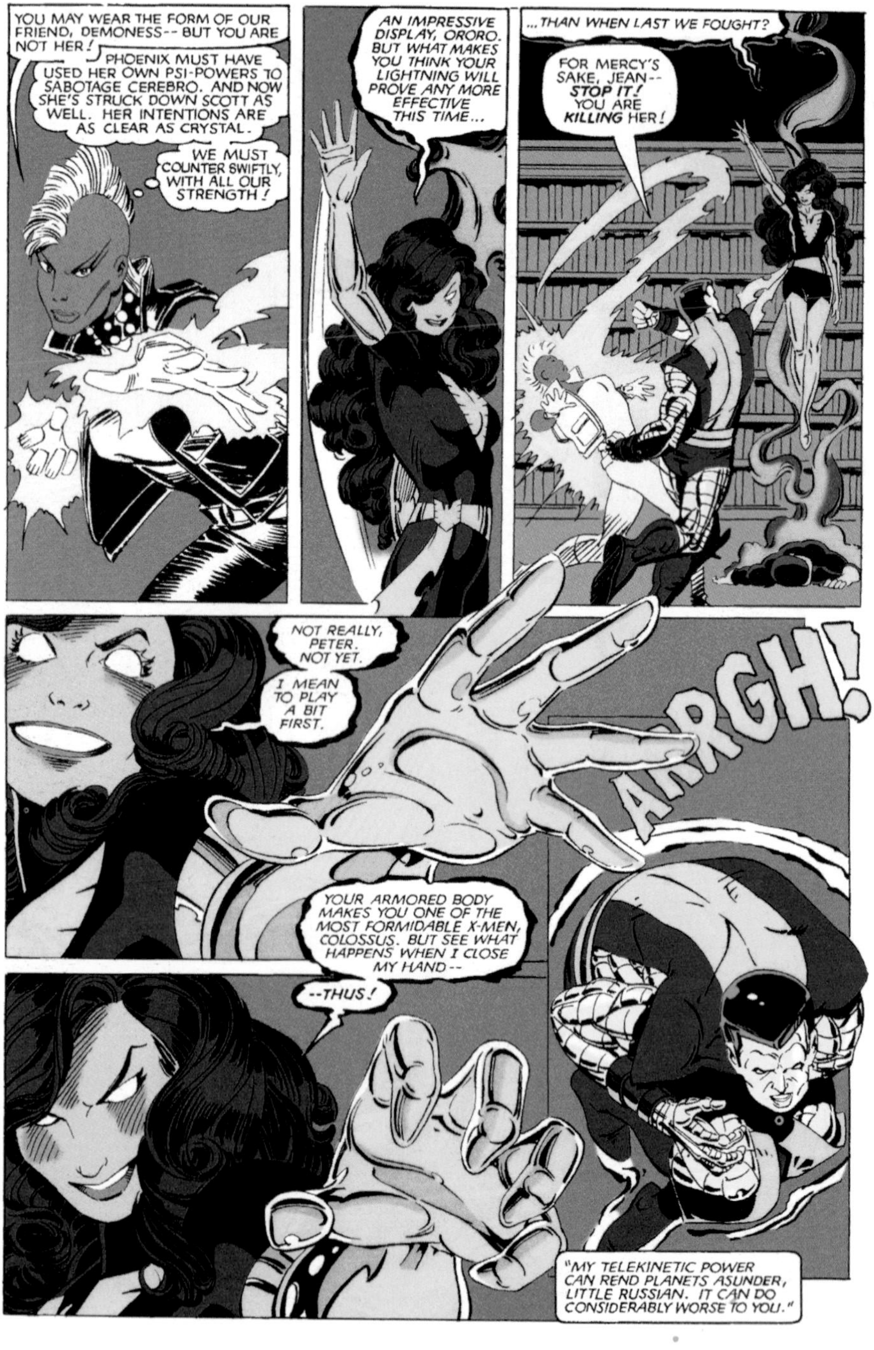
YOU MAY WEAR THE FORM OF OUR FRIEND, DEMONESS-- BUT YOU ARE NOT HER!
PHOENIX MUST HAVE USED HER OWN PSI-POWERS TO SABOTAGE CEREBRO. AND NOW SHE'S STRUCK DOWN SCOTT AS WELL. HER INTENTIONS ARE AS CLEAR AS CRYSTAL.
WE MUST COUNTER SWIFTLY, WITH ALL OUR STRENGTH!
AN IMPRESSIVE DISPLAY, ORORO. BUT WHAT MAKES YOU THINK YOUR LIGHTNING WILL PROVE ANY MORE EFFECTIVE THIS TIME...
...THAN WHEN LAST WE FOUGHT?
FOR MERCY'S SAKE, JEAN-- STOP IT! YOU ARE KILLING HER!
NOT REALLY, PETER. NOT YET.
I MEAN TO PLAY A BIT FIRST.
AARRGH!
YOUR ARMORED BODY MAKES YOU ONE OF THE MOST FORMIDABLE X-MEN, COLOSSUS. BUT SEE WHAT HAPPENS WHEN I CLOSE MY HAND--
--THUS!
"MY TELEKINETIC POWER CAN REND PLANETS ASUNDER, LITTLE RUSSIAN. IT CAN DO CONSIDERABLY WORSE TO YOU."

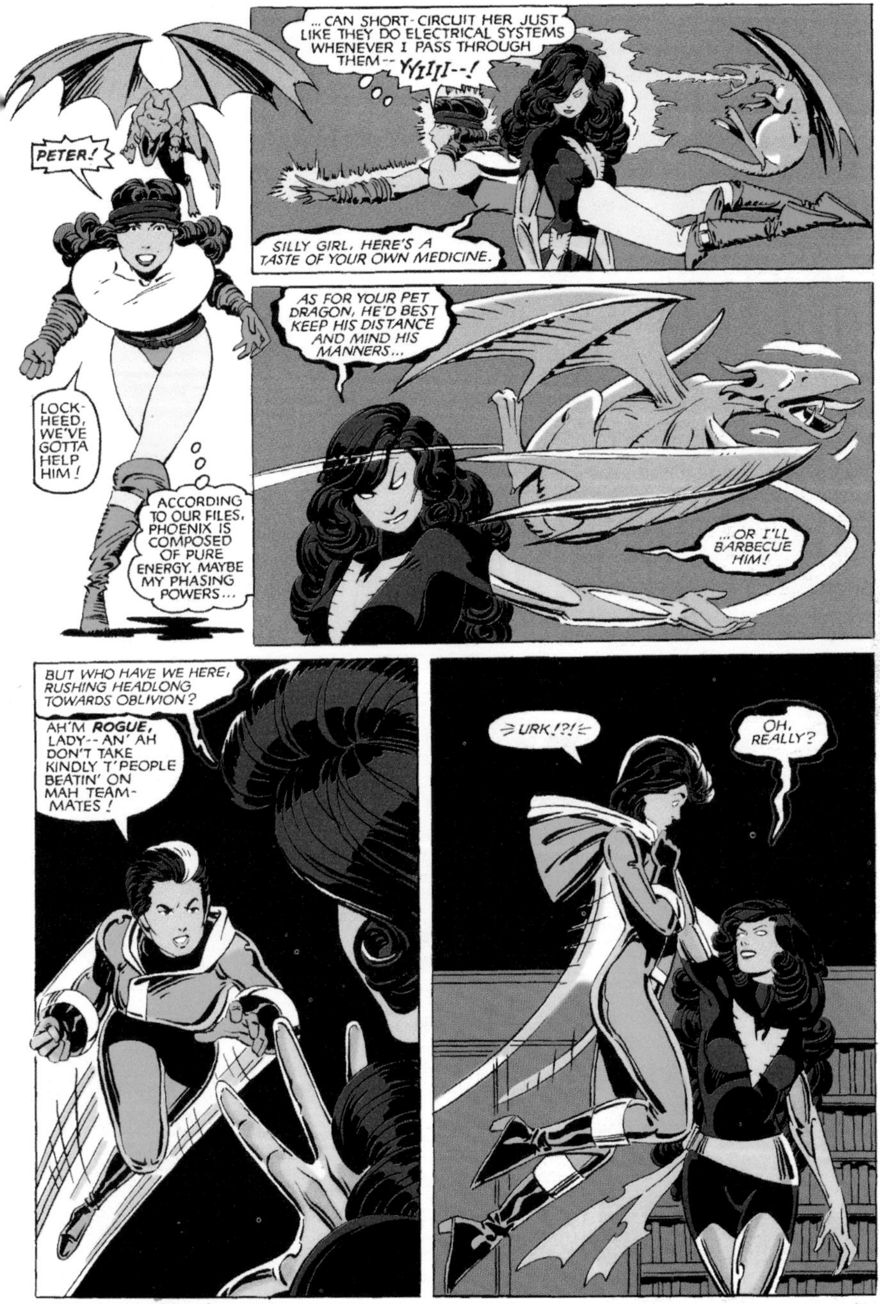
PETER!
LOCK-HEED, WE'VE GOTTA HELP HIM!
ACCORDING TO OUR FILES, PHOENIX IS COMPOSED OF PURE ENERGY. MAYBE MY PHASING POWERS...
...CAN SHORT-CIRCUIT HER JUST LIKE THEY DO ELECTRICAL SYSTEMS WHENEVER I PASS THROUGH THEM-- YYIIII--!
SILLY GIRL. HERE'S A TASTE OF YOUR OWN MEDICINE.
AS FOR YOUR PET DRAGON, HE'D BEST KEEP HIS DISTANCE AND MIND HIS MANNERS...
...OR I'LL BARBECUE HIM!
BUT WHO HAVE WE HERE, RUSHING HEADLONG TOWARDS OBLIVION?
AH'M ROGUE, LADY-- AN' AH DON'T TAKE KINDLY T'PEOPLE BEATIN' ON MAH TEAM-MATES!
URK!?!
OH, REALLY?

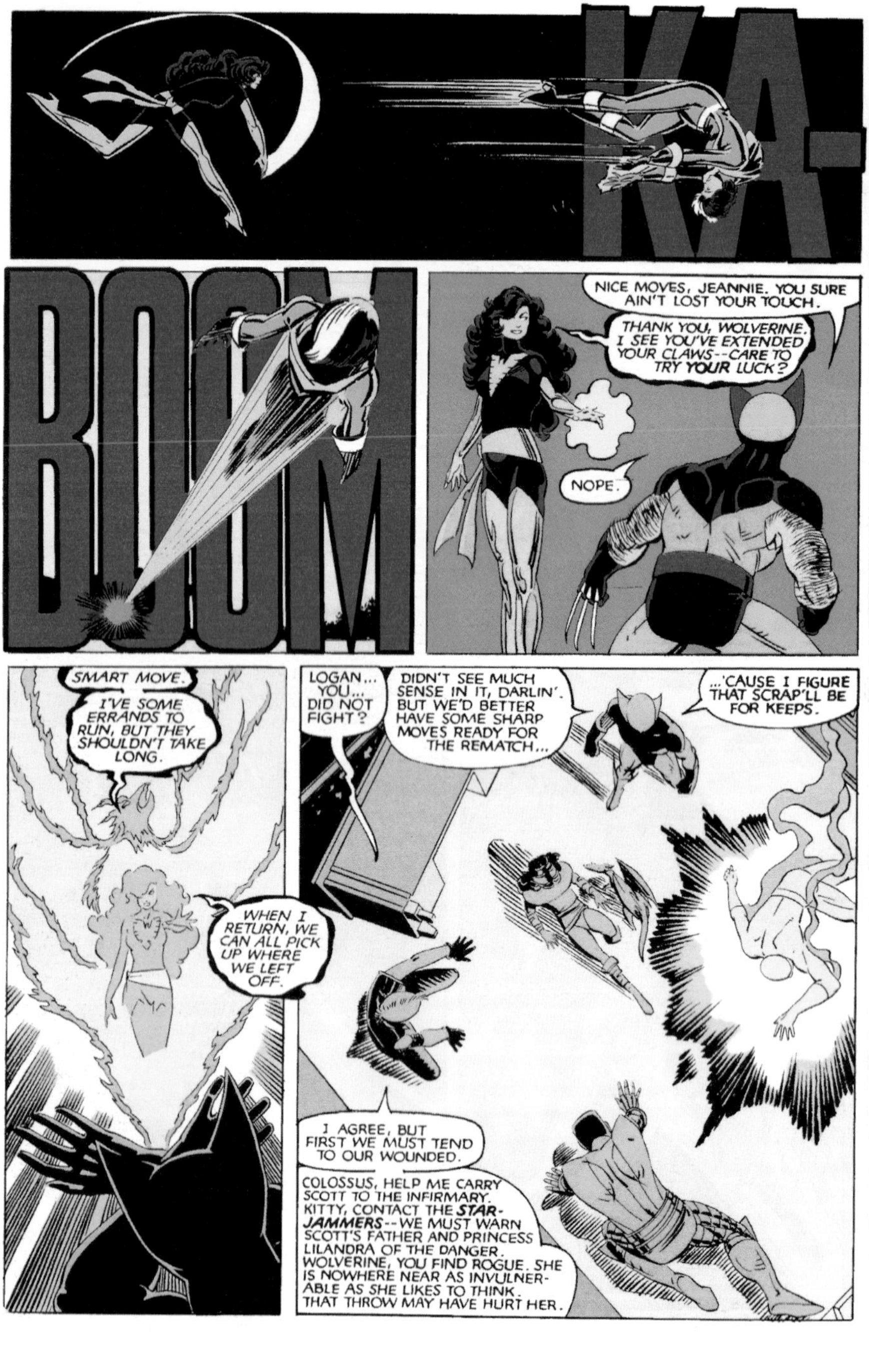
KA-
BOOM
NICE MOVES, JEANNIE. YOU SURE AIN'T LOST YOUR TOUCH.
THANK YOU, WOLVERINE. I SEE YOU'VE EXTENDED YOUR CLAWS--CARE TO TRY YOUR LUCK?
NOPE.
SMART MOVE.
I'VE SOME ERRANDS TO RUN, BUT THEY SHOULDN'T TAKE LONG.
WHEN I RETURN, WE CAN ALL PICK UP WHERE WE LEFT OFF.
LOGAN... YOU... DID NOT FIGHT?
DIDN'T SEE MUCH SENSE IN IT, DARLIN'. BUT WE'D BETTER HAVE SOME SHARP MOVES READY FOR THE REMATCH...
...'CAUSE I FIGURE THAT SCRAP'LL BE FOR KEEPS.
I AGREE, BUT FIRST WE MUST TEND TO OUR WOUNDED.
COLOSSUS, HELP ME CARRY SCOTT TO THE INFIRMARY. KITTY, CONTACT THE STAR-JAMMERS--WE MUST WARN SCOTT'S FATHER AND PRINCESS LILANDRA OF THE DANGER. WOLVERINE, YOU FIND ROGUE. SHE IS NOWHERE NEAR AS INVULNERABLE AS SHE LIKES TO THINK. THAT THROW MAY HAVE HURT HER.

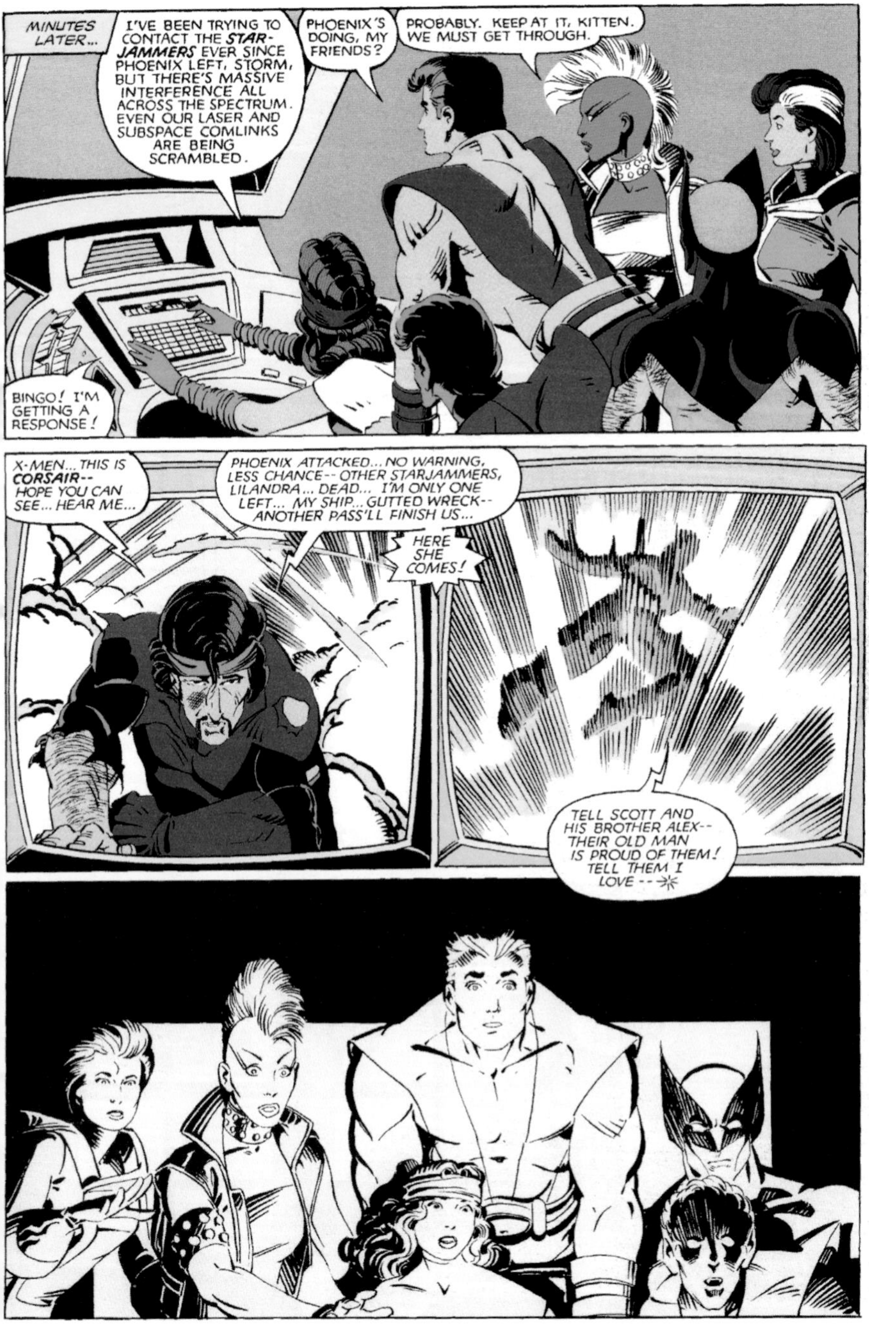
MINUTES LATER...
I'VE BEEN TRYING TO CONTACT THE STARJAMMERS EVER SINCE PHOENIX LEFT, STORM, BUT THERE'S MASSIVE INTERFERENCE ALL ACROSS THE SPECTRUM. EVEN OUR LASER AND SUBSPACE COMLINKS ARE BEING SCRAMBLED.
PHOENIX'S DOING, MY FRIENDS?
PROBABLY. KEEP AT IT, KITTEN. WE MUST GET THROUGH.
BINGO! I'M GETTING A RESPONSE!
X-MEN... THIS IS CORSAIR-- HOPE YOU CAN SEE... HEAR ME...
PHOENIX ATTACKED... NO WARNING, LESS CHANCE-- OTHER STARJAMMERS, LILANDRA... DEAD... I'M ONLY ONE LEFT... MY SHIP... GUTTED WRECK-- ANOTHER PASS'LL FINISH US...
HERE SHE COMES!
TELL SCOTT AND HIS BROTHER ALEX-- THEIR OLD MAN IS PROUD OF THEM! TELL THEM I LOVE --

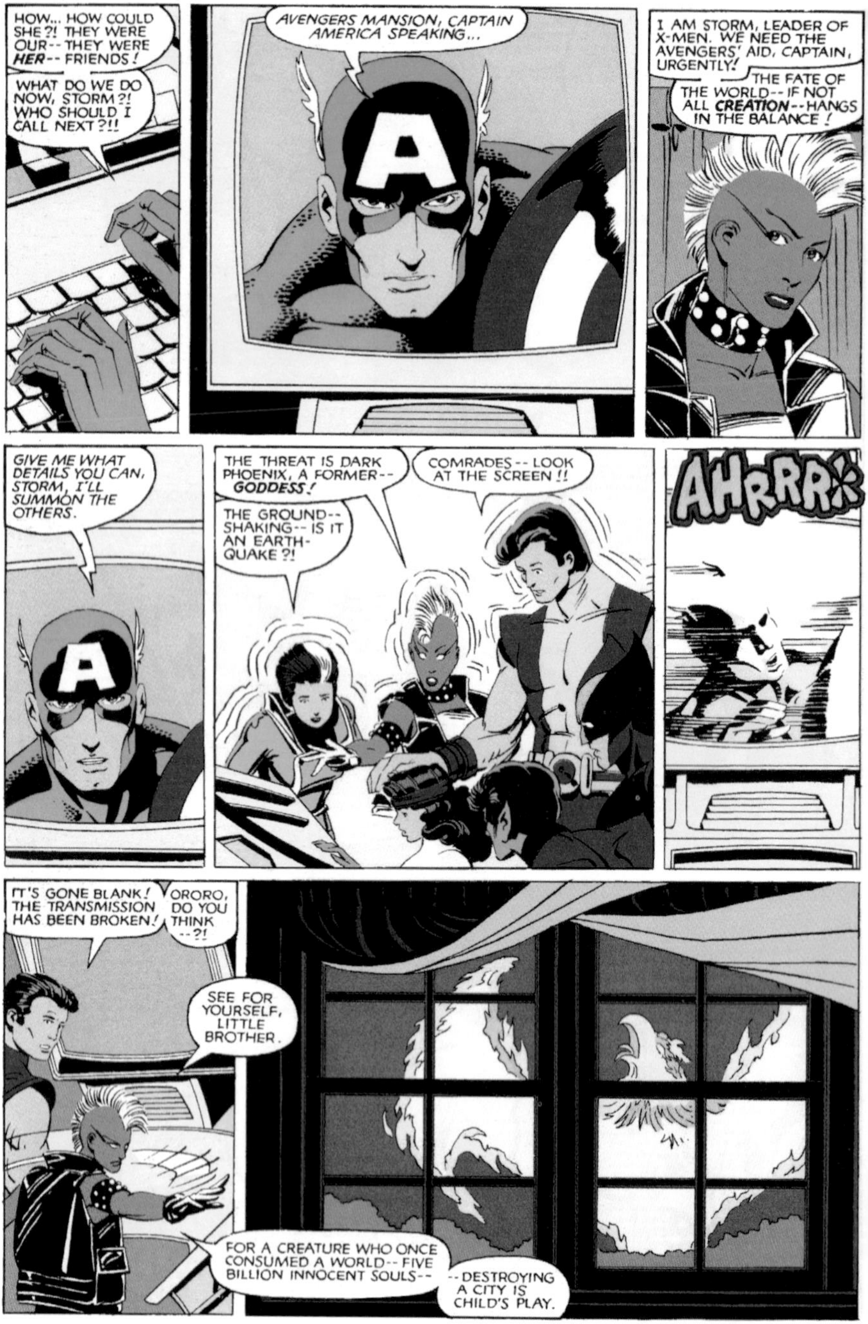

HOW... HOW COULD SHE?! THEY WERE OUR-- THEY WERE HER-- FRIENDS!
WHAT DO WE DO NOW, STORM?! WHO SHOULD I CALL NEXT?!!
AVENGERS MANSION, CAPTAIN AMERICA SPEAKING...
I AM STORM, LEADER OF X-MEN. WE NEED THE AVENGERS' AID, CAPTAIN, URGENTLY!
THE FATE OF THE WORLD-- IF NOT ALL CREATION--HANGS IN THE BALANCE!
GIVE ME WHAT DETAILS YOU CAN, STORM, I'LL SUMMON THE OTHERS.
THE THREAT IS DARK PHOENIX, A FORMER-- GODDESS!
THE GROUND-- SHAKING-- IS IT AN EARTH-QUAKE?!
COMRADES-- LOOK AT THE SCREEN!!
AHRRR!
IT'S GONE BLANK! THE TRANSMISSION HAS BEEN BROKEN!
ORORO, DO YOU THINK--?!
SEE FOR YOURSELF, LITTLE BROTHER.
FOR A CREATURE WHO ONCE CONSUMED A WORLD-- FIVE BILLION INNOCENT SOULS--
--DESTROYING A CITY IS CHILD'S PLAY.

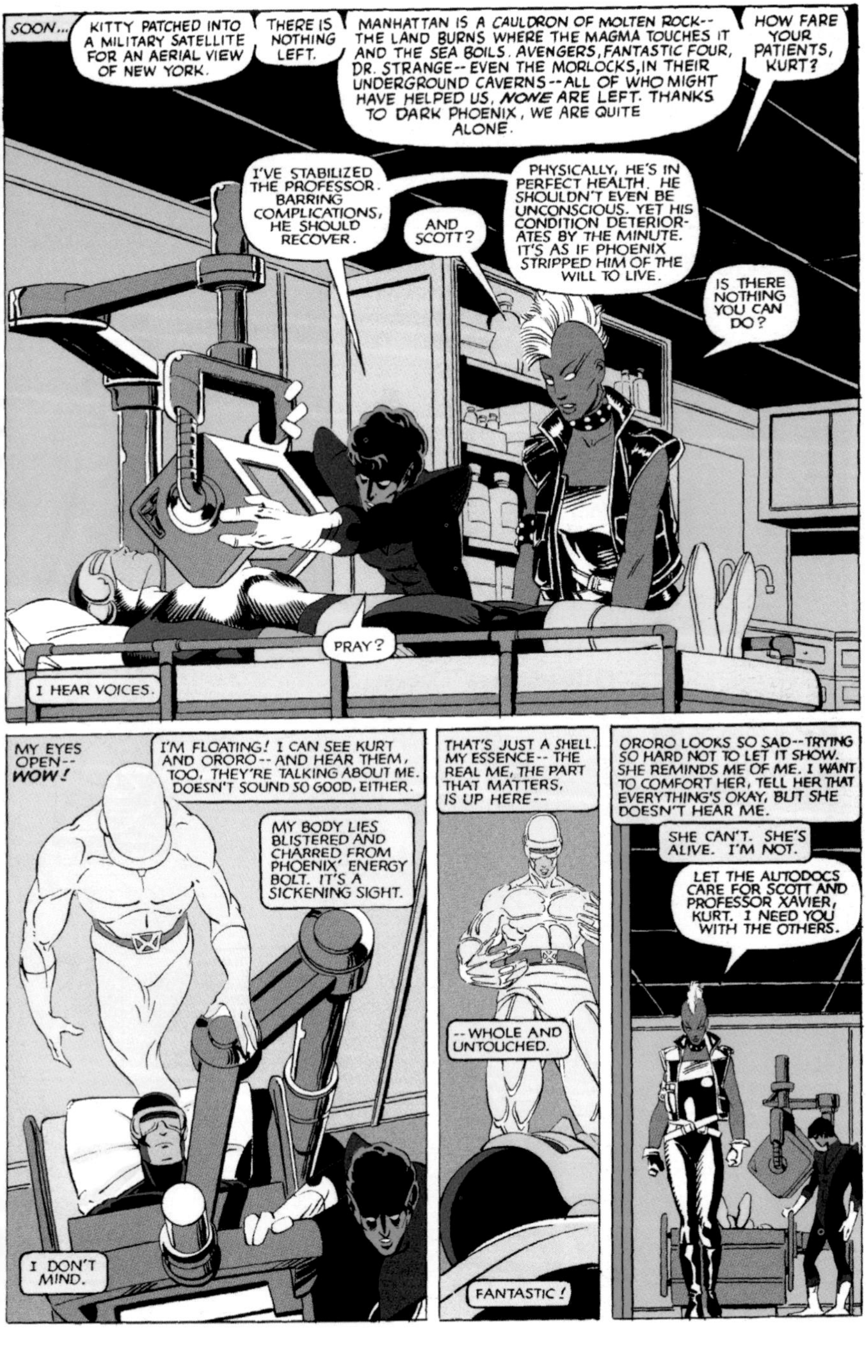

SOON...
KITTY PATCHED INTO A MILITARY SATELLITE FOR AN AERIAL VIEW OF NEW YORK.
THERE IS NOTHING LEFT.
MANHATTAN IS A CAULDRON OF MOLTEN ROCK-- THE LAND BURNS WHERE THE MAGMA TOUCHES IT AND THE SEA BOILS. AVENGERS, FANTASTIC FOUR, DR. STRANGE-- EVEN THE MORLOCKS, IN THEIR UNDERGROUND CAVERNS-- ALL OF WHO MIGHT HAVE HELPED US, NONE ARE LEFT. THANKS TO DARK PHOENIX, WE ARE QUITE ALONE.
HOW FARE YOUR PATIENTS, KURT?
I'VE STABILIZED THE PROFESSOR. BARRING COMPLICATIONS, HE SHOULD RECOVER.
AND SCOTT?
PHYSICALLY, HE'S IN PERFECT HEALTH. HE SHOULDN'T EVEN BE UNCONSCIOUS. YET HIS CONDITION DETERIORATES BY THE MINUTE. IT'S AS IF PHOENIX STRIPPED HIM OF THE WILL TO LIVE.
IS THERE NOTHING YOU CAN DO?
PRAY?
I HEAR VOICES.
MY EYES OPEN-- WOW!
I'M FLOATING! I CAN SEE KURT AND ORORO-- AND HEAR THEM, TOO. THEY'RE TALKING ABOUT ME. DOESN'T SOUND SO GOOD, EITHER.
MY BODY LIES BLISTERED AND CHARRED FROM PHOENIX' ENERGY BOLT. IT'S A SICKENING SIGHT.
I DON'T MIND.
THAT'S JUST A SHELL. MY ESSENCE-- THE REAL ME, THE PART THAT MATTERS, IS UP HERE--
--WHOLE AND UNTOUCHED.
FANTASTIC!
ORORO LOOKS SO SAD--TRYING SO HARD NOT TO LET IT SHOW. SHE REMINDS ME OF ME. I WANT TO COMFORT HER, TELL HER THAT EVERYTHING'S OKAY, BUT SHE DOESN'T HEAR ME.
SHE CAN'T. SHE'S ALIVE. I'M NOT.
LET THE AUTODOCS CARE FOR SCOTT AND PROFESSOR XAVIER, KURT. I NEED YOU WITH THE OTHERS.

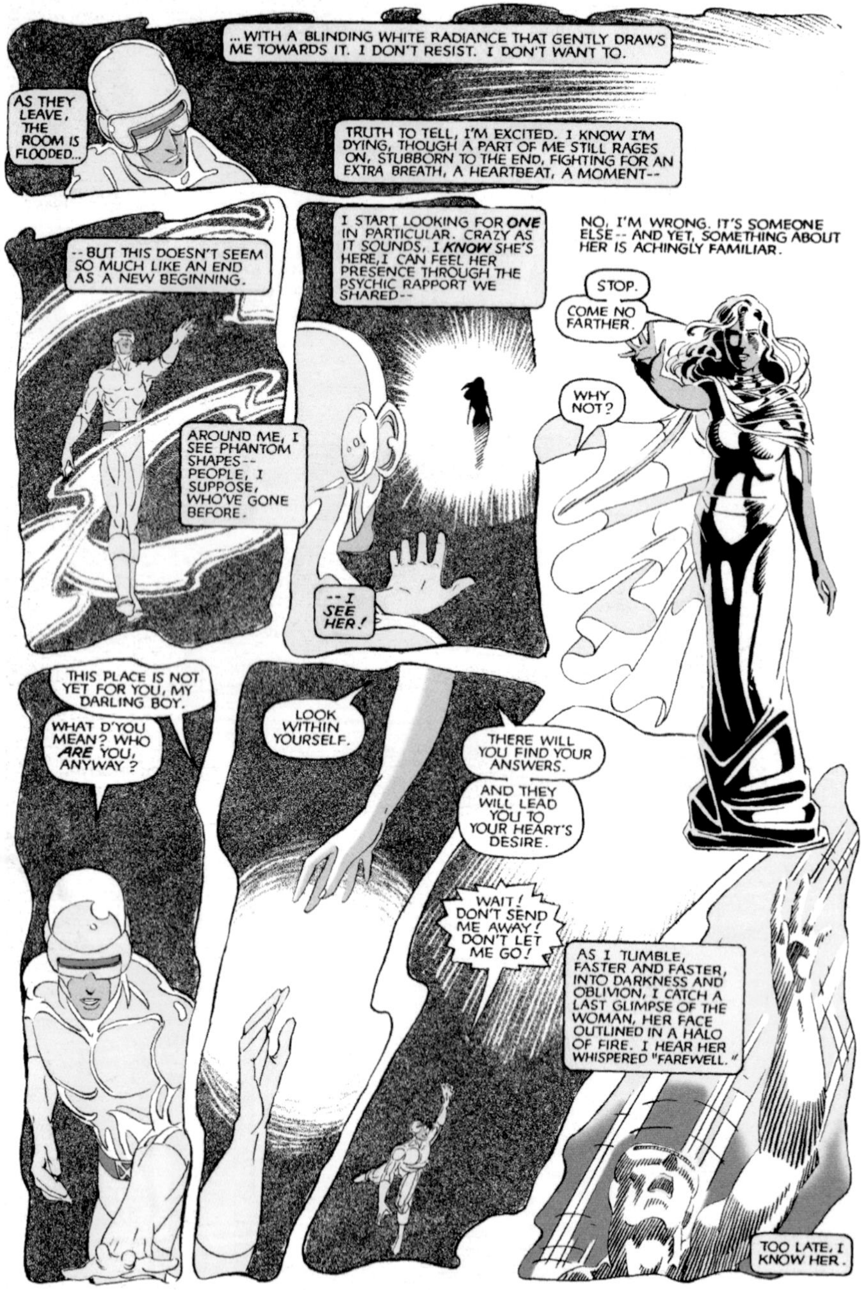
...WITH A BLINDING WHITE RADIANCE THAT GENTLY DRAWS ME TOWARDS IT. I DON'T RESIST. I DON'T WANT TO.
AS THEY LEAVE, THE ROOM IS FLOODED...
TRUTH TO TELL, I'M EXCITED. I KNOW I'M DYING, THOUGH A PART OF ME STILL RAGES ON, STUBBORN TO THE END, FIGHTING FOR AN EXTRA BREATH, A HEARTBEAT, A MOMENT--
--BUT THIS DOESN'T SEEM SO MUCH LIKE AN END AS A NEW BEGINNING.
AROUND ME, I SEE PHANTOM SHAPES--PEOPLE, I SUPPOSE, WHO'VE GONE BEFORE.
I START LOOKING FOR ONE IN PARTICULAR. CRAZY AS IT SOUNDS, I KNOW SHE'S HERE, I CAN FEEL HER PRESENCE THROUGH THE PSYCHIC RAPPORT WE SHARED--
--I SEE HER!
NO, I'M WRONG. IT'S SOMEONE ELSE--AND YET, SOMETHING ABOUT HER IS ACHINGLY FAMILIAR.
STOP.
COME NO FARTHER.
WHY NOT?
THIS PLACE IS NOT YET FOR YOU, MY DARLING BOY.
WHAT D'YOU MEAN? WHO ARE YOU, ANYWAY?
LOOK WITHIN YOURSELF.
THERE WILL YOU FIND YOUR ANSWERS.
AND THEY WILL LEAD YOU TO YOUR HEART'S DESIRE.
WAIT! DON'T SEND ME AWAY! DON'T LET ME GO!
AS I TUMBLE, FASTER AND FASTER, INTO DARKNESS AND OBLIVION, I CATCH A LAST GLIMPSE OF THE WOMAN, HER FACE OUTLINED IN A HALO OF FIRE. I HEAR HER WHISPERED "FAREWELL."
TOO LATE, I KNOW HER.

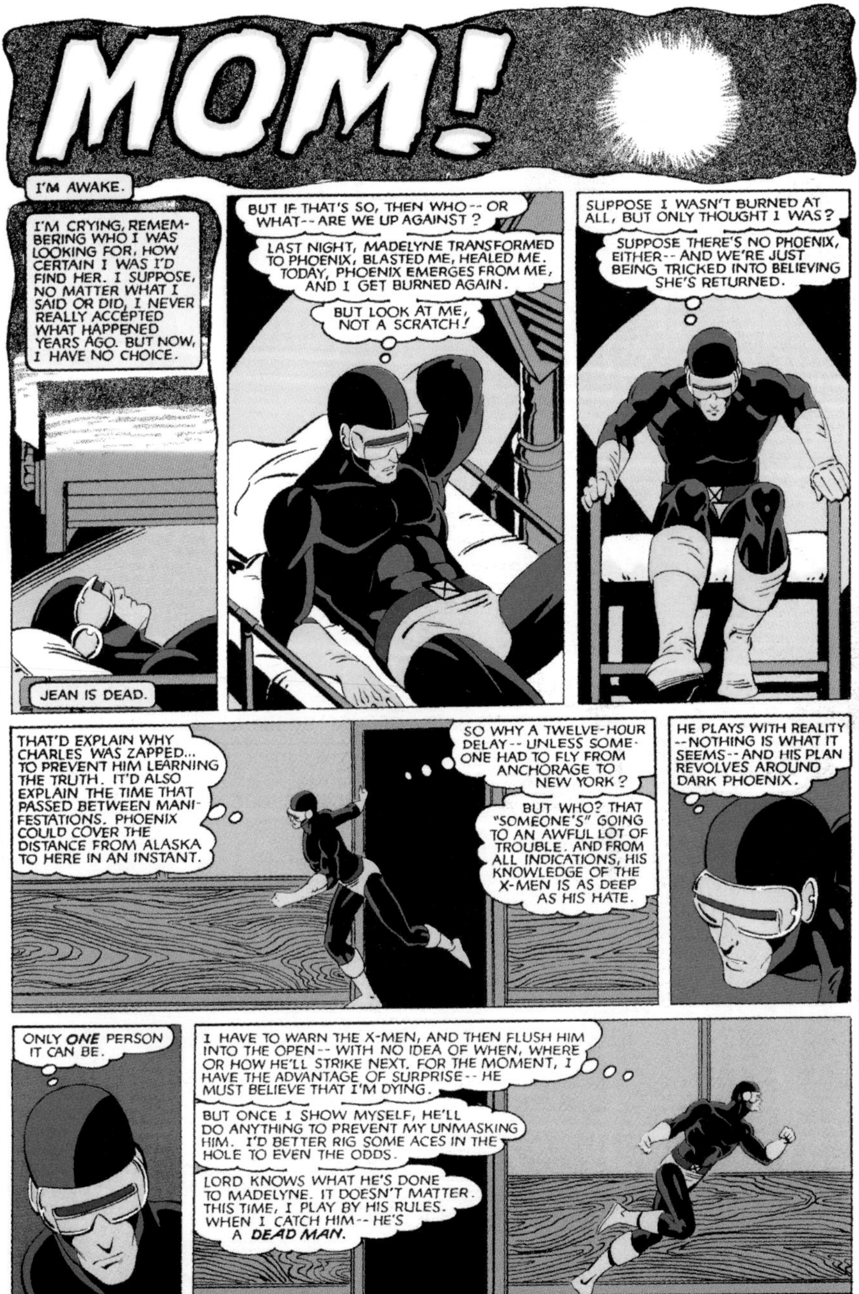
MOM!
I'M AWAKE.
I'M CRYING, REMEMBERING WHO I WAS LOOKING FOR, HOW CERTAIN I WAS I'D FIND HER. I SUPPOSE, NO MATTER WHAT I SAID OR DID, I NEVER REALLY ACCEPTED WHAT HAPPENED YEARS AGO. BUT NOW, I HAVE NO CHOICE.
JEAN IS DEAD.
BUT IF THAT'S SO, THEN WHO-- OR WHAT-- ARE WE UP AGAINST?
LAST NIGHT, MADELYNE TRANSFORMED TO PHOENIX, BLASTED ME, HEALED ME. TODAY, PHOENIX EMERGES FROM ME, AND I GET BURNED AGAIN.
BUT LOOK AT ME, NOT A SCRATCH!
SUPPOSE I WASN'T BURNED AT ALL, BUT ONLY THOUGHT I WAS?
SUPPOSE THERE'S NO PHOENIX, EITHER-- AND WE'RE JUST BEING TRICKED INTO BELIEVING SHE'S RETURNED.
THAT'D EXPLAIN WHY CHARLES WAS ZAPPED... TO PREVENT HIM LEARNING THE TRUTH. IT'D ALSO EXPLAIN THE TIME THAT PASSED BETWEEN MANIFESTATIONS. PHOENIX COULD COVER THE DISTANCE FROM ALASKA TO HERE IN AN INSTANT.
SO WHY A TWELVE-HOUR DELAY-- UNLESS SOMEONE HAD TO FLY FROM ANCHORAGE TO NEW YORK?
BUT WHO? THAT "SOMEONE'S" GOING TO AN AWFUL LOT OF TROUBLE. AND FROM ALL INDICATIONS, HIS KNOWLEDGE OF THE X-MEN IS AS DEEP AS HIS HATE.
HE PLAYS WITH REALITY --NOTHING IS WHAT IT SEEMS--AND HIS PLAN REVOLVES AROUND DARK PHOENIX.
ONLY ONE PERSON IT CAN BE.
I HAVE TO WARN THE X-MEN, AND THEN FLUSH HIM INTO THE OPEN-- WITH NO IDEA OF WHEN, WHERE OR HOW HE'LL STRIKE NEXT. FOR THE MOMENT, I HAVE THE ADVANTAGE OF SURPRISE-- HE MUST BELIEVE THAT I'M DYING.
BUT ONCE I SHOW MYSELF, HE'LL DO ANYTHING TO PREVENT MY UNMASKING HIM. I'D BETTER RIG SOME ACES IN THE HOLE TO EVEN THE ODDS.
LORD KNOWS WHAT HE'S DONE TO MADELYNE. IT DOESN'T MATTER. THIS TIME, I PLAY BY HIS RULES. WHEN I CATCH HIM-- HE'S A DEAD MAN.

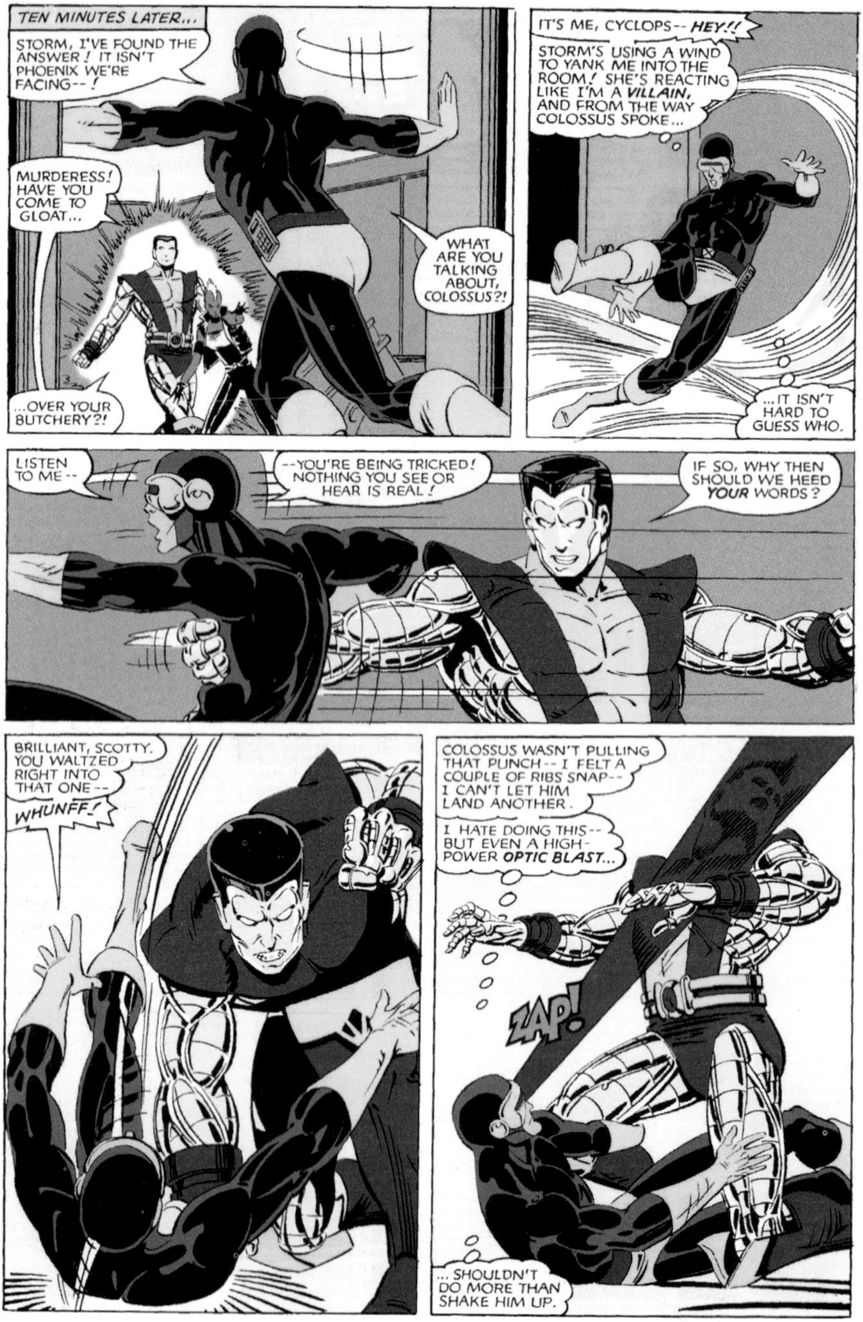
TEN MINUTES LATER...
STORM, I'VE FOUND THE ANSWER! IT ISN'T PHOENIX WE'RE FACING--!
MURDERESS! HAVE YOU COME TO GLOAT...
WHAT ARE YOU TALKING ABOUT, COLOSSUS?!
...OVER YOUR BUTCHERY?!
IT'S ME, CYCLOPS-- HEY!!
STORM'S USING A WIND TO YANK ME INTO THE ROOM! SHE'S REACTING LIKE I'M A VILLAIN, AND FROM THE WAY COLOSSUS SPOKE...
...IT ISN'T HARD TO GUESS WHO.
LISTEN TO ME--
--YOU'RE BEING TRICKED! NOTHING YOU SEE OR HEAR IS REAL!
IF SO, WHY THEN SHOULD WE HEED YOUR WORDS?
BRILLIANT, SCOTTY. YOU WALTZED RIGHT INTO THAT ONE--
WHUNFF!
COLOSSUS WASN'T PULLING THAT PUNCH-- I FELT A COUPLE OF RIBS SNAP-- I CAN'T LET HIM LAND ANOTHER.
I HATE DOING THIS-- BUT EVEN A HIGH-POWER OPTIC BLAST...
ZAP!
...SHOULDN'T DO MORE THAN SHAKE HIM UP.

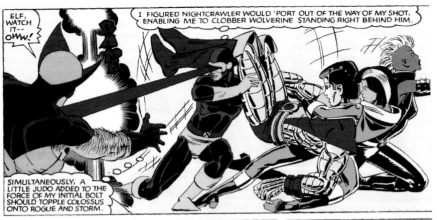

ELF, WATCH IT-- OWW!

I FIGURED NIGHTCRAWLER WOULD 'PORT OUT OF THE WAY OF MY SHOT, ENABLING ME TO CLOBBER WOLVERINE STANDING RIGHT BEHIND HIM.

SIMULTANEOUSLY, A LITTLE JUDO ADDED TO THE FORCE OF MY INITIAL BOLT SHOULD TOPPLE COLOSSUS ONTO ROGUE AND STORM.

NIGHTCRAWLER LIKES TO TACKLE FOES FROM ABOVE -- SO IF I SCYTHE MY BEAM ACROSS THE ENTIRE CEILING...

... I OUGHT TO CATCH HIM JUST AS HE MATERIALIZES.

BINGO!

≈UNNNGNH!≈

FLAMES?!!

KITTY'S DRAGON!!

I DON'T KNOW THE EXTENT OF LOCKHEED'S POWERS -- OR HOW MUCH PUNISHMENT HE CAN TAKE -- I CAN'T RISK FIGHTING HIM AS I DID THE X-MEN, I COULD TOO EASILY HURT HIM. BUT SINCE I DON'T WANT TO BE BARBECUED, EITHER ...

... IT'S TIME I MADE MY EXIT.

MY BUSTED RIBS ARE A PROBLEM I DIDN'T ANTICIPATE.

THEY'RE ALREADY STARTING TO SLOW ME DOWN

--ARRGH!

HOLD IT, LADY--

--YOU'RE NOT GETTING AWAY FROM US THAT EASILY!

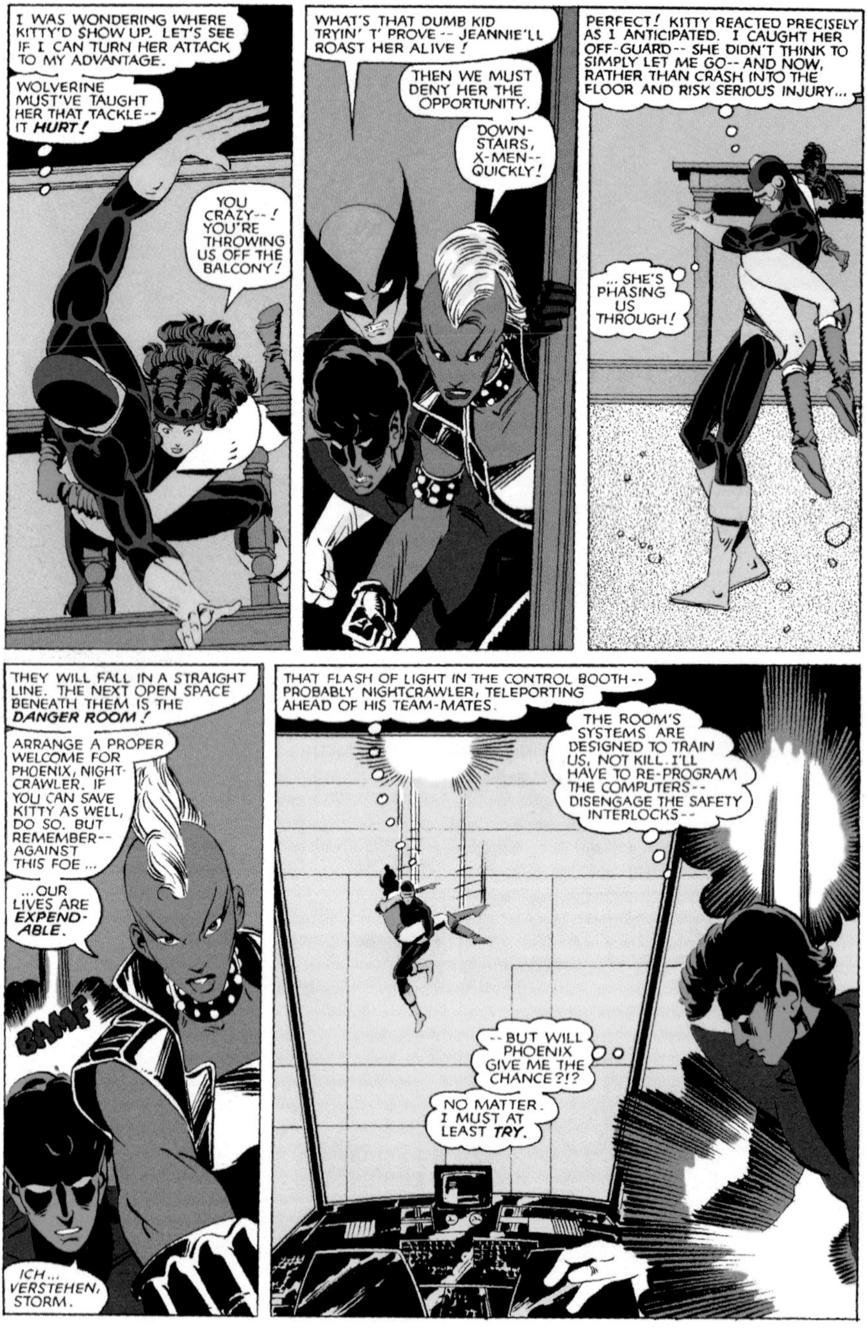
I WAS WONDERING WHERE KITTY'D SHOW UP. LET'S SEE IF I CAN TURN HER ATTACK TO MY ADVANTAGE.
WOLVERINE MUST'VE TAUGHT HER THAT TACKLE-- IT HURT!
YOU CRAZY--! YOU'RE THROWING US OFF THE BALCONY!
WHAT'S THAT DUMB KID TRYIN' T' PROVE-- JEANNIE'LL ROAST HER ALIVE!
THEN WE MUST DENY HER THE OPPORTUNITY.
DOWN-STAIRS, X-MEN-- QUICKLY!
PERFECT! KITTY REACTED PRECISELY AS I ANTICIPATED. I CAUGHT HER OFF-GUARD-- SHE DIDN'T THINK TO SIMPLY LET ME GO-- AND NOW, RATHER THAN CRASH INTO THE FLOOR AND RISK SERIOUS INJURY...
...SHE'S PHASING US THROUGH!
THEY WILL FALL IN A STRAIGHT LINE. THE NEXT OPEN SPACE BENEATH THEM IS THE DANGER ROOM!
ARRANGE A PROPER WELCOME FOR PHOENIX, NIGHT-CRAWLER. IF YOU CAN SAVE KITTY AS WELL, DO SO. BUT REMEMBER-- AGAINST THIS FOE...
...OUR LIVES ARE EXPEND-ABLE.
BAMF
ICH... VERSTEHEN, STORM.
THAT FLASH OF LIGHT IN THE CONTROL BOOTH-- PROBABLY NIGHTCRAWLER, TELEPORTING AHEAD OF HIS TEAM-MATES.
THE ROOM'S SYSTEMS ARE DESIGNED TO TRAIN US, NOT KILL. I'LL HAVE TO RE-PROGRAM THE COMPUTERS-- DISENGAGE THE SAFETY INTERLOCKS--
--BUT WILL PHOENIX GIVE ME THE CHANCE?!?
NO MATTER. I MUST AT LEAST TRY.

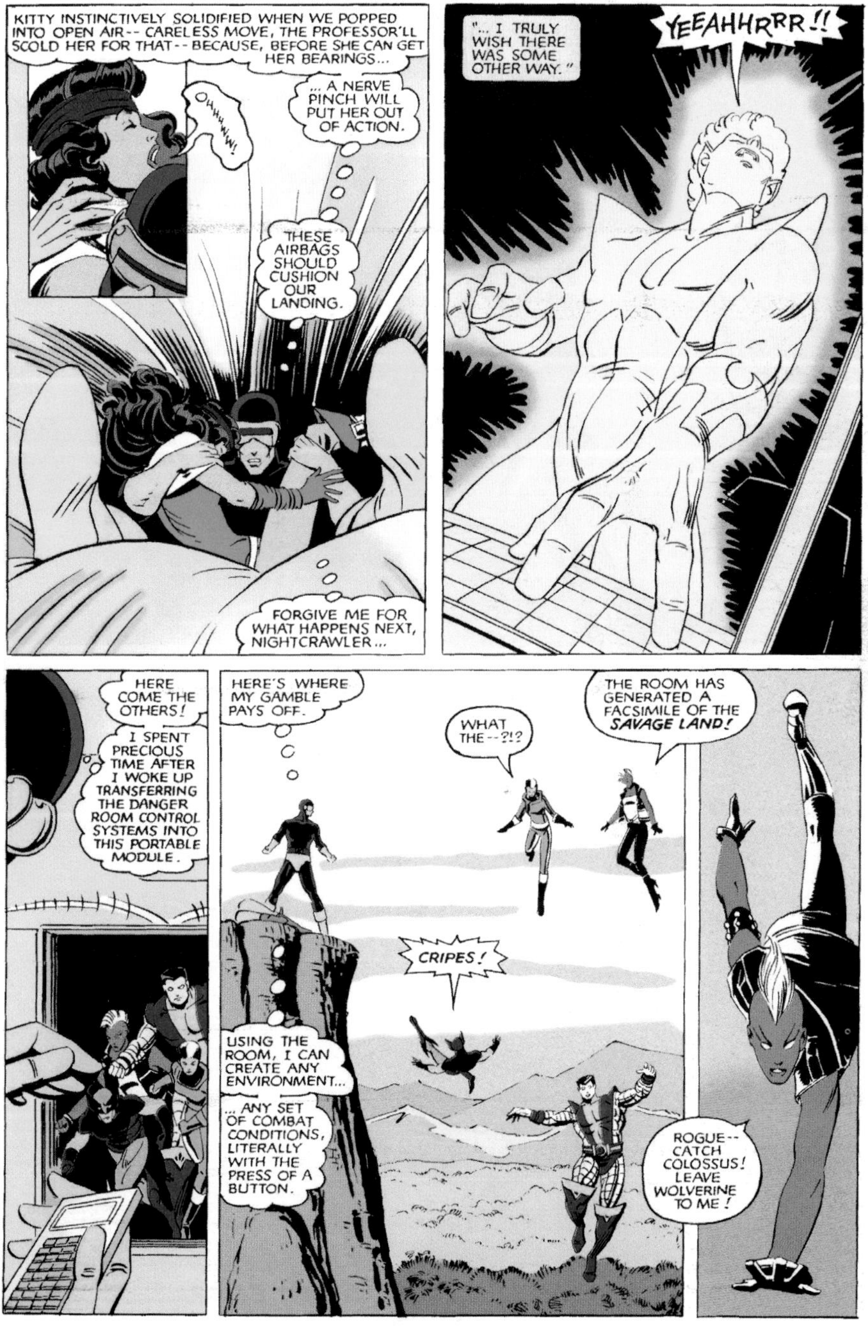

KITTY INSTINCTIVELY SOLIDIFIED WHEN WE POPPED INTO OPEN AIR-- CARELESS MOVE, THE PROFESSOR'LL SCOLD HER FOR THAT-- BECAUSE, BEFORE SHE CAN GET HER BEARINGS...
OHHHWW!
... A NERVE PINCH WILL PUT HER OUT OF ACTION.
THESE AIRBAGS SHOULD CUSHION OUR LANDING.
FORGIVE ME FOR WHAT HAPPENS NEXT, NIGHTCRAWLER...
"... I TRULY WISH THERE WAS SOME OTHER WAY."
YEEAHHRRR!!
HERE COME THE OTHERS!
I SPENT PRECIOUS TIME AFTER I WOKE UP TRANSFERRING THE DANGER ROOM CONTROL SYSTEMS INTO THIS PORTABLE MODULE.
HERE'S WHERE MY GAMBLE PAYS OFF.
WHAT THE--?!?
THE ROOM HAS GENERATED A FACSIMILE OF THE SAVAGE LAND!
CRIPES!
USING THE ROOM, I CAN CREATE ANY ENVIRONMENT...
... ANY SET OF COMBAT CONDITIONS, LITERALLY WITH THE PRESS OF A BUTTON.
ROGUE-- CATCH COLOSSUS! LEAVE WOLVERINE TO ME!

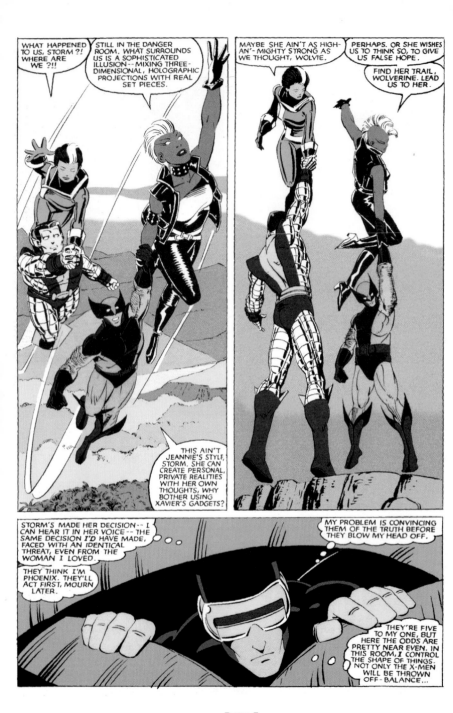

WHAT HAPPENED TO US, STORM?! WHERE ARE WE?!!

STILL IN THE DANGER ROOM. WHAT SURROUNDS US IS A SOPHISTICATED ILLUSION--MIXING THREE-DIMENSIONAL, HOLOGRAPHIC PROJECTIONS WITH REAL SET PIECES.

MAYBE SHE AIN'T AS HIGH-AN'-MIGHTY STRONG AS WE THOUGHT, WOLVIE.

PERHAPS. OR SHE WISHES US TO THINK SO, TO GIVE US FALSE HOPE.

FIND HER TRAIL, WOLVERINE. LEAD US TO HER.

THIS AIN'T JEANNIE'S STYLE, STORM. SHE CAN CREATE PERSONAL, PRIVATE REALITIES WITH HER OWN THOUGHTS, WHY BOTHER USING XAVIER'S GADGETS?

STORM'S MADE HER DECISION-- I CAN HEAR IT IN HER VOICE-- THE SAME DECISION I'D HAVE MADE, FACED WITH AN IDENTICAL THREAT, EVEN FROM THE WOMAN I LOVED.

THEY THINK I'M PHOENIX. THEY'LL ACT FIRST, MOURN LATER.

MY PROBLEM IS CONVINCING THEM OF THE TRUTH BEFORE THEY BLOW MY HEAD OFF.

THEY'RE FIVE TO MY ONE, BUT HERE THE ODDS ARE PRETTY NEAR EVEN. IN THIS ROOM, I CONTROL THE SHAPE OF THINGS. NOT ONLY THE X-MEN WILL BE THROWN OFF-BALANCE...

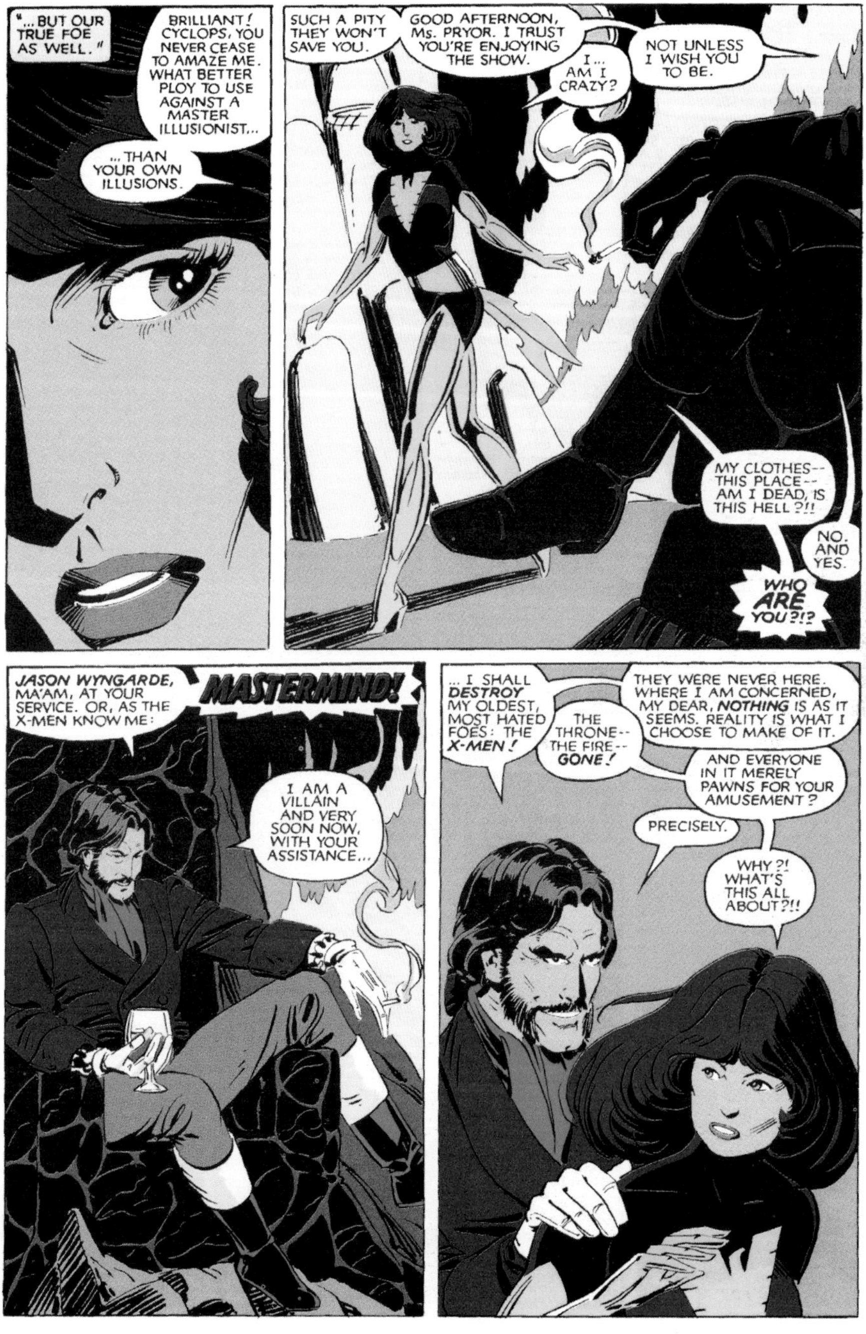
"...BUT OUR TRUE FOE AS WELL."
BRILLIANT! CYCLOPS, YOU NEVER CEASE TO AMAZE ME. WHAT BETTER PLOY TO USE AGAINST A MASTER ILLUSIONIST...
...THAN YOUR OWN ILLUSIONS.
SUCH A PITY THEY WON'T SAVE YOU.
GOOD AFTERNOON, Ms. PRYOR. I TRUST YOU'RE ENJOYING THE SHOW.
I... AM I CRAZY?
NOT UNLESS I WISH YOU TO BE.
MY CLOTHES-- THIS PLACE-- AM I DEAD, IS THIS HELL?!!
NO. AND YES.
WHO ARE YOU?!?
JASON WYNGARDE, MA'AM, AT YOUR SERVICE. OR, AS THE X-MEN KNOW ME:
MASTERMIND!
I AM A VILLAIN AND VERY SOON NOW, WITH YOUR ASSISTANCE...
...I SHALL DESTROY MY OLDEST, MOST HATED FOES: THE X-MEN!
THE THRONE-- THE FIRE-- GONE!
THEY WERE NEVER HERE. WHERE I AM CONCERNED, MY DEAR, NOTHING IS AS IT SEEMS. REALITY IS WHAT I CHOOSE TO MAKE OF IT.
AND EVERYONE IN IT MERELY PAWNS FOR YOUR AMUSEMENT?
PRECISELY.
WHY?! WHAT'S THIS ALL ABOUT?!!

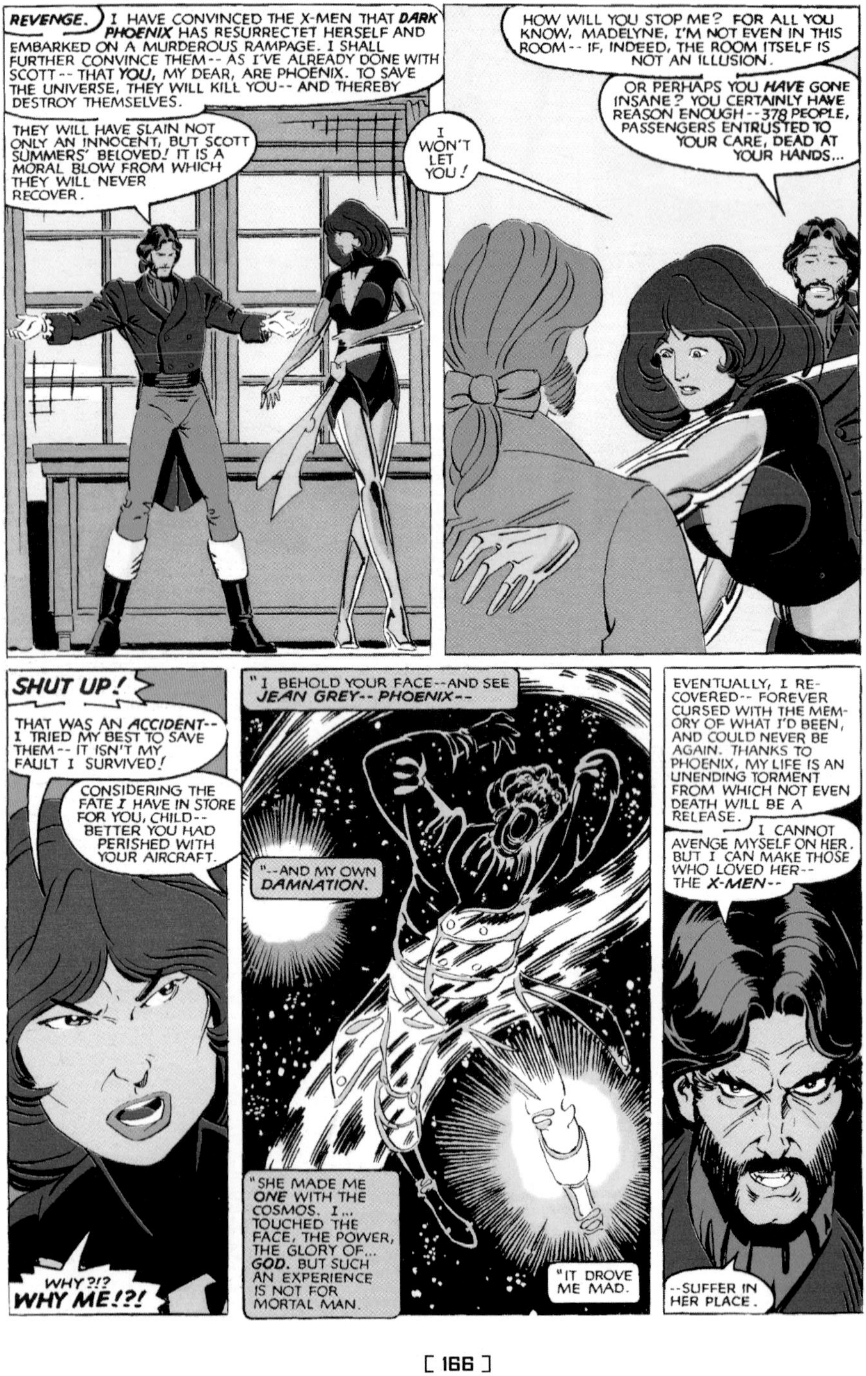
REVENGE. I HAVE CONVINCED THE X-MEN THAT DARK PHOENIX HAS RESURRECTET HERSELF AND EMBARKED ON A MURDEROUS RAMPAGE. I SHALL FURTHER CONVINCE THEM -- AS I'VE ALREADY DONE WITH SCOTT -- THAT YOU, MY DEAR, ARE PHOENIX. TO SAVE THE UNIVERSE, THEY WILL KILL YOU -- AND THEREBY DESTROY THEMSELVES.
THEY WILL HAVE SLAIN NOT ONLY AN INNOCENT, BUT SCOTT SUMMERS' BELOVED! IT IS A MORAL BLOW FROM WHICH THEY WILL NEVER RECOVER.
I WON'T LET YOU!
HOW WILL YOU STOP ME? FOR ALL YOU KNOW, MADELYNE, I'M NOT EVEN IN THIS ROOM -- IF, INDEED, THE ROOM ITSELF IS NOT AN ILLUSION.
OR PERHAPS YOU HAVE GONE INSANE? YOU CERTAINLY HAVE REASON ENOUGH -- 378 PEOPLE, PASSENGERS ENTRUSTED TO YOUR CARE, DEAD AT YOUR HANDS...
SHUT UP!
THAT WAS AN ACCIDENT -- I TRIED MY BEST TO SAVE THEM -- IT ISN'T MY FAULT I SURVIVED!
CONSIDERING THE FATE I HAVE IN STORE FOR YOU, CHILD -- BETTER YOU HAD PERISHED WITH YOUR AIRCRAFT.
WHY?!? WHY ME!?!
"I BEHOLD YOUR FACE -- AND SEE JEAN GREY -- PHOENIX --
"-- AND MY OWN DAMNATION.
"SHE MADE ME ONE WITH THE COSMOS. I... TOUCHED THE FACE, THE POWER, THE GLORY OF... GOD. BUT SUCH AN EXPERIENCE IS NOT FOR MORTAL MAN.
"IT DROVE ME MAD.
EVENTUALLY, I RECOVERED -- FOREVER CURSED WITH THE MEMORY OF WHAT I'D BEEN, AND COULD NEVER BE AGAIN. THANKS TO PHOENIX, MY LIFE IS AN UNENDING TORMENT FROM WHICH NOT EVEN DEATH WILL BE A RELEASE.
I CANNOT AVENGE MYSELF ON HER. BUT I CAN MAKE THOSE WHO LOVED HER -- THE X-MEN --
-- SUFFER IN HER PLACE.

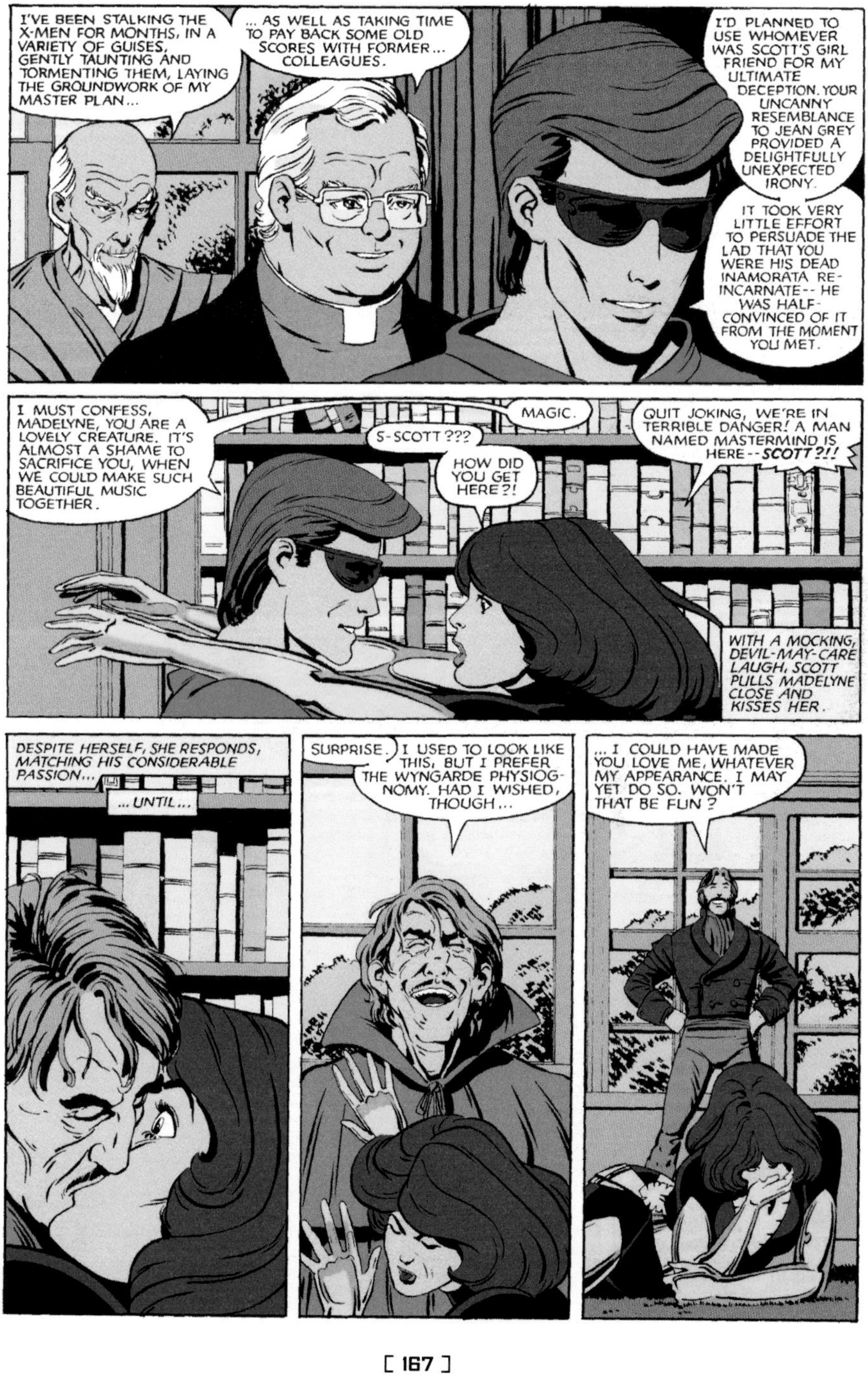

I'VE BEEN STALKING THE X-MEN FOR MONTHS, IN A VARIETY OF GUISES, GENTLY TAUNTING AND TORMENTING THEM, LAYING THE GROUNDWORK OF MY MASTER PLAN...
... AS WELL AS TAKING TIME TO PAY BACK SOME OLD SCORES WITH FORMER... COLLEAGUES.
I'D PLANNED TO USE WHOMEVER WAS SCOTT'S GIRL FRIEND FOR MY ULTIMATE DECEPTION. YOUR UNCANNY RESEMBLANCE TO JEAN GREY PROVIDED A DELIGHTFULLY UNEXPECTED IRONY.
IT TOOK VERY LITTLE EFFORT TO PERSUADE THE LAD THAT YOU WERE HIS DEAD INAMORATA RE-INCARNATE-- HE WAS HALF-CONVINCED OF IT FROM THE MOMENT YOU MET.
I MUST CONFESS, MADELYNE, YOU ARE A LOVELY CREATURE. IT'S ALMOST A SHAME TO SACRIFICE YOU, WHEN WE COULD MAKE SUCH BEAUTIFUL MUSIC TOGETHER.
MAGIC.
S-SCOTT???
HOW DID YOU GET HERE?!
QUIT JOKING, WE'RE IN TERRIBLE DANGER! A MAN NAMED MASTERMIND IS HERE--SCOTT?!!
WITH A MOCKING, DEVIL-MAY-CARE LAUGH, SCOTT PULLS MADELYNE CLOSE AND KISSES HER.
DESPITE HERSELF, SHE RESPONDS, MATCHING HIS CONSIDERABLE PASSION...
...UNTIL...
SURPRISE.
I USED TO LOOK LIKE THIS, BUT I PREFER THE WYNGARDE PHYSIOG-NOMY. HAD I WISHED, THOUGH...
...I COULD HAVE MADE YOU LOVE ME, WHATEVER MY APPEARANCE. I MAY YET DO SO. WON'T THAT BE FUN?

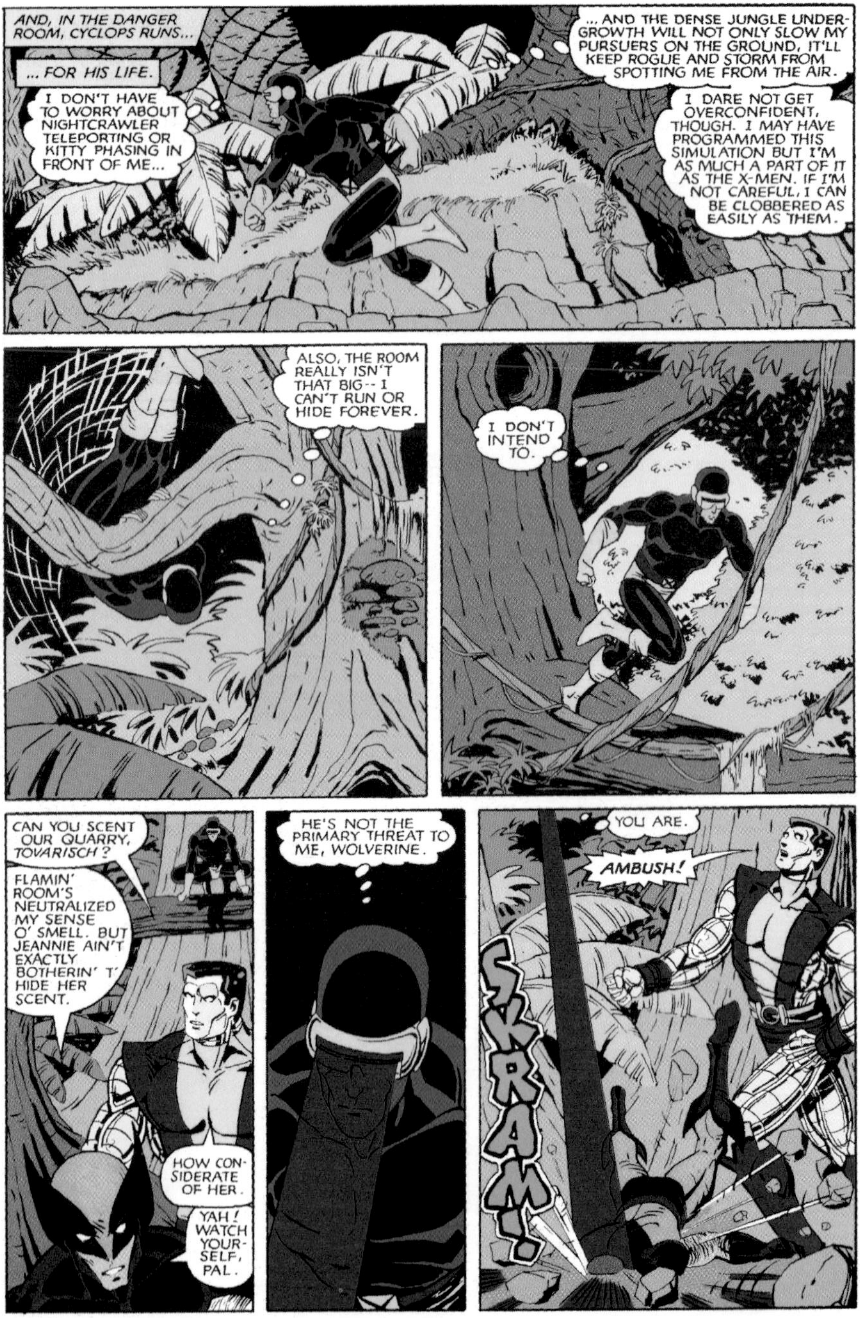
AND, IN THE DANGER ROOM, CYCLOPS RUNS...
... FOR HIS LIFE.
I DON'T HAVE TO WORRY ABOUT NIGHTCRAWLER TELEPORTING OR KITTY PHASING IN FRONT OF ME...
... AND THE DENSE JUNGLE UNDERGROWTH WILL NOT ONLY SLOW MY PURSUERS ON THE GROUND, IT'LL KEEP ROGUE AND STORM FROM SPOTTING ME FROM THE AIR.
I DARE NOT GET OVERCONFIDENT, THOUGH. I MAY HAVE PROGRAMMED THIS SIMULATION BUT I'M AS MUCH A PART OF IT AS THE X-MEN. IF I'M NOT CAREFUL, I CAN BE CLOBBERED AS EASILY AS THEM.
ALSO, THE ROOM REALLY ISN'T THAT BIG-- I CAN'T RUN OR HIDE FOREVER.
I DON'T INTEND TO.
CAN YOU SCENT OUR QUARRY, TOVARISCH?
FLAMIN' ROOM'S NEUTRALIZED MY SENSE O' SMELL. BUT JEANNIE AIN'T EXACTLY BOTHERIN' T' HIDE HER SCENT.
HOW CONSIDERATE OF HER.
YAH! WATCH YOURSELF, PAL.
HE'S NOT THE PRIMARY THREAT TO ME, WOLVERINE.
YOU ARE.
AMBUSH!
SKRAM!

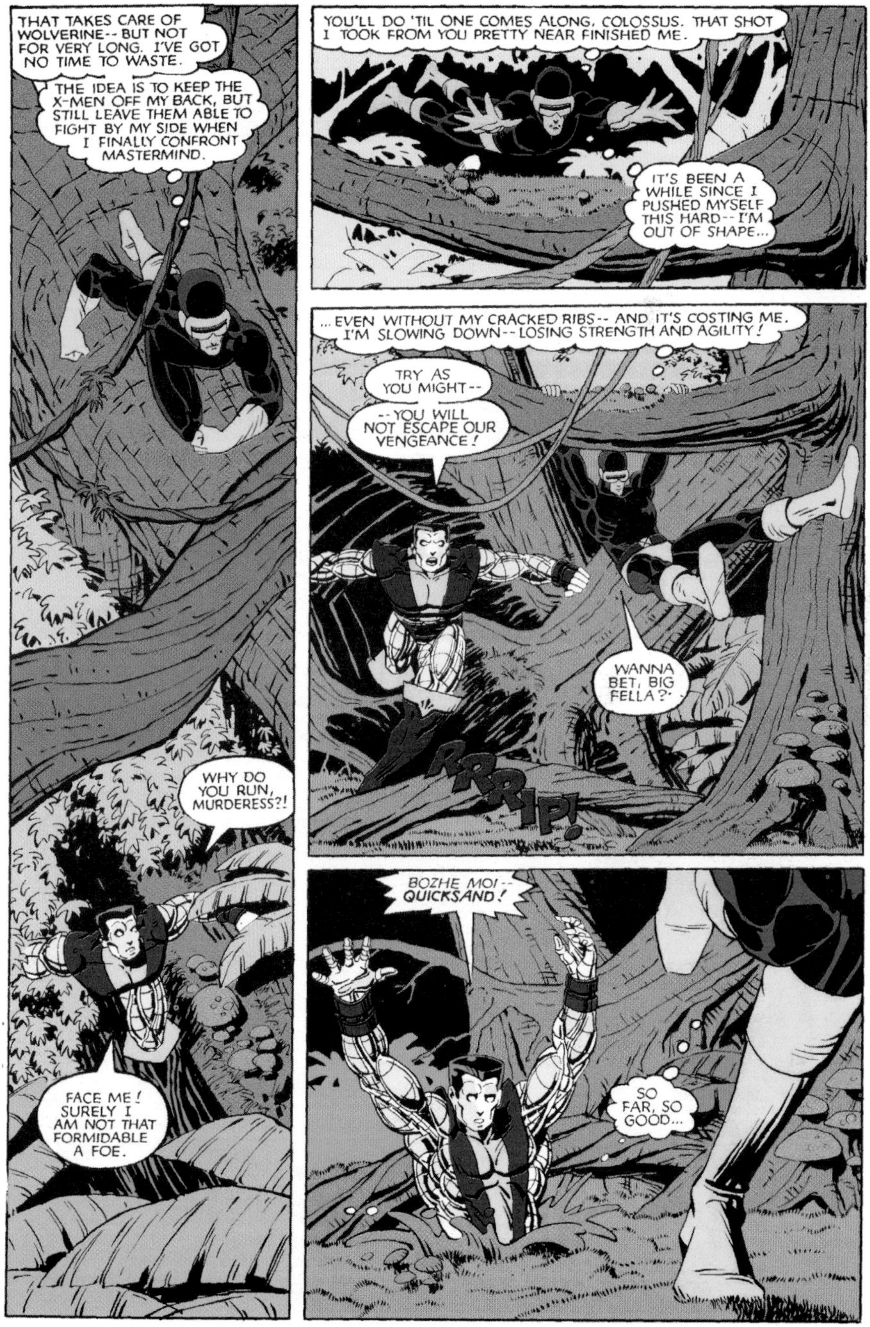
THAT TAKES CARE OF WOLVERINE-- BUT NOT FOR VERY LONG. I'VE GOT NO TIME TO WASTE.
THE IDEA IS TO KEEP THE X-MEN OFF MY BACK, BUT STILL LEAVE THEM ABLE TO FIGHT BY MY SIDE WHEN I FINALLY CONFRONT MASTERMIND.
WHY DO YOU RUN, MURDERESS?!
FACE ME! SURELY I AM NOT THAT FORMIDABLE A FOE.
YOU'LL DO 'TIL ONE COMES ALONG, COLOSSUS. THAT SHOT I TOOK FROM YOU PRETTY NEAR FINISHED ME.
IT'S BEEN A WHILE SINCE I PUSHED MYSELF THIS HARD--I'M OUT OF SHAPE...
...EVEN WITHOUT MY CRACKED RIBS-- AND IT'S COSTING ME. I'M SLOWING DOWN--LOSING STRENGTH AND AGILITY!
TRY AS YOU MIGHT--
--YOU WILL NOT ESCAPE OUR VENGEANCE!
WANNA BET, BIG FELLA?
RRRRIP!
BOZHE MOI-- QUICKSAND!
SO FAR, SO GOOD...

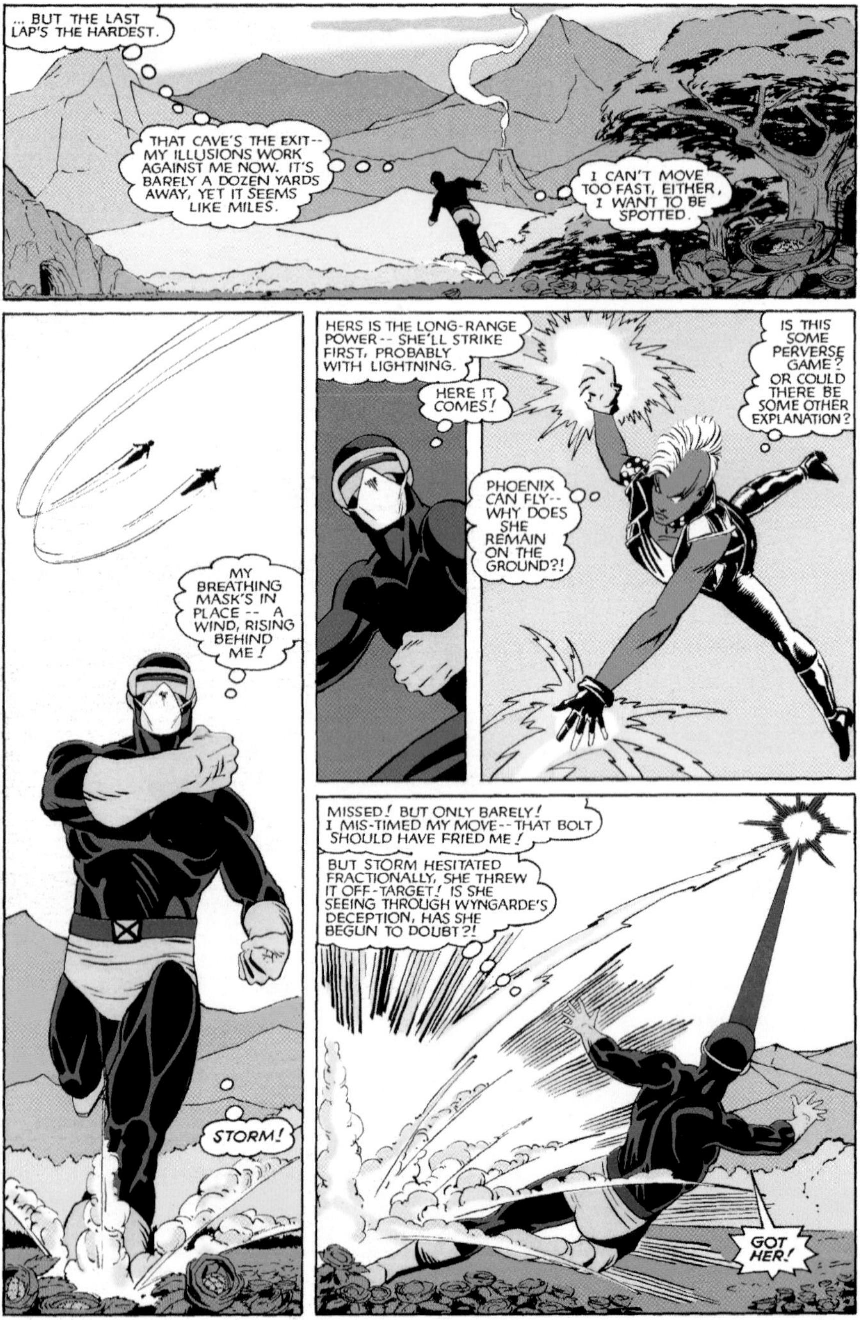

... BUT THE LAST LAP'S THE HARDEST.
THAT CAVE'S THE EXIT-- MY ILLUSIONS WORK AGAINST ME NOW. IT'S BARELY A DOZEN YARDS AWAY, YET IT SEEMS LIKE MILES.
I CAN'T MOVE TOO FAST, EITHER. I WANT TO BE SPOTTED.
MY BREATHING MASK'S IN PLACE -- A WIND, RISING BEHIND ME!
STORM!
HERS IS THE LONG-RANGE POWER -- SHE'LL STRIKE FIRST, PROBABLY WITH LIGHTNING.
HERE IT COMES!
IS THIS SOME PERVERSE GAME? OR COULD THERE BE SOME OTHER EXPLANATION?
PHOENIX CAN FLY-- WHY DOES SHE REMAIN ON THE GROUND?!
MISSED! BUT ONLY BARELY! I MIS-TIMED MY MOVE--THAT BOLT SHOULD HAVE FRIED ME!
BUT STORM HESITATED FRACTIONALLY, SHE THREW IT OFF-TARGET! IS SHE SEEING THROUGH WYNGARDE'S DECEPTION, HAS SHE BEGUN TO DOUBT?!
GOT HER!

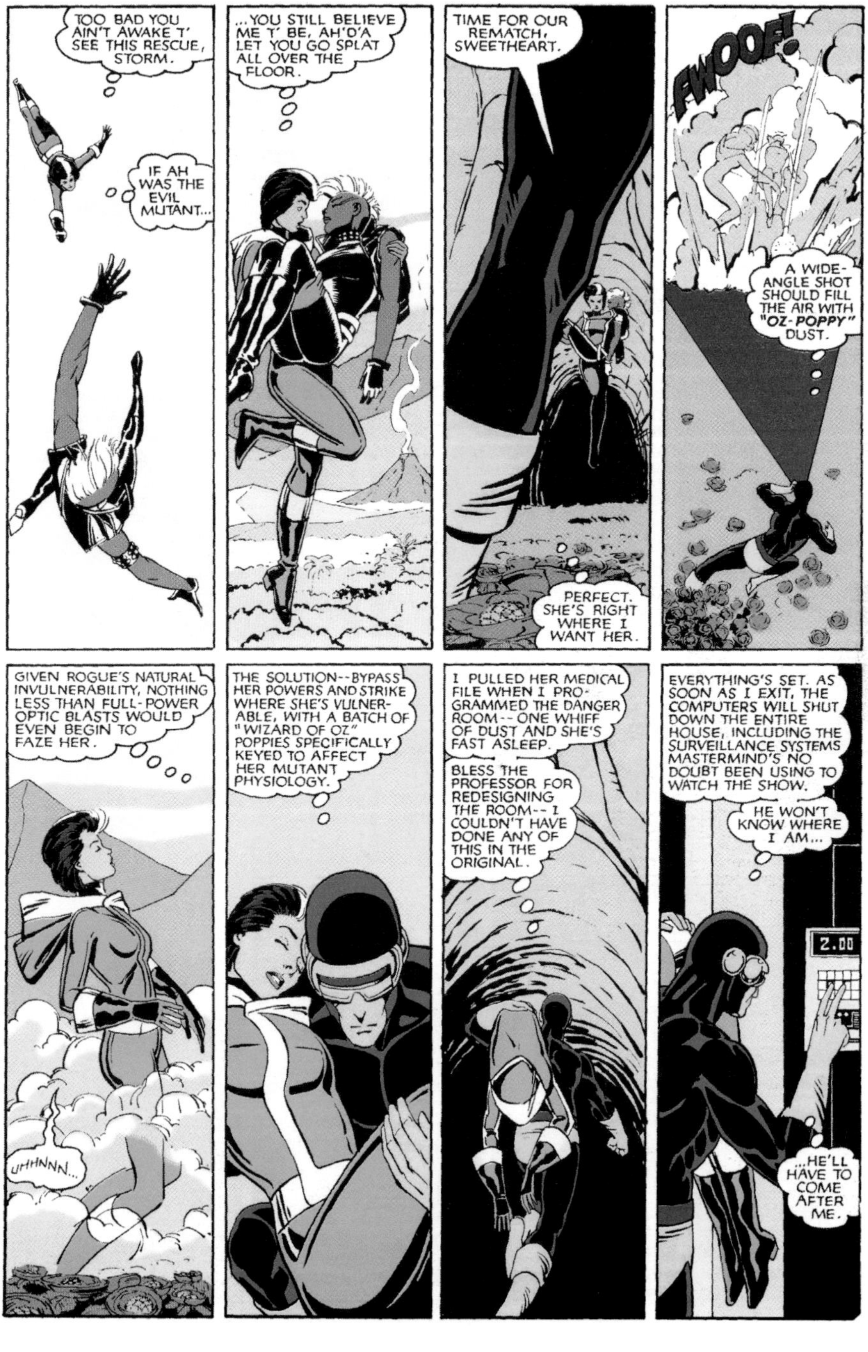

TOO BAD YOU AIN'T AWAKE T' SEE THIS RESCUE, STORM.
IF AH WAS THE EVIL MUTANT...
...YOU STILL BELIEVE ME T' BE, AH'D'A LET YOU GO SPLAT ALL OVER THE FLOOR.
TIME FOR OUR REMATCH, SWEETHEART.
PERFECT. SHE'S RIGHT WHERE I WANT HER.
FWOOF!
A WIDE-ANGLE SHOT SHOULD FILL THE AIR WITH "OZ-POPPY" DUST.
GIVEN ROGUE'S NATURAL INVULNERABILITY, NOTHING LESS THAN FULL-POWER OPTIC BLASTS WOULD EVEN BEGIN TO FAZE HER.
UHHNNN...
THE SOLUTION--BYPASS HER POWERS AND STRIKE WHERE SHE'S VULNERABLE, WITH A BATCH OF "WIZARD OF OZ" POPPIES SPECIFICALLY KEYED TO AFFECT HER MUTANT PHYSIOLOGY.
I PULLED HER MEDICAL FILE WHEN I PROGRAMMED THE DANGER ROOM--ONE WHIFF OF DUST AND SHE'S FAST ASLEEP.
BLESS THE PROFESSOR FOR REDESIGNING THE ROOM-- I COULDN'T HAVE DONE ANY OF THIS IN THE ORIGINAL.
EVERYTHING'S SET. AS SOON AS I EXIT, THE COMPUTERS WILL SHUT DOWN THE ENTIRE HOUSE, INCLUDING THE SURVEILLANCE SYSTEMS MASTERMIND'S NO DOUBT BEEN USING TO WATCH THE SHOW.
HE WON'T KNOW WHERE I AM...
2.00
...HE'LL HAVE TO COME AFTER ME.

THE INFIRMARY.

ROGUE'S THE KEY TO MY PLAN-- IT WAS READING HER FILE THAT GAVE ME THE IDEA.

THE PROFESSOR'S STILL UNCONSCIOUS, IN HIS CONDITION I CAN'T RISK WAKING HIM. BUT ROGUE HAS THE POWER TO ABSORB ANOTHER PERSON'S MEMORIES AND ABILITIES JUST BY TOUCHING THEM.

SHE CAN'T CONTROL HERSELF, EITHER-- THE SLIGHTEST CONTACT INITIATES THE TRANSFER. I SHOULD BE ABLE THEN TO SHIFT XAVIER'S PSI-POWERS TO HER WITHOUT DOING HIM ANY PHYSICAL HARM.

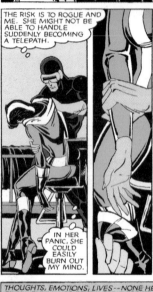

THE RISK IS TO ROGUE AND ME. SHE MIGHT NOT BE ABLE TO HANDLE SUDDENLY BECOMING A TELEPATH.

IN HER PANIC, SHE COULD EASILY BURN OUT MY MIND.

UNFORTUNATELY, I CAN'T SEE ANY ALTERNATIVE.

WHUNH..-!??!

HERE WE GO!

NO!

HER SCREAM MIXES RAGE AND TERROR...

...AS HER WORLD SHATTERS.

THOUGHTS, EMOTIONS, LIVES--NONE HER OWN--FLOOD HER BRAIN. SHE IS DROWNING, LOSING ALL SENSE OF SELF, TUMBLING GRATEFULLY TOWARDS OBLIVION.

ONE VOICE MAKES ITSELF HEARD ABOVE THE MULTITUDE-- GENTLE BUT UNYIELDING...

... SHOWING HER HOW TO RESTORE ORDER TO THE MADCAP CHAOS OF HER BRAIN.

SCOTT USES EVERYTHING TAUGHT HIM BY XAVIER...

... EVERYTHING LEARNED THROUGH THE PSYCHIC RAPPORT HE SHARED WITH JEAN GREY. THE STRAIN IS TERRIBLE, THE PAIN WORSE--

-- MADE NO LESS SO BECAUSE IT IS SHARED.

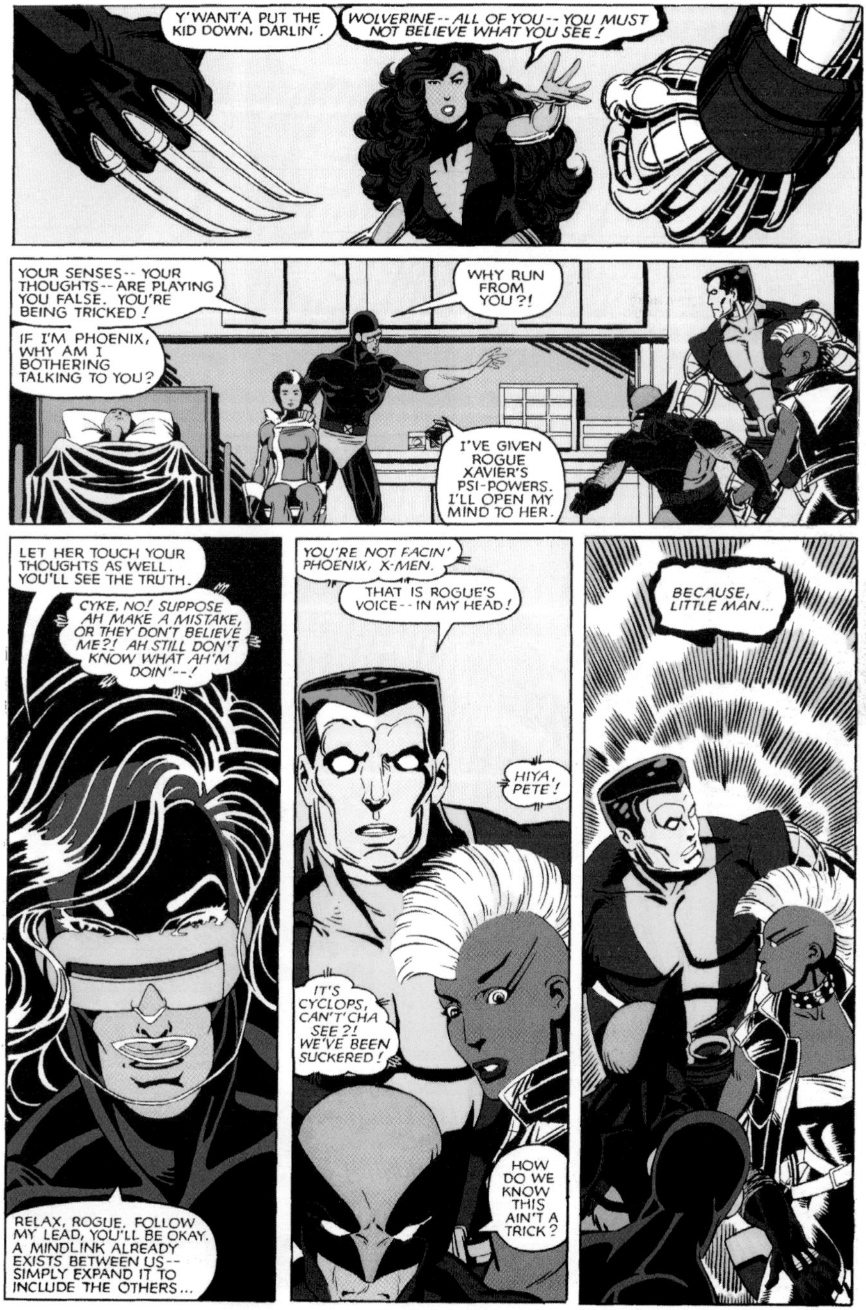

Y'WANT'A PUT THE KID DOWN, DARLIN'.
WOLVERINE--ALL OF YOU--YOU MUST NOT BELIEVE WHAT YOU SEE!
YOUR SENSES--YOUR THOUGHTS--ARE PLAYING YOU FALSE. YOU'RE BEING TRICKED!
IF I'M PHOENIX, WHY AM I BOTHERING TALKING TO YOU?
WHY RUN FROM YOU?!
I'VE GIVEN ROGUE XAVIER'S PSI-POWERS. I'LL OPEN MY MIND TO HER.
LET HER TOUCH YOUR THOUGHTS AS WELL. YOU'LL SEE THE TRUTH.
CYKE, NO! SUPPOSE AH MAKE A MISTAKE, OR THEY DON'T BELIEVE ME?! AH STILL DON'T KNOW WHAT AH'M DOIN'--!
RELAX, ROGUE. FOLLOW MY LEAD, YOU'LL BE OKAY. A MINDLINK ALREADY EXISTS BETWEEN US--SIMPLY EXPAND IT TO INCLUDE THE OTHERS...
YOU'RE NOT FACIN' PHOENIX, X-MEN.
THAT IS ROGUE'S VOICE--IN MY HEAD!
HIYA, PETE!
IT'S CYCLOPS, CAN'T'CHA SEE?! WE'VE BEEN SUCKERED!
HOW DO WE KNOW THIS AIN'T A TRICK?
BECAUSE, LITTLE MAN...

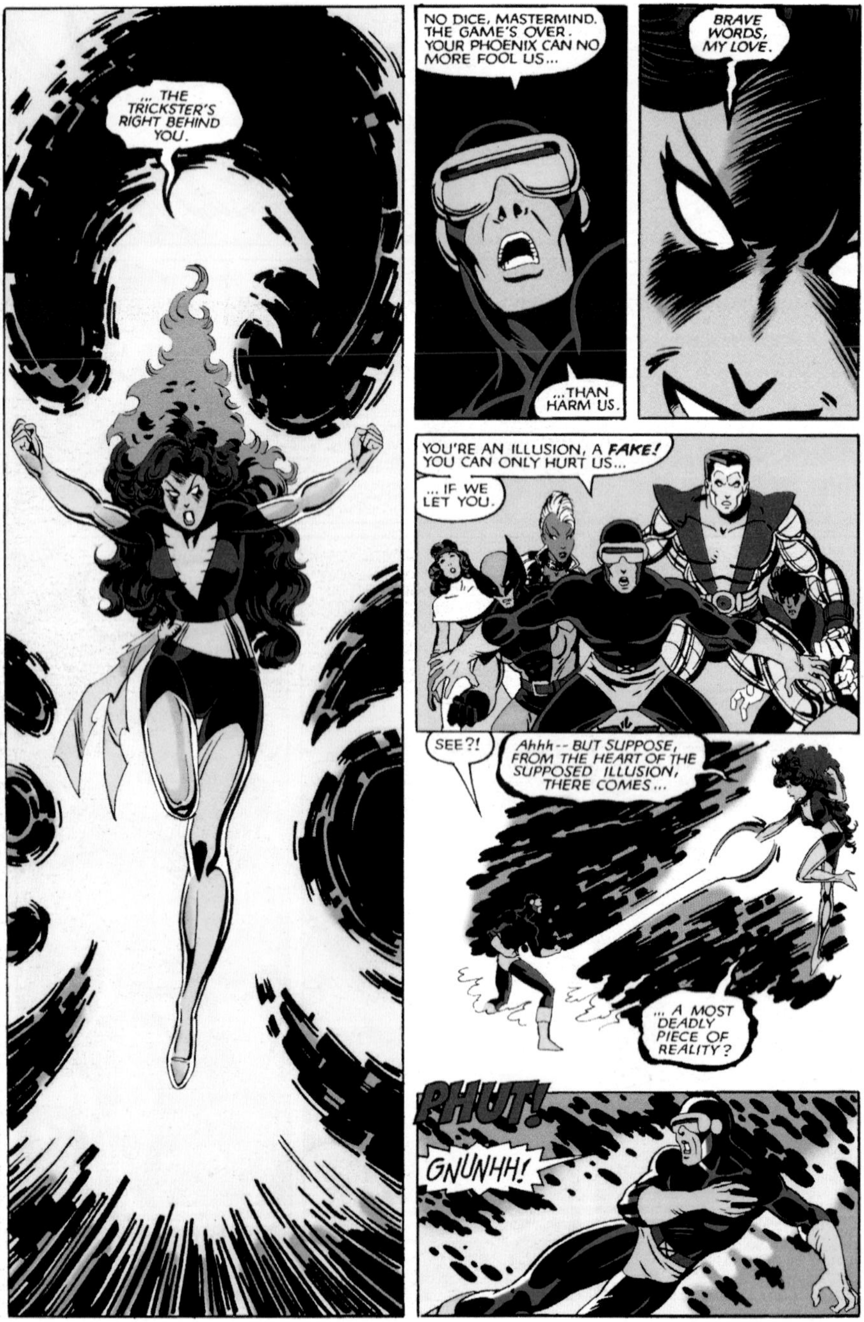
... THE TRICKSTER'S RIGHT BEHIND YOU.
NO DICE, MASTERMIND. THE GAME'S OVER. YOUR PHOENIX CAN NO MORE FOOL US...
...THAN HARM US.
BRAVE WORDS, MY LOVE.
YOU'RE AN ILLUSION, A FAKE! YOU CAN ONLY HURT US...
... IF WE LET YOU.
SEE?!
Ahhh-- BUT SUPPOSE, FROM THE HEART OF THE SUPPOSED ILLUSION, THERE COMES...
... A MOST DEADLY PIECE OF REALITY?
PHUT!
GNUNHH!

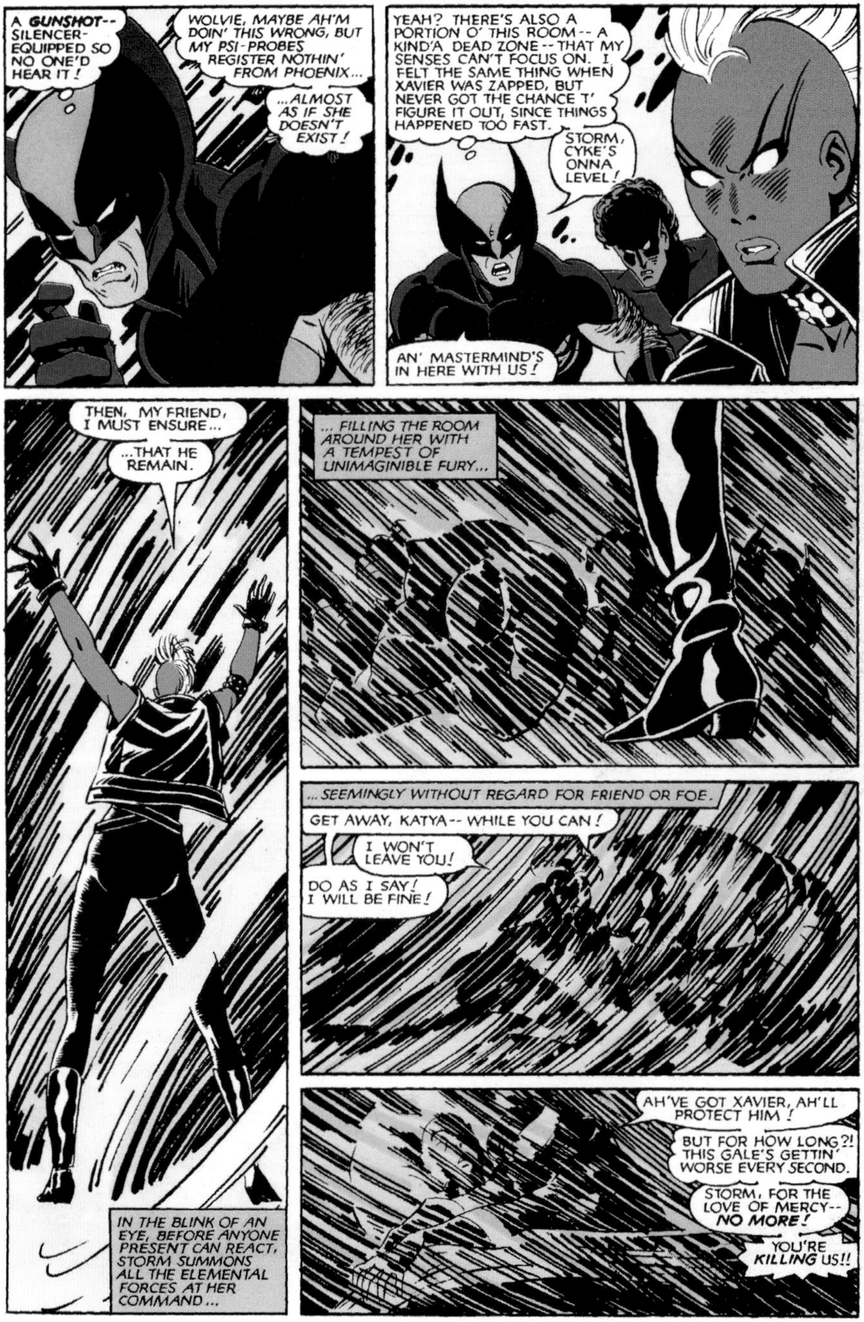

A GUNSHOT-- SILENCER-EQUIPPED SO NO ONE'D HEAR IT!
WOLVIE, MAYBE AH'M DOIN' THIS WRONG, BUT MY PSI-PROBES REGISTER NOTHIN' FROM PHOENIX...
...ALMOST AS IF SHE DOESN'T EXIST!
YEAH? THERE'S ALSO A PORTION O' THIS ROOM -- A KIND'A DEAD ZONE -- THAT MY SENSES CAN'T FOCUS ON. I FELT THE SAME THING WHEN XAVIER WAS ZAPPED, BUT NEVER GOT THE CHANCE T' FIGURE IT OUT, SINCE THINGS HAPPENED TOO FAST.
STORM, CYKE'S ONNA LEVEL!
AN' MASTERMIND'S IN HERE WITH US!
THEN, MY FRIEND, I MUST ENSURE...
...THAT HE REMAIN.
IN THE BLINK OF AN EYE, BEFORE ANYONE PRESENT CAN REACT, STORM SUMMONS ALL THE ELEMENTAL FORCES AT HER COMMAND...
... FILLING THE ROOM AROUND HER WITH A TEMPEST OF UNIMAGINIBLE FURY...
... SEEMINGLY WITHOUT REGARD FOR FRIEND OR FOE.
GET AWAY, KATYA -- WHILE YOU CAN!
I WON'T LEAVE YOU!
DO AS I SAY! I WILL BE FINE!
AH'VE GOT XAVIER, AH'LL PROTECT HIM!
BUT FOR HOW LONG?! THIS GALE'S GETTIN' WORSE EVERY SECOND.
STORM, FOR THE LOVE OF MERCY-- NO MORE!
YOU'RE KILLING US!!

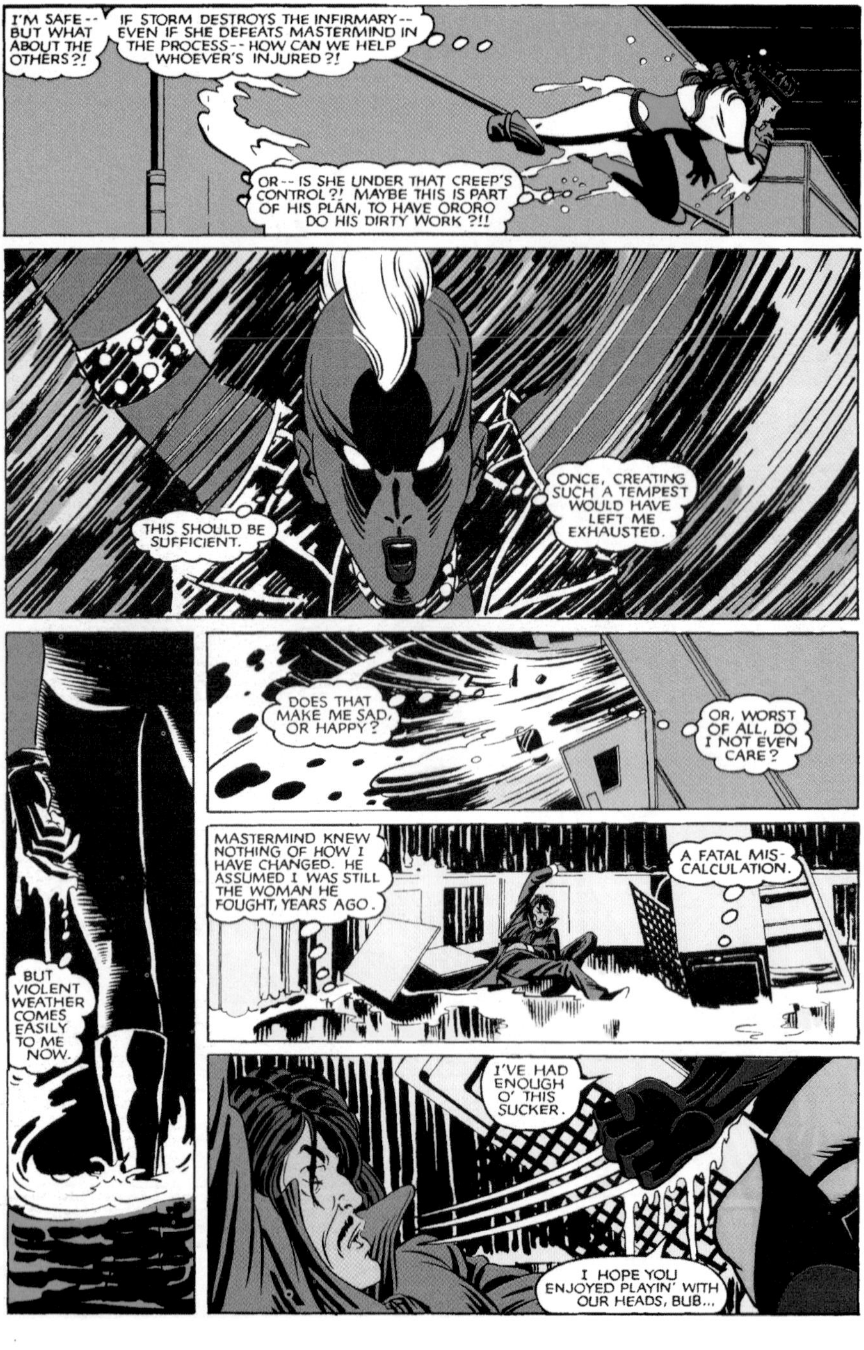

I'M SAFE-- BUT WHAT ABOUT THE OTHERS?!
IF STORM DESTROYS THE INFIRMARY-- EVEN IF SHE DEFEATS MASTERMIND IN THE PROCESS-- HOW CAN WE HELP WHOEVER'S INJURED?!
OR-- IS SHE UNDER THAT CREEP'S CONTROL?! MAYBE THIS IS PART OF HIS PLAN, TO HAVE ORORO DO HIS DIRTY WORK?!!
THIS SHOULD BE SUFFICIENT.
ONCE, CREATING SUCH A TEMPEST WOULD HAVE LEFT ME EXHAUSTED.
BUT VIOLENT WEATHER COMES EASILY TO ME NOW.
DOES THAT MAKE ME SAD, OR HAPPY?
OR, WORST OF ALL, DO I NOT EVEN CARE?
MASTERMIND KNEW NOTHING OF HOW I HAVE CHANGED. HE ASSUMED I WAS STILL THE WOMAN HE FOUGHT, YEARS AGO.
A FATAL MIS-CALCULATION.
I'VE HAD ENOUGH O' THIS SUCKER.
I HOPE YOU ENJOYED PLAYIN' WITH OUR HEADS, BUB...

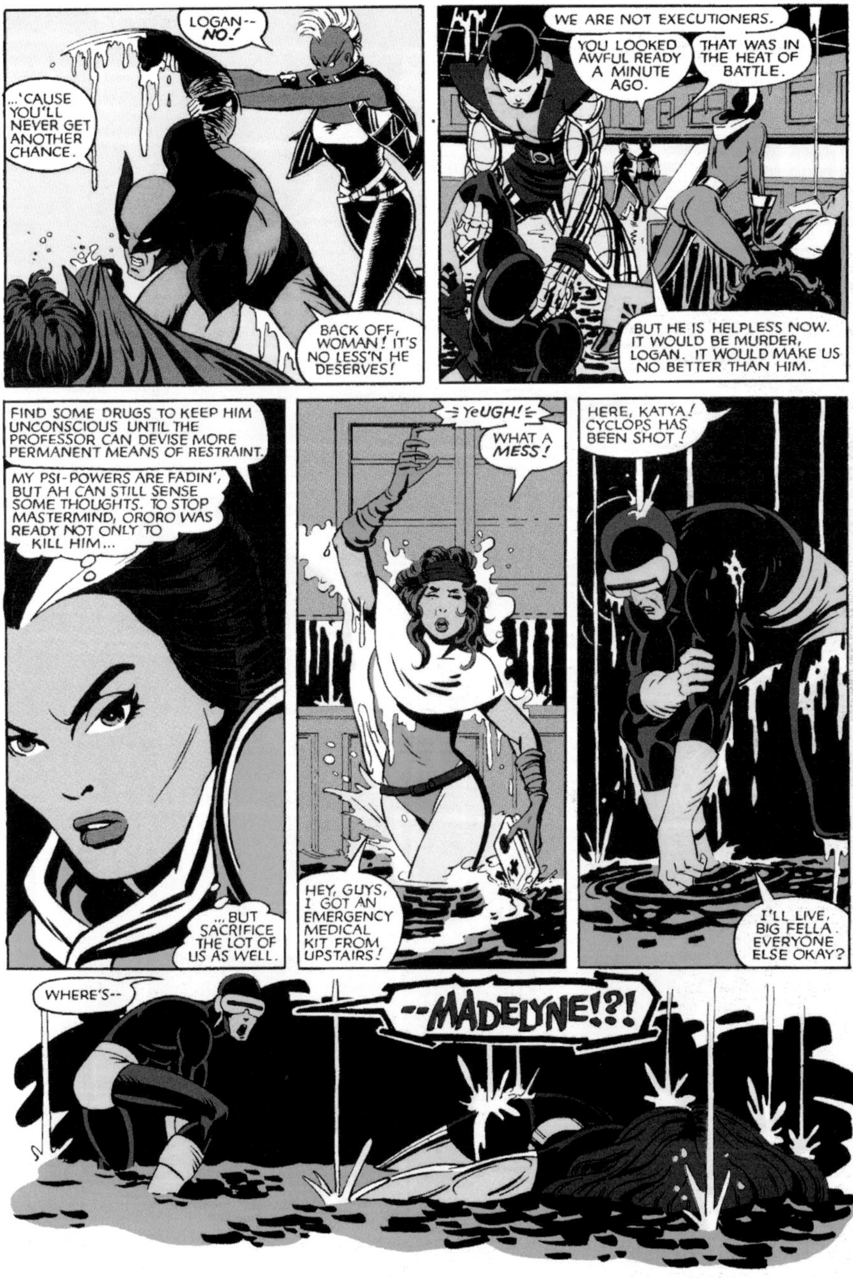
LOGAN-- NO!
...'CAUSE YOU'LL NEVER GET ANOTHER CHANCE.
BACK OFF, WOMAN! IT'S NO LESS'N HE DESERVES!
WE ARE NOT EXECUTIONERS.
YOU LOOKED AWFUL READY A MINUTE AGO.
THAT WAS IN THE HEAT OF BATTLE.
BUT HE IS HELPLESS NOW. IT WOULD BE MURDER, LOGAN. IT WOULD MAKE US NO BETTER THAN HIM.
FIND SOME DRUGS TO KEEP HIM UNCONSCIOUS UNTIL THE PROFESSOR CAN DEVISE MORE PERMANENT MEANS OF RESTRAINT.
MY PSI-POWERS ARE FADIN', BUT AH CAN STILL SENSE SOME THOUGHTS. TO STOP MASTERMIND, ORORO WAS READY NOT ONLY TO KILL HIM...
...BUT SACRIFICE THE LOT OF US AS WELL.
YeUGH!
WHAT A MESS!
HEY, GUYS, I GOT AN EMERGENCY MEDICAL KIT FROM UPSTAIRS!
HERE, KATYA! CYCLOPS HAS BEEN SHOT!
I'LL LIVE, BIG FELLA. EVERYONE ELSE OKAY?
WHERE'S--
--MADELYNE!?!

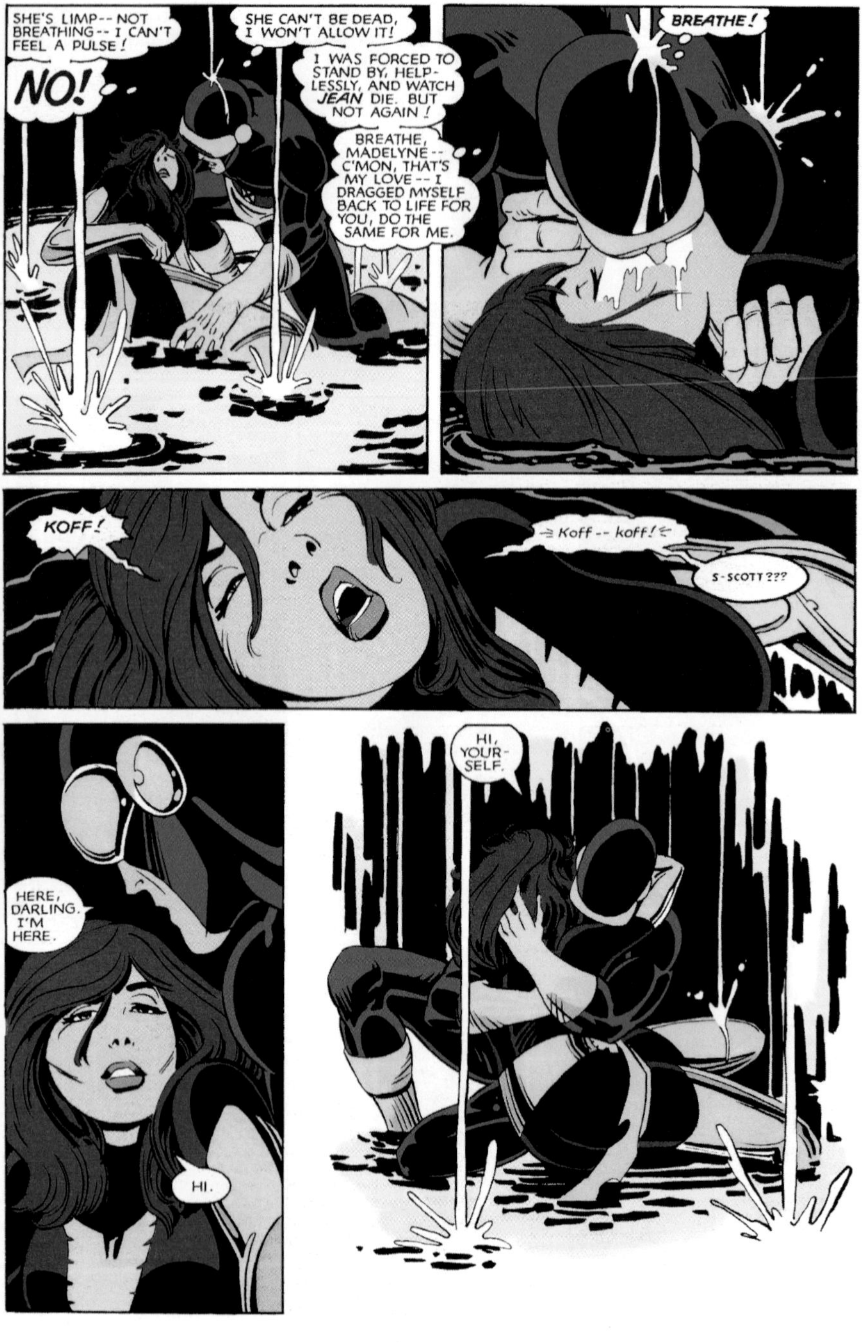
SHE'S LIMP-- NOT BREATHING-- I CAN'T FEEL A PULSE!
NO!
SHE CAN'T BE DEAD, I WON'T ALLOW IT!
I WAS FORCED TO STAND BY, HELP-LESSLY, AND WATCH JEAN DIE. BUT NOT AGAIN!
BREATHE, MADELYNE-- C'MON, THAT'S MY LOVE-- I DRAGGED MYSELF BACK TO LIFE FOR YOU, DO THE SAME FOR ME.
BREATHE!
KOFF!
Koff -- koff!
S-SCOTT???
HERE, DARLING. I'M HERE.
HI.
HI, YOUR-SELF.

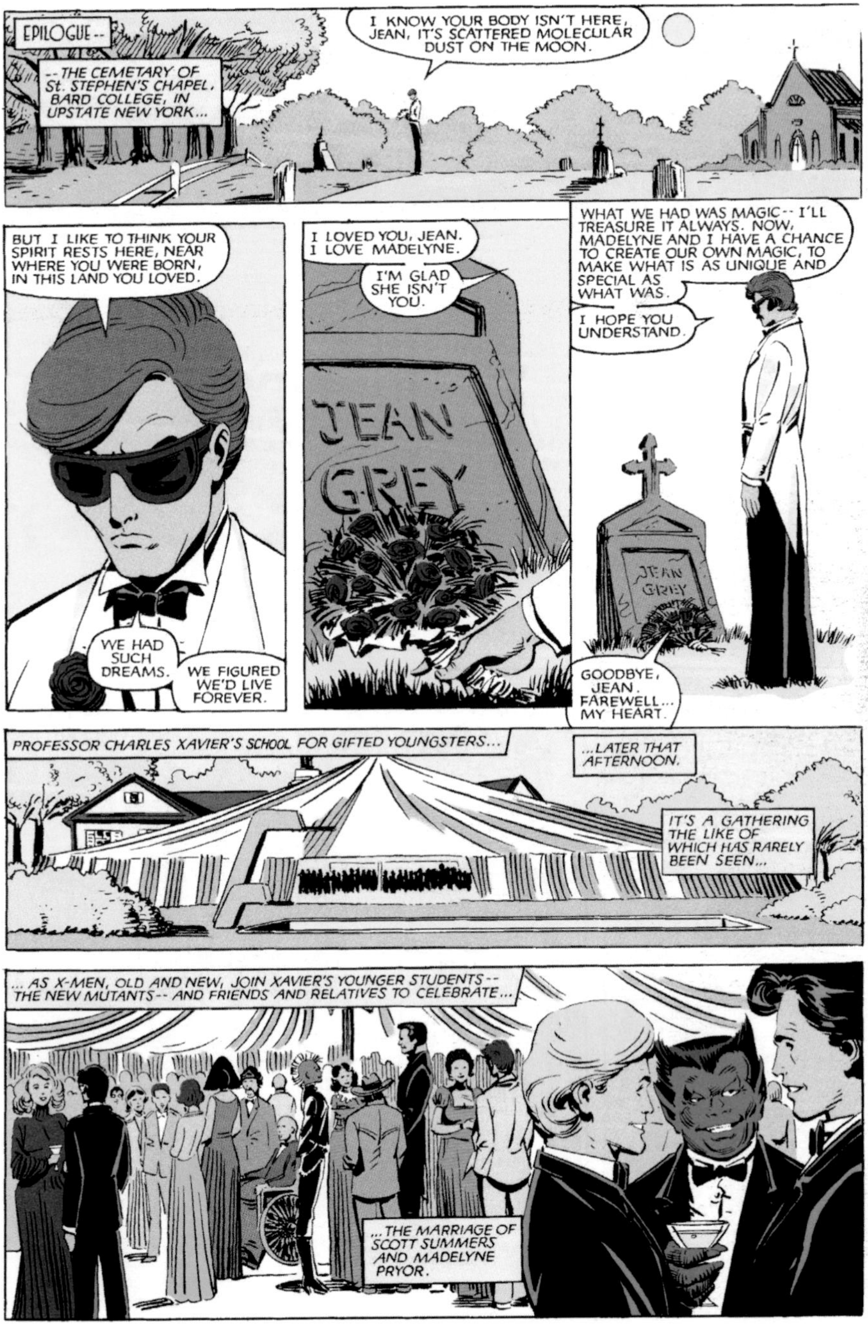
EPILOGUE--
--THE CEMETARY OF St. STEPHEN'S CHAPEL, BARD COLLEGE, IN UPSTATE NEW YORK...
I KNOW YOUR BODY ISN'T HERE, JEAN, IT'S SCATTERED MOLECULAR DUST ON THE MOON.
BUT I LIKE TO THINK YOUR SPIRIT RESTS HERE, NEAR WHERE YOU WERE BORN, IN THIS LAND YOU LOVED.
WE HAD SUCH DREAMS.
WE FIGURED WE'D LIVE FOREVER.
I LOVED YOU, JEAN. I LOVE MADELYNE.
I'M GLAD SHE ISN'T YOU.
JEAN GREY
WHAT WE HAD WAS MAGIC-- I'LL TREASURE IT ALWAYS. NOW, MADELYNE AND I HAVE A CHANCE TO CREATE OUR OWN MAGIC, TO MAKE WHAT IS AS UNIQUE AND SPECIAL AS WHAT WAS.
I HOPE YOU UNDERSTAND.
JEAN GREY
GOODBYE, JEAN. FAREWELL... MY HEART.
PROFESSOR CHARLES XAVIER'S SCHOOL FOR GIFTED YOUNGSTERS...
...LATER THAT AFTERNOON.
IT'S A GATHERING THE LIKE OF WHICH HAS RARELY BEEN SEEN...
... AS X-MEN, OLD AND NEW, JOIN XAVIER'S YOUNGER STUDENTS -- THE NEW MUTANTS -- AND FRIENDS AND RELATIVES TO CELEBRATE...
...THE MARRIAGE OF SCOTT SUMMERS AND MADELYNE PRYOR.

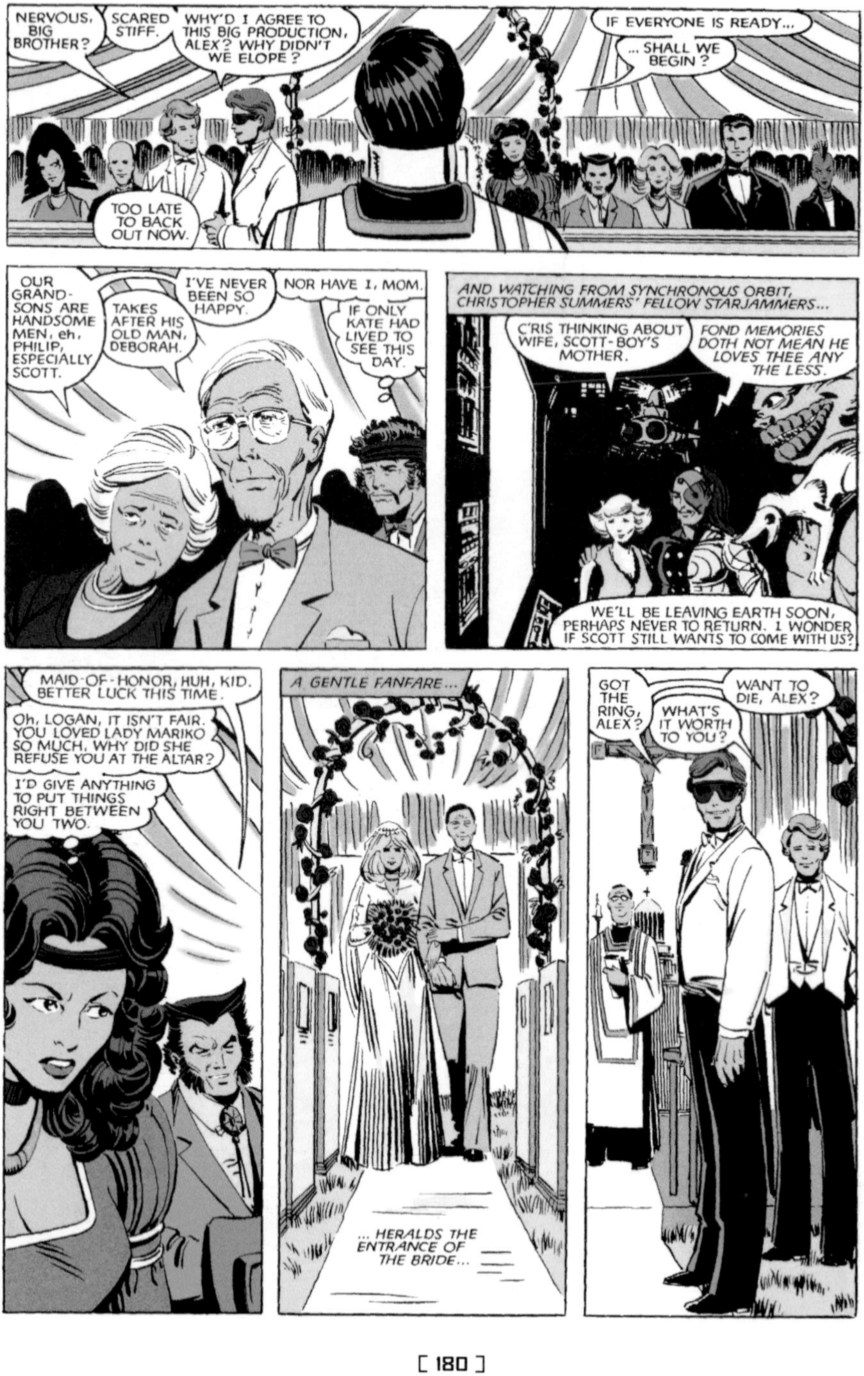

NERVOUS, BIG BROTHER?
SCARED STIFF.
WHY'D I AGREE TO THIS BIG PRODUCTION, ALEX? WHY DIDN'T WE ELOPE?
TOO LATE TO BACK OUT NOW.
IF EVERYONE IS READY...
... SHALL WE BEGIN?
OUR GRANDSONS ARE HANDSOME MEN, eh, PHILIP, ESPECIALLY SCOTT.
TAKES AFTER HIS OLD MAN, DEBORAH.
I'VE NEVER BEEN SO HAPPY.
NOR HAVE I, MOM.
IF ONLY KATE HAD LIVED TO SEE THIS DAY.
AND WATCHING FROM SYNCHRONOUS ORBIT, CHRISTOPHER SUMMERS' FELLOW STARJAMMERS...
C'RIS THINKING ABOUT WIFE, SCOTT-BOY'S MOTHER.
FOND MEMORIES DOTH NOT MEAN HE LOVES THEE ANY THE LESS.
WE'LL BE LEAVING EARTH SOON, PERHAPS NEVER TO RETURN. I WONDER IF SCOTT STILL WANTS TO COME WITH US?
MAID-OF-HONOR, HUH, KID. BETTER LUCK THIS TIME.
Oh, LOGAN, IT ISN'T FAIR. YOU LOVED LADY MARIKO SO MUCH. WHY DID SHE REFUSE YOU AT THE ALTAR?
I'D GIVE ANYTHING TO PUT THINGS RIGHT BETWEEN YOU TWO.
A GENTLE FANFARE...
... HERALDS THE ENTRANCE OF THE BRIDE...
GOT THE RING, ALEX?
WHAT'S IT WORTH TO YOU?
WANT TO DIE, ALEX?

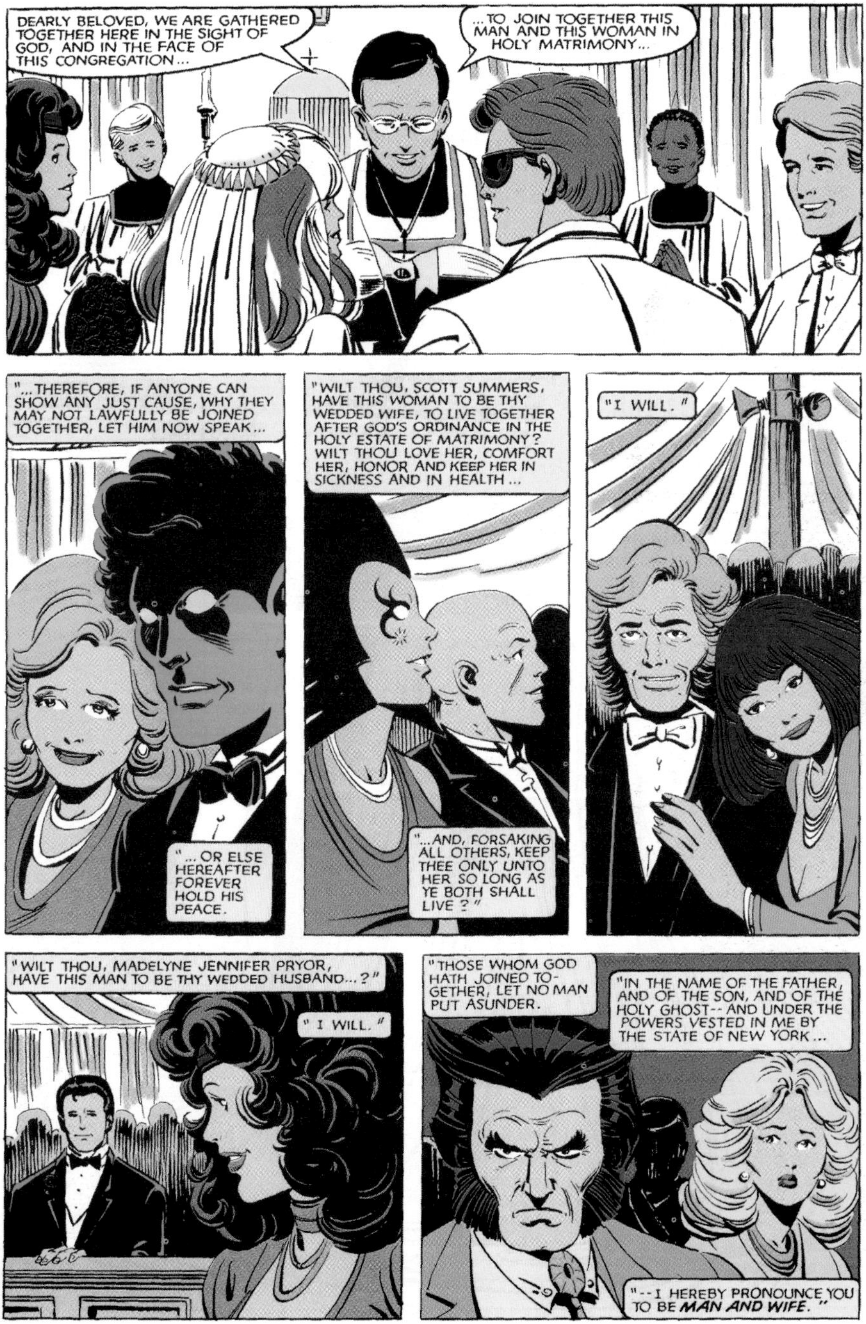
DEARLY BELOVED, WE ARE GATHERED TOGETHER HERE IN THE SIGHT OF GOD, AND IN THE FACE OF THIS CONGREGATION...
...TO JOIN TOGETHER THIS MAN AND THIS WOMAN IN HOLY MATRIMONY...
"...THEREFORE, IF ANYONE CAN SHOW ANY JUST CAUSE, WHY THEY MAY NOT LAWFULLY BE JOINED TOGETHER, LET HIM NOW SPEAK...
"...OR ELSE HEREAFTER FOREVER HOLD HIS PEACE.
"WILT THOU, SCOTT SUMMERS, HAVE THIS WOMAN TO BE THY WEDDED WIFE, TO LIVE TOGETHER AFTER GOD'S ORDINANCE IN THE HOLY ESTATE OF MATRIMONY? WILT THOU LOVE HER, COMFORT HER, HONOR AND KEEP HER IN SICKNESS AND IN HEALTH...
"...AND, FORSAKING ALL OTHERS, KEEP THEE ONLY UNTO HER SO LONG AS YE BOTH SHALL LIVE?"
"I WILL."
"WILT THOU, MADELYNE JENNIFER PRYOR, HAVE THIS MAN TO BE THY WEDDED HUSBAND...?"
"I WILL."
"THOSE WHOM GOD HATH JOINED TOGETHER, LET NO MAN PUT ASUNDER.
"IN THE NAME OF THE FATHER, AND OF THE SON, AND OF THE HOLY GHOST-- AND UNDER THE POWERS VESTED IN ME BY THE STATE OF NEW YORK...
"--I HEREBY PRONOUNCE YOU TO BE MAN AND WIFE."

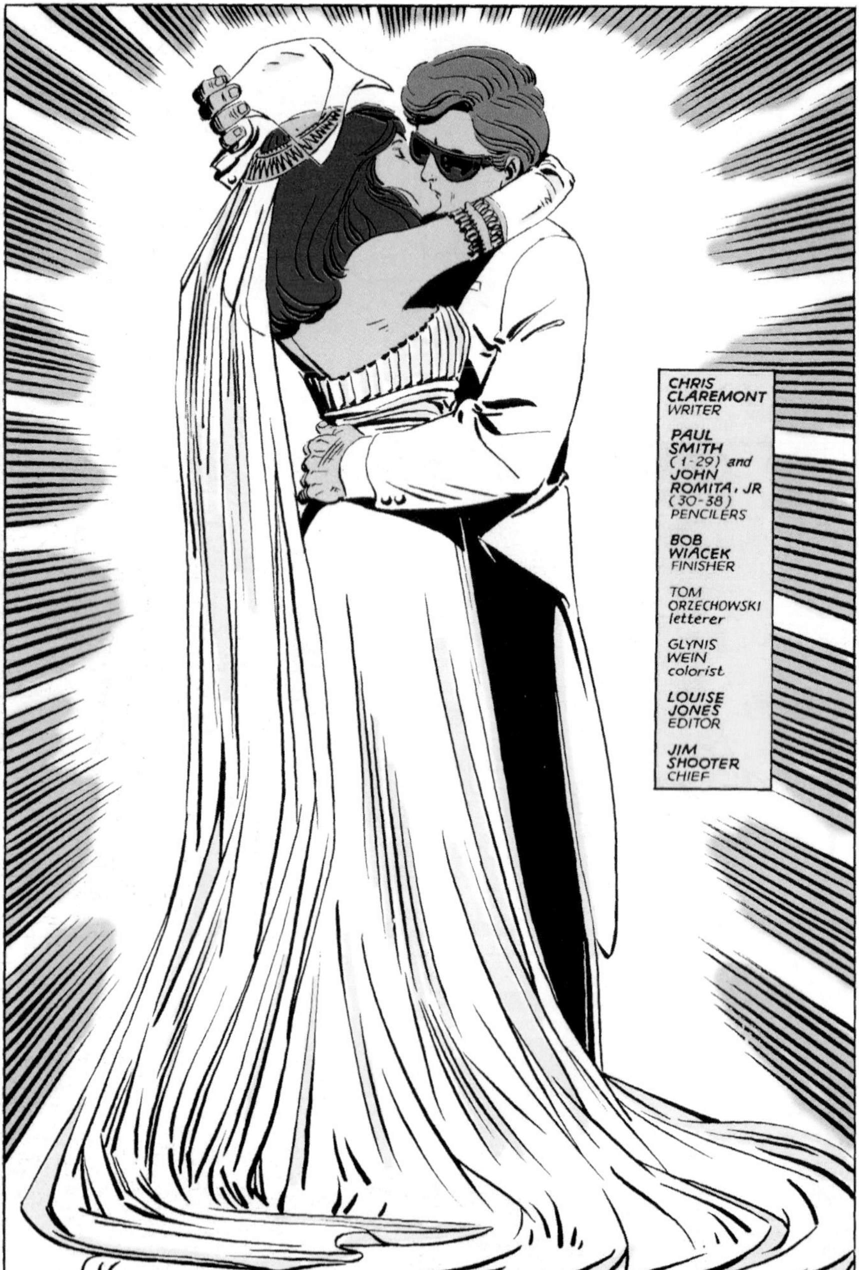
CHRIS CLAREMONT WRITER
PAUL SMITH (1-29) and JOHN ROMITA, JR (30-38) PENCILERS
BOB WIACEK FINISHER
TOM ORZECHOWSKI letterer
GLYNIS WEIN colorist
LOUISE JONES EDITOR
JIM SHOOTER CHIEF

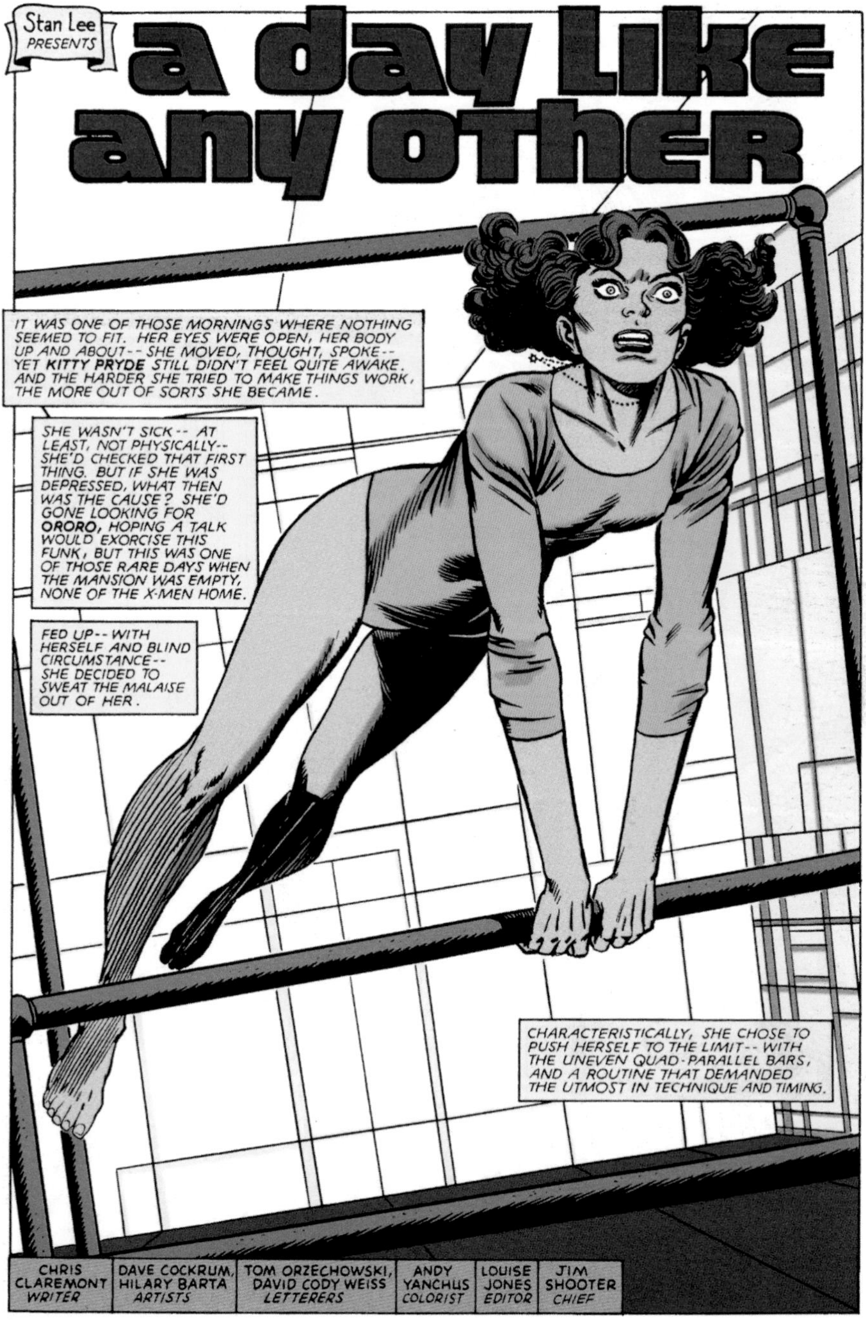
Stan Lee PRESENTS
a day like any other
IT WAS ONE OF THOSE MORNINGS WHERE NOTHING SEEMED TO FIT. HER EYES WERE OPEN, HER BODY UP AND ABOUT-- SHE MOVED, THOUGHT, SPOKE-- YET KITTY PRYDE STILL DIDN'T FEEL QUITE AWAKE. AND THE HARDER SHE TRIED TO MAKE THINGS WORK, THE MORE OUT OF SORTS SHE BECAME.
SHE WASN'T SICK-- AT LEAST, NOT PHYSICALLY-- SHE'D CHECKED THAT FIRST THING. BUT IF SHE WAS DEPRESSED, WHAT THEN WAS THE CAUSE? SHE'D GONE LOOKING FOR ORORO, HOPING A TALK WOULD EXORCISE THIS FUNK, BUT THIS WAS ONE OF THOSE RARE DAYS WHEN THE MANSION WAS EMPTY, NONE OF THE X-MEN HOME.
FED UP-- WITH HERSELF AND BLIND CIRCUMSTANCE-- SHE DECIDED TO SWEAT THE MALAISE OUT OF HER.
CHARACTERISTICALLY, SHE CHOSE TO PUSH HERSELF TO THE LIMIT-- WITH THE UNEVEN QUAD-PARALLEL BARS, AND A ROUTINE THAT DEMANDED THE UTMOST IN TECHNIQUE AND TIMING.
CHRIS CLAREMONT WRITER
DAVE COCKRUM, HILARY BARTA ARTISTS
TOM ORZECHOWSKI, DAVID CODY WEISS LETTERERS
ANDY YANCHUS COLORIST
LOUISE JONES EDITOR
JIM SHOOTER CHIEF

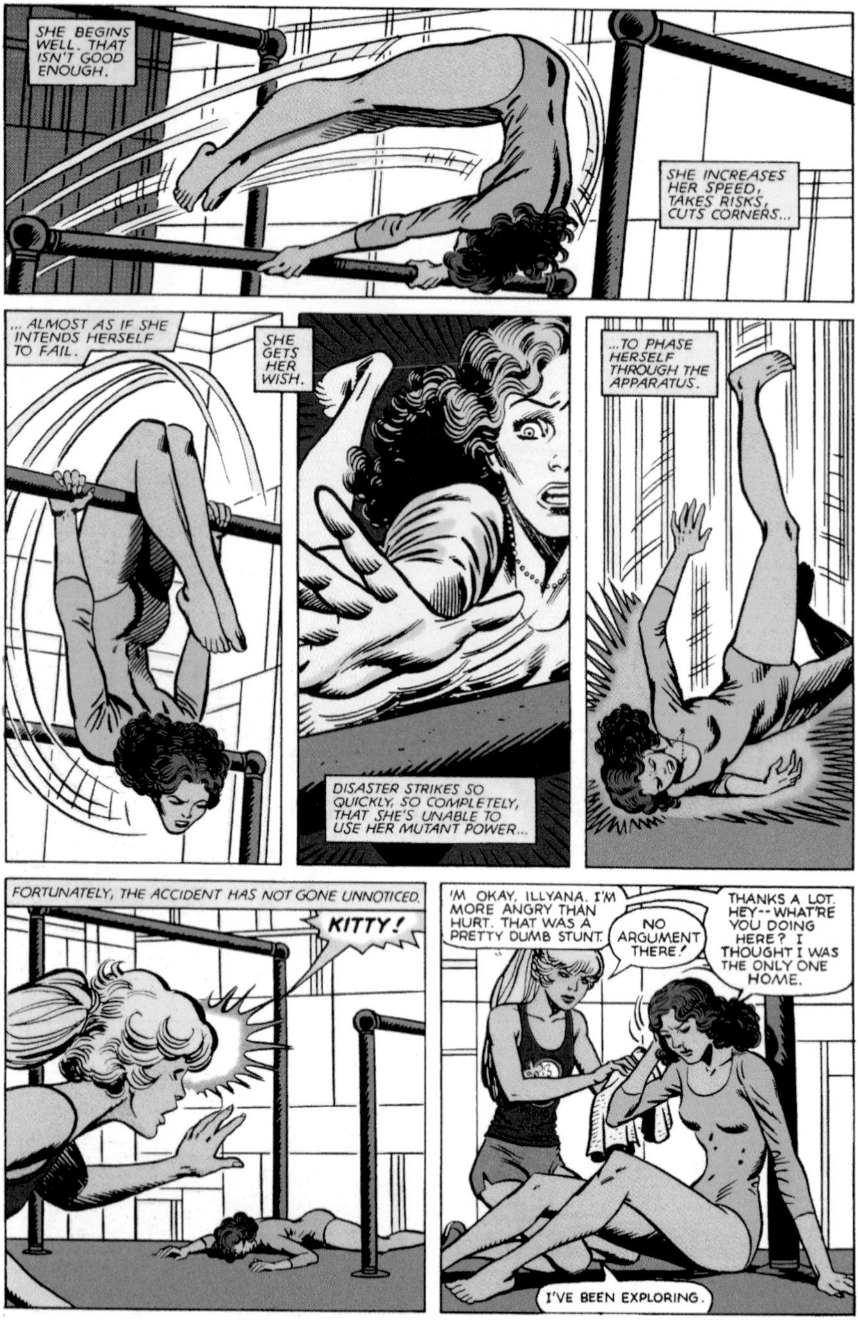
SHE BEGINS WELL. THAT ISN'T GOOD ENOUGH.
SHE INCREASES HER SPEED, TAKES RISKS, CUTS CORNERS...
... ALMOST AS IF SHE INTENDS HERSELF TO FAIL.
SHE GETS HER WISH.
DISASTER STRIKES SO QUICKLY, SO COMPLETELY, THAT SHE'S UNABLE TO USE HER MUTANT POWER...
...TO PHASE HERSELF THROUGH THE APPARATUS.
FORTUNATELY, THE ACCIDENT HAS NOT GONE UNNOTICED.
KITTY!
I'M OKAY, ILLYANA. I'M MORE ANGRY THAN HURT. THAT WAS A PRETTY DUMB STUNT.
NO ARGUMENT THERE!
THANKS A LOT. HEY--WHAT'RE YOU DOING HERE? I THOUGHT I WAS THE ONLY ONE HOME.
I'VE BEEN EXPLORING.

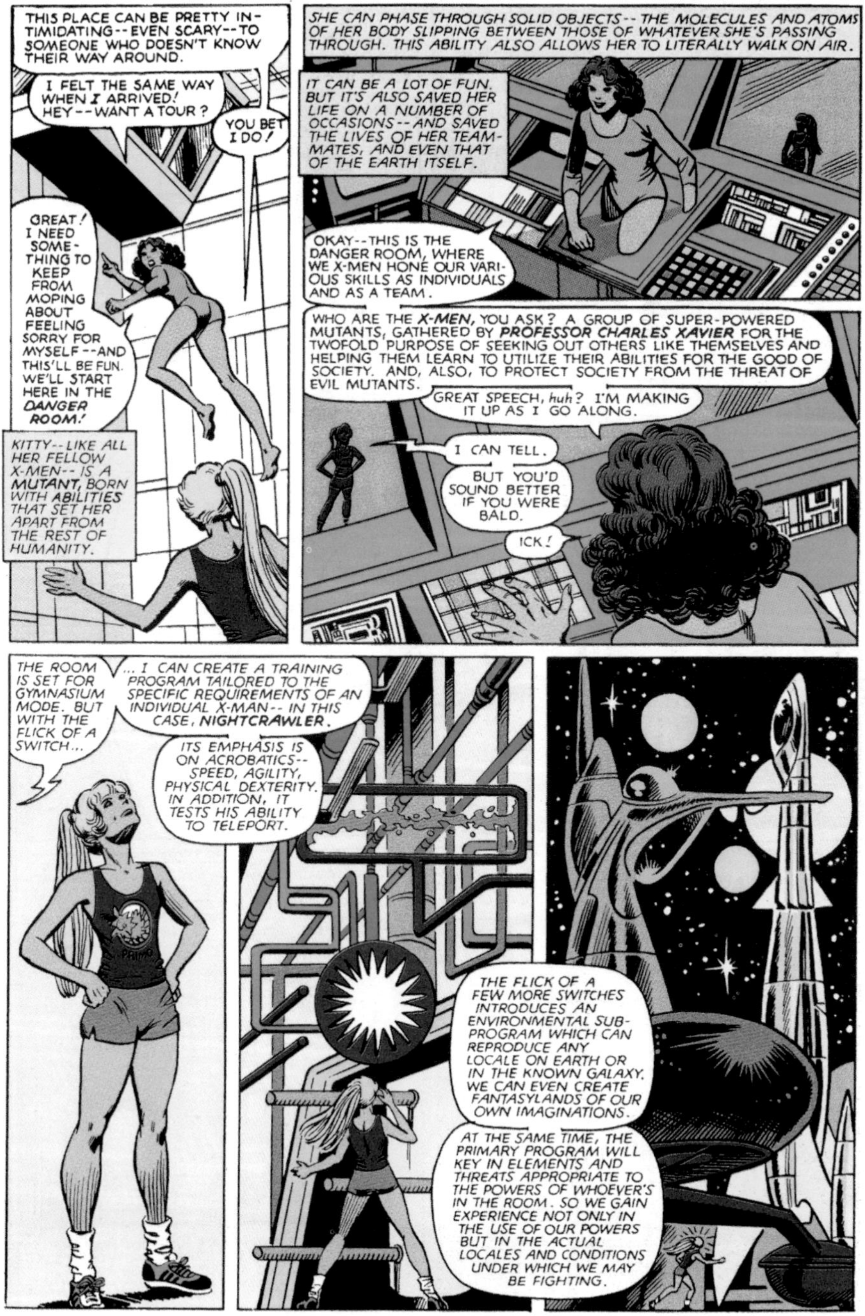
THIS PLACE CAN BE PRETTY INTIMIDATING--EVEN SCARY--TO SOMEONE WHO DOESN'T KNOW THEIR WAY AROUND.
I FELT THE SAME WAY WHEN I ARRIVED! HEY--WANT A TOUR?
YOU BET I DO!
GREAT! I NEED SOMETHING TO KEEP FROM MOPING ABOUT FEELING SORRY FOR MYSELF--AND THIS'LL BE FUN. WE'LL START HERE IN THE DANGER ROOM!
KITTY--LIKE ALL HER FELLOW X-MEN--IS A MUTANT, BORN WITH ABILITIES THAT SET HER APART FROM THE REST OF HUMANITY.
SHE CAN PHASE THROUGH SOLID OBJECTS--THE MOLECULES AND ATOMS OF HER BODY SLIPPING BETWEEN THOSE OF WHATEVER SHE'S PASSING THROUGH. THIS ABILITY ALSO ALLOWS HER TO LITERALLY WALK ON AIR.
IT CAN BE A LOT OF FUN, BUT IT'S ALSO SAVED HER LIFE ON A NUMBER OF OCCASIONS--AND SAVED THE LIVES OF HER TEAMMATES, AND EVEN THAT OF THE EARTH ITSELF.
OKAY--THIS IS THE DANGER ROOM, WHERE WE X-MEN HONE OUR VARIOUS SKILLS AS INDIVIDUALS AND AS A TEAM.
WHO ARE THE X-MEN, YOU ASK? A GROUP OF SUPER-POWERED MUTANTS, GATHERED BY PROFESSOR CHARLES XAVIER FOR THE TWOFOLD PURPOSE OF SEEKING OUT OTHERS LIKE THEMSELVES AND HELPING THEM LEARN TO UTILIZE THEIR ABILITIES FOR THE GOOD OF SOCIETY. AND, ALSO, TO PROTECT SOCIETY FROM THE THREAT OF EVIL MUTANTS.
GREAT SPEECH, huh? I'M MAKING IT UP AS I GO ALONG.
I CAN TELL.
BUT YOU'D SOUND BETTER IF YOU WERE BALD.
ICK!
THE ROOM IS SET FOR GYMNASIUM MODE. BUT WITH THE FLICK OF A SWITCH...
...I CAN CREATE A TRAINING PROGRAM TAILORED TO THE SPECIFIC REQUIREMENTS OF AN INDIVIDUAL X-MAN--IN THIS CASE, NIGHTCRAWLER.
ITS EMPHASIS IS ON ACROBATICS--SPEED, AGILITY, PHYSICAL DEXTERITY. IN ADDITION, IT TESTS HIS ABILITY TO TELEPORT.
THE FLICK OF A FEW MORE SWITCHES INTRODUCES AN ENVIRONMENTAL SUB-PROGRAM WHICH CAN REPRODUCE ANY LOCALE ON EARTH OR IN THE KNOWN GALAXY. WE CAN EVEN CREATE FANTASYLANDS OF OUR OWN IMAGINATIONS.
AT THE SAME TIME, THE PRIMARY PROGRAM WILL KEY IN ELEMENTS AND THREATS APPROPRIATE TO THE POWERS OF WHOEVER'S IN THE ROOM. SO WE GAIN EXPERIENCE NOT ONLY IN THE USE OF OUR POWERS BUT IN THE ACTUAL LOCALES AND CONDITIONS UNDER WHICH WE MAY BE FIGHTING.

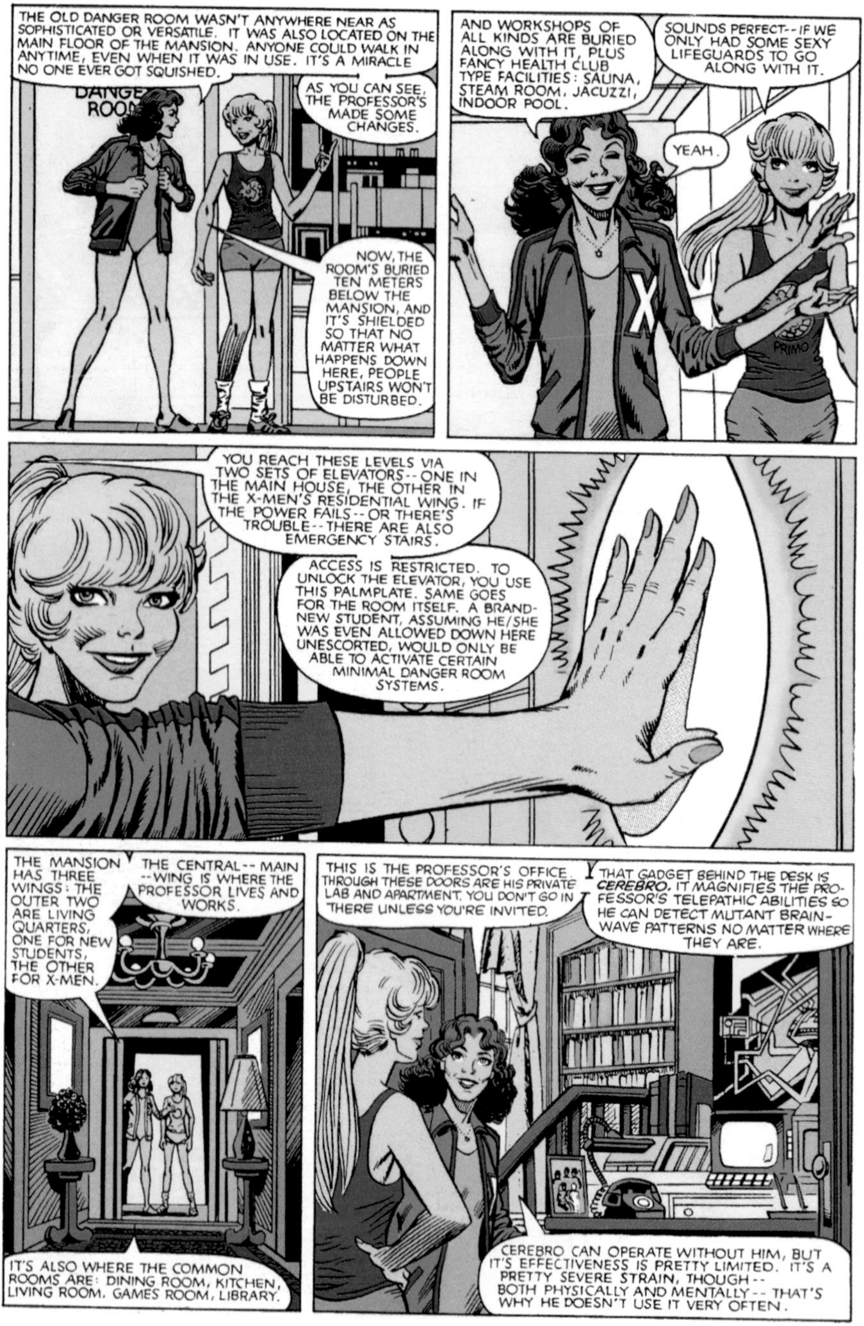
THE OLD DANGER ROOM WASN'T ANYWHERE NEAR AS SOPHISTICATED OR VERSATILE. IT WAS ALSO LOCATED ON THE MAIN FLOOR OF THE MANSION. ANYONE COULD WALK IN ANYTIME, EVEN WHEN IT WAS IN USE. IT'S A MIRACLE NO ONE EVER GOT SQUISHED.
AS YOU CAN SEE, THE PROFESSOR'S MADE SOME CHANGES.
NOW, THE ROOM'S BURIED TEN METERS BELOW THE MANSION, AND IT'S SHIELDED SO THAT NO MATTER WHAT HAPPENS DOWN HERE, PEOPLE UPSTAIRS WON'T BE DISTURBED.
AND WORKSHOPS OF ALL KINDS ARE BURIED ALONG WITH IT, PLUS FANCY HEALTH CLUB TYPE FACILITIES: SAUNA, STEAM ROOM, JACUZZI, INDOOR POOL.
SOUNDS PERFECT-- IF WE ONLY HAD SOME SEXY LIFEGUARDS TO GO ALONG WITH IT.
YEAH.
YOU REACH THESE LEVELS VIA TWO SETS OF ELEVATORS-- ONE IN THE MAIN HOUSE, THE OTHER IN THE X-MEN'S RESIDENTIAL WING. IF THE POWER FAILS-- OR THERE'S TROUBLE-- THERE ARE ALSO EMERGENCY STAIRS.
ACCESS IS RESTRICTED. TO UNLOCK THE ELEVATOR, YOU USE THIS PALMPLATE. SAME GOES FOR THE ROOM ITSELF. A BRAND-NEW STUDENT, ASSUMING HE/SHE WAS EVEN ALLOWED DOWN HERE UNESCORTED, WOULD ONLY BE ABLE TO ACTIVATE CERTAIN MINIMAL DANGER ROOM SYSTEMS.
THE MANSION HAS THREE WINGS: THE OUTER TWO ARE LIVING QUARTERS, ONE FOR NEW STUDENTS, THE OTHER FOR X-MEN.
THE CENTRAL-- MAIN --WING IS WHERE THE PROFESSOR LIVES AND WORKS.
IT'S ALSO WHERE THE COMMON ROOMS ARE: DINING ROOM, KITCHEN, LIVING ROOM, GAMES ROOM, LIBRARY.
THIS IS THE PROFESSOR'S OFFICE. THROUGH THESE DOORS ARE HIS PRIVATE LAB AND APARTMENT. YOU DON'T GO IN THERE UNLESS YOU'RE INVITED.
THAT GADGET BEHIND THE DESK IS CEREBRO. IT MAGNIFIES THE PROFESSOR'S TELEPATHIC ABILITIES SO HE CAN DETECT MUTANT BRAIN-WAVE PATTERNS NO MATTER WHERE THEY ARE.
CEREBRO CAN OPERATE WITHOUT HIM, BUT IT'S EFFECTIVENESS IS PRETTY LIMITED. IT'S A PRETTY SEVERE STRAIN, THOUGH-- BOTH PHYSICALLY AND MENTALLY-- THAT'S WHY HE DOESN'T USE IT VERY OFTEN.

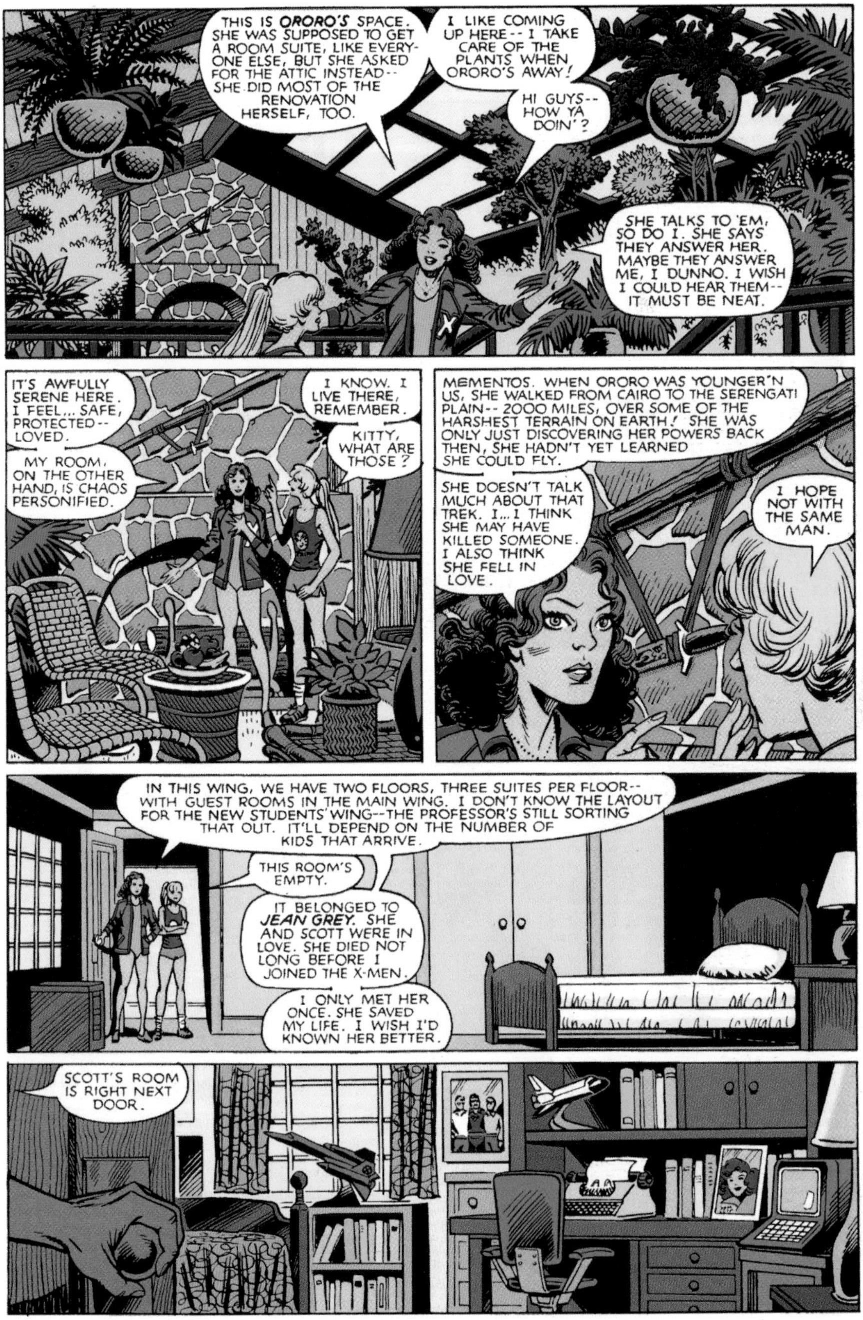
THIS IS ORORO'S SPACE. SHE WAS SUPPOSED TO GET A ROOM SUITE, LIKE EVERYONE ELSE, BUT SHE ASKED FOR THE ATTIC INSTEAD-- SHE DID MOST OF THE RENOVATION HERSELF, TOO.
I LIKE COMING UP HERE-- I TAKE CARE OF THE PLANTS WHEN ORORO'S AWAY!
HI GUYS-- HOW YA DOIN'?
SHE TALKS TO 'EM, SO DO I. SHE SAYS THEY ANSWER HER. MAYBE THEY ANSWER ME, I DUNNO. I WISH I COULD HEAR THEM-- IT MUST BE NEAT.
IT'S AWFULLY SERENE HERE. I FEEL... SAFE, PROTECTED-- LOVED.
MY ROOM, ON THE OTHER HAND, IS CHAOS PERSONIFIED.
I KNOW. I LIVE THERE, REMEMBER.
KITTY, WHAT ARE THOSE?
MEMENTOS. WHEN ORORO WAS YOUNGER'N US, SHE WALKED FROM CAIRO TO THE SERENGATI PLAIN-- 2000 MILES, OVER SOME OF THE HARSHEST TERRAIN ON EARTH! SHE WAS ONLY JUST DISCOVERING HER POWERS BACK THEN, SHE HADN'T YET LEARNED SHE COULD FLY.
SHE DOESN'T TALK MUCH ABOUT THAT TREK. I... I THINK SHE MAY HAVE KILLED SOMEONE. I ALSO THINK SHE FELL IN LOVE.
I HOPE NOT WITH THE SAME MAN.
IN THIS WING, WE HAVE TWO FLOORS, THREE SUITES PER FLOOR-- WITH GUEST ROOMS IN THE MAIN WING. I DON'T KNOW THE LAYOUT FOR THE NEW STUDENTS' WING--THE PROFESSOR'S STILL SORTING THAT OUT. IT'LL DEPEND ON THE NUMBER OF KIDS THAT ARRIVE.
THIS ROOM'S EMPTY.
IT BELONGED TO JEAN GREY. SHE AND SCOTT WERE IN LOVE. SHE DIED NOT LONG BEFORE I JOINED THE X-MEN.
I ONLY MET HER ONCE. SHE SAVED MY LIFE. I WISH I'D KNOWN HER BETTER.
SCOTT'S ROOM IS RIGHT NEXT DOOR.

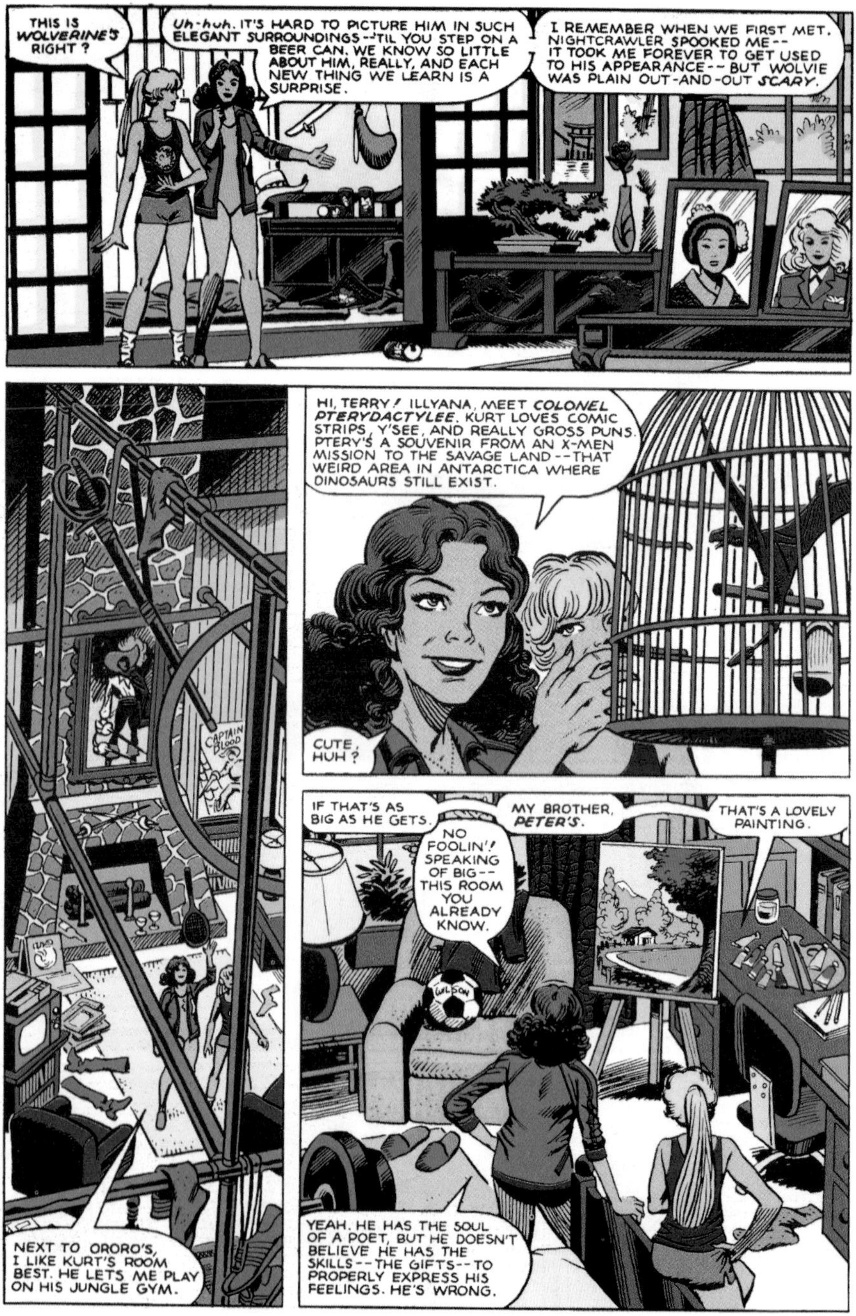
THIS IS WOLVERINE'S RIGHT ?
Uh-huh. IT'S HARD TO PICTURE HIM IN SUCH ELEGANT SURROUNDINGS--'TIL YOU STEP ON A BEER CAN. WE KNOW SO LITTLE ABOUT HIM, REALLY, AND EACH NEW THING WE LEARN IS A SURPRISE.
I REMEMBER WHEN WE FIRST MET. NIGHTCRAWLER SPOOKED ME-- IT TOOK ME FOREVER TO GET USED TO HIS APPEARANCE-- BUT WOLVIE WAS PLAIN OUT-AND-OUT SCARY.
CAPTAIN BLOOD
NEXT TO ORORO'S, I LIKE KURT'S ROOM BEST. HE LETS ME PLAY ON HIS JUNGLE GYM.
HI, TERRY! ILLYANA, MEET COLONEL PTERYDACTYLEE. KURT LOVES COMIC STRIPS, Y'SEE, AND REALLY GROSS PUNS. PTERY'S A SOUVENIR FROM AN X-MEN MISSION TO THE SAVAGE LAND--THAT WEIRD AREA IN ANTARCTICA WHERE DINOSAURS STILL EXIST.
CUTE, HUH ?
IF THAT'S AS BIG AS HE GETS.
NO FOOLIN'! SPEAKING OF BIG-- THIS ROOM YOU ALREADY KNOW.
MY BROTHER, PETER'S.
THAT'S A LOVELY PAINTING.
WILSON
YEAH. HE HAS THE SOUL OF A POET, BUT HE DOESN'T BELIEVE HE HAS THE SKILLS--THE GIFTS--TO PROPERLY EXPRESS HIS FEELINGS. HE'S WRONG.

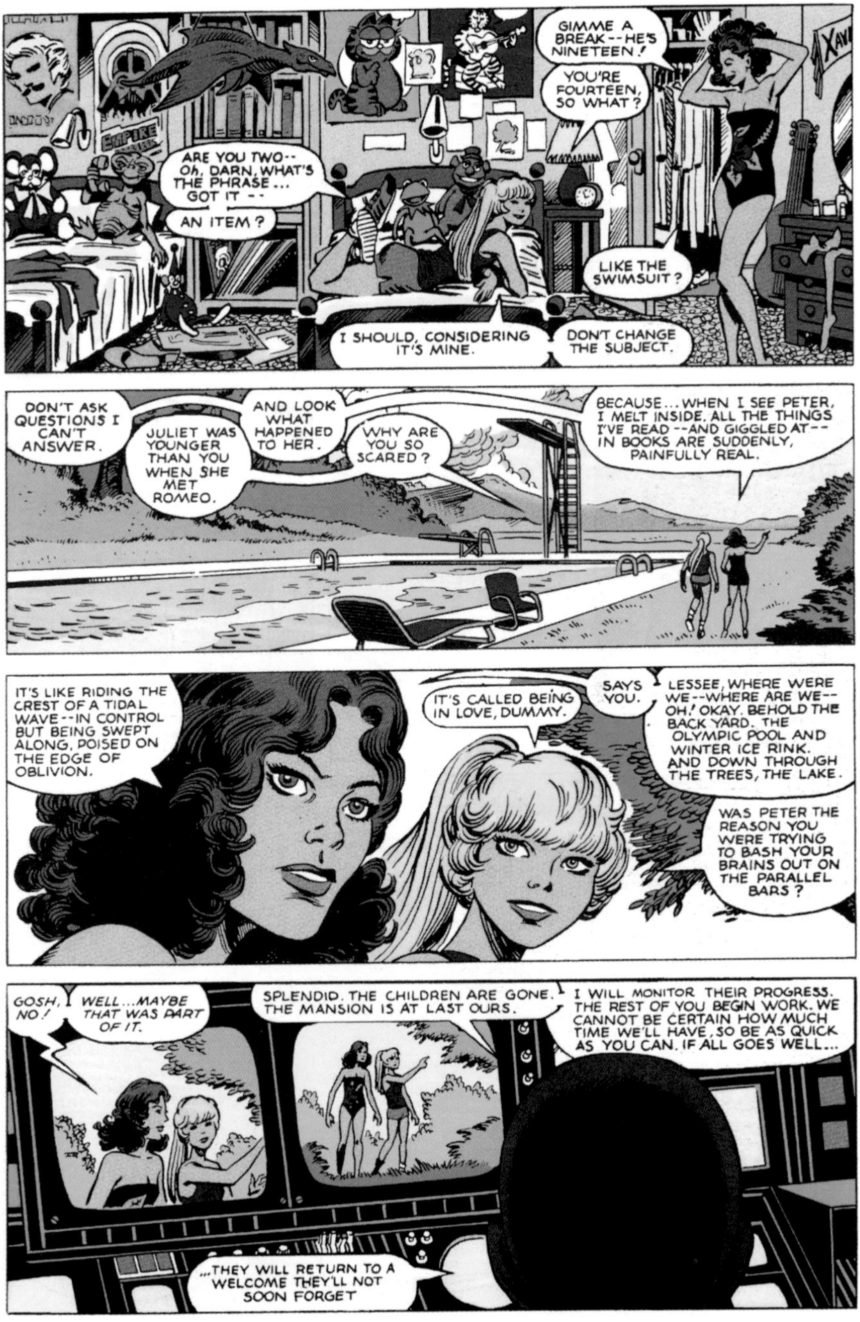

ARE YOU TWO-- Oh, DARN, WHAT'S THE PHRASE... GOT IT --
AN ITEM?
GIMME A BREAK--HE'S NINETEEN!
YOU'RE FOURTEEN, SO WHAT?
LIKE THE SWIMSUIT?
I SHOULD, CONSIDERING IT'S MINE.
DON'T CHANGE THE SUBJECT.
DON'T ASK QUESTIONS I CAN'T ANSWER.
JULIET WAS YOUNGER THAN YOU WHEN SHE MET ROMEO.
AND LOOK WHAT HAPPENED TO HER.
WHY ARE YOU SO SCARED?
BECAUSE... WHEN I SEE PETER, I MELT INSIDE. ALL THE THINGS I'VE READ--AND GIGGLED AT-- IN BOOKS ARE SUDDENLY, PAINFULLY REAL.
IT'S LIKE RIDING THE CREST OF A TIDAL WAVE--IN CONTROL BUT BEING SWEPT ALONG, POISED ON THE EDGE OF OBLIVION.
IT'S CALLED BEING IN LOVE, DUMMY.
SAYS YOU.
LESSEE, WHERE WERE WE--WHERE ARE WE-- OH! OKAY. BEHOLD THE BACK YARD. THE OLYMPIC POOL AND WINTER ICE RINK. AND DOWN THROUGH THE TREES, THE LAKE.
WAS PETER THE REASON YOU WERE TRYING TO BASH YOUR BRAINS OUT ON THE PARALLEL BARS?
GOSH, NO!
WELL... MAYBE THAT WAS PART OF IT.
SPLENDID. THE CHILDREN ARE GONE. THE MANSION IS AT LAST OURS.
I WILL MONITOR THEIR PROGRESS. THE REST OF YOU BEGIN WORK. WE CANNOT BE CERTAIN HOW MUCH TIME WE'LL HAVE, SO BE AS QUICK AS YOU CAN. IF ALL GOES WELL...
...THEY WILL RETURN TO A WELCOME THEY'LL NOT SOON FORGET

"MY FOLKS CAME TO VISIT A FEW WEEKS BACK. THINGS ARE LOUSY BETWEEN 'EM. I DON'T UNDERSTAND--HOW CAN PEOPLE FALL OUT OF LOVE?"

"I KEEP WONDERING IF MY BEING HERE HAS ANYTHING TO DO WITH THEIR DIVORCE. IF WE'D DONE MORE TOGETHER--IF I'D BEEN WITH THEM, SAY, INSTEAD OF IN OUTER SPACE WITH THE X-MEN--MAYBE WE'D STILL BE A FAMILY."

AS I RECALL, THIS TOUR WAS SUPPOSED TO MAKE YOU FEEL *BETTER*.

SORRY. OVER THERE IS OUR BOATHOUSE. IT'S ALSO WHERE WE STASH THE SCUBA GEAR. IN THE MOOD FOR A SWIM?

OVERRIDING ILLYANA'S PROTESTS ABOUT NOT HAVING A SUIT, KITTY SOON HAS HER FRIEND IN THE LAKE.

ONLY ONE AIR TANK IS CHARGED...

...WHICH FORCES THEM TO "BUDDY-BREATHE" ALONG THE SHORELINE UNTIL THEY REACH AN UNDERWATER AIRLOCK.

TH-THAT WAS *F-F-FREEZING!* OF ALL THE MEAN, NASTY, ROTTEN--!

YOU AGREED TO IT.

YOU SHOVED ME INTO THE LAKE! WHERE ARE WE ANYWAY?

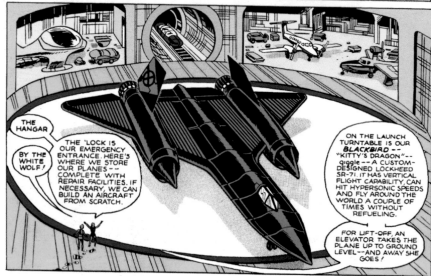

THE HANGAR

BY THE WHITE WOLF!

THE 'LOCK IS OUR EMERGENCY ENTRANCE. HERE'S WHERE WE STORE OUR PLANES--COMPLETE WITH REPAIR FACILITIES. IF NECESSARY, WE CAN BUILD AN AIRCRAFT FROM SCRATCH.

ON THE LAUNCH TURNTABLE IS OUR *BLACKBIRD*-- "KITTY'S DRAGON"-- giggle -- A CUSTOM-DESIGNED LOCKHEED SR-71. IT HAS VERTICAL FLIGHT CAPABILITY, CAN HIT HYPERSONIC SPEEDS AND FLY AROUND THE WORLD A COUPLE OF TIMES WITHOUT REFUELING.

FOR LIFT-OFF, AN ELEVATOR TAKES THE PLANE UP TO GROUND LEVEL--AND AWAY SHE GOES!

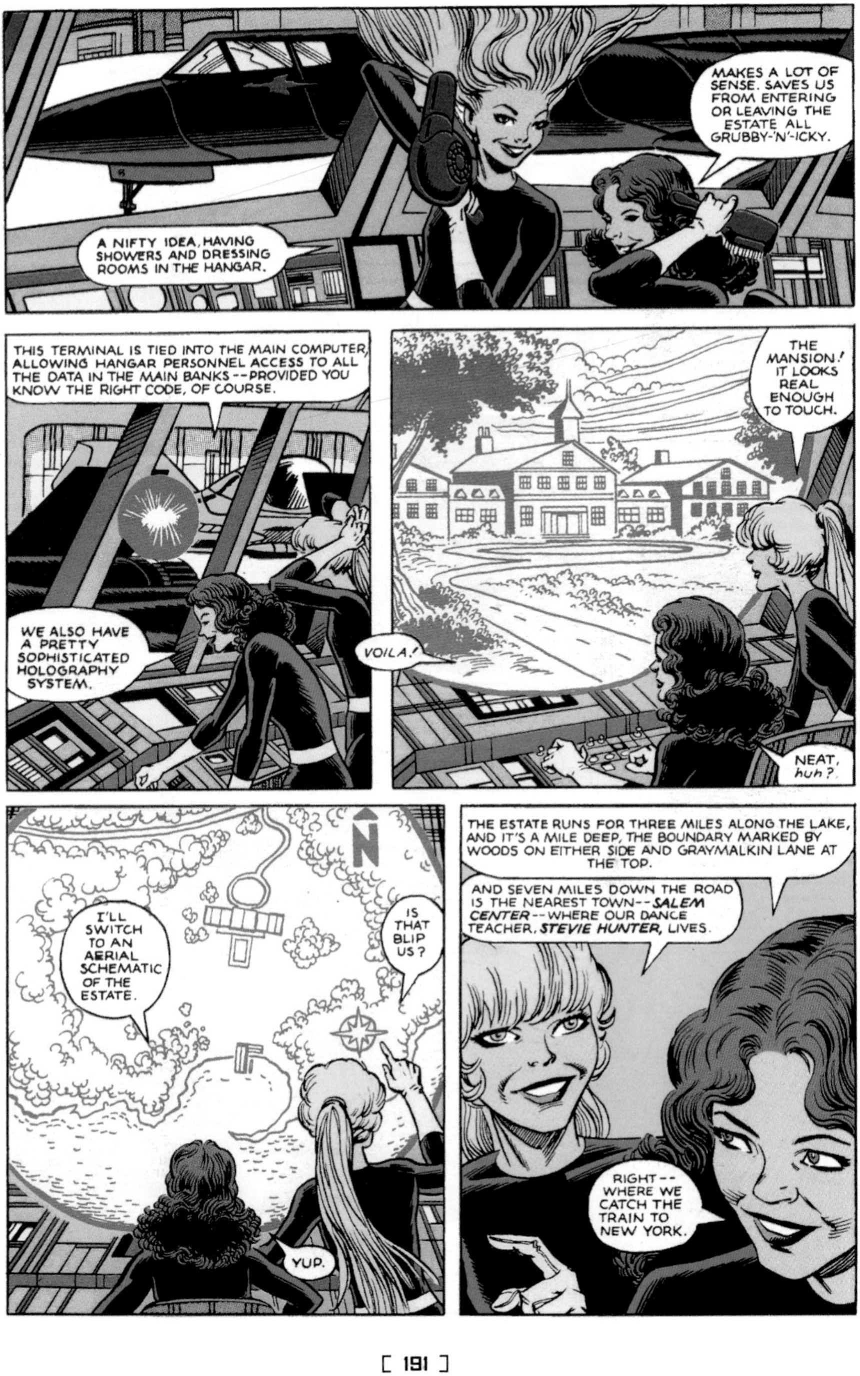
MAKES A LOT OF SENSE. SAVES US FROM ENTERING OR LEAVING THE ESTATE ALL GRUBBY-'N'-ICKY.
A NIFTY IDEA, HAVING SHOWERS AND DRESSING ROOMS IN THE HANGAR.
THIS TERMINAL IS TIED INTO THE MAIN COMPUTER, ALLOWING HANGAR PERSONNEL ACCESS TO ALL THE DATA IN THE MAIN BANKS--PROVIDED YOU KNOW THE RIGHT CODE, OF COURSE.
WE ALSO HAVE A PRETTY SOPHISTICATED HOLOGRAPHY SYSTEM.
VOILA!
THE MANSION! IT LOOKS REAL ENOUGH TO TOUCH.
NEAT, huh?
I'LL SWITCH TO AN AERIAL SCHEMATIC OF THE ESTATE.
IS THAT BLIP US?
YUP.
THE ESTATE RUNS FOR THREE MILES ALONG THE LAKE, AND IT'S A MILE DEEP, THE BOUNDARY MARKED BY WOODS ON EITHER SIDE AND GRAYMALKIN LANE AT THE TOP.
AND SEVEN MILES DOWN THE ROAD IS THE NEAREST TOWN--SALEM CENTER--WHERE OUR DANCE TEACHER, STEVIE HUNTER, LIVES.
RIGHT--WHERE WE CATCH THE TRAIN TO NEW YORK.

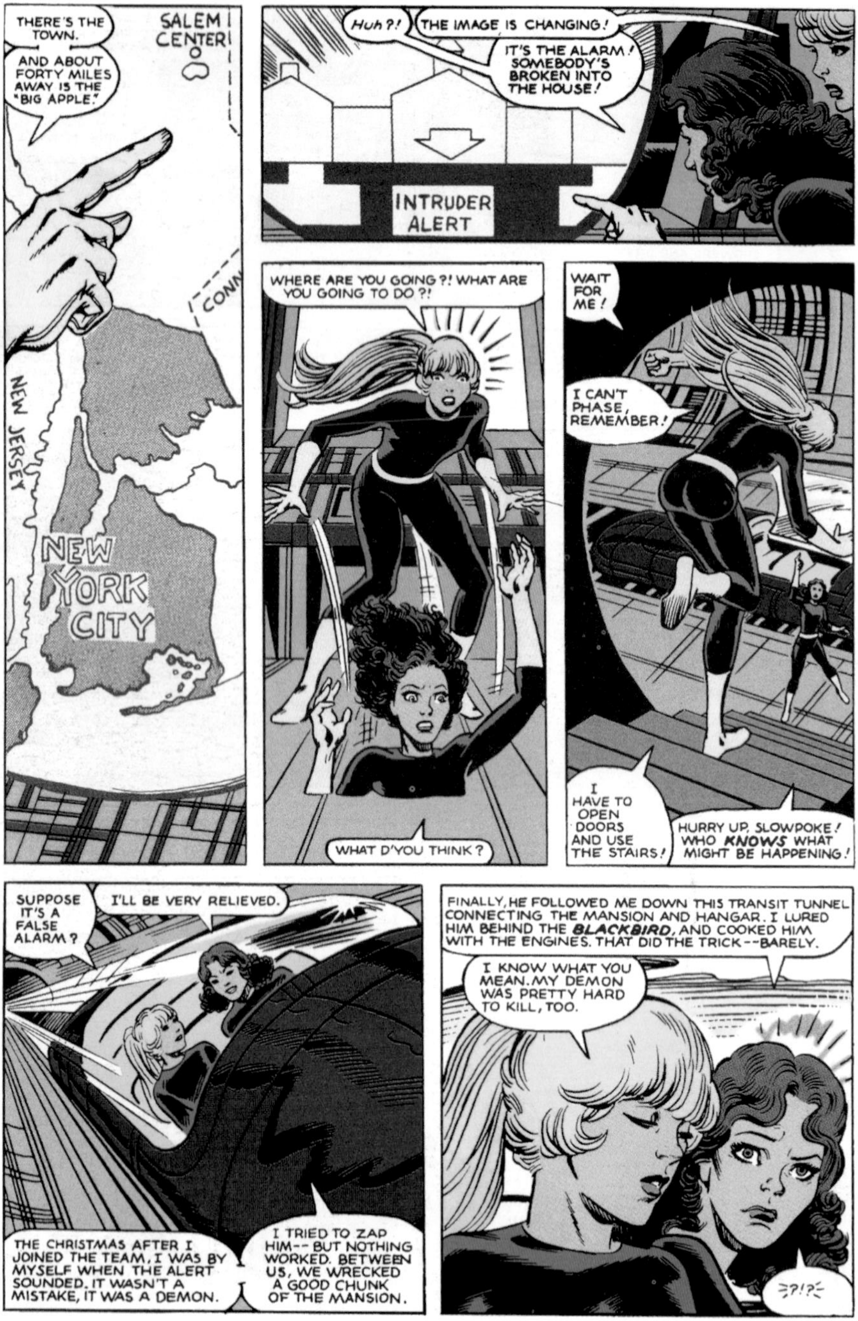
THERE'S THE TOWN.
SALEM CENTER
AND ABOUT FORTY MILES AWAY IS THE "BIG APPLE."
CONN
NEW JERSEY
NEW YORK CITY
Huh?!
THE IMAGE IS CHANGING!
IT'S THE ALARM! SOMEBODY'S BROKEN INTO THE HOUSE!
INTRUDER ALERT
WHERE ARE YOU GOING?! WHAT ARE YOU GOING TO DO?!
WHAT D'YOU THINK?
WAIT FOR ME!
I CAN'T PHASE, REMEMBER!
I HAVE TO OPEN DOORS AND USE THE STAIRS!
HURRY UP, SLOWPOKE! WHO KNOWS WHAT MIGHT BE HAPPENING!
SUPPOSE IT'S A FALSE ALARM?
I'LL BE VERY RELIEVED.
THE CHRISTMAS AFTER I JOINED THE TEAM, I WAS BY MYSELF WHEN THE ALERT SOUNDED. IT WASN'T A MISTAKE, IT WAS A DEMON.
I TRIED TO ZAP HIM-- BUT NOTHING WORKED. BETWEEN US, WE WRECKED A GOOD CHUNK OF THE MANSION.
FINALLY, HE FOLLOWED ME DOWN THIS TRANSIT TUNNEL CONNECTING THE MANSION AND HANGAR. I LURED HIM BEHIND THE BLACKBIRD, AND COOKED HIM WITH THE ENGINES. THAT DID THE TRICK--BARELY.
I KNOW WHAT YOU MEAN. MY DEMON WAS PRETTY HARD TO KILL, TOO.
?!?

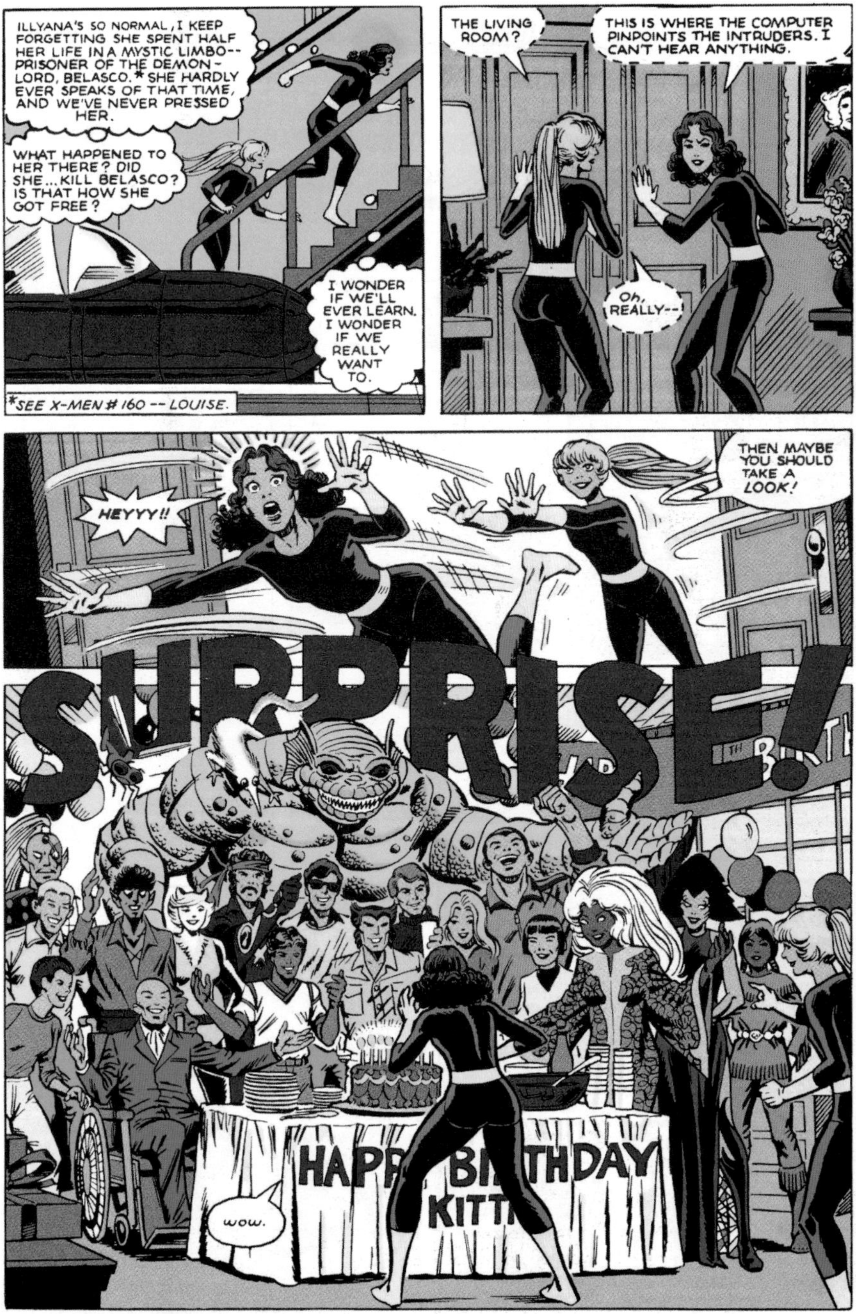
ILLYANA'S SO NORMAL, I KEEP FORGETTING SHE SPENT HALF HER LIFE IN A MYSTIC LIMBO-- PRISONER OF THE DEMON-LORD, BELASCO.* SHE HARDLY EVER SPEAKS OF THAT TIME, AND WE'VE NEVER PRESSED HER.
WHAT HAPPENED TO HER THERE? DID SHE... KILL BELASCO? IS THAT HOW SHE GOT FREE?
I WONDER IF WE'LL EVER LEARN. I WONDER IF WE REALLY WANT TO.
*SEE X-MEN #160 -- LOUISE.
THE LIVING ROOM?
THIS IS WHERE THE COMPUTER PINPOINTS THE INTRUDERS. I CAN'T HEAR ANYTHING.
Oh, REALLY--!
HEYYY!!
THEN MAYBE YOU SHOULD TAKE A LOOK!
SURPRISE!
HAPPY BIRTHDAY KITTY
WOW.

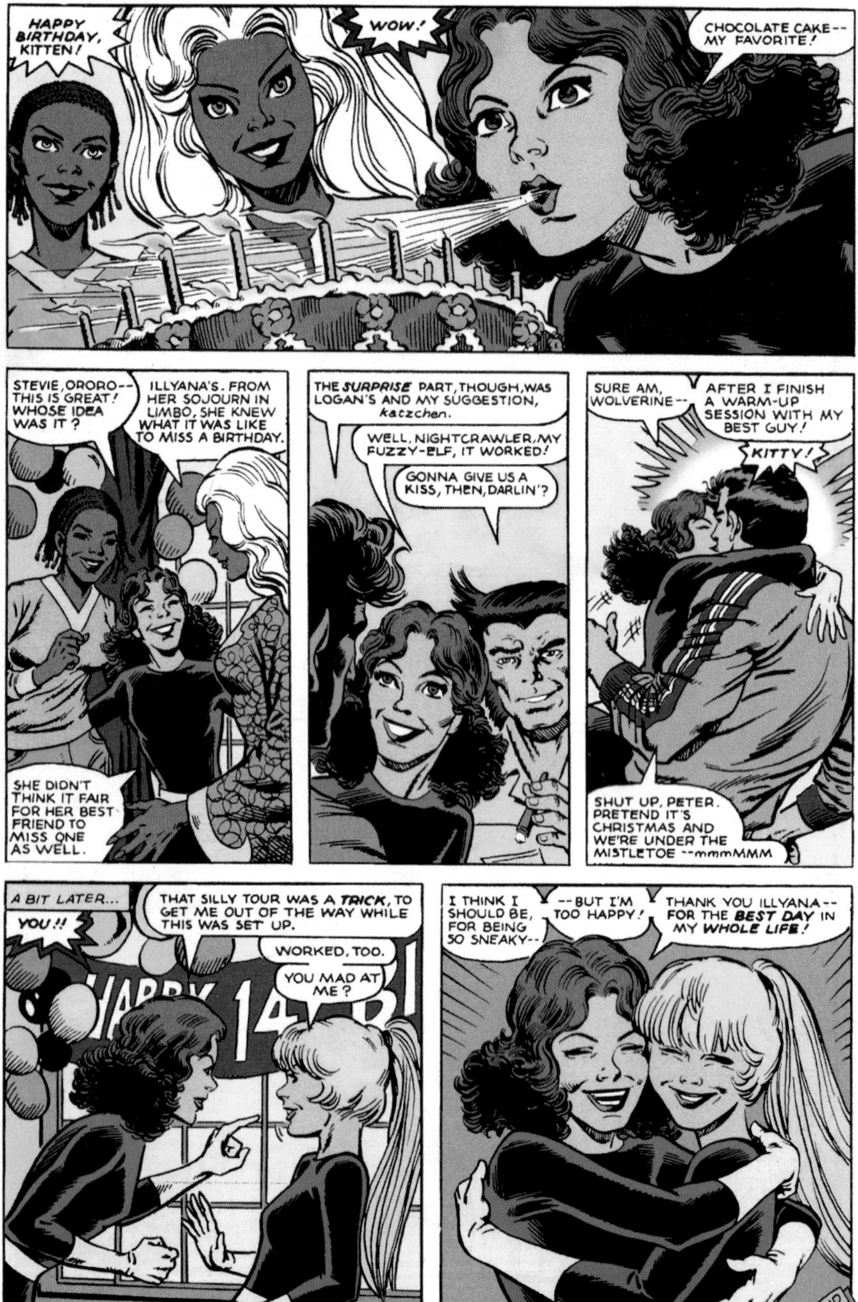

HAPPY BIRTHDAY, KITTEN!
WOW!
CHOCOLATE CAKE-- MY FAVORITE!
STEVIE, ORORO-- THIS IS GREAT! WHOSE IDEA WAS IT?
ILLYANA'S. FROM HER SOJOURN IN LIMBO, SHE KNEW WHAT IT WAS LIKE TO MISS A BIRTHDAY.
SHE DIDN'T THINK IT FAIR FOR HER BEST FRIEND TO MISS ONE AS WELL.
THE SURPRISE PART, THOUGH, WAS LOGAN'S AND MY SUGGESTION, katzchen.
WELL, NIGHTCRAWLER, MY FUZZY-ELF, IT WORKED!
GONNA GIVE US A KISS, THEN, DARLIN'?
SURE AM, WOLVERINE--
AFTER I FINISH A WARM-UP SESSION WITH MY BEST GUY!
KITTY!
SHUT UP, PETER. PRETEND IT'S CHRISTMAS AND WE'RE UNDER THE MISTLETOE --mmmMMM
A BIT LATER...
YOU!!
THAT SILLY TOUR WAS A TRICK, TO GET ME OUT OF THE WAY WHILE THIS WAS SET UP.
WORKED, TOO.
YOU MAD AT ME?
I THINK I SHOULD BE, FOR BEING SO SNEAKY--
--BUT I'M TOO HAPPY!
THANK YOU ILLYANA-- FOR THE BEST DAY IN MY WHOLE LIFE!
END